BENDING BODIES

Bending Bodies

Moulding Masculinities, Volume 2

Edited by

SØREN ERVØ and THOMAS JOHANSSON

ASHGATE

Published by
Ashgate Publishing Limited
Gower House
Croft Road
Aldershot
Hants GU11 3HR
England

Ashgate Publishing Company
Suite 420
101 Cherry Street
Burlington, VT 05401-4405
USA

Ashgate website: http://www.ashgate.com

British Library Cataloguing in Publication Data
Bending bodies : moulding masculinities
   Vol. 2
   1. Masculinity - Congresses 2. Men - Identity - Congresses
   3. Body, Human - Philosophy - Congresses 4. Body image in men
   - Congresses
   I. Ervø, Søren II. Johansson, Thomas III. Nordic Summer
   University
   305.3'2

Library of Congress Control Number: 99-073638

ISBN 1 84014 803 9

Printed and bound by Athenaeum Press, Ltd.,
Gateshead, Tyne & Wear.

Contents

Acknowledgements   *vii*
List of Contributors   *viii*
Foreword by Victor Jeleniewski Seidler   *xi*

1   Introduction   1
    Søren Ervø and Thomas Johansson

2   The Body, the Will and the Fear of Falling: 16
    The History of Masculine Self-Control
    Claes Ekenstam

3   Consuming Manhood: The Feminization of   47
    American Culture and the Recreation of the
    Male Body, 1832–1920
    Michael S. Kimmel

4   Men, Bodies and Identities   77
    Victor Jeleniewski Seidler

5   What's Behind the Mask? Bodybuilding and   92
    Masculinity
    Thomas Johansson

6   Putting on Make-up with Red Gloves: Masculine   107
    Aesthetics in an Exclusive Male Culture
    Geir A. Øygarden

7   When Boys Become Men: The Martial Arts as   125
    Young People's Revolt against the Youth Rebellion
    Hans Bonde

8   Sylvester Stallone's Body: "A Peculiar, Not To   140
    Say Pathological, Interest"
    Martti Lahti

9   Searching for the Body: Making Connections   170
    between Health, Bodies and Men's Violence
    Jeff Hearn

10 Male Ways of Giving Birth   193
    Klaus Theweleit

11 The Psychodynamics of Shame in the   208
    Autobiographies of Modern Finnish Men
    Juha Siltala

12 Asthma: The Construction of the Masculine Body   224
    Arto Tiihonen

13 Disabling Men: Masculinity and Disability in   238
    Al Davison's Graphic Autobiography *The Spiral Cage*
    Paul McIlvenny

14 Ethos of Sexual Liberation and the Masculine   259
    Other
    Ilpo Helén

15 Coming Out to be Straight: 272
    Young Men's Constructions of Heterosexualities
    Stephan W. Cremer

16 "There has always been ..."   288
    Gay History in Politics and in Reality
    Wilhelm von Rosen

17 Coming of Age in England: 305
    Black Gay Young Men's Schooling Experiences
    Mairtin Mac an Ghaill

Index   *321*

Acknowledgements

We would like to thank the authors for trusting us with their material. The financial support we have received from "The Nordic Summer University" has allowed most of the contributors to meet at different conferences and enabled their papers to be proofread. Also thanks to Sidsel Ervø for technical assistance. And finally we praise the eminent work by our "proofreader" Rictor Norton, without whom this task would have been less manageable and the result less successful.

The article by Michael Kimmel was earlier published in *Michigan Quarterly Review*, vol. 33, no. 1, Winter 1994.
The article by Arto Tiihonen was earlier published in *International Review for Sociology of Sport*, vol. 29, no. 1, 1994.

List of Contributors

(for both volumes)

Hans Bonde, Ph.D., Assistant Professor, Deptartment of Sports Science, University of Copenhagen, Denmark. <HBonde@ifi.ku.dk>

Mikael Carleheden, Ph.D., Associate Professor, Department of Sociology, University of Örebro, Sweden. <Mikael.Carlehede@sam.oru.se>

R. W. Connell, Professor of Education, Faculty of Education, University of Sydney, Australia. <r.connell@edfac.usyd.edu.au>

Stephan W. Cremer, Ph.D., Department of Health Service of the City of Utrecht, Netherlands. <S.Cremer@Utrecht.nl>

Claes Ekenstam, Ph.D., Associate Professor at the Department of the History of Ideas and Education, University of Göteborg, Sweden. <claes.ekenstam@idehist.gu.se>

Søren Ervø, M.A. in Film and History, Department of Film and Media Studies, University of Copenhagen, Denmark. <serv@vip.cybercity.dk>

Lena Eskilsson, Ph.D., Associate Professor, Department of the History of Science and Ideas, University of Umeå, Sweden. <Lena.eskilsson@idehist.gu.se>

Katrine Fangen, Ph.D., Assistant Professor, Department of Sociology, University of Oslo, Norway. <Katrine.fangen@sosiologi.uio.no>

Jeff Hearn, Professor of Sociology, Department of Sociology, Åbo Akademi University, Finland. <jhearn@ra.abo.fi>

Ilpo Helén, Ph.D., Assistant Professor, Department of Sociology, University of Helsinki, Finland. <IHELEN@valt.helsinki.fi>

Øystein Gullvåg Holter, Ph.D., Associate Professor, Department of Sociology, University of Oslo, Norway. <ogh@afi-wri.no>

Ella Johansson, Ph.D., Associate Professor, Nordeuropa-Institut, Humboldt-Universität zu Berlin, Germany. <Ella.Johansson@etn.lu.se>

Thomas Johansson, Ph.D., Professor, Department of Social Work, University of Gothenburg, Sweden. <Thomas.Johansson@socwork.gu.se>

Michael S. Kimmel, Professor in Sociology, State University of New York at Stony Brook, USA. <103321.1076@compuserve.com>

Christian Kullberg, Ph.D., Associate Professor, Department of Social Science, University of Örebro, Sweden.<Christian.Kullberg@sam.oru.se>

Martti Lahti, Chair, Department of Communication and Media Design, Laurea Polytechnic, Vantaa, Finland. <Martti-lahti@laurea.fi>

Philip Lalander, Ph.D., Associate Professor, SoRAD, University of Stockholm, Sweden. <Philip.Lalander@hik.se>

Jørgen Lorentzen, Ph.D., Assistant Professor, Department of Gender Studies, University of Oslo, Norway. <J.l.lorentzen@skk.uio.no>

Mairtin Mac an Ghaill, Ph.D., Professor, Department of Education, University of Sheffield, England. <M.m.a.ghaill@sheffield.ac.uk>

Paul McIlvenny, Ph.D., Associate Professor, Department of Languages and Intercultural Studies, Aalborg University, Denmark. <paul@sprog.auc.dk >

Ulf Mellström, Ph.D., Associate Professor, Department of Technique and Social Change, University of Linköping, Sweden. <UlfMe@tema.liu.se>

Michael Meuser, Ph.D., Assistant Professor, Department of Sociology, University of Bremen. <meuser.michael@t-online.de>

Wilhelm von Rosen, Dr. Phil. in History from the University of Copenhagen, Senior Researcher at the National Archives of Denmark. <wr@ra.sa.dk>

Victor Jeleniewski Seidler, Professor of Social Theory, Department of Sociology, Goldsmiths College, University of London, England. <soa01vjs@gold.ac.uk>

Juha Siltala, Ph.D., Professor, Department of History, University of Helsinki, Finland. <Juha.siltala@helsinki.fi>

Klaus Theweleit, Dr.Phil., freelance lecturer and author in Freiburg, Germany. <thewelei@ruf.uni-freiburg.de>

Arto Tiihonen, Ph.D., Department of Social Sciences of Sport, University of Jyväskylä, Finland. <artot@congcreator.com>

Helena Wahlström, Ph.D., Assistant Professor, Department of English, Gävle University College, Sweden. <hen@hig.se>

Geir A. Øygarden, Ph.D., Department of Sociology, University of Uppsala, Sweden. <Geir.Oygarden@soc.uu.se>

Foreword

VICTOR JELENIEWSKI SEIDLER

Why has it become so important to focus upon men's relationships with their bodies as we approach the new millennium? Is it because for many people it becomes a time to think of new beginnings and for critical thinking in relation to men and masculinities this has come to mean thinking in new ways about men's diverse relationships with their bodies? It is clear that much contemporary exploration in the visual arts concerns testing the boundaries of bodies and refusing the distinction so crucial to an Enlightenment vision of modernity, between nature and culture, through treating the body as machine.

There seems to be a pervasive desire within contemporary culture to test the limits against which we can re/invent ourselves in relation to the new technologies that seem to potentially transform the reach of human senses. Unsure of the utopian dreams for social and political emancipation which have governed so much of European thought of the last two centuries, people now seem able to trust only in themselves and the work they can do on their own bodies. There is a conviction that if people can remake their bodies, then they can recreate themselves. At some level this can seem to continue a secularized Protestant inheritance that informs modernity, for it can grow out of an unease and uncertainty in relation to the body, which Max Weber in *The Protestant Ethic and the Spirit of Capitalism* connects to an inherited sense that natures are evil. This has a particular resonance for men who can be left to feel that they must constantly prove themselves. It often makes it difficult for men to sit quietly with themselves, for they constantly have to move into an arena of action, for only here can they prove that they are not "good for nothing," as their parents might have accused them of being.

Traditionally work became the site within the public realm in which men learnt to affirm their male identities. Men learnt to be active as a way of assuaging their feelings of guilt and unease and they learnt to identify passivity with the "feminine." This meant that male bodies were constantly on the move and men felt that they constantly had to prove themselves. Often this meant that they had to prove themselves against their own bodies, testing themselves against their tiredness or hunger. These were limits that they learnt to break through, rather than to listen to and respect. The notion of "men listening to their bodies" ceased to make any sense at all – the thought had been made unthinkable. Rather men's relationships with their bodies were instrumental. They proved their self-control, and thereby their masculinities, through proving that they could exercise control over their own bodies. Within modernity this also meant exerting control over the bodies of their wives and children. For these bodies were also deemed to be men's property.

Within liberal moral theory, freedom was largely defined as the freedom to dispose of your property in any way that you chose. This was set in patriarchal terms and it meant that men were free to exercise their control over women and children, who were deemed to be "closer to nature." This meant that they could not think for themselves, but rather they were dependent upon men to be able to guide their lives through reason. Traditionally this meant that women were considered to be irrational, because they were under the influence of their emotions and feelings. This meant that they could not be "reasoned with" and men had to accept their duty and responsibility to discipline their wives and children. There could be no communication across the genders, rather the only language that women could supposedly understand was the language of force. This served to legitimate male violence, as men learnt that they owed it to their wives to show them "the back of the hand."

As men learnt to assume an instrumental relationship with their own bodies, bodies became a crucial testing ground for diverse masculinities. Men could rarely feel "man enough" and they constantly felt they had to prove their superiority in relation to women as a way of affirming their male identities. But there was also a sense in which the body had to be disciplined and controlled because at some level it was defined as "feminine." There was a fear of emotions, particularly of vulnerability, sadness and fear that seemed to bring masculinity into question. So it is that boys often grew up *not* wanting to acknowledge whatever emotions were beginning to surface, because they could so easily threaten their male identities. A fear of these "soft" emotions is linked to homophobia, so that men often learn to silence their emotions as part of learning how to discipline their bodies. These different regimes of body discipline need to be carefully explored, for they are at the same time disciplining the emotional life of the body. Within diverse masculinities, we discover different ways in which men learn to endure bodily pain as well as to inflict pain on others, as ways of affirming their own male identities. Often the fear of homosexuality gives a particular edge to this process.

With the crisis in traditional industries that used to provide so much unskilled and semi-skilled work for working-class men, it has become difficult to draw upon work as the traditional arena within which male identities are affirmed. Work was often crucial for men because this was the space in which their masculinities could be proved. Family life was honored in name, but men knew that as regards their male identities, their loyalties lay elsewhere. They did not expect women to understand this. Even if they knew that they were working for their wives and children, it was difficult not to recognize that their primary loyalties seemed to lie elsewhere, for it remained crucial to be able to prove that they were "man enough." It has been the crisis in male employment that has been crucial in precipitating what we identified in *Achilles Heel* as a "crisis in masculinity" in the early 1980s. This crisis has deepened because of the concurrent breakdown in relationships, which has meant that men could no longer count on marriage and fatherhood as settings in which they could prove themselves. The social supports for male identities that were so often taken for granted within patriarchal societies have been radically challenged and men feel uneasy about what it means "to be a man" in the closing years of the twentieth century.

For younger men this often has less to do with the challenges of feminism than it has for men who first learnt to question their masculinities in relation to feminism. Sometimes younger men feel easier in their relationships with women, but they want to explore the possibilities of different masculinities. They are more concerned for themselves and what it means for them to grow up into manhood and what this could also mean for redefining notions of fatherhood and parenting. Often there are also concerns with men's relationships with their bodies, for as the traditional supports for male identity have gone, so the body has assumed a new centrality in the redefining of masculinities. Often it is through the body that men can prove themselves. This has helped to create different body cultures for men, but also new anxieties and uncertainties in men's diverse relationships with their bodies. This has been an issue for both gay and straight men, for it has been linked to ways men learn to think about their own sexualities. Not wanting to be fixed within given categories, there is a greater emphasis upon the fluidity of postmodern masculinities. This appeals to younger men who want to insist upon the freedom to create their own masculinities, while learning from the histories and experiences of diverse masculinities.

The explorations of men's bodies that are offered here begin to share the significant theoretical and empirical work that is being done. They offer different ways of opening up these crucial issues and show the diverse ways in which men have learnt to think and feel their relationships with their bodies. But they also open up the possibilities of dialogue between the different traditions of work that are represented here. There are many different voices present in this text and they are all to be welcomed as contributions to the remaking of masculinities and the fostering of different visions of gender equality as we face the new millennium.

Victor Jeleniewski Seidler is Professor of Social Theory in the Department of Sociology, Goldsmiths College, University of London. He was part of the founding collective of Achilles Heel, the journal of men's sexual politics. He is the author of *Rediscovering Masculinity: Reason, Language and Sexuality; Recreating Sexual Politics: Men, Feminism and Politics.* He also edited *The Achilles Heel Reader* and *Men, Sex and Relationships.* His recent work includes *Unreasonable Men: Masculinity and Social Theory; Recovering the Self: Morality and Social Theory* and most recently *Man Enough: Embodying Masculinities.*

Chapter 1

Introduction

SØREN ERVØ AND THOMAS JOHANSSON

This two-volume anthology is the result of our efforts to collect innovative articles that in different ways represent a field, which we prefer to label pragmatically as "studies of men and masculinities." [1]

Many of the articles have earlier been presented at six conferences held between 1995 and 1997 by the Nordic Network for Masculinity Studies within the Nordic Summer University, arranged by the editors and financed by the Nordic Ministry Council. This early collection has been complemented by a few additional articles that have been presented at other seminars on "masculinities" in the Scandinavian countries during the same period. Finally we have included contributions from some of our visitors, among them some of the major researchers on masculinities, who have been promoting this hitherto predominantly Anglo-American subject. [2]

By enabling the first collective contribution from mainly Nordic scholars to "studies of men and masculinities" we hope to encourage further reading and research in other non-English cultures, which can contribute to an understanding of masculinities in a global context.

Instead of selecting articles with similar approaches, we have chosen to maintain a multi-disciplinary selection. This is not done in order to attempt a systematic overview, but rather to include the many different kinds of research that have been presented in the Nordic region under the label of "masculinity studies." Because the subject of gender transcends traditional structures and institutions in society, including the boundaries within academia, "studies of men and masculinities" necessitate a multi-disciplinary approach. The multi-disciplinary approach also helps to establish interesting links between otherwise very different subject areas. Though we welcome the "mainstreaming" of gender studies, and hope that our anthologies will contribute further to this development, we also believe that a multi-disciplinary approach is important in order to preserve the political and critical dimension of gender studies. "Studies of men and masculinities" is necessarily linked to the political struggle for a more equal society. If this were not the case, we might fall back to a kind of research on gender that merely reproduced traditional gender categories and cultivated an uncritical notion of the gender order.

The concept of masculinity is analyzed in a variety of ways – as forms of behavior, as specific ethics, codes and historical traits. Common to most of the authors is the belief that gender is socially constructed and negotiated, and that we need to maintain a close relationship between gender theory and case-studies in order to understand and demonstrate the dynamic and contradictory nature of gender. Our aim has been to show how different masculinities continuosly intersect and interact with specific individuals, groups and historical settings, in order to deconstruct static views of gender and gender relations.

Though "studies of men and masculinities" have grown steadily over the last few years, especially in the Anglo-American countries, the field is still very tentative and needs further development in many regards. This development may depend on more contributions from other parts of the world, enabling us to develop less ethnocentric perspectives. And though we acknowledge the need for more clarified theoretical agendas,[3] we also believe that diversity is still the best prerequsite for theoretical growth. The different approaches in our anthologies will hopefully enable the reader to envision "studies of men and masculinities" even beyond the present level of theoretical sophistication and diversity of subjects. We believe that it is too soon to evaluate the potential of "studies of men and masculinities" until they have been integrated into further subject areas and have been more developed internationally. Despite our belief that there is a need to develop the theoretical work – for instance to scrutinize and employ the dominant concepts of male crisis and hegemonic masculinity more critically[4] – we do not wish to distance ourselves from the multifaceted work already published, but are content to contribute further "pieces to the puzzle," believing that development in depth presupposes development in breadth.

The discussions surrounding the political implications of men engaging in feminism and gender studies have obscured the fact that "women's studies" have also always been "studies of men and masculinities." And if these concepts had been investigated with the same curiosity as women and femininity, "studies of men and masculinities" might have been integrated into gender studies much sooner. The monolithic accounts of masculinity as well as the lack of empirical studies of men and male cultures have neccesitated a late corrective (and not merely a supplement): trying to find its place within the dispersed field of gender studies, and distinguish itself from the omnipresent public debates on "new men" and "fatherhood" fueled by women's magazines, popular psychology and the agendas of different "men's movements."[5] While "studies of men and masculinities" ought to challenge all accounts of men and masculinities (including these concepts) as well as omissions of these within gender studies, they also, supportive of feminism in general, entail criticism of traditional scholarship for its failure to include a gender concept and incorporate the insights produced by gender studies.

Basically, we feel that "studies of men and masculinities" are interesting and important, because they raise questions that are still unanswered. Though self-critical awareness and sincere respect for the many implications of men "tampering with feminism" are essential,[6] we should not let these concerns prevent us from developing the field beyond the constraints of political correctness. The important political loyality toward feminism and theoretical dependency toward gender studies in general should not prevent us from committing ourselves professionally and critically when dealing with specific theories of gender.

The editors do not perceive "studies of men and masculinities" as a possible vehicle for contemporary men's rights or masculinist movements, nor has there been any evidence for such a connection yet. On the contrary, many of the authors included here have declared themselves as pro-feminists, and have on several occasions been active in pointing out backlash tendencies within different men's movements. Despite honoring the aspirations toward a politically engaged or even activistic scholarship, we do not believe that labelling research "critical," "pro-feminist," "gay-affirmative" and so on is sufficient to legitimize or establish the field within academia. Respectable political intentions do not produce new insights, nor do they prevent anybody from using this research with a different agenda.

Overall, we have tried to collect articles that employ the concept of masculinity in order to enhance or develop a gender perspective within areas where gender already seems to be so visible that conflicts, crises and changes within masculine identities would have profound effects on the perception and embodiment of masculinities and consequently on gender relations. In other words, we assumed that the best strategy would be to focus on dominant gender arenas, such as sexuality, the body, the family and subcultures dominated by men and male values. *Among Men – Moulding Masculinities, Volume 1* aims to contribute to the investigation of relational aspects of masculinity, in order to describe how different masculinities are moulded within specific structures and settings, especially how men interact with each other, and how they collectively react to and embody the changing concepts of masculinity within male-dominated subcultures. *Bending Bodies – Moulding Masculinities, Volume 2* aims to study changes within masculine identity and subjectivity and to discuss the constructions of masculinities that result from the relationship and understanding men develop toward their own and other men's bodies, sexualities and masculine dis/abilities.

By centering on the struggle and negotiation between different groups and discourses of masculinity and investigating the origin of dominant images and ideals of masculinity, the two volumes hope to widen our understanding of how historic forms of masculinities are interpreted, revived and combined in the process of moulding masculinities.

Bending Bodies – Moulding Masculinities, Volume 2

Claes Ekenstam rereads a case-story by the psychotherapist Alexander Lowen in order to examine how the split between mind and body can affect men, and to discuss modern men's relationship to their bodies and emotional lives. Ekenstam examines the construction of the modern ego through the concepts of Foucault and suggests that "the disciplined ego, which achieves stategic leverage by subjecting feelings to conscious goals, is masculine." Ekenstam turns toward historical "mentalities" to describe pre-industrial masculine ideals, while stressing the importance of an analytical distinction between emotional ideals and actual feelings. Ekenstam analyzes a publication from 1770, titled "Anecdotes concerning renowned and remarkable Swedish men." One of the signs of masculinity at that time was the beard, a privilege God had given only to men, which was also regarded as a sign of sexual prowess. The new tradition of shaving, dictated by fashion, created some uneasiness among more traditional men – shaving was equivalent to renouncing one's masculinity and was thus unfitting. Ekenstam also describes the contradictory concepts of masculinity within the Christian tradition as well as their mutual conflict with the images of masculinity embraced by the aristocracy.

Victor Seidler argues that the "modern" was defined in terms of the male mind being "human", whereas the male body remained "animal." Modernity insisted upon a radical separation between nature and culture, which was reflected in the categorical split between body and mind. As men learn to identify with their minds they literally come to live in their heads. According to Seidler they become observers of their own bodily experience, because the body is deemed to be part of a disenchanted nature. The language of the body comes to be depersonalized, for bodies come to be treated as men's property. Within modernity men come to assume an instrumental relationship with their bodies. And as long as men continue to conceive of the body as a machine that serves to carry our heads around, it will be difficult for men to rethink relations between mind and body, thoughts and emotions, spirit and flesh. It will also be difficult to acknowledge the emotional life of the body and the ways that particular forms of hypermasculinity can make one ill. But in the 1990s men began to engage more critically with the inherited masculinities of their fathers. There is the beginning of a widespread movement to re-vision masculinities, especially so that young fathers can be more involved with their children than their fathers were with them. Though Seidler thinks change is possible, he remains critical toward postmodernism, because in crucial respects it remains a project of a dominant masculinity. Seidler believes that only as men learn to value their relationships with other men, can they also learn to live differently embodied masculinities.

Michael Kimmel examines some of the efforts to rescue and retrieve masculinity during a pivotal moment of historical transition, during which masculinity was widely perceived as being in crisis and in radical need of such restoration. He describes the ways in which a secure sense of masculinity was gradually destabilized in the first few decades of the nineteenth century, and the mechanisms that men employed to reground their eroding sense of manhood. These included increasing restrictions on the male body through proscriptions of sexuality; the exclusion of all "others" – such as women, non-native-born whites, men of color and, later in the century, homosexuals – from the increasingly problematic public area; and fantasies of escape. Kimmel lastly explores the rediscovery of the male body at the turn of the century as a gendered testing ground, a site of demonstration of masculinity, especially in consumerist fantasies of physical prowess.

Thomas Johansson argues that the cultural changes that result from different body-altering techniques, most extreme in plastic surgery, become obvious when we enter the world of the gym. Through their grotesque bodies, male and female bodybuilders are good examples of "bodies that matter" (Butler). Johansson uses a case-study to describe the experiences of a certain bodybuilder and investigate the fascination surrounding bodybuilding seen from within, such as the "possibilities of body perfection" and the discipline necessary to obtain a "perfect body."

Discussing an autobiography by another bodybuilder, Johansson proposes
that his description of bodybuilding also becomes a study of masculinity,
because the hard body must be seen foremost as a male body, a body that is
threatened by soft bodies and by ambiguities. Bodies that historically have
belonged to warriors or patriarchs – men who had to defend their families
and countries – today are merely aesthetic objects of desire. Muscles are
still closely linked to masculinity, but the masculine body has also become
a floating signifier and is consequently also tied to femininity. More
generally, the hard body may be read as a sign of the fight against
ambivalence and ambiguity inherent in modernity. The disciplining of the
body also involves the making of a specific identity; an identity that is
clearly opposed to the fat, slim, badly defined soft body. The dynamics of
discipline and desire, empowerment and disempowerment and narcissism
and fragmentation are all central to contemporary culture. When looking
into bodybuilding and the fitness industry, we are also studying central
aspects of modernity/postmodernity.

Geir Øygarden's chapter explores an exclusive male room with
particular reference to those rites, norms, and values constructing
masculinity. He discusses how bodily symbolic actions function as
"exemplares," a perspective that is illustrated by empirical examples from
the fields of boxing, bodybuilding and boxercise. Scar tissues, cuts and
fractures – earned in boxing – are understood as part of a masculine
aesthetics, and as a search for reality. Øygarden suggests that boxing can
be considered as a space where men are still left mostly to themselves –
and as an exclusive male room offers some advantages when studying
masculine culture. Øygarden suggests that boxing and bodybuilding
represent different concepts of the body – while the bodybuilder is
concerned with visual constructs, the boxer exposes an internal quality
through a pattern of physical movements. But simultaneously they are
united in the same negation, because both cultures challenge good taste,
through either aesthetic or ethical deviation. They also share the
submission to discipline, and the relationship to other bodybuilders and
boxers serves as a disciplinary mechanism. Øygarden also discusses why
fractures seem so integral to the masculine "make-up" culture and proposes
that its meaning is to write experiences onto the body, in a style that
opposes symmetry. Women's make-up, on the contrary, is designed to
conceal symmetrical flaws, so that female experiences can be kept hidden
or invisible. In contrast to boxing, bodybuilding comes across as anything
but masculine – because it revolves around an aesthetic dimension and its
(promise of) masculinity is never put to the test.

Taking as his example the Oriental martial arts, Hans Bonde explains that female dominance in the education of modern boys is not total. Within the Oriental martial arts he discovers a number of rituals and a kind of manhood test where boys and young men are taught masculine codes of behavior. In much of the present-day educationalist debate and research female dominance is emphasized when discussing the education of modern boys. It is asserted that family structure and children's institutions do not always offer the boys opportunities for finding masculine figures of identification. It is easily overlooked that throughout our century movements like sports and the Boy Scouts have offered important means for the teaching of masculine behavior. In the latter end of the century especially, the Oriental martial arts seem to have had a particular attraction for young males. Bonde attempts to show how martial arts became a modern voluntary introduction to masculine codes, a kind of manhood test. Going in for rituals and authority, martial arts may be interpreted as young people's rebellion against the youth rebellion of the 1960s, and also against the paucity of sensuous experience and the cultivation of literary and verbal-abstract abilities of our modern society.

Martti Lahti suggests that masculinity and the body do not always reject each other, not even in the ideal representations of masculinity. According to Lahti, a long list of male body genres (for example Biblical epics, porn films, musicals, action cinema, Westerns, horror movies) are built on the presence of the male body and specifically emphasize the connection between masculinity and the regime of the visible. Lahti suggests that although representations of masculinity often incorporate the fantasy of an omniscient and disembodied male subjectivity, we should not ignore the cases in which masculinity is constructed specifically in and through the body. His paper explores how Sylvester Stallone's star image has evolved during the past two and a half decades, in response to Rosalind Coward's provocative comment that "In spite of the ideology that would have us believe that women's sexuality is an enigma, it is in reality men's bodies, men's sexuality which is the true 'dark continent' of this society." Lahti demonstrates how this relatively unscrutinized male body has provided a privileged representational space for the articulation of tensions between fantasies of power and powerlessness.

Jeff Hearn's focus is on health, bodies and men's violence, and the connections between them, which have often been left unstated. Following an initial discussion of definitions of violence, Hearn focuses on the relative lack of separation of the study of health, illness and the body, and the study of violence, especially men's violence. This is followed by an examination of some of the ways in which men's violence bears on health, illness and bodies – of men, women, young people and children. According to Hearn, the impacts of men's violence are both short-term/immediate/psychological and long-term/less immediate/indirect. Hearn stresses that the doing of violence involves action on the body of others, and also involves the construction of the body of the violator, in this context the bodies of men. In his final section Hearn explores these themes in terms of men's violence toward women, drawing on research on men's accounts of their own violence, and the responses of agencies, friends and family. In examining these questions, Hearn believes that it is necessary to place men's actions and experiences, including those involving violence, in the context of men's social relations, both structural and interpersonal, with women, and especially the effects of men's violence on women. In bringing together health, bodies and men's violence, Hearn's study is located in the intermediate zone between the study of health, illness, and the body, and the study of violence.

Klaus Theweleit's paper unfolds as a response to and appraisal of Sara Ruddick's book *Maternal Thinking*, in order to describe male ways of thinking/male ways of giving birth. Theweleit develops the concept of "caring labor", which to him means "a way of living, of thinking, a way of producing reality that (though it can be or perhaps even has to be militant) disconnects itself from making war, disconnects itself from the common male ways of destruction, disconnects itself from the common (male) way of linking labor to a sort of productivity that expresses its worth or worthlessness only in money relations of economic victory or defeat." Theweleit analyzes the language used to describe the first nuclear tests by some of the male witnesses. Their language establishes a parallel between this evolution in destruction and the birth of a baby – a parallel Theweleit believes to be symptomatic of these men – because it betrays the truth of bodies that never really had the chance to experience the differences between being emotionally dead or alive. Though women seem to learn "caring labor" and "maternal thinking" through childbirth, Theweleit is certain that men can also learn it through involvement with children. Overall, he stresses the need for men to learn to distinguish between ways of making things and people grow, or making them die.

Juha Siltala has analyzed 55 autobiographies from a sample of 350, collected in the writing contest "Hurray for man!" during 1993 by the Council for Equality in the Ministry of Social Affairs and Health. This material has allowed him to make some observations on cultural regulation of self-feeling common to almost all of the participants. In spite of the optimistic title of the writing contest, most of these stories describe men's lives as a series of losses, anxieties and a continual battle to maintain their self-esteem. It has been suggested that the participants of an autobiographical contest are self-absorbed losers – healthy and lucky Finnish men do not bother, they are playing ice hockey or repairing their houses. Siltala's approach is different; he analyzes these autobiographies from a psychoanalytical perspective as descriptions of common men in crisis, not of uncommon anti-men, believing that a psychoanalytically oriented researcher must recognize the same mental processes at work in both losers and winners – the difference is rather gradual, not qualitative. Siltala finds that old and young, educated and uneducated, employed and unemployed are ruled by shame in these autobiographies. Dependence fills them with overwhelming shame, because it reminds them of the position of a helpless child, a passive victim at the mercy of powers beyond their control. Siltala points out how a man's honor is experienced as physical potency, as being an agent – not a victim. Shame is equivalent to the loss of one's psychological borders and one's exposure to the eyes of others as a passive victim.

Arto Tiihonen focuses on understanding the social construction of male identity in Finland in the 1960s and 1970s, and is based on autobiographic experiences by the author. He employs his sporting biography as material for "memory work" (a method developed by Frigga Haug), the key experience here being illness (asthma). By writing through it, the author thematicized the healthy, sporting, and disciplined body inscribed in hegemonic masculinity. According to Tiihonen, changing from a boy into a man is not the easiest task in Finnish culture. Suicides, the dangers of life, fear of the unknown, the pressure to succeed, and the fear of failure are all too well known. Tiihonen believes that his change to manhood was made easier through his orientation toward sport. Sports made him appreciated outside the home and enabled him to find a place among people of his own age. Tiihonen describes how a physical barrier – asthma – made it difficult for him to follow common expectations to separate notions of the body and spirit, the physical and the mental. His experience was a totality – because the constricted breathing of asthma creates a very corporeal feeling. Pursuing sports taught him to instrumentalize his body and separate it from reason to become an object of reason. Exercises for different limbs, for durability, power and acceleration taught him also the vocabulary for which this kind of dismemberment worked easily. However, asthma shattered that machine world. He could no longer function like a nippy sports car, but rather had to warm up with considerable use of the "gas pedal." Breathing and relaxation exercises, as well as yoga, taught him to know his corporeality in different ways. He was forced to realize the meaning of slowing down, listening, relaxing – though the will to succeed still held an attraction.

Paul McIlvenny examines the autobiographical comics of Al Davison in order to explore the everyday assumptions of male ability in Western culture that conceal dis/ability and the "failures" of masculinity. His particular focus is on the relations between several men when only one of them is "disabled." Unfortunately, these relations are often violent, insidious, and marginalizing. McIlvenny spotlights the autobiographical work of Al Davison, an English man born with severe spina bifida. Davison has published a comic called *The Spiral Cage* that relates in graphic style the trials and joys of growing up "disabled" in English society. In his sometimes distressing autobiography we have a chance to observe the self-representation and visualization of the fragmented and abject male body in relation to other men and a disabling society and body politics. In order to tackle Davison's autobiography McIlvenny discusses a number of issues that cut across gender, sexuality and ability. The social model of disability rejects medical and constructionist perspectives because able society is often the disabler. A disabled man often fails to measure up to the dominant culture's definition of masculinity – as strength and autonomy – which means that the disabled man is often seen as dependent and emasculated. According to McIlvenny we can discern from Davison's autobiography that the disabled male body in comics can pose a double threat to hegemonic masculinity: as well as being vulnerable, and so providing an echo of failure, it can actively refuse to remain invisible, defined by the regulating gaze of other men.

Writing about our "culture of sexual liberation" in Ilpo Helén traces the various figurations, categories and generalizations that enable modern, "liberal" Western men and women to articulate and evaluate our relation to our bodies and pleasures. According to Hélen sexual liberation is essentially an ethos. It consists of ethical problematizations of proper sexual conduct in general and of individuals, of ideals of good sex life, and of the relation to the sexual self, to one's own desires, pleasures and experiences. In addition, sexual liberation has political dimensions: it is related to the questions of power and individual liberties and rights. In a sense, the most influential current of sexual liberation in the 1960s and 1970s was the expansion of pornography. In addition, there are two discourses and projects that since the late 1960s and the early 1970s have most significantly formulated contemporary "liberal" views of nature, meaning, norms and practices of sexual pleasures and form the basis of sexual liberation's politics and ethics. The first is orgasmology, based on William Masters's and Virginia Johnson's sex research and therapy, which also influences and has parallels to the second major current of sexual liberation, radical feminism. Hélen juxtaposes these two currents to elaborate his thesis, that man and the masculine become shadowed, even outcast in the feminized world of sexual liberation. Whereas the picture and problematics of feminine sexuality touch the whole of woman's human condition, personality and self, the figuration of man and manliness is concentrated on the penis and its capabilities.

Stephan Cremer explores the following questions: How do boys relate images of masculinity to (hetero)sexuality? How do they construct heterosexualities in different situations: being together with the girlfriend or being in an all-male group? How do they combine these different constructions in a male heterosexual identity? Cremer tries to answer these questions on the basis of his research on images about sexuality among boys. He discusses the results on two levels: of male socialization in the light of feminist object-relation theory; and of power in the light of Connell's theory of hegemonic masculinity. Cremer has conducted biographical interviews with 15 boys, a method he believes provides the boys with room for "retrospective self-definitions": they can express their expectations and experiences of sexuality in their own words. One of Cremer's findings is that the boys thought more about what the girl would want than what they themselves wanted. They especially want to do sex well, and for them this meant operating in a way that the girl takes pleasure from. They hardly stop to think about their own desires and have no idea of their own boundaries. Their care, their thoughts orientate themselves around the (assumed) desires of the girl. According to Cremer it is noticeable that most of the boys interviewed sketched a negative impression about the sexuality of "other boys", who are the machos, criminals, and tough types who just use girls. The boys see themselves as an exception to the male kind. Through exaggeration about sexual experiences in peer groups, boys gain a ranking order in the group. This ranking order as well as guiding the girl in her sexual experiences produces masculinity for the boys.

According to Wilhelm von Rosen the discourse concerning the cause of homosexuality is a measure of the degree to which gays have become integrated into the male sex and thereby to a lesser degree are perceived as deviants and a minority. He believes that only when the question of the cause of homosexuality is no longer asked and when scientific hypotheses about the etiology of homosexuality are no longer formulated, will gays be fully integrated in a single unified male sex. This will mean that homosexuality as well as heterosexuality will have lost its relevance and be without social significance. Both generalizations will then become of only historical interest. In spite of sexual politically correct invocations in scientific publications about the cause of homosexuality, all phrases expressing a hypothesis based on the biological cause of homosexuality are master narratives, a discourse that socially and culturally maintains marginalization and indicates that a man may not simply be – man.

During the past decade Mairtin Mac an Ghaill has been involved in exploring the construction of young people's identity within schooling contexts. The black young gay men, of Asian and African-Caribbean origin, involved in his qualitative study were aged between 16 and 19 years. They were all attending local post-16 educational institutions, and Mac an Ghaill taught a number of them. He collected much of the material reported here from observation, informal discussions and recorded semi-structured interviews with the students and their teachers at their schools and colleges. The material is taken from life and school histories that involved discussion of family/kinship networks, peer groupings, work experience, political views/activities and school/college experiences. This methodological approach helped to locate schooling within wider socio-political processes. Mac an Ghaill's main argument is that in order to grasp what is going on in schools with reference to sexual identity formation, it is necessary to bring together young gay people's accounts of schooling and recent theoretical developments in sexual politics. From both these sources sexual/gender categories can be seen as being shaped by and shaping the processes of colonization, racism, class hegemony, male domination, heterosexism and other forms of oppression. In short, sexual/gender relations can be seen as a crucial point of intersection of different forms of power, stratification, desire and subjective identity formation. According to Mac an Ghaill the main focus in this theory-led empirical work is a rethinking of sexual/gender categories in relation to the complex interconnections of multiple forms of oppression. Of key significance here is the deconstruction of dominant forms of heterosexuality.

Notes

1.   As these two volumes also demonstrate, "studies of men and masculinities" is not a coherent or unified research paradigm, despite some dominant

tendencies, such as the affinities toward Marxist sociology and psychoanalytical gender-theories. Maybe this explains why the discussion about an appropriate label continues. But the search for a common descriptive label is hardly worth the effort, considering the many different approaches already present, and the fact that no label gives a satisfactory presentation of all of the methods and theories employed. The efforts to agree on normative terms are similarly bound to fail. Whether we label it "men's studies," "pro-feminist research" or "male dominance studies," such labels will not be sufficient or even particularly helpful in solving the political challenges confronting each researcher differently, nor protect against unwarranted criticism. Only further research can hope to do that.

2. Although their work has created an important incentive to develop "studies of men and masculinites," an uncritical implementation of this work on a global level also risks obscuring its dependence on a certain geographical and historical context, as well as preventing the development of concepts and theories of a less generalizing nature, which in time could contribute to a more detailed and thoroughly researched global perspective on masculinities. For instance, the relative absence of racial and class differences in the Nordic countries, characterized by cultures of sameness, has led few Nordic scholars to evaluate theories based on differences attributed to gender, race and class. Though gender identities and gender relations are certainly structured and influenced in many ways by international relations and global instiutions (mainly dominated by American culture, through advertisements for Coca-Cola and Marlboro or Levis clothing, through Hollywood blockbusters, through MTV and CNN, but also promoted by international organizations through implementation of Western policies concerned with birth control, AIDS, or gender equality), we urgently need more research into national and regional differences in order to understand how masculinities are intertwined and juxtaposed according to regional differences and national myths.

3. So far it has primarily been the concept of masculinities that has been scrutinized for its lack of theoretical clarity and coherence. McMahon warns against the tendency that "all the attributes of men discussed in the literature [on men] are spoken of as aspects of masculinity" and that writers on masculinity seldom explicitly indicate what kind of concept they take masculinity to be, risking the reduction of the concept "masculinity" to an explanatory cliché (*Theory and Society*, 22 (5), 1993, pp. 675–96). Jeff Hearn (in *Understanding Masculinities*, 1996) lists a number of dangers resulting from certain usages of "masculinity" as an explanatory term and suggests that the term should be used more precisely, and particularly that we move back from the concept of "masculinities" to the concept of "men," that we further explore the multiplicity of "discourses on masculinities," and that we develop concepts that more accurately reflect women's and men's differential experiences of men. Hearn insists that "to begin the analysis of men

with "masculinity/masculinities," or to search for the existence of masculinity/masculinities is likely to miss the point." According to Hearn "It cannot be assumed *a priori* that masculinity/masculinities exist. To do so is to reproduce a heterosexualizing of social arrangements" (p. 214). Suggesting that "gender, in the sense of an actually existing identity or social characteristic of men and women, does not exist," John MacInnes (in *The End of Masculinity*, Open University Press, 1998) proposes the abandonment of the concept of masculinity, understood as "the property, character trait or aspect of identity of individuals" (p. 2). He concludes that "trying to define masculinity or masculinities is a fruitless task," but immediately reinvents the concept by arguing that "masculinity exists only as various ideologies or fantasies, about what men should be like, which men and women develop to make sense of their lives." MacInnes's argument is directed against any confusion of identities with ideologies, thereby "reducing identity directly to ideology." Instead he proposes that we study "the specific historical conditions under which men and women ever come to believe that such a thing as masculinity exists in the first place, the different forms such beliefs take and the consequences that they have within such historical conditions" (p. 77). Kenneth Clatterbaugh has recently concluded that "It may well be the best kept secret of the literature on masculinities that we have an extremely ill-defined idea of what we are talking about" (in *Men and Masculinities*, 1 (1), July 1998). Clatterbaugh's article is excellent, but unfortunately he does not seem to distinguish between conceptual clarity within a single text or research project, and the entire field of "masculinity studies." There is certainly a need for a clear concept of masculinity within every single research project, but there is not the same need for all researchers to agree upon a common concept of masculinity.

4. The concept of hegemonic masculinity is often used as an explanatory concept, albeit seldom discussed or developed beyond the formulaic description given by Connell. This may explain why the concept hasn't been modified or challenged, even when employed outside the theoretical framework presented by Connell. Mostly it simply refers, in a rather descriptive sense, to the mere existence of some kind of power structure between different groups of men, to emphasize the common notion of plural antagonistic masculinities (where masculinities can imply very different things). The concept of "male crisis" only makes real sense opposite a "normal" situation, that is hardly ever described in detail, for good reasons. According to both psychoanalytical and postmodern theories masculine identity is perceived as a permanent crisis, making the contribution made by the concept of crisis seem rather redundant.

5. There are many examples among gender scholars that this insight has already been incorporated; one example is given by Lynne Joyrich, who writes: "The investigation of the construction and embodiment of the previously unmarked category of masculinity is part of this effort to emphasize the differences

among and within (not simply between) definitions of masculine and feminine, men and women, male and female" (*Re-viewing Reception. Television, Gender and Postmodern Culture* (Bloomington and Indianapolis: Indiana University Press, 1996), p. 71). Susan Jeffords has also acknowledged the need for feminst discussions of masculinity because "there is an increasing understanding that many of the issues that affect women's lives cannot be adequately understood without a companion understanding of the intricate interrelationships between the constructions of women's and men's lives by and through the gender system" ("The Big Switch: Hollywood Masculinity in the Nineties," in Collins, Radner and Collins (eds), *Film Theory Goes to the Movies* (New York and London: Routledge, 1993), p.197).

6. We include two examples of the criticism directed against the field of "masculinity studies," and encourage the reader to evaluate herself whether each of the authors included in these volumes has been sufficiently forthcoming in regard to the concerns raised here. Unfortunately there is a tendency among some critics to generalize from criticism of specific research to "studies of men and masculinities" in general. We would like to suggest that criticism of certain "studies of men and masculinities" could also be read as an argument for improving these, rather than rejecting the project altogether. Andrea Cornwall and Nancy Lindisfarne emphasize that "the scrutiny of men, as men, must also embrace prior studies of women and femaleness and locate discussions of masculinity in the history of gender studies" (in *Dislocating Masculinity*, 1994, p. 28). Christine Skelton expresses her concern that much of "the new men's studies canon is characterised by omissions or distortions of fundamental elements of feminism" (in "Feminism and Research into Masculinities and Schooling", in *Gender and Education*, 10 (2), 1998, p. 220) and that "these investigations do not sufficiently engage with what feminism is 'about' to provide insights which usefully satisfy and complement existing feminist studies of gender relations" (p. 221). Both arguments could be challenged, especially because of their attempt to simplify the rather difficult task of locating "studies of men and masculinities" within existing feminist studies/history of gender studies, their belief that this embedding is a prerequisite for complementing gender studies, and the implicit accusation that omissions of any kind are politically motivated. It would be a simple task to find other examples within more traditional gender studies, which could be blamed for distorting or omitting earlier views. And these tendencies might also simply characterize new approaches and interpretations.

Chapter 2

The Body, the Will and the Fear of Falling: The History of Masculine Self-Control

CLAES EKENSTAM

Because there is nothing simple about our relationship to our own body, which is the site of a painful division, the abode of a fundamental conflict. On the one hand, it is the foundation and source of our existence. On the other hand, as a result of the continual presence of the desire that never ceases howling in it, it contradicts and shocks and calls into question the consciousness we have construed of ourselves. This tormentor ... is "the Other" that dwells within us and that tears us apart. As such it is our most intimate enemy, threatening us and denying us. And we turn its arguments against it and deny it as well.

Jaques Revel and Jean-Pierre Peter[1]

The splitting of the body

The two French historians of mentalité quoted above suggest that there is a split within the human being. They claim that while the body is the source and foundation of our existence, it finds itself in a hostile relationship to consciousness because of alien desire, "our most intimate enemy." Since desire proceeds from the depths of our physical being, we may assume that this antagonistic situation affects our attitude to our entire body. Thus, body and desire are united, whereas consciousness is another thing altogether, an abstract and non-physical essence, albeit often cryptically associated with the gray matter of the brain. "We" refers not to our bodies; the abode of the identity is shifted to consciousness and its ideas.

The conflict between the human being's physical and mental components is a consistent theme in the work of psychotherapist Alexander Lowen. Now in his mid-eighties, Lowen has written a series of books since the 1950s in which he discusses the modern human being's complex relationship to his own body. A disciple of psychoanalyst Wilhelm Reich, Lowen has developed a method of body-centered psychotherapy which he calls bioenergetic analysis.

Not unlike the French historians cited above, Lowen attributes the conflict primarily to an antagonism between, on the one hand, the individual's consciousness and volition, and, on the other hand, his physical needs, emotions and sexual impulses. But the split also runs through the body itself, divides it, separates physical functions from each other, rechannels, blocks or inhibits energy currents, emotions and sensory impressions. As opposed to the historians cited above, who appear to argue that such conflicts are basic to the human condition, Lowen claims that they are due primarily to certain peculiarities of Western culture.[2] In one of his earlier works, *The Betrayal of the Body* (1967), Lowen offers an interesting case history that illustrates one way in which the conflict between a human being's consciousness and his physical identity can manifest itself.[3]

An introductory case

Lowen relates the story of a patient whom he calls Bill, a man who has come to him because of prolonged depression and inability to work. A mathematician by profession, Bill is described as a young man "with a cool, precise mind that could analyze a problem clearly, except where he was personally concerned."[4] The prevailing sense in Bill's life is that "nothing happens," and that is what plagues him the most.[5] This feeling of stagnation and uneventfulness leads Bill to fantasize about touching high-voltage lines and jumping in front of speeding cars.

Lowen describes his patient's body as thin and tense. Although his arms and legs are powerful, they are not integrated with the rest of his body. A split exists here, just as with Bill's entire personality. On occasion this split manifests itself as oscillation between exhilaration and depression, tempting him into perilous activities.

Bill is a rock climber and prides himself at being among the best in his field. He claims never to have experienced either giddiness or fear of heights, despite the fact that a number of serious incidents have occurred while climbing steep mountains. One time he lost his foothold while climbing all by himself. For a while he hung onto a narrow cliff ledge with one hand, his feet dangling in the air.

Lowen characterizes his patient as a desperate person who exposes himself to unnecessary dangers simply to prove that he can survive them. Bill longs for the sense of excitement and thrill that danger provides; nevertheless, he is frightened by what might happen if he were to lose control of the situation. He is caught in a psychological conflict from which he is incapable of escaping. Metaphorically speaking, he is still dangling over the chasm. He can neither struggle to his feet nor let go.

Lowen sees Bill as an extremely strong-willed person, but says that if he is to bring himself out of his depression, he must learn to surrender. His will must relinquish its hold on his body. Lowen, whose therapy also focuses on clearing away the patient's emotional blockages at the physical level, instructs Bill to assume a position employed by athletes to strengthen their leg muscles. The purpose of this therapeutic exercise is to give concrete form to the patient's emotional attitudes and make him aware of his physical rigidity. Lowen argues that there is a direct connection between psychological problems and chronic muscle tensions.

Lowen tells Bill to stand on the edge of a couch, bend his knees and lean forward with his entire body weight at the base of his big toes. A normal athlete is able to maintain this strenuous posture for a minute at the very most. However, Bill assures Lowen that he can stand there indefinitely. And sure enough, he keeps the position for more than five minutes – enduring severe pain and violently trembling legs – before being forced to give up. At this point he throws himself to his knees, despite having been instructed to fall onto a soft mattress. Lowen repeats the exercise until Bill realizes that he is scared to death of experiencing what it feels like to fall.

Lowen's interpretation of Bill's attitude is that he is subconsciously resolved to remain on his feet, cost what it may. This resolve is manifested physically in a pair of legs so tense that they are hardly able to bend. On a psychological level, Bill is avoiding any and all dependence on other people, thus suppressing his need for intimacy and human contact. There is a clear connection between the absence of meaningful relationships in his life and his sense of being shut off within himself. Bill's consciousness has been severed from anything having to do with the body's spontaneous functions, particularly the emotions.

According to Lowen, it can be demonstrated analytically that people like Bill who fear falling from heights are also frightened of falling asleep or in love.[6] Falling represents the antithesis of maintaining control. To fall requires letting go and allowing spontaneous feelings to outflank the will – be it a question of love, grief or anger. Even falling asleep involves similar issues, since you have to relinquish control and abandon yourself to the subconscious and its dreams. What's more, falling is often seen as equivalent to failure, a frightening prospect for many people in our achievement-oriented culture.[7]

What Lowen is saying is that a person who is afraid of falling in a physical sense also fears losing control of his feelings. This fear is not always a conscious one, but it often comes to the surface in the course of psychotherapeutic treatment. In Bill's case this connection is unambiguous. On the unconscious level he is just as afraid of falling as of letting out his feelings. For example, he has never been deeply in love. Insomnia is also a recurrent problem for him. All this comes to light shortly after the exercise described above. On the very next night Bill has a nightmare that clears the way for the release of repressed memories and feelings dating back to childhood.

Masculine self-control

This case study illustrates the severe consequences that a split between mind and body can have on a person. I have not chosen this example in order to argue that Bill is a typical representative of our culture. Nevertheless, he illustrates – albeit in exaggerated form – some recurring tendencies. Although such phenomena are not gender specific, one of my assumptions is that the gulf between mind and body is normally more pronounced in men than in women.[8] Thus, the case of Bill can serve as a springboard for a discussion of men's relationship to their bodies and emotional life.

Lowen describes Bill as a man who possesses a cold, incisive intellect. There is nothing wrong with his ability to analyze problems. However, he is totally incapable of understanding himself. He scrupulously avoids intimate personal relationships. His emotions are so rigorously repressed that he barely feels anything at all. Though his body is tense and rigid, it obeys the dictates of his mind with machine-like precision. In order to experience even the slightest sensation that something is happening, Bill must expose himself to physical danger. Clearly he carries a great deal of destructive potential within him.

Only after Bill lets go, after he has "fallen" in the symbolic sense that Lowen speaks of, can he emerge from his depression. According to Lowen, a person who finds himself in such a predicament must loosen the grip that the will has on the body and let out his suppressed feelings. This is the key to finding a way out of his depression toward more meaningful relationships and a richer life. The rigid self-control that such a person has cultivated becomes such a serious problem for him that the only way out is to give free reign to his body's natural spontaneity. The fact that Bill "lives exclusively in his head" and has cut himself off from a more vital relationship with his body constitutes his fundamental dilemma.

Are not these personality traits the very ones that the public debate of the past two decades has put forth as the source of men's difficulties? Have we not read over and over about young men who risk their lives by willfully engaging in perilous activities? Do we not find rigid attitudes similar to Bill's headstrong indomitability everywhere we look, particularly in men who have attained high positions in society? A great deal has been written about men like Bill who have little or no contact with their own feelings and who cannot handle intimate relationships. Many observers have speculated as to the causes of violence, drug abuse, sexual assault and other forms of destructive behavior, all of which are committed overwhelmingly by men.

I would argue that Bill is not essentially different from many people in contemporary Western society, particularly men, who identify almost wholly with their thoughts and consequently "live in their heads." Of course, this tendency varies in strength from individual to individual. I have to agree with Lowen that this development is a major contributing factor to a whole host of personal and societal problems. This by no means implies that I want to denigrate the work of the intellect, but I am leveling a critique against the dissociation from the body and emotional life that has been brought about by the type of rationality currently promoted by our society, especially in failing to take seriously the inner life of human beings.[9] I would go even further and assert that this process is one pillar of the perpetuation of rigid masculine power structures and the depersonalization of contemporary social relations. Despite a widespread belief to the contrary, such tendencies also exacerbate destructive behavior, the underlying cause of which is not lack of control over our basic drives, but rather inadequate integration of mind and body, a phenomenon we may assume to be a consequence of specific historical developments.

Identifying exclusively with a type of rationality that is detached from the body reinforces the kind of split personality described in the quotation at the beginning of this paper. The body is renounced. This is a frequent occurrence in our culture, both in scholarly discourse and in everyday life. To take just one example, even clearly physical phenomena such as sexual desire and intercourse are often portrayed in newspaper advice columns as belonging primarily to the mental sphere. Ruth Westheimer, the American sexologist who is better known as Dr. Ruth, provides a good example of this approach when she writes that "orgasm is in the head."[10] According to this idealistic point of view, notions of sexuality are more basic to our sexual experience and behavior than physical desire and sensation.

Michel Foucault and Richard Sennet suggest in a joint essay that the concept of sexuality as a mental phenomenon is the consequence of an historic process in the West. The medieval church father St. Augustine – as well as other early theological and medical authorities – treats sexuality as a singularly somatic phenomenon. St. Augustine describes orgasm as a kind of convulsion during which the body is seized by intense spasms. He writes that "the sexual act assumes complete control of a person's being, both physiological and emotional; it leads to the greatest possible pleasure on the level of the senses, and when this culmination is attained, all intentional thought is shunted aside."[11] However, subsequent writers begin to describe sexuality in another manner altogether. The explicit physicality that characterizes St. Augustine's depiction makes way for a more psychological narrative. According to Foucault, it is possible "that after St. Augustine we have come to experience sexuality in our minds."[12]

The hypothesis that our view of the nature of sexuality now emphasizes the mind over the body is an extremely interesting one. We can only speculate as to whether this intellectual shift has been matched by an actual change in our relationship to our bodies. From Lowen's point of view, such a social and psychological transformation is theoretically plausible. In fact, he indirectly confirms Foucault's and Sennet's thesis. Lowen argues that contemporary concepts of sexuality proceed from mental images that emphasize technique and achievement, the ultimate result of which is "sex in our heads." In this scheme of things, intercourse tends more to be a defence against emotions than a means of expressing them. He locates the underlying cause of this state of affairs in the particular regulation of sexuality currently dominant in the West. However, he asserts that a sexuality based more on the body is possible, given other societal and cultural conditions than those that exist now.[13]

A belated introduction: The intellectual history of men

Without rejecting the possibility that a splitting of the personality may be inherent to the human condition, I will assume that this phenomenon originates primarily from the changes that have taken place in our culture with regard to mentalité. Scholars such as Norbert Elias and Michel Foucault have convincingly argued that a human being's relationship to his body and drives has undergone a major transformation since pre-industrial times.[14] As a result, the relationship between our minds and bodies has also shifted.

Clearly I have no intention of treating this transformation as though it began at a specific point in history. As Elias points out, there is no zero point with regard to human development, just as there is no zero point for the human community. Both "primitive" and "civilized" peoples establish a series of behavioral prohibitions and restrictions, all of which directly affect the individual psyche.[15] Nevertheless, such prohibitions and restrictions differ significantly from one culture and epoch to the next. They can become stronger or weaker, or other more subtle variations can arise. Assuming this to be the case, cleavages in human experience should manifest themselves in different ways and attain different degrees of visibility.

As has long been emphasized within women's studies, biological sex is always interpreted through a cultural screen. The newer discipline of men's studies has gleaned a growing body of knowledge that confirms this thesis by demonstrating that the ways in which masculinity finds expression vary with societal conditions. If one proceeds, as Lowen does, from the assumption that the psyche is somatically grounded and intimately connected to the life of the emotions, it follows that the various forms that masculinity assumes can also vary with attitudes toward the body and its urges.

In the tradition of Elias and Foucault, I want to emphasize that we must take into consideration long-term historical processes if we are to understand the emergence of the modern subject. At the same time, these two scholars have opened themselves to criticism by not having paid attention to the fact that the process of civilization and discipline, a process which they maintain has engendered the modern ego, is related to gender. The individual who, according to Elias, plans out his life and calculates the possible advantages associated with maintaining self-control is a man. The disciplined ego, which achieves strategic leverage by subjecting feelings to conscious goals, is masculine in the same way that femininity is associated with the body and the emotions and is assumed to constitute their ultimate expression rather than being the product of emotional restraint.[16]

Social historian Peter N. Stearns discusses the evolution of modern masculinity from such a long-range perspective, although in this context he does not refer to either Elias or Foucault. According to Stearns, masculine ideals have always been shaped by the material and societal circumstances under which men have lived, but they have also been influenced by the tenacious traditions of bygone eras. Thus, the ideologies surrounding contemporary males have roots that extend deep into the strata of human history.

Stearns considers industrialism to be an important watershed in men's history. He argues that the crisis of contemporary masculinity is largely a result of the changes in mentalities that the emergence of industrial society gave rise to. Up until that time there were more generally accepted concepts about what it meant to be a man. That's not to say that images of masculinity were totally harmonious or lacking in internal contradictions. Rather than one masculine ideal, we should assume that there were several, each tied to a particular social class. The various ideals both complemented and contradicted each other.[17]

What I intend to take up below is one particular pre-industrial masculine ideal. My example is from the years around 1700. On the one hand, it represents a distinct contrast to the masculinity of our own day and age, thereby illustrating the mutability of such ideals. On the other hand, Stearns's argument suggests that the masculine ideal I will discuss has affected more recent developments in our views of men. My presentation will focus on the attitudes that this ideal reveals about the male body and men's emotional life. Critical research on men's history – particularly more distant periods – is still in its beginning stages; thus the knowledge we have at our disposal is highly inadequate. Nor can a single example serve as a complete illustration of a particular ideal, much less of an entire society's outlook. Instead of attempting to define the universal features intrinsic to a certain way of looking at men, I want to offer a case study, which needs to be more fully developed and compared to similar analyses.[18] Nevertheless, I hope that this example can say something important about the masculine ideal of that time, and that, despite its limitations, it possesses some degree of general applicability.

In discussing this case, I will employ the distinction between emotional ideals and actual feelings developed by Peter N. Stearns and Carol Z. Stearns.[19] They point out that a differentiation must be made between the standards by which feelings in a society or group are evaluated or regulated and people's actual emotional experiences. Scholars have frequently confused these two levels. Tensions and discrepancies between the ideals that society holds up and people's concrete experiences are not uncommon. Over-hasty conclusions have been drawn about the presence or absence of specific emotions at a particular time in history merely on the basis of normative statements from the period.

The prescriptive level – "the emotional rules" – is what Stearns calls "emotionology." But this level is not the same thing as people's real experiences and ways of expressing their feelings, granted that there must exist a series of connections between emotionology and actual emotions. For example, norms that restrict and model the expression of emotions can certainly affect real life, but there may be a significant time delay and the effect may differ significantly from the original intention.

Pastor, sinner and troublemaker

Beginning in 1770, several volumes of a publication titled Anecdotes Concerning Renowned and Remarkable Swedish Men (referred to as Swedish Men from now on) were issued in Stockholm. This sweeping work is a curious combination of encyclopedic entries, genealogical tables, diaries and biographies of Swedish men. Fervent, highly personal presentations alternate with gossip and low-keyed, semi-official portraits. Despite the fact that a number of famous men – most of them aristocrats – emerge out of the past, it would be difficult to find a common thread in the messages that the variegated presentations are intended to convey.

The foreword to the work asserts that portrayals of renowned men have always been regarded as an effective way of providing their successors "with a spur to virtue as well as a warning against error and weakness."[20] One of the figures who appears to be included more as an admonitory example than as an illustration of virtue is the outspoken Mora priest Jacob Boëthius (1647-1718). According to Swedish Men, Boëthius's fear of God and benevolence toward his country are beyond reproach. Nevertheless, he exemplifies "an injurious enthusiasm" that "discloses an overwrought zeal and impetuosity."[21] Due to his relentless attacks on the Carolingian autocracy of his time, Boëthius was branded as an instigator and blasphemer, for which he was sentenced to death in 1697. The death penalty was lifted, but he still had to spend 13 years in jail.[22]

Although it would not be difficult to find other men with temperaments just as fiery as Boëthius's during Sweden's period as a great power (the seventeenth century), he went further than most. As pointed out by Carl Gustaf Boëthius, one of Jacob's descendants, his contemporaries were startled and horrified by his severity and his radical break with all worldly considerations.[23] He was an observant Lutheran with pietistic leanings who took his religion with the utmost seriousness. Though he was not unique in this respect, what distinguished him was his extraordinary consistency. But even extreme cases can sometimes illuminate more universal patterns. Since many of Boëthius's public and private writings have been preserved, his life can help shed light on the relationship between ideals and reality, emotionology and actual feelings.

"The body is a beast, swine and monster"

In a ten-page letter to his son Simon, Boëthius offers a fascinating picture of human beings as spiritual and corporeal creatures. The fact that the letter is from a father to his son is of particular interest for our purposes, since there is little cause to doubt that it deals with the writer's view of the male body.[24] Boëthius explains that the soul is synonymous with the human being, whereas the body is not. The soul is "divine spirit, a vigorous, magnificent, indivisible and immortal essence," while "the body is a beast, swine and monster."[25] Thus, he emphasizes from the very first the chasm that separates the positive qualities associated with the soul from the despicable bestiality that characterizes the body.

Boëthius concedes that the body is a marvelous work of God, created from ashes and dust; nonetheless, "because of sin, it must turn back to nasty and fetid earth."[26] The soul, on the other hand, will live forever, either in bliss and glory or in "shame, infamy and anguish," depending on how one has conducted his life. So he admonishes his son to cleanse his soul with "the tears of daily penance"[27] In so doing, he will spare himself the eternal torments of hell.

According to Boëthius, the soul cannot be totally free from sin and its contagion as long as it resides in an impure body. The principal abode of sin is the body and its organs. Boëthius provides a detailed catalogue of where the various sins are located. The head is the seat of folly, abuse and imprudence, particularly with respect to dereliction of one's duty to God and contempt for his commandments. The head is also the habitat of vanity, superstition, fury and "haughty glances."[28] The mouth and tongue are the culprits when God's name is taken in vain or slanderous oaths are uttered.The further Boëthius descends, the greater his titillation and abhorrence:

> The chest gives rise to self-love and hatred toward others, as well as envy, ill-will, rage, bitterness, murderous impulses and insubordination. In the belly and abdomen sit a wolf and swinish gluttony, revelry, inebriation and

drunkenness, wicked desires, larcenous proclivities that spread out to the hands and feet; further down in the loins resides an odious lasciviousness, debility worse than a dog's, the lust for fornication and copulation. All these heinous sins dwell in the body or the flesh and its carnal members, and they are a human being's most implacable foes.[29]

As this passage demonstrates, Boëthius does not pull any punches in his denunciation of the human being's corporeal weaknesses. He assigns each sin to a specific part of the body. Actions and feelings associated with sympathy and antipathy toward other people (or toward one's self) reside in the chest, that is near the heart. The stomach is linked to everything having to do with greed, whether it is a question of food or other people's property. Sexual desire is centered in the area of the genitals. Since "odious lasciviousness" and "the lust for fornication and copulation" are found "further down in the loins," one thing you cannot say about Boëthius is that he regards sex as being "in the head." For him the propensity to carnal sin is located primarily in the body.

By no means does Boëthius claim that there exists a simple antithetical relationship between the body and soul, where the soul maintains its purity and domination over the body by means of rejecting everything physical. His analysis is a good deal more complex than that. The soul must be mobilized to employ just those qualities and hostile forces which threaten the Christian's inner purity. A person who is prone to rage, bravery and revenge should demonstrate those same attributes by suppressing them. A person should harness his impulses in order to free his soul from the sinfulness of the flesh. Through prayers and invocations – backed up by a genuine fear of God, Christian love, self-denial, and divine grace – the struggle for the body must be pursued so as to promote the purity of the soul.

That damn French conceit

Though Boëthius's instructions to his son as to how to lead a true Christian life belong to a genre that flourished in the seventeenth and eighteenth centuries, his aestheticism stands out as unusually severe. Simon is not only to shun "the voluptuousness of the flesh," he is also to avoid "costly apparel" and "sumptuous food".[30] He is even forbidden to wear a wig. In addition, he is urged to groom his hair and maintain a generally tidy appearance. Of course, Boëthius also emphasizes the importance of adhering to commonly accepted virtues, such as honesty, humility and obedience.

Boëthius prescribes a similar kind of asceticism for his wife Helena. In one of his letters to her, he takes offence at her vanity. She has disobeyed him by refusing to conceal her throat and face with an appropriate hood. As a sign of humility and submission, she should appear "in civilized apparel that demonstrates modesty and chastity, instead of braided hair, gold or pearls, and expensive attire."[31] Despite his exhortations, she has been reluctant to stop wearing "French ornaments ... artificial curls over the forehead ... ribbons and frills, or other pretentious and strange embellishments."[32] By dressing in that manner, she exhibits conceit and conformity to the world's wicked, haughty ways; this is particularly despicable in a member of the ecclesiastical estate. Furthermore, in view of the fact that a royal decree has been issued assessing a fine for anyone wearing artificial curls, Boëthius appeals to his wife to cease and desist with "all that provocative behavior." It would be a "devilish shame" if a member of his family were required to pay a fine, especially since he himself had publicly decried "that damn costume of conceit."[33]

Sweden's transformation during the seventeenth century to a great European power had led to a rising standard of living, especially for the high nobility. Beginning in the 1630s, consumption of luxury items and an exuberant lifestyle were increasingly common in noble circles, though other classes were affected as well. Expensive banquets, ornate buildings and elegant clothing often demanded greater resources than were available, a situation which often led to profound indebtedness. Nevertheless, the Swedish aristocracy stopped at nothing in its imitation of the lifestyle and dress of the French nobility. During Sweden's period as a great power, this love of luxury assumed such far-reaching proportions that the King felt called upon to impose restrictions. By the end of the century, criticism of the aristocracy's extravagant habits was commonplace.

Not infrequently the clergy objected to the age's vanity, inconsistent as it was with the ideal of an ascetic life. Nevertheless, many of the clergy were themselves far from immune to the temptations of French gallantry.[34] This conflict can be seen in Boëthius's anxiety about his family's sartorial habits. But, as we shall soon see, even he was not exempt from the battle between asceticism and hedonism.

Men, pastors and beards

In the above discussion, Boëthius emerges almost as a caricature of a strict
Carolingian pastor. Since we are familiar with Archbishop Angermanus's
ravings at the end of the sixteenth century – as well as the ethical zeal of
subsequent pastors and bishops – we know that Boëthius was far from
alone.[35] However, I should point out that such an attitude never reigned
supreme among Swedish clergy, not even during the height of Old
Testament orthodoxy. But for Boëthius everything connected with physical
desire or vanity is repugnant and sinful, or so it seems. Nonetheless, his
view of the body is hardly as unequivocal as it may appear in the writings I
have cited so far.

In the first place, even though Boëthius condemns carnality and such
passions as hatred and fury, he does not reject all expressions of feeling.
For example, he regards weeping – at least the remorseful tears and
laments of the sinful – as a good thing to do.[36] Nor is hatred against his
principles, assuming that it is directed against an object – such as one's
own sinfulness – that is deserving of it.[37] Not even lust is contemptible if it
is connected to sensations freed from erotic urges, what he calls "heavenly
lust."[38]

In the second place, a less derogatory image of the body surfaces in
some of his other writings. In a couple of unpublished manuscripts, he
deals with the question as to whether men should wear beards, a hotly
debated topic at the time. According to Magnus von Platen, Boëthius draws
up a whole series of correspondences between the different parts of a
man's face and the qualities possessed by God. For instance, he writes that
the ears correspond to God's gentleness and the mouth to his words.[39] The
beard "signifies the fruit and divine qualities of the words, as well as being
in their service," that is performing the work of the ministry.[40] Thus, this
more exalted image of the male body is based on its resemblance to the
divine form, to a being devoid of sin.

That Boëthius attributes so much importance to the matter of beards
may seem peculiar, but it is a question that had great symbolic significance
in the sexual politics of his time. The Reformation had brought about a
realignment of gender relations within Christian ideology. Despite the
essentially patriarchal structure that had characterized the Catholic church
and faith earlier, this framework had allowed for a sometimes ambivalent
and far from unequivocally disparaging attitude toward the female sex.
During certain periods female saints were worshipped just as reverently as
the male God and Savior. Venerable old church fathers were occasionally

ascribed positive qualities traditionally associated with women.[41]

Nonetheless, early Protestantism purged the faith of many feminine elements, thus honing the church's masculine profile. It is in this connection that the issue of beards becomes relevant. Von Platen claims that from the sixteenth to the eighteenth centuries, "a bushy beard was almost regarded as part of a pastor's official dress."[42] Of course, the beard has often been looked upon as an archetypal symbol of eminent old age, grandeur, wisdom and strength of character. It has even been associated with bravado and physical strength. Since only men can have beards, these same qualities were identified as masculine.[43] The clergy of Boëthius's time were evidently interested in projecting this particular image.

A popular idea in the early eighteenth century was that God had awarded the privilege of wearing a beard to men in general and to clergymen in particular. Nevertheless, some pastors had begun to follow the dictates of fashion and started shaving, a trend that aroused uneasiness among their more traditional colleagues. Bishop Jesper Swedberg of Skara warned the clergy in a 1704 circular not to go along with the fad and its departure from the course of "clerical gravity."[44] An epistle issued after a pastoral meeting six years later decreed that clergy neither wear wigs nor shave, lest they "appear to fall victim to the lustful vagaries of youth."[45]

What is especially noteworthy in terms of this masculine ideal among the early eighteenth-century clergy is that a beard is not associated with either sexual desire or potency. More often than not, copious hair growth, either on the scalp or face, has been tied to passion and sexual prowess. That can be explained in terms of the fact that a boy's beard is one of the first signs of puberty. Thus, incipient facial hair has traditionally been regarded as evidence of sexual maturity.[46] However, it is clear that the clergy of the time did not look at things that way, least of all Boëthius. A beard should be permitted to grow unconstrained, the new custom of shaving oneself being nothing less than "spiritual fornication."[47] As his day's most ardent proponent of ecclesiastical beards, Boëthius reasoned that facial hair was God's gift to adult males, the proof of which was the fact that it had been denied to women and children. Shaving was equivalent to renouncing one's masculinity and was thus unbefitting a pastor.

In the presence of God, I, poor sinner, confess

Considering the persistence with which Boëthius concerned himself with other people's chastity, you might expect that he himself would have lived in accordance with his ideals. However, such was apparently not the case. On the contrary, it would appear that the frenzy of his assaults on worldly vanity and the temptations of the flesh were in direct proportion to the strength he had to rally in order to ensure the purity of his own soul. In the confessions he sent to the Stockholm pastorate at the end of his life, he discloses with almost shocking candor his lifelong struggle with iniquity. He claims that his sins are as innumerable as the hairs of his head.[48]

Boëthius relates that his wicked career began at the age of ten when some vicious lads led him down the nefarious path of masturbation: "As an adult, I continued to practise this extremely despicable and unnatural vice on the sly – God help me – sometimes even in the saddle when riding all alone, and on all other kinds of occasions."[49]

Not even after his marriage was he able to resist this evil temptation, he confesses contritely. Despite repeated resolutions to mend his ways, he submitted over and over again "to the incitements of the devil and the allurements of the flesh".[50] Only when nearing the age of 50 did he manage – thanks to the Bible, prayer and medication (it is not clear what kind) – to get the better of his depravity. However, the wicked spirit of lustfulness has laid siege to his body in many other ways as well.

When sleeping in the same bed as young boys, he has occasionally "fondled" their private parts, albeit "in repose and without committing any other outrage."[51] Once, due to indecorous curiosity and lechery, he placed his hand on a guest's groin. The same erotic obsession has beguiled him into spying on "the private parts of young girls."[52] He has also been drawn to observe copulating dogs and other animals.

Not even in the case of his wife has Boëthius been able to observe the boundaries of Christian decency. If she has been upright, chaste, and virtuous, he has been wanton and steeped in vice. At times he has compelled her to have sex against her will, for example when she is having her menstrual period, thus committing a frightful sin. On occasion they have had intercourse on Sunday morning before church services. But what he is most ashamed of is the time they heard footsteps outside the door while in the middle of lovemaking:

> She pulled away and wanted to get up, but I held her on top of me and consummated the act of fornication in such a way that my seed spilled out, contaminating both my body and the bed. We were both immediately penitent and beseeched God to forgive us our sin.[53]

Boëthius says that he remained faithful to his wife, despite the fact that "this damn lust to fornicate has been so powerful ... including my secret craving for women."[54] Nevertheless, his urgent desires seem to have gotten the better of him on occasion, at which times he is not very particular about the object of his lust. Based on his confessions above, he would no doubt be classified as a pedophile if he lived today. All in all, it would appear that he was obsessed by his erotic cravings.

Of course, it is by no means unusual in the Christian confessional genre for the author to portray himself as an inveterate sinner inside whom an unceasing battle rages between God and the devil. So we cannot be sure that Boëthius was wholly truthful in his claims. The only thing we can base our assessment on is what he himself wrote. Relevant in that regard is the violent conflict that his opposing images of the body give rise to. The lechery that he condemns in such harsh terms appears to have beset him like an irresistible force. Despite never-ending resolutions to reform and attempts to control his appetites, he constantly submits to temptation. He is literally unable to keep his hands to himself or govern his desires. Time after time his sexual drives overpower his will, despite his commitment to mortify his flesh, to deny himself and the earthly pleasures.[55]

But it is not only the memory of carnal sins that plagues Boëthius. Although he does not confess to a penchant for alcohol, he has contaminated his body with excessive food and drink, especially during his university years. On a number of occasions he has violated his sacred resolution not to become intoxicated; once he even appeared at a funeral in an inebriated state. His list of sins includes gambling at cards for money and beer, as well as engaging in fisticuffs, including pulling an opponent's hair.[56]

Boëthius bewails his inflammable temper, his general impulsiveness and arrogance. He confesses to having vexed his disciples with harsh words and insulting names, such as ass, blockhead, lazybones and dirty dog. His conceit has led him to strive after worldly accolades. He is all too eager to adopt cosmopolitan manners instead of imitating Christ's life of poverty and simplicity. As it turns out, it is not only his wife who has sinned by parading herself in unbecoming attire; he has also formed the habit of dressing elegantly and carrying slim canes with silver handles. Furthermore, he has shaved off his sideburns and put on a wig, although there are mitigating circumstances in the case of the wig: he does it for health reasons.[57]

Emotionology, feelings and the Christian image of men

The inverse relationship between the admonitions Boëthius showers on his son (and others) and his own behavior is startling. He forbids his son to do exactly what he himself has done. In the realm of the emotions, there is a clear discrepancy between the ideals he strives to realize, that is emotionology, and his actual feelings. As opposed to mathematician and mountain climber Bill, Boëthius has an underdeveloped ability to master his impulses. Time after time he falls short of his goal due to the ravages of the flesh. Nor does his prohibition against the mortal sin of anger appear to have been particularly successful in holding his wrath at bay. All his well-meaning resolutions to restrain himself are frustrated the first time he has a chance to act out his impulses. Boëthius clearly has a hard time living up to his lofty ideals. Does this mean that we should discard the clerical emotionology of his time as an unrealistic ideology without any real significance, like a banquet speech to which nobody pays any attention?

Even though Boëthius constantly fails in his attempts to live a chaste life, there is no reason to suspect that he does not subscribe to his ideals. His confessions demonstrate that there really is a constant battle within him between his reason and the carnal impulses that thwart his resolutions. He never stops struggling to rise above himself toward purity and spirituality, toward God. In his mind this ascendancy also represents a withdrawal from the devil, an attempt to extract himself from all that is profane and corporeal.

Thus, despite constant setbacks in his attempt to live up to his ideals, his emotional life and actions are influenced by this effort to elevate himself above his body and his physical desires. Immediately after having sex with his wife in a manner wholly inconsistent with his own ideology, he is overwhelmed by contrition and must ask God to forgive him. While his desires are clearly more powerful than his self-imposed restrictions (he can neither resist nor stop in time), genuine enjoyment is rendered impossible by his importunate guilt feelings. His fall from the spheres of the angels into lust and sin occasions him great despair. Instead of being a source of joy and pleasure, his body is a scourge.

Boëthius's entire life, both internal and external, seems to have been characterized by the conflict between mind and body. His guilt feelings lead to self-torment as well as to finding fault with those around him.[58] All his strivings are focused on trying to get the better of his carnal desires. The account offered in his confessions of the crisis he underwent in the mid-1690s implies that his struggle finally bore fruit. After this turning point in his life, he has "greater fortitude, strength and steadfastness to resist the devil and the impure cravings of the flesh."[59]

The source of this conflict between the will and the instincts is nothing more r less than Boëthius's own notions of the sinfulness of the flesh, notions that are certainly not unique to him but rather were part and parcel of the clerical ideology and emotionology in fashion at the time. Like all of his contemporaries, he interprets the Bible literally.[60] Boëthius is a proponent, albeit an extreme one, of the clerical thinking of his age, which emphasized a division between spirituality and corporeality. Human beings were expected to elevate themselves above their carnal desires. Failure to do so was equivalent to falling.

Regardless of the fact that the Christian clerical tradition was neither homogeneous nor static, its long-term historical significance for the development of the Western mind can scarcely be exaggerated. When Michel Foucault examines the growth of modern disciplinary techniques, he traces their origins to the cloisters and clerical milieus of the Middle Ages and the Renaissance.[61] Peter Stearns emphasizes the central role played by the clerical tradition in the development of Western manly ideals. The injunctions to self-control, asceticism, prayer and contemplation have deep roots in the Judeo-Christian tradition and thus are of great importance for the Western male. In order to achieve salvation, he must struggle against his carnal nature; in other words, he expresses his masculinity by harnessing his sexuality rather than by satisfying it.

Perhaps the most distinctive feature of the history of the Western male that emerges from this tradition is the glorification of the patriarchal system. It was Christianity that brought to Europe the image of the omnipotent father, the highest authority, all-knowing, severe and implacable in his judgments. Stearns argues that patriarchy was particularly useful to a socio-economic system like that of the West, which has traditionally been based on the preservation of the status and property of the upper classes, while assigning petty allotments to the peasant majority.

Once the system had been established, it propagated itself. At the same time that sons were subjected to discipline and prevented from rebelling, they were encouraged to become fathers themselves. The angry God of the Old Testament vindicated and inspired fathers who sought to maintain their authority through threats and physical punishment.[62] During Sweden's time as a great power, that is when Boëthius was writing, this clerical image of the authoritarian father was a living reality. The notion of a severe, admonitory father figure looms large in his letter to his son. Prayer, asceticism and self-control are consistent themes, as well as filial obedience.[63]

However, there was another side to the male ideal advanced by the Christian church. According to Stearns, Christianity also introduced the image of the gentle and amiable man, one who loved and sought love, who was merciful to the weak and able to inspire others. In this connection, some men were honored for virtues normally ascribed to women, thus rendering the boundaries between the sexes more difficult to delineate. The Christ image came to be the chief example of this particular masculine ideal. This by no means implies that Christianity abandoned the image of the patriarchal man. On the contrary, it was stressed more than ever after the Reformation. Nevertheless, there was a tension within Christianity's male ideal that could be neither circumvented nor resolved. Christianity was a religion for the angry, powerful man as well as for those – both men and women – who feared him. This was a dualistic image of how men were to behave. Severe/forgiving, brutal/gentle, authoritarian/vulnerable: the list of opposites is a long one.[64]

Masculinities, self-control and historical change

If the Christian tradition provided contradictory concepts of what it meant to be a man in pre-industrial society, the matter is complicated even further when we widen our perspective to include other groups of men. Stearns maintains that the early Middle Ages in the West witnessed a fusing of different cultural influences, a development that was to create an unprecedented ambiguity in our culture's view of men. In addition to the Christian tradition, the legacy of classical antiquity and the Germanic tribes that had brought down the Roman Empire contributed to this course of events.

The tribal chiefs of the Germanic culture embodied an aggressive masculinity far different from both the Christian ideal and the high cultures of Mediterranean antiquity. The medieval culture that was built on the ruins of Rome's political and economic system raised these coarse warrior-hunters to the new aristocracy. The emphasis on virility, hunting and military prowess bequeathed by these men was to live on among the European nobility for many centuries to come, even after a high degree of refinement and sophistication had evolved.[65]

The image of masculinity embraced by the aristocracy emerges unambiguously in a book titled *The Courtier's Calling: Showing the Ways of Making a Fortune, and the Art of Living at the Court*, the Swedish edition of which was published in 1699, that is during the same period when Boëthius penned the words we have been analyzing here. Written by Frenchman Jacque de Caillières, the book is intended for young noblemen who wish to make a career for themselves at court or in the army. Without a trace of embarrassment, Caillières maintains that the true goal of the nobleman is honor, wealth and pleasure.[66] Thus, as opposed to Boëthius, Caillières affirms the value of worldly achievement, and the same thing applies to sexuality. He calls lovemaking "the very soul of nature, the essence of bourgeois life and the source of all pleasure and amusement."[67] The attitude toward anger in this aristocratic emotionology is more permissive than in the case of Boëthius, though the nobleman is also advised to exercise restraint when necessary.[68]

In an outspoken polemic against the Church, Caillières admits that his sometimes ruthless advice for dealing with court rivals and competing for the prince's favor is not particularly Christian. But he reminds us that the teachings espoused in the Sunday service are not always applicable to real life at the court. If we place all our bets on the life hereafter, we will never accomplish great things in this one. When it comes down to it, we must look to ourselves first.[69]

Just as the Christian male image has shifted from time to time and place to place, the same is true for that of the nobility. For example, Caillières attacks the stoic ideals popular among the nobility of his time, especially in Sweden during its period as a great power. According to the teachings of stoicism, a philosophy going back to ancient Greece and the upper classes of the Roman Empire, a person should liberate himself from his emotions and strive for total self-control if he wishes to achieve wisdom and peace of mind. Caillières says that this ideal of virtue is unrealistic and undesirable. The emphasis on voluptuousness advocated by the Epicureans conforms more closely to the essential nature of body and soul; sensual pleasure is the highest good that a human being can aspire to.[70]

Space limitations do not permit a thorough treatment of the aristocratic masculine ideal. Nevertheless, my examples have illustrated some of the differences between this image and that promulgated by the Christian church. These two very different concepts of manliness demonstrate how hazardous it is to speak of a single or unchanging image of masculinity, even when discussing pre-industrial society. We would complicate the question even further if we took up the beliefs of those who constituted the majority of the male population, namely the peasants. It is unlikely that the view among Sweden's general population of what it meant to be a man had much in common with that of the nobility, and we can presume that it was only in partial accord with that of orthodox Lutheranism. In virtually all manuals on behavior written for aristocrats, "real" (noble)men are opposed to those coming from the lower classes. Caillières writes that a "nobleman's state is wholly inconsonant with the nature of the inferior soul possessed by the serf."[71] In Lord Chesterfield's manual for young men, publicized a century later, good manners are constantly contrasted with the crude, rustic customs of the common folk.[72]

However, if we ignore such complicating factors and focus on possible similarities between the male images set forth in the writings of Boëthius and Caillières, we find that such similarities actually exist. Perhaps the most interesting aspect of their view of the male is that they both proceed from his passionate nature. Although his aims are different, the pastor's energetic striving to overcome worldly conceit and carnal lust bears a striking resemblance to the court aristocrat's fierce struggle to gain personal prerogatives. Both men write that anger must be restrained; but where Boëthius – despite his ideals – loses his temper all too readily, Caillières expressly recommends that one should be aggressive when circumstances are appropriate (for example, on the battlefield or when trying to eliminate rivals at court).[73] Boëthius affirms the value of tears; Caillières admits that it is difficult to hold them back when someone else is crying. These more sensitive proclivities appear in no way to exclude the pronounced masculine tendencies that ordinarily characterize both of these male images.

Despite the fact that both Boëthius and Caillières advocate masculine restraint in principle, they portray men as extremely emotional creatures. It is true that according to the emotionology implicit in the male image offered by Boëthius, there are many situations in which a man is forbidden to express anger and sexual desire. Nevertheless, his emotions frequently have more power over his actions than do his ideals. The emotionology embraced by Caillières is not as severe, and he has a more positive attitude toward feelings in general. At the same time, he points out time and again the importance of exercising restraint in order to achieve one's goals. But for Caillières' court aristocrat, feelings are never very far off.

To summarize the view of the emotions suggested by these two male images, they both evince profound ambivalence, albeit not the same kind. In the case of Boëthius, a violent struggle rages between carnal desires and the efforts of the will to suppress them. The normative masculine ideal presented by Caillières is not as laden with conflict (though it may have been so in real life). Nevertheless, a battle appears to be going on here as well between the importunate emotions and the mind's deliberations as to whether to express or suppress them. Such profound emotional ambivalence, the oscillation between fully expressing one's feelings and bridling them, seems to have been common during that time.[74]

What should be emphasized here is that both Boëthius and Caillières acknowledge the power of the emotions despite their conflicting attitudes as to how they should be expressed. These men could apparently identify what they felt without a great deal of difficulty. They could experience and express feelings such as anger, hatred, lust, love, envy, jealousy and sorrow, granted that it was not always considered desirable to do so. In that respect both the priest and the court aristocrat stand in stark contrast to Lowen's patient Bill, whose emotions are so repressed that he is not even aware that they exist. The kind of man he represents has an entirely different relationship to his emotional life from the man envisaged in the other two male ideals I have discussed.

Were there men like Bill during Sweden's period as a great power? And do the choleric Boëthius or the self-controlled but passionate Caillières have counterparts among today's men? To the latter question we can respond with an unequivocal yes; even if it is not likely that such men are very common today, literature written before the industrial revolution is replete with such figures. With regard to the first question, I am much more reluctant to answer in the affirmative, although it certainly is possible. However, there is a great deal to indicate that the particular personality type represented by Bill – with his highly developed capacity for self-control, his near-total repression of feelings, and his mechanical behavior – is mostly a product of post-industrial society. This kind of masculinity is highly visible in movies, novels and the writings of psychologists in the post-war era, though seldom before that. Emotional muteness – or what has also been called emotional autism – is more and more common in literature and in film the closer we come to our own time.

Do the various ways of relating to the body and emotions described in this essay show that there has been a historical transformation from pre-industrial times to the present in the mentality of the Western male? Of course, it is wholly impossible to prove anything definite about historical processes and how they have affected the male psyche on the basis of a few random cases. Clearly a far more comprehensive study than this one would be required. However, the examples I have provided represent one way to examine men's attitudes to their bodies and emotional life at different times in history. Obviously the male personality is not a simple or unchanging phenomenon, not even if we limit ourselves to a specific time period; class and individual variations are much too great to permit that. Nevertheless, it should be possible to identify certain recurrent structural features in an historical era's concept of what constitutes manliness. These features can then be compared to those of other eras.

Be that as it may, two recent studies offer support for my suspicion that the modern Western male has developed a more effective and intricate form of self-control than has ever existed previously. Despite the fact that one of the studies was carried out by a social historian and the other by a practising psychotherapist, they confirm each other's findings in an interesting and troubling way. Peter Stearns's study summarizes the research he has been conducting for a number of years on the history of the emotions in the West. As opposed to the image we generally have of ourselves, Stearns maintains that – with the exception of sex – contemporary Americans have a more derogatory and controlling attitude toward their emotions than was the case during the Victorian era.[75] By the same token, Alexander Lowen maintains in his latest study that the people who seek his help today tend to have a more complex relationship to their bodies than those he treated when starting off as a psychotherapist some 50 years ago. According to Lowen, his current patients are frequently more dissociated from their physical being, experience greater physical tension, are less vigorous and have poorer contact with their feelings. They live more in their heads; the division between their minds and bodies has widened. Lowen claims that this trend is not peculiar to people who enter into psychotherapy, but rather is a commonplace phenomenon in our culture.[76]

Although the objection may be raised that both Stearns and Lowen limit their research to American society, they both argue that, despite national differences, modern developments throughout the Western world exhibit certain common features. Thus, it is a good guess that the split between mind and body is wider than ever before in Western culture as a whole. As the emphasis on self-control increases and becomes more closely identified with the body, the fear of falling is likely to be exacerbated as well. If my thesis is correct, this would be particularly true for contemporary males. But is it possible that I am painting an overly gloomy picture of modern society? Are not increasing numbers of men beginning to question the roles that society has assigned to them and seeking less orthodox ways to explore what it means to be a man, husband and father?

A wonderful example of such a search for a new male sensibility is

Wim Wender's movie *Wings of Desire*. The angel Damiel, superbly played by Bruno Gantz, is immortal and invulnerable as long as he remains in his invisible world. It is a secure, though often drab, existence that renders him unable to participate in the lives of mortals. He can see and hear everything that happens on earth but has no way of affecting it.

One day Damiel becomes deeply enamored of a trapeze artist. But the only way for him to live with her is to give up his invisibility and become human, that is leave the world of the angels and descend to earth. In other words, he must acknowledge his vulnerability and embrace mortality. He hesitates at first, but the desire to be with his beloved finally gets the better of him. He falls, both metaphorically and literally – he leaps from a helicopter and lands by the Berlin Wall, which was still intact at the time. Carrying a coat of mail, which symbolizes the emotional shield he has cast off during the fall, he wanders toward the center of the city. No longer protected by his armor, but not imprisoned by it either, he finds himself in a world of color and taste. In Wenders' rendition, it is the only world where real love is possible. In order to touch other people, you must be willing for them to touch you as well.

Acknowledgement

This essay was written as part of my research project, "The History of Manliness: The Masculine Ideals in Sweden 1750-1850," financed by the Research Council for the Humanistic Social Sciences. Translated by Ken Schubert.

Notes

1.   Jaques Revel and Jean-Pierre Peter, "Kroppen: Den sjuka människan och hennes historia" ("The Body: The Sick Person and His History"), J. Le Goff and P. Nora (eds), Att skriva historia: Nya infallsvinklar och objekt (Writing History: New Perspectives and Objects) (Stockholm, 1978), p. 278.
2.   Ibid., pp. 276f. Revel and Peter offer a contradictory analysis, arguing "that the suppression of drives is a universal psychological process ... just as basic as the subconscious," maintaining at the same time that this "rigidity in relation to the body, the deafness with which one removes or neutralizes it, is the result of an entire culture, our own, and that has been the case ever since Empedokles."
3.   Alexander Lowen, *The Betrayal of the Body*, second edition (New York, 1969). Lowen discusses Bill's case on pp. 95ff, 104ff.

4.   Ibid., p. 95.
5.   Ibid.
6.   Ibid., p. 97.
7.   Alexander Lowen, *Fear of Life*, second edition (New York, 1981), pp. 271f.
8.   Lowen has orally confirmed that this is his decided opinion, based on long years of psychotherapy with both women and men (Lowen, presentation at the conference, "The Passion for Life III," arranged by the International Institute for Bioenergetic Analysis, Pawling, State of New York, April 9, 1995). See also English psychotherapist Roger Horrock's interesting discussion in Masculinity in Crisis: Myths, Fantasies and Realities (London, 1994), especially chapter 7, "Male Autism," pp. 107-24.
9.   See discussion in Victor Seidler, 'Recreating Sexual Politics: Men, Feminism and Politics' (London, 1991).
10. Dr. Ruth Westheimer, "Så får du henne att tända" ("How to Turn Her On"), Expressen Newspaper, Stockholm, February 14, 1988.
11. Michel Foucault and Richard Sennet, "Sexualitet och avskildhet" ("Sexuality and Privacy"), Res Publica, nr. 3 (1985), p. 40. See also St. Augustine, "The City of God Against the Pagans," vol. IV, book XIV, chapter XVI, originally "De Civitate Dei Contra Paganos," circa 420 (London: The Loeb Classical Library, 1966), p. 353.
12. Foucault and Sennet, "Sexualitet och avskildhet", p. 42.
13. Alexander Lowen, Love and Orgasm, second edition (New York, 1975).
14. See Norbert Elias, The History of Manners: The Civilising Process, Vol. 1 (orig. Über den Prozess der Zivilisation, vol. 1, 1939) (Oxford, 1978); Michel Foucault, The History of Sexuality: Vol. I. An Introduction (Harmondsworth, 1981), and Discipline and Punish: The Birth of the Prison (Harmondsworth, 1991).
15. Elias, The History of Manners, p. 160.
16. See Robert van Krieken, "The Organisation of the Soul: Elias and Foucault on Discipline and the Self," Archives Européennes de Sociologie, 31 (2), 1990, pp. 364f; see also Louis McNay, Foucault and Feminism: Power, Gender and the Self (Cambridge, 1992), p. 11-47.
17. Peter N. Stearns, 'Be a Man! Males in Modern Society,' second revised edition (New York, 1990), pp. 8ff, 17f. James A. Rotundo describes, although not as emphatically, a similar course of development in American Manhood, Transformations in Masculinity from the Revolution to the Modern Era (New York, 1990), passim. In a number of books that discuss the dilemma of the modern male, industrial society is also assumed to have had a decisive and partially negative influence on men, particularly with regard to the father/son relationship. See Richard Rohr, Vildmannen: Om sökandet efter genuin manlighet, trans. from German edit. Der Wilde Mann: Geistliche Reden zur Männerbefreiung, 1990 (Alingsås, 1992), p. 28; Sam Keen, Fire in the Belly: On Being a Man, second edition (New York, 1990), pp. 20f; Robert Bly, Iron John: A Book About Men (New York, 1990), pp. 19ff.

18. See Stephen Menells' discussion of "ideal types" as opposed to "real types" in Norbert Elias: An Introduction, second edition (Oxford, 1992), pp. 88, 257.
19. Carol Z. Stearns and Peter N. Stearns, "Emotionology: Clarifying the History of Emotions and Emotional Standards," The American Historical Review, 90 (4) (October 1985), pp. 813-36; Anger: The Struggle for Emotional Control in America's History (Chicago, 1986), pp. 12ff.
20. Sam Loenbom, "Foreword," Anecdoter Om Namnkunniga Och Märkwärdiga Swenska Män (Anecdotes Concerning Renowned and Remarkable Swedish Men), vol. 1, section 1 (Stockholm, 1770).
21. Ibid., "Jacob Boëthius," vol. 1, part 4 (1770), p. 3.
22. Besides the biographical details about Boëthius in Swedish Men, my presentation is based on Sven Arvid Boëthius, "En kort levernebeskrivning" ("A Short Biography") and Carl Gustaf Boëthius, "Mäster Jacobs Syndabekännelse" ("Master Jacob's Confessions"), both in Mora-Prosten "Mäster Jacob Boëthius' Syndabekännelse" 1707, published by Hjalmar Sundén (Stockholm, 1977), respectively pp. 7-17 and pp. 23-34.
23. C. G. Boëthius, "Mäster Jacobs Syndabekännelse", p. 23.
24. According to Thomas Laquer, a description of the male body is all that can be expected, since at that time even the female body was defined as masculine, though less perfect and in inverted form; see Making Sex: Body and Gender from the Greeks to Freud (Cambridge, Massachusetts, 1990).
25. Jacob Boëthius, "Prosten Boëthii Bref till sin Son Simon Boëthius," ("Pastor Boëthius' Letter to His Son Simon"), Swenska Män, vol. 1, part 4 (1770), p. 55.
26. Ibid.
27. Ibid., p. 56.
28. Ibid., p. 57.
29. Ibid.
30. Ibid., p. 52.
31. Jacob Boëthius, "Utdrag af Prosten Boëthii Bref till sin fru Helena Löfgren, dat. Stockholm den 7 Julii 1710" ("Excerpts from Pastor Boëthius' Letter to His Wife Helena Löfgren, Stockholm, July 7, 1710"), Swenska Män, vol. 1, part 4 (Stockholm, 1770), p. 43.
32. Ibid., pp. 43f.
33. Ibid., p. 44.
34. See Peter Englund, Det hotade huset: Adliga föreställningar om samhället (The Endangered Edifice: Aristocratic Concepts of Society) (Stockholm, 1989), pp. 70-89, 205-20; Per-Johan Ödman, Kontrasternas spel: En svensk mentalitets- och pedagogikhistoria (The Play of Opposites: A Mental and Pedagogic History of Sweden), vol. 1 (Stockholm, 1995), pp. 163f, 218-25.
35. See Hilding Pleijel, Hustavlans värld: Kyrkligt folkliv i äldre tiders Sverige (The World of Domestic Regulations: Churchgoers in the Sweden of Old) (Stockholm, 1970), pp. 20ff, 66-83; David Gaunt, Familjeliv i norden (Family Life in Scandinavia) (Stockholm, 1983), pp. 70ff; Ödman, Kontrasternas spel

(1995), pp. 118-29, 162-71.

36. See Jacob Boëthius, "Syndabekännelse", Mora-Prosten "Mäster Jacob Boëthius' Syndabekännelse" av år 1700 (1977), pp. 39, 123ff, 143ff; "Prosten Boëthii Bref till sin Son Simon Boëthius" (1770), p. 56.

37. Jacob Boëthius, "Syndabekännelse," p. 165.

38. Ibid., p. 127.

39. Magnus von Platen, Svenska skägg: Våra manshakor genom tiderna (Swedish Beards: Our Men's Chins Throughout History) (Stockholm, 1995), pp. 57ff.

40. Jacob Boëthius, quoted in ibid., p. 60.

41. Peter N. Stearns, Be a Man!, p. 33; Lyndal Roper, "Was There a Crisis in Gender Relations in Sixteenth-Century Germany", Oedipus and the Devil: Witchcraft, Sexuality and Religion in Early Modern Europe (London, 1994), pp. 37-52; Merry Wiesner, "Luther and Women: The Death of Two Marys", Disciplines of Faith: Studies in Religion, Politics and Patriarchy, J. Obelkevich, L. Roper and R. Samuel (eds) (London, 1987), pp. 295-308; Caroline W. Bynum, Fragmentation and Redemption: Essays on Gender and the Human Body in Medieval Religion (New York, 1991), passim.

42. Platen, Svenska skägg, p. 57.

43. Ibid., pp. 8f.

44. Swedberg, quoted in ibid., p. 59.

45. Quoted in ibid., p. 59.

46. Ibid., p. 9. See also Carl-Herman Tillhagen, Vår kropp i folktron (Our Bodies in Popular Belief) (Stockholm, 1989), pp. 102-37.

47. Jacob Boëthius, quoted in Platen, Svenska skägg, p. 60; see also p. 59.

48. Jacob Boëthius, "Syndabekännelse", p. 37.

49. Ibid., p. 41.

50. Ibid., p. 43.

51. Ibid.

52. Ibid.

53. Ibid., pp. 45f.

54. Ibid., p. 125.

55. See ibid., p. 61.

56. Ibid., pp. 49, 53ff, 103ff.

57. See ibid., pp. 73ff, 103, 141.

58. See C. G. Boëthius, "Mäster Jacobs Syndabekännelse," p. 23.

59. Jacob Boëthius, "Syndabekännelse," p. 147.

60. See C. G. Boëthius, "Mäster Jacobs Syndabekännelse," p. 23.

61. See especially Foucault, The History of Sexuality: Vol. I. An Introduction.

62. Stearns, Be a Man!, pp. 30ff.

63. One of the things Jacob Boëthius regrets in his confessions is that he has not listened sufficiently to or obeyed his father's admonitions. See "Syndabekännelse," pp. 95ff.

64. Stearns, Be a Man!, pp. 30ff; see also pp. 38ff.

65. Ibid., pp. 30f.

66. Jacques de Caillières, Skickelige och Förnäme Personers samt Unga Ädlingars Lycka (The Courtier's Calling: Showing the Ways of Making a Fortune, and the Art of Living at Court) (Stockholm, 1699), pp. 12f.
67. Ibid., p. 313.
68. See ibid., pp. 57f, 99ff.
69. Ibid., pp. 78-85.
70. Ibid., pp. 14f.
71. Ibid., p. 237.
72. Lord Chesterfield, Första Grunder til et belefvadt uppförande i sällskap och allmänna lefvernet för ynglingar (Letters to His Son, 1779) (Lund, 1795), passim.
73. Cailliéres, Skickelige och Förnäme Personers, pp. 73ff, 100.
74. See Claes Ekenstam, Kroppens idéhistoria: Disciplinering och karaktärsdaning i Sverige 1700-1950 (The History of Ideas of the Body: Discipline and Character Formation in Sweden 1700-1950) (Hedemora, 1993), pp. 40ff, 181ff.
75. Peter N. Stearns, American Cool: Constructing a Twentieth-Century Emotional Style (New York, 1995), passim.
76. Alexander Lowen, Joy: The Surrender to the Body and to Life (New York, 1995), pp. 290f; see also his "Healing the Split in the Modern Personality," excerpt from a talk given at a conference titled "The Evolution of Psychotherapy," Newsletter, 16 (1), Winter 1996, The International Institute for Bioenergetic Analysis (New York).

References

Ambjörnsson, Ronny, *Mansmyter: Liten guide till manlighetens paradoxer* (Stockholm, 1990) (*Male Myths: A Little Guide to the Paradoxes of Masculinity*).

Anonym, "Om Jacob Boèthius", *Swenska Män*, bd 1, Fjerde stycket (1770) (Anonymous, "Jacob Boèthius, Swedish Men, volume 1, part 4).

Augustinus, *The City of God Against the Pagans*, vol. IV, orig. De civitate dei contra paganos, circa 420 (London, 1966).

Bly, Robert, *Iron John: A Book About Men* (New York, 1990).

Boèthius, Carl Gustaf, "Mäster Jacobs Syndabekännelse," *Mora-Prosten Mäster Jacob Boèthius' Syndabekännelse av år 1707* (Stockholm, 1977) ("Master Jacob's Confessions", *Mora Pastor Jacob Boèthius' Confessions 1707*).

Boèthius, J., "Syndabekännelse," *Mora-Prosten Mäster Jacob Boèthius' Syndabekännelse av år 1707*, utg. av Hjalmar Sundén (Stockholm, 1977) ("Confessions," *Mora Pastor Master Jacob Boèthius' Confessions" of 1707*, published by Hjalmar Sundén).

Boèthius, J., "Utdrag af Prosten Boèthii Bref till sin fru Helena Löfgren, dat. Stockholm den 7 Julii 1710," *Swenska Män*, bd 1, Fjerde stycket (Stockholm,

1770) ("Excerpts From Pastor Boèthius' Letter to His Wife Helena Löfgren, Stockholm, July 7, 1710," *Swedish Men,* volume 1, part 4).

Boèthius, Jacob, "Prosten Boèthii Bref till sin Son Simon Boèthius," *Swenska Män,* bd 1 (1770) ("Pastor Boèthius' Letter to His Son Simon," *Swedish Men,* volume 1).

Boèthius, Sven Arvid, "En kort levernebeskrivning," *Mora-Prosten Mäster Jacob Boèthius´ Syndabekännelse av år 1707* (Stockholm, 1977) ("A Short Biography," *Mora Pastor Master Jacob Boèthius' Confessions of 1707).*

Bynum, Caroline W., *Fragmentation and Redemption: Essays on Gender, and the Human Body in Medieval Religion* (New York, 1991).

Cailliéres, Jaques de, *Skickelige och Förnäme Personers samt Unga Ädlingars Lycka,* orig. La Fortune des gens de qualité, 1661 (Stockholm, 1699) (*The Courtier´s Calling: Showing the Ways of Making a Fortune, and the Art of Living at Court).*

Chesterfield, greve av (Philip Dormes Stanhope), *Första Grunder til et belefvadt uppförande i sällskap och allmänna lefvernet för ynglingar /.../,* translated from English orig. Lord Chesterfield, *Letter to His Son, 1779* (Lund, 1795).

Ekenstam, Claes, *Kroppens idéhistoria: Disciplinering och karaktärsdaning i Sverige 1700-1950* (Hedemora, 1993) (*The History of Ideas of the Body: Discipline and Character Formation in Sweden 1700-1950).*

Elias, Norbert, *The History of Manners: The Civilising Process,* Vol. 1, orig. Über den Prozess der Zivilisation, vol. 1, 1939 (Oxford, 1978).

Englund, Peter, *Det hotade huset: Adliga föreställningar om samhället* (Stockholm, 1989) (*The Endangered Edifice: Aristocratic Concepts of Society).*

Foucault, M., *The History of Sexuality: Vol. I. An introduction,* orig. Histoire de la sexualité: La volonté de savoire, 1976 (Harmondsworth, 1981).

Foucault, M., *Discipline and Punish: The Birth of the Prison,* orig. Survellier et punir, 1974 (Harmondsworth, 1991).

Foucault, Michel and Sennet, Richard, "Sexualitet och avskildhet," *Res Publica,* nr 3 (Stockholm, 1985) ("Sexuality and Privacy").

Gaunt, David, *Familjeliv i norden* (Stockholm, 1983) (*Family Life in Scandinavia).*

Horrocks, Roger, *Masculinity in Crisis: Myths, Fantasies and Realities* (London, 1994).

Keen, Sam, *Fire in the Belly: On Being a Man,* second edition (New York, 1990).

Krieken, Robert van, "The Organisation of the Soul: Elias and Foucault on Discipline and the Self," *Archives Européennes de Sociologie,* 31 (2), 1990.

Laqueur, Thomas, *Making Sex: Body and Gender from the Greeks to Freud* (Cambridge, Massachusetts, 1990).

Loenbom, Sam, "Företal," *Swenska Män,* bd 1 (Stockholm, 1770) ("Foreword," *Swedish Men,* volume 1).

Lowen, A., *Fear of Life,* 2nd edition (New York, 1981).

Lowen, A., "Healing the Split in the Modern Personality," excerpt from a talk given at the Conference *The Evolution of Psychotherapy, Newsletter,* vol. 16, nr 1, Winter, The International Institute for Bioenergetic Analysis (New York, 1996).

Lowen, A., *Joy: The Surrender to the Body and to Life* (New York, 1995).

Lowen, A., *Love and Orgasm,* 2nd edition (New York, 1975).

Lowen, Alexander, *The Betrayal of the Body,* orig. 1967, 2nd edition (New York, 1969).

McNay, Lois, *Foucault and Feminism: Power, Gender and the Self* (Cambridge, 1992).

Menell, Stephen, *Norbert Elias: An Introduction,* 2nd edition (Oxford, 1992).

Platen, Magnus von, *Svenska skägg: Våra manshakor genom tiderna* (Stockholm, 1995) (*Swedish Beards: Our Men's Chins Throughout History*).

Pleijel, Hilding, *Hustavlans värld: Kyrkligt folkliv i äldre tiders Sverige* (Stockholm, 1970) (*The World of Domestic Regulations: Churchgoers in the Sweden of Old*).

Revel, Jaques and Jean-Pierre Peter, "Kroppen: Den sjuka människan och hennes historia" ("The Body: The Sick Person and His History"), J. Le Goff and P. Nora (eds.), *Att skriva historia: Nya infallsvinklar och objekt* (*Writing History: New Perspectives and Objects*), orig., Faire de l'histoire l-lll, 1974, Swedish edition with selections and introduction by B. Odén, (Stockholm, 1978).

Rohr, Richard, *Vildmannen: Om sökandet efter genuin manlighet,* trans. from revised German edition Der Wilde Mann: Geistliche Reden zur Männerbefreiung, 1990 [orig. A Man's Approach to God] (Alingsås, 1992).

Roper, Lyndal, *Oedipus and the Devil: Witchcraft, Sexuality and Religion in Early Modern Europe* (London, 1994).

Rotundo, J. Anthony, *American Manhood: Transformations in Masculinity from the Revolution to the Modern Era* (New York, 1990).

Seidler, Victor, *Recreating Sexual Politics: Men, Feminism and Politics* (London, 1991).

Stearns, Carol Z. and Peter N., "Emotionology: Clarifying the History of Emotions and Emotional Standards," *The American Historical Review,* vol. 90, nr 4, October (1985).

Stearns, Carol Z. and Peter N., *Anger: The Struggle for Emotional Control in America's History* (Chicago, 1986).

Stearns, P. N., *Be a Man! Males in Modern Society,* 2nd rev. ed. (New York, 1990).

Stearns, P. N., *American Cool: Constructing a Twentieth-Century Emotional Style* (New York, 1995).

Swenska Män,= Anecdoter Om Namnkunniga Och Märkwärdiga Swenska Män, published by S. Loenbom (Stockholm, 1770-71) (*Anecdotes Concerning Renowned and Remarkable Swedish Men*).

Tillhagen, Carl-Herman, *Vår kropp i folktron* (Stockholm, 1989) (*Our Bodies in Popular Belief*).

Westheimer, Ruth, "Så får du henne att tända" ("How to Turn Her On"), *Expressen* Newspaper, Stockholm, February 14 (1988).

Wiesner, Merry, "Luther and Women: The Death of Two Marys", *Disciplines of Faith: Studies in Religion, Politics and Patriarchy*, J. Obelkevich, L. Roper and R. Samuel (eds.) (London, 1987).

Ödman, Per-Johan, *Kontrasternas spel: En svensk mentalitets- och pedagogikhistoria*, volume 1 (Stockholm, 1995) (*The Play of Opposites: A Mental and Pedagogic History of Sweden*).

Chapter 3

Consuming Manhood: The Feminization of American Culture and the Recreation of the Male Body, 1832–1920

MICHAEL S. KIMMEL

> You can't have a firm will without firm muscles.
>
> *G. Stanley Hall*

It's a psychoanalytic commonplace that what we lose in reality we recreate in fantasy. Those objects, relationships, and experiences that give life meaning, that make us feel full, satisfied, secure, are snatched from us, leaving us insecure, frightened, and desperate. Part of our normal, garden-variety neurosis is the creation of a stockpile of symbols that remind us of those lost qualities, a secret symbolic treasure chest we can occasionally raid to recreate earlier moments of fulfilment.

American men have been searching for their lost manhood since the middle of the nineteenth century. Plagued by chronic anxiety that our masculinity is constantly being tested, American men have raided that cultural treasure chest for symbolic objects that might restore this lost manhood. At times such raids exhibit neurotic tendencies of psychic retreat to earlier mythic times of gender identity security; at other times, though, men have been subject to more serious breaks with reality and the effort to live in that symbolic fantasy world.

This essay will examine some of those efforts to rescue and retrieve masculinity during a pivotal moment of historical transition during which masculinity was widely perceived as being in crisis and in radical need of such restoration. First, I will describe the ways in which a secure sense of masculinity was gradually destabilized in the first few decades of the nineteenth century, and describe some of the mechanisms that men employed to reground their eroding sense of manhood. These included increasing restrictions on the male body through proscriptions of sexuality; the exclusion of all "others" such as women, non-native-born whites, men of colors and, later in the century, homosexuals from the increasingly problematic public area; and fantasies of escape. I will also explore the rediscovery of the male body at the turn of the century as a gendered testing ground, a site of demonstration of masculinity, especially in consumerist fantasies of physical prowess.

The terrors of the self-made man

At the turn of the nineteenth century, the term "manhood" was synonymous with the term "adulthood," the opposite of "childhood." Virility was counterpoised to puerility, not femininity. To be manly was to accept adult responsibilities as a provider, producer, and protector of a family. Manhood was grounded in property ownership, whether of landed estates or of the working man's physical body which was his to deploy as he saw fit. Two models of manhood prevailed. The term "Genteel Patriarch" describes the manhood of the landed gentry: refined, elegant, and given to casual sensuousness, he was a devoted father who spent his time on his estate with his family. Urban craftsmen and shopkeepers subscribed to a model of "Heroic Artisan," who embodied the physical strength and republican virtue of the Jeffersonian yeoman farmer and independent artisan. Also a devoted father, the Heroic Artisan taught his sons his craft, supporting them through ritual apprenticeship to master status, as his father had earlier initiated him. An economic liberal who cherished his workplace autonomy, he was also a democrat, delighting in the participatory democracy of the town meeting.

By the 1830s, a new version of masculinity emerged in the eastern cities. "Marketplace Manhood" describes this "new man" who derived his identity entirely from success in the capitalist marketplace, from his accumulated wealth, power, and capital. The manhood of the urban entrepreneur, the businessman, was restless, agitated, devoted to his work in the homosocial public arena. He was thus an absentee landlord at home and an absent father to his children. When Henry Clay called America "a nation of self-made men," it was of Marketplace Man that he was speaking.

The frenzy for self-making spelled the historic doom of both Heroic Artisans and Genteel Patriarchs. Even today, once-heroic artisans fight against being transformed into faceless proletarians, which means the loss of workplace autonomy, small-town communal political power and domestic patriarchy, while the gentility of the old gentry is now ridiculed as the effeminacy of the urban dandy and fop. The triumph of marketplace masculinity pushed these two remnants of the old regime into the realms of the non-men.

For Marketplace Man himself, the psychological consequences of self-making were striking, and immediately evident to the sensitive eye. As manhood became dislodged from traditional moorings, it was thrown into constant question in the unstable world of economic competition. Masculinity became a homosocial enactment, to be proved in the marketplace, a "site of humiliation" according to Henry David Thoreau. No wonder that perceptive French aristocrat Alexis de Tocqueville noticed this irony at the core of the American temperament:

> An American will build a house in which to pass his old age and sell it before the roof is on; he will plant a garden and rent it just as the trees are coming into bearing; he will rear a field and leave others to reap the harvest; he will take up a profession and leave it, settle in one place and soon go off elsewhere with his changing desires. ... At first sight there is something astonishing in this spectacle of so many lucky men restless in the midst of abundance.[1]

What a lucky man, indeed chronically restless, temperamentally anxious, a man in constant motion to prove what ultimately cannot be proved: that he is a real man and that his identity is non-threatened by the actions of other men.

How could American middle-class men, these new self-made men, ever find relief from their relentless efforts to prove their manhood? Participants in the marketplace, which promises orderly rational accounting, ultimately became preoccupied with a world increasingly out of control. To a young man seeking his fortune in such a free and mobile society, identity was no longer fixed, and there were no firm familial foundations on which to ground a secure sense of himself as a man. Achieving manhood became a concern for men; for the first time in American history, young men experienced "identity crises." "Sons had to compete for elusive manhood in the market rather than grow into secure manhood by replicating fathers. Where many could never attain the self-made manhood of success, middle class masculinity pushed egotism to extremes of aggression, calculation, self-control and unremitting effort."[2]

These young men solved this first "crisis of masculinity" in American history in a variety of ways: they went to work, making sure to keep women out of the workplace and ensuring it as a homosocial preserve. They went to war, pitting the manhood of the industrial workers and Heroic Artisans of the north against the chivalric yeoman farmers of the south. They also went to war against their selves, pitting their manly will and resolve against the raging desires and animal lusts that their bodies experienced. And they went

West, to start over, to make their fortunes, to escape the civilizing constraints of domestic life represented by the Victorian woman.

To succeed in the market, the American middle-class man had to first gain control over his self. And by this he increasingly meant his body its desires, its sensations. In the 1830s and 1840s, a spate of advice manuals counselled these young men on how to do just that.[3] The concern was so widespread, the advice books so popular, and the link between economic and sexual behavior so explicit, in fact, that one modern writer coined the phrase "spermatic economy" to describe the fusion of sexual and marketplace activities. Simply put, the self-control required of marketplace success required the sexual control of a disciplined body, a body controlled by the will. Conservation of sperm signified conservation of energy for its deployment in the market. "Sturdy manhood," one writer claimed, "loses its energy and bends under too frequent expenditure of this important secretion."[4]

Conforming to the spermatic economy meant, first of all, gaining control over the body, often imagined in these advice books as a well of carnal desires and diffuse energy. Like premature Freudians, advice manual writers sought to control these desires and harness the energy toward productive activity. Young men were counselled to avoid certain behaviors and activities likely to elicit carnal appetites over their more productive competition. Above all, these manuals were frantically concerned about masturbation, which would sap men's vital energies and enervate them for the tasks ahead.

The American edition of S. A. Tissot's classic French work *A Treatise on the Diseases Produced by Onanism* in 1832 captured the public imagination and allowed fears to congeal on the secret vice. Self-control, so necessary for success in the world of men, meant sexual control control over what the body did and control over appetite for vice. By the 1850s, several advice books, among them William Alcott's *The Young Man s Guide* (1846), George Burnap's *Lectures to Young Men* (1848), George Peek's *The Formation of a Manly Character* (1853), and Timothy Arthur's *Advice to Young Men* (1855) addressed men's need for self-control over passion and temptation directly, and masturbation indirectly, occasionally in a coded language that readers no doubt understood.

Among the most successful of these advice books were Sylvester Graham's *A Lecture to Young Men* (1834), and his later *Lectures on Science and Human Life* (1839) and John Todd's *The Student's Manual* (1835). Todd, a New England minister, who became one of the nation's foremost campaigners against women's rights, and Graham, a health reformer and the inventor of the cracker that bears his name, were the pre-eminent experts who addressed themselves to the problems of becoming and remaining a successful man in the mid-nineteenth century. In his autobiographical work, *John Todd, The Story of his Life, Told Mainly By Himself* (1876), Todd claimed to have been "an orphan, shelterless, penniless" as a boy; he was, therefore, a prime example of the self-made man. (With one small exception, it was all a lie. Todd had been raised by his mother and two aunts after his father died.) *The Student's Manual* struck a nerve among American youth; by 1854 it had gone through 24 editions.

Graham laid out an elaborate plan for dietary and behavioral reforms that would allow men to live secure, happy, and successful lives. Concerned that the inner "vital economy" of the body was becoming enervated and insecure because of sexual excess, vice, and masturbation, Graham offered a set of bodily do's and don't's, a prescription of dietary and sexual temperance. All desire, Graham wrote, "disturbs and disorders all the functions of the system." To combat desire, Graham advocated a diet of farinaceous foods, properly prepared, like "good bread, made of coarsely ground, unbolted wheat, or rye-meal, and hominy, made of cracked wheat, or rye, or Indian corn." Young men should avoid full and large suppers, and should eat no animal meat whatever, since he was convinced that one is more susceptible to sins of the flesh if one eats another's flesh, advice for which Graham was twice attacked by Boston butchers. He advocated strenuous exercise, the avoidance of "every kind of stimulating and heating substances" and sleeping on a hard wood bed, since feather beds would wrap the sleeper in indolent luxury and thereby enervate him. Graham warned that socializing boys to bad habits of "luxury, indolence, voluptuousness and sensuality" (many of the qualities once praised among Genteel Patriarchs), would lead them to surrender their "nobleness, dignity, honor, and manhood" and become

> the wretched transgressor [who] sinks into a miserable fatuity, and finally becomes a confirmed and degraded idiot, whose deeply sunken and vacant, glossy eye, and livid shrivelled countenance, and ulcerous, toothless gums, and fetid breath, and feeble, broken voice, and emaciated and dwarfish and crooked body, and almost hairless head covered perhaps with suppurating blisters and running sores denote a premature old age! a blighted body and a ruined soul![5]

Such dire warnings indicate that, for Graham, the real demon that haunted young men was the specter of male sexual desire. Male sexuality was, by definition, predatory, lustful, and amoral, the chief obstacle to public order. Sexuality in all its forms must be suppressed and controlled. Sexual relations between husbands and wives needed to be regulated and their frequency curtailed Graham suggested no more than once a month lest a variety of illnesses befall the husband.[6] Even sexual fantasies, "those lascivious day-dreams and amorous reveries", which are so common among "the idle, and the voluptuous, and the sedentary, and the nervous" must be suppressed, Graham argued, lest the daydreamer succumb to "debility, effeminacy, disordered functions, and permanent disease, and even premature death, without the actual exercise of the genital organs!" Seemingly harmless sexual fantasies lead to desire and motivation, a boiling lust, that must find an outlet, either with a woman or by oneself.

Many other members of this antebellum vice squad were eager to assist self-made men in their efforts at self-control. Dr Augustus Kingsley Gardner advised parents that even if their children attempt to hide their practice of the solitary vice, sooner or later the "hysterias, epilepsies, spinal irritations, and a train of symptoms" would give them away to a watchful eye. Another writer counselled parents to employ several innovative treatments for sexual intemperance and especially masturbation, including a straight-jacket, to help boys keep their hands to themselves, and tying the feet so that the thighs would remain separate. If these didn't work, he contrived "cork cushions" which could be placed inside the thighs to pry them apart, and a "genital cage," a metal truss of silver or tin in which the boy's penis and scrotum were placed and held by springs. (Several patents for these devices, including one that sounded an electrical alarm in the event of an erection, were issued at the turn of the century, as competition in the war against venery heated up.) R. J. Culverwell invented a chair that served as a kind of douche-bidet for the sexually tempted. An armchair was fitted with an open seat, beneath which a pan of cold water, or "medicated refrigerant fluid" would be placed. By means of a pump, a young man could direct this cold water to his genitals, thus "cooling" his sexual urges, and making himself more capable of self-control.[7]

This obsessive repression of all things sexual indicates more than sexual prudishness or puritanical repression. It reveals an increasing preoccupation with the body and a correspondingly decreasing interest in the soul. That body was a sexual body, a body of desires, of dangerous fluids, of blind passions. This preoccupation with carnality, fuelled by fears of loss of control, led to extraordinary measures to reassert control. If the young man wanted to become a successful Marketplace Man, he would have to control his body, to turn it into a tempered instrument that he could, by his will, deploy in an uncertain sea of fortune, confident that it was able to withstand fitful storms and still remain afloat.

This sexual panic had serious consequences, not only for the young men involved, but also for women, and for non-white, or immigrant men those screens against which white, native-born American men constructed their identities. These "repressed middle class sexual energies were then channelled into a xenophobic hostility toward the immigrant and the black, then projected into fantasies incorporating the enviable and fully expressed sexuality of these alien groups" as well as projected onto women, who were cast simultaneously as seductive temptresses, brimming with carnal desires they were unable to control, or pious, asexual angels, for whom the merest mention of the body and its desires, would cause them to faint straightaway.[8] Sexual anxieties projected onto blacks, women, and immigrants prompted men to devise social, economic, political, and ideological controls, to keep others out of the way, clearing the field for white, native-born men.

The crisis of masculinity at the turn of the century

By the last few decades of the century, the realm of production had been so transformed that men could no longer anchor their identity in their position in the market. Now, new symbols were created, the consumption of which reminded men of that secure past, before identity crises, before crises of masculinity. Manhood had earlier meant economic autonomy control over one's own labor, cooperative control over the labor process, ownership of the products of one's labor. It had meant political patriarchy the control of domestic and political life by native-born white men whose community spirit and republican virtue were respected in small-town life. And it had meant the freedom symbolized by the West vast, uncivilized, primitive where men could test and prove their manhood away from the civilizing influence of women! When these avenues of demonstrating manhood were suddenly closed, it touched off a widespread cultural identity crisis. As historian Elliot I. Corn writes:

> Where would a sense of maleness come from for the worker who sat at a desk all day? How could one be manly without independence? Where was virility to be found in increasingly faceless bureaucracies? How might clerks or salesmen feel masculine doing "women's work"? What became of rugged individualism inside intensively rationalized corporations? How could a man be a patriarch when his job kept him away from home for most of his waking hours?[9]

And so men began to search for ways to reconstitute gender identity, to recreate ways to feel secure and confident as men. Some sought to return to those earlier years, by proclaiming the Heroic Artisan as working-class hero, by excluding women, blacks, and immigrants, or by globalizing the frontier through imperial expansion. But the most striking efforts had to do with the body, both in renewed efforts to control the disorderly body, and the fantasy efforts to clothe the body in the accoutrements of a wild and rugged, primitive masculinity. "As men felt their own sense of masculinity eroding, they turned to fantasies that embodied steroid physical action, reading novels of the Wild West and cheering the exploits of baseball and football players."[10] If manhood could no longer be produced, then it could be consumed, by the appropriation of symbols and props that signified earlier forms of stability.

Historians have long noted the turn of the century as an era of transition from a "culture of production" to a "culture of consumption." Identity was based less on what one did and more upon how one lived. In his classic study *The Lonely Crowd*, sociologist David Riesman discerned the shift in identities and ethics, between the "inner directed" nineteenth-century man, a man of strong character animated by an inner sense of morality, and the twentieth-century "other directed" man, a sensitive personality animated by a need to fit in, to be liked. Inner directed men went their own way, could stand alone, tuned to the hum of an internal gyroscope; other directed men scanned a mental radar screen for fluctuations in public opinion. For the other directed man, having a good personality was the way to win friends and influence people.

The new man was perfectly suited for the emerging culture of consumption. These new values were reinforced in new institutions such as the department store, vaudeville stage, baseball diamonds, and the advertising industry. They also underscored the search for a new foundation upon which to ground manhood for the coming century. Such a search involved a sweeping critique of the "feminization" of American culture. As the traditional bases for manhood were eroding, Americans had lost the hardy virtues of rugged manliness and were becoming soft, effete, enervated. To some, this was a symptom of a widespread cultural degeneration, of race mixing, the dilution of native blood stock. To others, rapid industrialization and urbanization had created a class of robotic workers and a new class of "brain workers," men who sit at desks all day and never physically exert themselves. Others were preoccupied with the feminization of young boys: since the separation of spheres required that men be away from home all day, the socialization of young boys had been completely taken over by women as mothers, teachers, and Sunday School instructors. To reconstitute

American manhood meant literally to rescue boys from the feminizing clutches of adult women.

Efforts to reconstitute male identity in the realm of consumption required several psychological and cultural inversions of earlier ways to demonstrate manhood. Early nineteenth-century capitalism required adventurous producers, men willing to take risks in the marketplace. Late nineteenth-century industrial capitalism, by contrast, required adventurous consumers and cautious, timid, and obedient workers. As historian Stephanie Coontz poses the problem:

> As an impersonal work and political order ignored men's individual values, skills, and reputation, masculinity lost its organic connection with work and politics, its material base. The loss of opportunities for middle-class men to succeed to self-employment and the growing subordination of skilled workers to management contradicted traditional definitions of manliness. The qualities men now needed to work in industrial America were almost feminine ones: tact, teamwork, the ability to accept direction. New definitions of masculinity had to be constructed that did not derive directly from the workplace.[11]

New definitions, for example, that indicated a historic shift in language from *manhood*, the inner directed autonomous American producer, to *masculinity*, the set of qualities that denoted the acquisition of gender identity. While "manhood" had historically been contrasted with "childhood," to suggest that manhood meant being fully adult, responsible, and autonomous, the new opposite of "masculinity" was "femininity," traits and attitudes associated with women, not children. Manhood was an expression of inner character; masculinity was constantly in need of validation, of demonstration, of proof.

It was in patterns of consumption, leisure, and recreation that American men found the danger, adventure, and risk-taking that used to be their experience in their working lives. Now they found the excitement at the baseball park, at the gymnasium, or sitting down to read *Tarzan* or a good Western novel. Suddenly, books appeared about the urban "jungle" or "wilderness," so that men could experience risk and excitement without ever leaving the city books like Upton Sinclair's classic muckraking expose of the Chicago meat-packing industry, *The Jungle* (1902), or Robert Worst's work on settlement houses, *The City Wilderness* (1898). Or they could flip through the pages of *National Geographic* to experience the primitive "other."

One could replace the inner experience of manhood with a sense of security that radiated outward from the virtuous self into a sturdy and muscular frame that had taken shape from years of hard physical labor and transform it into a set of physical characteristics obtained by hard work in the gymnasium. The ideal of the self-made man gradually assumed increasingly physical connotations, so that by the 1870s, the idea of "inner strength" was replaced by a doctrine of physicality and the body. By the turn of the century, a massive, nationwide health and athletics craze was in full swing, as men compulsively attempted to develop manly physiques as a way of demonstrating that they possessed the virtues of manhood. The self-made man of the 1840s "shaped himself by acting upon the material world and [testing] himself in the crucible of competition"; by the century's end, he was making over his physique to appear powerful physically, perhaps to replace the lost real power he once felt. If the body revealed the virtues of the man, then working on the body could demonstrate the possession of virtues that one was no longer certain one possessed.[12]

The feminization of American culture

In his popular novel *The Bostonians* (1885), Henry James confronted the feminization of American culture. After pursuing the young feminist visionary Verena Tarrant for what seems like an eternity, Basil Ransome explodes in a rhetorical torrent:

> The whole generation is womanized; the masculine tone is passing out of the world, it's a feminine, nervous, hysterical, chattering, canting age, an age of hollow phrases and false delicacy and exaggerated solicitudes and coddled sensibilities, which, if we don't soon look out, will usher in the reign of mediocrity, of the feeblest and flattest and most pretentious that has ever been. The masculine character, the ability to dare and endure, to know and yet not fear reality, to look the world in the face and take it for what it is ... that is what I want to preserve, or rather ... recover; and I must tell you that I don't in the least care what becomes of you ladies while I make the attempt.[13]

Here was the critique of the feminization of American culture in condensed form. Something had happened to American society that had led to a loss of cultural vitality, a loss of national virility.

Some writers believed that cultural feminization was the natural consequence of the invasion of cultural outsiders, the "others," whose manhood was suspect to begin with. Fears of cultural degeneration were fuelled by the entry of supposedly weaker and less virile races and ethnicities into the growing northern industrial city. To others, it was the city itself that bred feminization, with its conformist masses scurrying to work in large bureaucratic offices, sapping innate masculine vitality in the service of the corporation. "Your cities are populated by weaklings," wrote health reformer Bernard MacFadden in a letter to President Theodore Roosevelt in 1907. A few years earlier, Frank Lloyd Wright had hurled a series of expletives at the city as evidence of his disdain for its enervating qualities:

> ... a place fit for banking and prostitution and not much else ... a crime of crimes ... a vast prison ... triumph of the herd instinct ... outgrown and-overgrown ... the greatest mouth in the world ... humanity preying upon humanity ... carcass ... parasite ... fibrous tumor ... pig pile ... incongruous mantrap of monstrous dimensions ... Enormity *devouring manhood*, confusing personality by frustration of individuality. Is this not Anti-Christ? The Moloch that knows no God but more?[14]

Many believed that feminization of American culture was synonymous with the feminization of American boyhood, the result of the predominance of women in the lives of young boys as mothers left alone at home with their young sons, and as teachers in both elementary and Sunday schools. The turn of the century witnessed a gradual feminization of public school teaching. In 1870, about two-thirds of all teachers in public and private school were women; by 1900, nearly three-fourths were women, and almost 80 percent by 1910. The "preponderance of women's influence in our public schools," warned Rabbi Solomon Schindler in 1892, was feminizing our boys; a "vast horde of female teachers" were teaching boys how to become men, added psychologist J. McKeen Cattell. A 1904 report of a British group sent to the United States to observe American education and head off a similar problem in Britain concluded that the preponderance of women teachers meant that "the boy in America is not being brought up to punch another boy's head; or to stand having his own punched in an healthy and proper manner" (although the report did not specify the proper manner for having one's head punched).[15]

Observers were alarmed about the effect of pedagogical feminization on young boys. One writer posed two unpleasant outcomes: the "effeminate babyish boy" and "the bad boy," and suggested that masculine influence "is necessary for the proper development" of young boys. Another writer in *The Educational Review* in 1914 complained that women teachers had created "a feminized manhood, emotional, illogical, non-combative against public evils." This psychic violence to "masculine nature," he argued, was beginning to "warp the psyches of our boys and young men into femininity."[16]

To others, the problem wasn't women but the demands of the culture itself that made men "weak, effeminate, decaying and almost ready to expire from sheer exhaustion and decrepitude" as an editorial in the *North Carolina Presbyterian* put it in 1867. The demands of the workplace, the rapid pace of urban life, the changing, roaring, churning energy of a society driven by marketplace masculinity relentlessly on the go, anxious and eager to succeed had simply worn men out by the end of the century. Over-civilization had made men "over-sophisticated and effete;" their energies had been spent, not saved their manhood dissipated into countless economic and social directions. Suddenly new words such as "pussyfoot" and "stuffed shirt" were in common parlance, as men sought to demarcate themselves from those who had fallen victim to moral and gendered lassitude. Women "pity weakly men," O. S. Fowler warned, but they love and admire those "who are red faced, not white livered; right hearty feeders, not dainty; sprightly, not tottering; more muscular than exquisite, and powerful than effeminate, in mind and body."[17]

Most terrifying to men, and most indicative of this fear of cultural feminization, was the specter of the sissy. The term "sissy" was also coined in the last decade of the century, and came to encapsulate all the qualities that men were not. Above all, the sissy was outwardly feminine in demeanor, comportment, and affect. If manhood is defined by justice, courage, generosity, modesty, wrote Rafford Pyke in his 1902 diatribe against sissies in *Cosmopolitan* magazine, then the sissy was "flabby, feeble, mawkish," "chicken-hearted, cold and fearful." He was "a slender youthful figure, smooth faced, a little vacuous in the expression of the countenance, with light hair and rather pale eyes a little wide apart; a voice not necessarily weak, but lacking timbre, resonance, carrying power." Dr Alfred Stille, president of the American Medical Association, weighed in with a claim that "a man with feminine traits of character, or with the frame and carriage of a female, is despised by both the sex he ostensibly belongs to, and that of which he is at once a caricature and a libel."[18]

The emergence of a visible gay male subculture in many large American cities at the turn of the century gave an even greater moral urgency to men's hysterical flight from the perception of being a sissy. Here were real-live gender inverts, men acting like women and therefore any manner of behavior or action that was reminiscent of these inverts might be a man's undoing. To be seen as a sissy was the worst thing imaginable it meant being everything that a man wasn't. And everything that a woman (and therefore gay man) was. Thus did masculinity become a set of attitudes, traits, and characteristics that were defined by their opposition to femininity, to the realm of women. Men were fanatical in their resolute avoidance of all emotions or behaviors seen as even remotely feminine. This concern with the sissification of

American manhood was so pronounced by the turn of the century that men sought to demarcate themselves from women by any means at their disposal. Beards and moustaches experienced a cultural revival, as men sought to sharpen the distinctions in manner, appearance, and style between the sexes as a way of muting the increasing similarities of everyday life, and thus mask men's increasing gender anxiety. To those concerned with feminization, American manhood was seen as listless, lifeless, lethargic. It needed a quick pick-me-up, a jolt of energy, a vitality booster. American manhood needed to pump up.

Men's bodies, men's selves

And pump up men did in droves. The turn of the century witnessed a nationwide health craze, as thousands of American men sought to acquire manly physiques, shore up flagging energy, or develop masculine hardiness as ways of countering the perceived feminization of culture. The health craze was vital to the perpetuation of a virile nation; claimed one contemporary observer:

> Gymnasiums, athletic clubs, outdoor sports, and methods of exercise and other artificial means of contributing to and continuing the physical vigor and virility of the race take the place of the hard physical labor of the earlier periods, or the love of luxury and ease, when physical development is no longer a necessity, overcomes the promptings of intelligence and experience, and the moral illness of the civilization has begun its work of devastation and destruction.[19]

This preoccupation with the physical body facilitated the transition from inner directed men, who expressed their inner selves in the workplace and at home that is, in their "real" lives to other directed men, concerned with acquiring the culturally defined trappings that denoted manhood. The increasing importance of the body, of physicality, meant that men's bodies carried a different sort of weight than expressing the man within. The body did not contain the man; it was the man.

Turn-of-the-century men flocked to healers who prescribed tonics and elixirs guaranteed to put hair on their chests and life in their step. Men like Russell Trail, founder of the New York Hydropathic and Physiological School, who proclaimed the virtues of hydropathy the famed "water cure" which involved steam-induced sweats or plunges in ice water. Or Robert Edis, who saw impurities hiding everywhere in the feminized household and railed against wallpaper, draperies, carpets and Europeanized furniture. Or Horace Fletcher, whose proposal that we masticate each bit of food 1000 times before swallowing was proclaimed as a way to recover health and challenge the "gobble, gulp, and go" table manners of marketplace masculinity. Or Bernard MacFadden, the celebrated founder of Physical Culture, who promoted a new muscular manhood to be built from purified blood, deep breathing exercises, vigorous workouts with barbells, and large doses of his breakfast cereal, Strengthro. (MacFadden was also the proud inventor of a "peniscope," a cylindrical glass tube with a rubber hose at one end attached to a vacuum pump, designed to enlarge the male organ.)

And men consumed vast quantities of these manly concoctions. Like Sylvester Graham's crackers earlier in the century, or C. W. Post's new Grape Nuts (1901) promoted as brain food for the burgeoning white-collar class because "Brain workers must have different food than day laborers." Or J. H. Kellogg's rolled flakes of whole corn, which were but a part of his total health regimen. In 1900 one firm published a list of 63 imported and 42 domestic bottled waters for sale, complete with the geographic source of each water, and a brief note alerting potential purchasers to their specific medicinal properties. And men bought enormous numbers of the advice manuals and guide books to find out how to become and remain manly in the face of constant threats books such as William Haikie's *How to Get Strong and How to Stay So* (1879), and MacFadden's own *Superb Manhood* were turned into best-sellers, the first self-help books of the new century.[20]

As earlier in the century, when the world is experienced as being out of control, one remedy is to gain control over the body. Many turn-of-the-century health reformers continued their predecessors' morbid fascination with controlling male sexuality, especially the body's fluids, as a way to gain control of the forces that were sapping men's energies. A recurring economic metaphor marks many post-bellum advice books, as men were encouraged to save, conserve, and invest their seed, the fruits of their productive bodies, and to avoid unnecessary expenditure or profligate waste.[21]

Crusaders against masturbation were divided about the immediate effects of the solitary vice. To some, it resulted in the immediate onset of sexual depravity consorting with prostitutes, unbridled lusts that the young man could no longer contain and, ultimately, insanity and early death. Masturbation was a crime that "blanches the cheek, that shakes the nervous system into ruin, that clouds the intellect, that breaks down the integrity of the will, that launches emasculated ruin into asylums of hopeless insanity, collapsing in premature death," wrote G. Douglas in 1900. To others, masturbation would so drain its practitioner that he would have no ardor left over for sexual activity. Winfield Hall's advice book, *From Youth to Manhood?* published by the YMCA in 1900, claimed that since masturbation is unnatural, it is "more depleting than is normal sexual intercourse." Thus, as if in compensation, nature would exact its revenge, "removing, step by step, his manhood."[22]

One could counteract these tendencies through physical and dietary regimens. Eating Corn Flakes for breakfast, for example, designed by J. H. Kellogg as a massive anaphrodisiac, to temper and eventually reduce sexual ardor in American men. Kellogg was perhaps the most creative and hysterical turn-of-the-century health reformer. Kellogg's books, such as *Man the Masterpiece* (1886) and *Plain Facts for Young and Old* (1888), were best-sellers of popular self-improvement, providing a guide for young men and their parents about clean and healthful living.

Kellogg was fanatical in his pursuit of masculine purity. His general health regime included:

1. Kneading and pounding on the abdomen each day to promote evacuation before sleep and thus avoid "irritating" congestions.
2. Drinking hot water, six to eight glasses a day (same end in view).
3. Urinating several times each night (same end in view).
4. Avoiding alcohol, tobacco, and tea because they stimulated lecherous thoughts.
5. Taking cold enemas and hot sitz baths each day.
6. Wearing a wet girdle to bed each night.[23]

But Kellogg's chief concern was masturbation. In *Plain Facts for Old and Young*, Kellogg provided anxious parents with a frighteningly systematic list of 39 signs of masturbation, including physical and behavioral changes. Such a list could provoke anxiety in virtually every parent. What could they do about this plague? In a chapter called "Treatment for Self-Abuse and Its Effects," Kellogg listed a set of chilling home remedies. In addition to bandaging the genitals, and covering the organs with cages, and tying the hands, Kellogg also recommends circumcision, "without administering an anaesthetic, as the brief pain attending the operation will have a salutary effect upon the mind, especially if it be connected with the idea of punishment." Parents of older boys may be forced to have silver sutures placed over the foreskin of their sons' penises to prevent erection. "The prepuce, or foreskin, is drawn forward over the glans, and the needle to which the wire is attached is passed through from one side to the other. After drawing the wire through, the ends are twisted together, and cut off close. It is now impossible for an erection to occur, and the slight irritation thus produced acts as a most powerful means of overcoming the disposition to resort to the practice." (Although the extent to which Kellogg's sadistic suggestions were followed by terrified parents is impossible to know, one can only cringe at the possibility that any did.)

By the 1910s, much of this sexual panic began to subside, in part because of the popularization of Freudian psychoanalysis. If nothing else, Freud was a fierce opponent of sexual puritanism, and the ideology of the spermatic economy. To Freud the sexual instinct was just that, an instinct, inherited and normal. In "Sexual Morality and Modern Nervousness" (1908), Freud argued that the notion of physical depletion had it backward it was *continence* rather than expenditure of semen, that was injurious to men. The only harm from masturbation was the guilt that traditionally attended it. "Masturbation as a rule does not much harm beyond that which we believe it to be wrong," was how one physician put it as close as one can come to an iatrogenic, or, more accurately, a cultural etiology of disease.

Yet no sooner was the fear of depletion through masturbation ushered out as a problem for men than problems with male sexuality found another new, or, rather, a very old, cause. Dr William Robinson's *Sexual Impotence* (1912) was an enormously popular treatment of male sexual problems, going through 13 editions. Robinson argued that "older doctors" had exaggerated the ills associated with masturbation; it certainly was not the cause of impotence. In fact, men were not to be blamed for impotence: women were, since it was women's lack of responsiveness to male sexual ardor which exacerbated and sometimes even caused impotence. The problem was, as he coined the term, "frigidity" in women, which "will not call out his virility." Once again, male sexuality was women's concern.[24]

By the end of the century, psychiatrists and psychologists were blaming modern society for many of men's psychological problems. Some reformers suggested that it was the pace of society that caused men's problems the rush of the modern, the clanking barrage of stimuli, the productive frenzy. Men simply wore themselves out mentally as well as physically. Dr Edward Jarvis, speaking before the American Institutions for the Insane in 1851, pointed his finger at mobility and industrialization:

> No son is necessarily confined to the work ... of his father ... all fields are open ... all are invited to join the strife. ... They are struggling ... at that which they cannot reach ... their mental powers are strained to their utmost tension. ... Their minds stagger ... they are perplexed with the variety of insurmountable obstacles; and they are exhausted with the ineffectual labor.

And Dr Peter Bryce, head of the Alabama Insane Hospital, found in 1872 that mental illness was most common among men "at the most active time of life," ages 35 to 40. Habitual intemperance, sexual excesses, overstrain in business, in fact all those habits that tend to keep up too rapid cerebral action, are supposed to induce this form of disease. It is especially a disease "of fast life, and fast business in large cities."[25]

No one understood the psychological and somatic effects of modern civilization better than George Beard and Dr S. Weir Mitchell.Beard's *American Nervousness* (1881) and *Sexual Neurasthenia* (1884; revised 1902) introduced a new psychological malady into American life: neurasthenia, or, as it quickly became known in the popular press, "brain sprain." Neurasthenia, Beard claimed, was the result of "overcivilization" changes such as steam power, the periodical press, the telegraph, the sciences. The outcome was a host of symptoms, including insomnia, dyspepsia, hysteria, hypochondria, asthma, headache, skin rashes, hay fever, baldness, inebriety, hot flashes, cold flashes, nervous exhaustion, brain collapse. "Modern nervousness is the cry of the system struggling with its environment."[26]

Mitchell agreed. In his best-selling *Wear and Tear: Hints for the Overworked* (1891), Mitchell observed that the "growth of nerve maladies has been inordinate" because the "nervous system of certain classes of Americans is being sorely overtaxed." The cause was modern life itself:

> the cruel competition for the dollar, the new and exacting habits of business, the racing speed which the telegraph and railway have introduced into commercial life, the new value which great fortunes have come to possess as means towards social advancement, and the overeducation and overstraining of our young people.

As a result of this "wear and tear," the "incessant cares of overwork, of business anxiety," Americans were suffering from "dyspepsia, consumption, and maladies of the heart."[27]

Never before had a cultural diagnosis resulted in a more gendered prescription and cure. Neurasthenia tended to invert gendered health, masculinizing women and feminizing men. So neurasthenic women were therefore to be confined to their beds, to remain completely idle and unstimulated; they had to reinvent their femininity. For example, Charlotte Perkins Gilman was diagnosed as having neurasthenia in 1885, when she was 25, by none other than Dr Mitchell. "Live as domestic a life as possible," he advised her. "Have your child with you all the time. Lie down an hour after each meal. Have but two hours intellectual life a day. And never touch a pen, brush, or pencil as long as you live." Gilman was obedient; she "went home, followed those directions rigidly for months, and came perilously close to losing my mind," she wrote in her diary. (Her short story "The Yellow Wallpaper" offers a chilling description of her experience, and what might have happened had she not had the strength to get out of bed.) Men, by contrast, were pushed out to Western dude ranches to take in the masculinizing freshness of the out-of-doors. Men, after all, had to reinvent their masculinity. Riding the range, breathing the fresh country air, and exerting the body and resting the mind were curative for men, and in the last two decades of the century large numbers of weak and puny Eastern city men like Theodore Roosevelt, Owen Wister, Frederic Remington and Thomas Eakins all went West to find a cure for their insufficient manhood. That each returned a dedicated convert, trumpeting the curative value of the strenuous life, is part of the story of how we were won over to the West.

Recreating manhood in the out-of-doors

The effort to recreate American manhood went outside the home or the bedroom, outside the factory or the corporation, into leisure and recreation, to include the rediscovery of the tonic freshness of the wilderness. Teenagers, college students, and young male clerks filled diaries with an endless list of their outdoor activities everything from boxing to hiking, from ice skating to football and baseball. One physician proposed that a certain cure for hay fever was a "season of farm work," not because contact with the allergen would cure the malady, but because outdoor work would cure virtually anything. "Get your children into the country," one real estate advertisement for Wilmington, Delaware urged potential buyers in 1905. "The cities murder children. The hot pavements, the dust, the noise, are fatal in many cases and harmful always. The history of successful men is nearly always the history of country boys." And if not to purchase, at least to rent or visit. "Thousands of tired, nerve-shaken, over-civilized people are beginning to find out that going to the mountains is going home; that wilderness is a necessity," wrote John Muir. And George Evans advised:

> Whenever the light of civilization falls upon you with a blighting power, and work and pleasure become stale and flat, go to the wilderness. The wilderness will take hold on you. It will give you good red blood; it will turn you from a weakling into a man.

Perhaps, but for many wilderness explorers or visitors to newly minted "dude ranches," which were often nothing more than failed cattle ranches reopened as consumer health spas the West had been transformed into a gigantic theme park, safely unthreatening, whose natural beauty was protected as in an art museum. The three men who so graphically memorialized the premodern West, novelist Owen Wister, painter Frederic Remington, and naturalist Presid nt Theodore Roosevelt, were all effete Eastern intellectuals who spent time on these civilized Western ranches and rediscovered their manhood and spent the rest of their adult lives sharing news of their conversion.[28]

Hunting experienced a renaissance at the turn of the century. Just as modern methods of slaughtering beef had been developed, and the hunt was no longer a material necessity for survival, it returned as recreation and fantasy in the proving of manhood. Theodore Roosevelt organized the Boone and Crockett Club to encourage big-game hunting. "Hunting big game in the wilderness," he and cofounder George Bird Grinnell wrote in 1893, "is a sport for a vigorous and masterful people." William Kent, a California congressman concerned about the degeneration of the race since the disappearance of the cave man, rejoiced in the savagery of the hunt. After a kill, Kent declared, "you are a barbarian, and you're glad of it. It's good to be a barbarian ... and you know that if you are a barbarian, you are at any rate a man."[29]

Some commentators didn't care how the meat was obtained, as long as it was consumed. Many health reformers, including Graham, had shunned meat eating, believing that it excited the system and stimulated animal passions. To the masculinist health reformers, meat eating was a potent answer to feminized manhood; some claimed that a diet devoid of red meat would prevent the building of full manly power. George Beard described his encounter with a vegetarian in gendered terms; the hiker's "pale and feminine features, tinged with an unnatural flush" repelled Beard. Following a popular medical belief, Woods Hutchinson claimed that one needs blood to make blood, muscle to make muscle, and that the way to health was through consumption of large quantities of barely cooked beef. Hutchinson taunted vegetarians for being repelled by "Meat! R-r-red meat, dr-r-ripping with b-l-lood, r-r-reeking of the shambles." By eating red meat, men were literally consuming manhood.[30]

Sports crazy

In the late nineteenth century, America went "sports crazy," as the nation witnessed a bicycle craze, a dramatic increase in tennis, golf, bicycling, weight-lifting, and boxing, new excitement over football and racing, keen

interest in basketball, and the spectacular rise of baseball. Sports were heralded as character-building; health reformers promised that athletic activity
would make young men healthier and instill moral virtues. Sports were a
central element in the fight against feminization; sports made boys into
men. Sports were necessary, according to D. A. Sargent, to "counteract the
enervating tendency of the times and to improve the health, strength, and
vigor of our youth" since they provide the best kinds of "general exercise
for the body, and develop courage, manliness, and self-control." Sports
aided youth in "the struggle for manliness," wrote G. Walter Fiske in *Boy
Life and Self-Government*. Manhood required proof; sports were its central
testing ground, where men proved they were men, and not women or homosexuals. One English newspaper championed athletics for substituting
the "feats of man for the 'freak of the fop,' hardiness for effeminacy, and
dexterity for luxurious indolene."[31]

More than physical manhood, sports were celebrated for instilling
moral virtue as well. Here, especially, the masculinist response to the crisis
of masculinity resonated with the anti-urban sentiments of those who
feared modern industrial society. Sports developed "courage, steadiness of
nerve," "resourcefulness, self-knowledge, self-reliance," "the ability to
work with others" and "readiness to subordinate selfish impulses, personal
desires, and individual credit to a common end," claimed Frances Walker,
president of MALT, in an address to the Phi Beta Kappa at Harvard in
1893. The Wesleyan University *Bulletin* observed in 1895 that the end of
the century "is an era of rampant athleticism. But these contests play their
part in making sturdy citizens, and training men in the invaluable qualities
of loyalty, self-sacrifice, obedience, and temperance." Sports could rescue
American boys from the "haunts of dissipation" that seduced them in the
cities, the taverns, gambling parlors, and brothels, according to the *Brook-
lyn Eagle*. Youth needs recreation, the *New York Herald* claimed, and "if
they can't get it healthily and morally, they will seek it unhealthily and
immorally at night, in drink saloons or at the gambling tables, and from
these dissipations to those of a lower depth, the gradation is easy."[32]

So America went off to the sporting green. The first tennis court was
built in Boston in 1876, the first basketball court in 1891. The American
Bowling Congress was founded in 1895, and the Amateur Athletic Union
in 1890. Sports offered a counter to the "prosy mediocrity of the latter-day
industrial scheme of life," as Thorstein Veblen put it in *The Theory of the
Leisure Class*, revitalizing American manhood while it replaced the frontier as "the outlet through which the pressure of urban populations was
eased." Nowhere was this better expressed than in boxing and in the rapid

rise of baseball, both as participatory and as spectator sports. These were among the central mechanisms by which masculinity was reconstituted at the turn of the century, as well as vehicles by which the various classes, races, and ethnicities that were thrown together into the urban melting pot accommodated themselves to class society and developed the temperaments that facilitated the transition to a consumer culture.[33]

Here is what one boxing fan wrote in 1888: "This vaunted age needs a saving touch of honest, old fashioned barbarism, so that when we come to die, we shall die leaving men behind us, and not a race of eminently respectable female saints."[34] He certainly got his wish; boxing was increasingly popular at the turn of the century. As with other sports, boxing was defended as a counter to the "mere womanishness," of modern, overcivilized society. But boxing was more than mere manhood; it heralded the triumphant return of the Heroic Artisan as mythic hero. No sooner had the Heroic Artisan virtually disappeared into enormous, impersonal factories lined with rows and rows of unskilled workers, than he staged his triumphant return in the boxing ring. If the workaday world undermined working-class manhood requiring obedience to rules and docility toward managers then boxing celebrated his traditional virtues: toughness, prowess, ferocity. If men could not make things with the skill of their hands, they could, at least, destroy things, or others, with them.

In his fascinating study of bare-knuckle prize fighting in America, *The Manly Art*, Elliot Corn describes the way that working-class bachelor subcultures in the late nineteenth-century city resurrected the language of skilled artisans in their descriptions of boxing matches. Just as industrialization had destroyed traditional skills and crushed artisanal autonomy, boxing revived it in a frenzied fantasy of violence. Boxing was a "profession," and boxers were "trained" in various "schools" of fighting. Newspapers reported that the combatants "went to work," or one "made good work" of his opponent. Admirers spoke of the way that particular fighters "plied their trades" or understood the "arts and mysteries" of the pugilistic metier.

Figure 1:   Charles Atlas advertisement
Figure 2:   Eugen Sandow
Figure 3:   Bernarr McFadden (Frontierspiece from the "Virile Powers
               Of Superb Manhood" by Bernarr McFadden (New York: Physical
               culture Publishing Company, 1990)

Words like "art," "science" and "craft" were tossed about as often as in universities. Boxers resisted proletarianization; they controlled their own labor and were free of work discipline and authority relations. Here was a "manly art," which instilled and expressed violent masculine power, and required craftsmanlike skill and artistic deftness. Boxers symbolized autonomous artisanal manhood at the very moment of its disappearance.[35]

No one symbolized this cult of "elemental virility" better than John L. Sullivan, a walking embodiment of the remasculinization of America, perhaps the "greatest American hero of the late 19th century." With his manly swagger and well-waxed moustache, this Irish fighter recalled a lost era of artisanal heroism, "the growing desire to smash through the fluff of bourgeois gentility and the tangle of corporate ensnarements to the throbbing heart of life." And no one could symbolize the demise of this triumphant return of artisanal manhood than the emergence of Jack Johnson, the first black heavyweight boxing champion. Flamboyant and powerful, Johnson was the black specter that haunted white working-men's sense of manhood in antebellum days the specter that unskilled free blacks would triumph over skilled white workers in the workplace, the bedroom, and now, in the sporting world they held dearest in their artisanal hearts: the boxing ring.[36]

Baseball, too, encapsulates how sports were used to recreate a threatened manhood at the turn of the century. Theodore Roosevelt cited baseball in his list of "the true sports for a manly race." Just as horse racing had resulted in better horse breeding, Edward Marshall claimed in 1910, so baseball "resulted in improvement in man breeding." "No boy can grow to a perfectly normal manhood today without the benefits of at least a small amount of baseball experience and practice," wrote William McKeever in his popular advice manual, *Training the Boy* (1913). Perhaps novelist Zane Grey said it best. "All boys love baseball," he wrote. "If they don't they're not real boys."[37]

And they're not real Americans, for baseball was heralded as promoting civic, as well as gendered, virtue. A. J. Spalding enumerated, alliteratively, in his *America's National Game* (1911):

American Courage. Confidence. Combativeness; American Dash. Discipline, Determination, American Energy. Eagerness, Enthusiasm; American Pluck, Persistence, Performance: American Spirit, Sagacity. Success; American Vim, Vigor, Virility.

Such American values were Christian values, replacing the desiccated immorality of a dissolute life with the healthy vitality of American manhood, a "remedy for the many evils resulting from the immoral associations boys and young men of our cities are apt to become connected with" and therefore deserving "the endorsement of every clergyman in the country." Baseball was good for men's bodies and souls, imperative for the health and moral fiber of the body social. From pulpits and advice manuals, the virtues of baseball were sounded.[38]

Those virtues stressed, on the surface, autonomy and aggressive independence but they simultaneously reinforced obedience, self-sacrifice, discipline, and a rigid hierarchy. While sport "gives a product of exotic ferocity and cunning," a "rehabilitation of the early barbarian temperament," as Thorstein Veblen put it, its training regimen also "conduces to economic serviceability." Sports reproduced those character traits required by industrial capitalism, and participation by working-class youths was hailed as a mechanism of insuring obedience to authority and acceptance of hierarchy. Baseball's version of masculinity thus cut with a contradictory edge: if the masculinity expressed on the baseball field was exuberant, fiercely competitive, wildly aggressive, it was so only in a controlled and orderly arena, closely supervised by powerful adults. As such, the masculinity reconstituted on the baseball field also facilitated a docility and obedience to authority that would serve the maintenance of the emerging industrial capitalist order.[39]

Baseball was fantasy, and it was diversion, a safety valve, allowing the release of potential aggression in a healthy, socially acceptable way. "One thing in common absorbs us," wrote the Rev. Roland D. Sawyer in 1908, "we rub shoulders, high and low; we speak without waiting for an introduction; we forget everything clannish, all the petty conventionalities being laid aside." Novelist and former minor league ballplayer Zane Grey echoed these sentiments:

> Here is one place where caste is lost. Ragamuffins and velvet-breached, white collared boys stand in that equality which augurs well for the future of the stars and stripes. Dainty clothes are no bar to the game if their owner is not afraid to soil them.[40]

It was not just "masculinity" that was reconstituted through sports, but a particular kind of masculinity: white and middle class. Baseball perpetuated hierarchy even as it seemed to challenge it. By the end of the second decade of the century, some of the innocence of this illusory solution was lost. In 1919, this world was shaken during the World Series scandal that involved the infamous Chicago "Black Sox," who had apparently "fixed" the series. The scandal captivated American men. Commercialism had "come to dominate the sporting quality of sports;" heroes were venal and the pristine pastoral was exposed as corrupt, part of the emergent corporate order, and not the alternative to it that people had imagined.[41] But by then it was too late: the corporate order would face less and less organized opposition from a mobilized and unified working class. The reconstituted masculinity that was encouraged by baseball had replaced traditional definitions of masculinity, and was fully accommodated to the new capitalist order. The geographic frontier was replaced by the outfield fence, workplace autonomy by watching a solitary pitcher and batter square off against one another.

From the bedroom to the baseball diamond, from health bars to barbells, from the cleansing sanitarium to the neighborhood gymnasium, American men went searching for a sense of manhood that had somehow been lost. The turn of the century found men looking, as we have always looked, for increasing control over our bodies, an indication that we had mastered an unruly self, and were able to turn ourselves into productive machines. How ironic that our efforts to resist being turned into machines in the arena of production had us turn ourselves into machines of consumption; the secular body was less a temple than a template of the healthy, self-controlled and therefore self-possessed man. Alongside these increasingly desperate efforts to control the body and its desires and appetites, American men retreated to masculinist fantasy camps, the untamed outdoor baseball diamond or dude ranch, to experience vicariously the rugged manhood that we imagined of our mythic ancestors.

Today, of course, the body remains no less a site of masculine proof, the ultimate testing ground for identity in a world in which collective solutions to the problem of identity seem all but discredited. If manhood-as-character does not emanate from inside to be expressed through the body, perhaps mascunlinity-as-personality can be applied to the body, as evidence of that inner experience, even in its absence. If we do not experience that manhood in the workplace, we metaphorically recreate the workplace in the realm of consumption, as we "work out," or as we experience "performance anxiety" that our "tools" will not perform adequately to "get the job done" this in an activity that was once considered pleasure. Or we head off to the corporate "jungle" replete with signifiers of earlier rugged manhood driving Jeep Cherokees, wearing power ties, Timberland shoes, Stetson or Chaps cologne, before we head off to bond with other men for the weekend at a Robert Bly retreat. Now, as then, what we lose in reality we recreate in fantasy.

Notes

1. Alexis de Tocqueville, *Democracy in America*, trans. George Lawrence, ed. J. P. Mayer (New York: Anchor, 1969), p. 536.
2. Charles Sellers, *The Market Revolution: Jacksonian America, 1815-1846* (New York: Oxford University Press, 1992), p. 246.
3. Such books were enormously popular. William Alcott's *The Young Man's Guide* (1833) ran through 21 editions by 1858. The first edition of Daniel Eddy's *The Young Man's Friend* sold 10,000 copies. In 1857, Albert Barnes noted "the unusual number of books that are addressed particularly to Poling men" and the way in which "our public speakers everywhere advert to their character, temptations, dangers and prospects with deep solicitude." Cited in Joseph Kett, *Rites of Passage* (New York: Basic Books, 1977), p. 95.
4. Cited in G. J. Barker-Benfield, *The Horrors of the Half-Known Life: Male Attitudes Toward Women and Sexuality in Nineteenth Century America* (New York: Harper and Row, 1976), p. 179. "Men were preoccupied with the fear of a toss of sperm, connected as it was to the whole question of manhood and to a man's hopes for some kind of immortality," the author remarks. "Men believed their expenditure of sperm had to be governed according to an economic principle" (p. 180; see also chapters 15-16).
5. Sylvester Graham, *A Lecture to Young Men* (Providence: Weeden and Cory, 1834), pp. 25, 33-4, 39, 58, 73.
6. These included: Languor, lassitude, muscular relaxation, general debility and heaviness, depression of spirits, loss of appetite, indigestion, faintness and sinking at the pit of the stomach, increased susceptibilities of the skin and lungs to all the atmospheric changes, feebleness of circulation, chilliness, headache, melancholy, hypochondria, hysterics, feebleness of all the senses, impaired vision, loss of sight, weakness of the lungs, nervous cough, pulmonary consumption, disorders of the liver and kidneys, urinary difficulties, disorders of the genital organs, weakness of the brain, loss of memory, epilepsy, insanity, apoplexy and extreme feebleness and early death of offspring. ...In part, the cautions against sexual expression were based on a volcanic theory of the orgasmic eruption. The nervous system, Graham warned, is almost unbearably fragile, and is unable to bear "the convulsive paroxysms attending venereal indulgence":"The brain, stomach, heart, lungs, liver, skin and the other organs feel it sweeping over them with the tremendous violence of a tornado. The powerfully excited and convulsed heart drives the blood, in fearful congestion, to the principal viscera, producing oppression, irritation, debility, rupture, inflammation, and sometimes disorganization; and this violent paroxysm is generally succeeded by great exhaustion, relaxation, lassitude, and even prostration" (1834, p. 20).
7. Gardner, cited in Barker-Benfield, *The Horrors*, pp. 272-3. See also John Hatter and Robin Hailer, *The Physician and Sexuality in Victorian America* (New York: Norton, 1977), p. 208. R. J. Culverwell, *Professorial Records: The*

Institutes of Marriage, Its Intent, Obligations, and Physical and Constitutional Disqualifications (New York, 1846), p. 5.

8. Charles Rosenberg and Carroll Smith-Rosenberg, "The Female Animal: Medical and Biological Views of Woman and Her Role in Nineteenth Century America," *Journal of American History*, 2 (1973), p. 353.

9. Elliot I. Corn, *The Manly Art: Bare-Knuckle Prize Fighting in America* (Ithaca: Cornell University Press, 1986), p. 192.

10. Anthony Rotundo, "Body and Soul: Changing Ideals of American Middle-Class Manhood, 1770-1920," *Journal of Social History*, 16 (4) (1983), p. 32. See also his *American Manhood* (New York: Basic Books, 1993), which appeared too late to be incorporated into this essay.

11. Stephanie Coontz, *The Social Origins of Private Life* (New York: Verso, 1988), p. 339.

12. Roberta J. Park, "Physiologists, Physicians, and Physical Education: Nineteenth Century Biology and Exercise, Hygienic and Educative," in Berryman, I. W. and Park, R. I. (eds), *Sport and Exercise Science* (Urbana: University of Illinois Press, 1992), p. 141.

13. Henry James, *The Bostonians* (New York: Modern Library, 1984), p. 293.

14. Bernard MacFadden, "An Open Letter to President Roosevelt," *Physical Culture*, 18 (1907), p. 75. Frank Lloyd Wright is cited in Herbert Mlischamp, *Man About Town: Frank Lloyd Wright in New York City* (Cambridge: The MIT Press, 1983), p. 13. Anti-urbanism as a theme in the critique of feminization is discussed by T. J. Jackson Lears, *No Place of Grace: Anti-Modernism and the Transformation of American Culture, 1880-1920* (New York: Pantheon, 1981).

15. Rabbi Solomon Schindler, "A Flaw in our Public School System," *Arena*, 6 (June 1892), p. 60; I. McKeen Cattell cited in William O'Neill, *Divorce in the Progressive Era* (New Haven: Yale University Press, 1967), p. 221. The British report is mentioned in Luther Culick, "The Alleged Feminization of Our American Boys," *American Physical Education Review*, 10 (September 1905), p. 214.

16. Alfred Cleveland, "The Predominance of Female Teachers," *Pedagogical Seminary*, 12 (September 1905), pp. 301, 303. A. Chadwick, "The Woman Peril," *Educational Review*, 47 (February 1914), pp. 115-16, 118.

17. See John Higham, *Strangers in the Land: Patterns of American Nativism, 1860-1925* (New York: Atheneum, 1970), pp. 78-9. O. S. Fowler, *Private Lectures on Perfect Men, Women and Children in Happy Families ...* (Sharon Station, New York, privately printed by M. K. O. S. Fowler, 1883), p. 5. William James argued that "there is no more contemptible type of human character than that of the nervous sentimentalist and dreamer, who spends his life in a weltering sea of sensibility and emotion, but who never does a concrete manly deed." Cited in Robert N. Bellah *et al.*, *Habits of the Heart* (New York: Harper and Row, 1985), p. 120. See also Henry Childs Merwin, "On Being Civilized Too Much," *Atlantic Monthly*, 79 (June 1897).

18. Rafford Pyke, "What Men Like in Men," *Cosmopolitan* (August 1902), pp. 405-6. Stille cited in Morris Fishbein, *A History of the American Medical*

Association (Philadelphia: W. B. Saunders, 1947), pp. 82-3.

19. George Ruskin Phoebus, "Civilization - Physical Culture," *Physical Culture*, 3 (1900), pp. 21-2.

20. See Harvey Green, *Fit for America: Health, Fitness, Sport and American Society* (New York: Pantheon, 1986). See also G. Carson, *Cornflake Crusade* (New York: Rinehart and Co., 1957).

21. One medical text in 1883 anthropomorphized and assigned political tendencies to male and female reproductive cells, claiming that "the male element is the originating factor, and the female the perpetuating factor; the ovum is conservative, the male cell progressive." William Keith Brooks, *The Law of Heredity* (Baltimore: J. Murphy, 1883), p. 94; see also Cynthia Eagle Russett, *Sexual Science: The Victorian Construction of Womanhood* (Cambridge: Harvard University Press, 1989), p. 94, and H. W. Foster, "Physical Education and Degeneracy," *The Independent*, 52 (2 August 1900).

22. G. Douglas, "Social Purity," in *Official Report of the 12th International Christian Endeavor Convention* (New York, 1900), p. 254; Winfield Hall, *From Youth to Manhood* (New York: Association Press, 1900), p. 54. Hall was elaborate in his advice on the methods to avoid the evils of masturbation. He counselled boys and young men to sleep on hard beds, "throw your whole energy into your work," and perform a regimen of ritual ablution and purification: "Arise three quarters of an hour before breakfast every morning, take a cold sponge or shower bath; drink two glasses of cold water; dress and go out and walk around the block before breakfast" (p. 58).

23 J. H. Kellogg, *Man the Masterpiece, or Plain Truths Plainly Told About Boyhood, Youth and Manhood* (Burlington, Iowa: I. F. Segner, 1886), pp. 445-53; see also J. H. Kellogg, *Plain Facts for Old and Young, Embracing the Natural History and Hygiene of Organic Life* (Burlington, Iowa: I. F. Segner, 1888); Joseph Kett, *Rites of Passage*, p. 165; John Money, *The Destroying Angel* (Buffalo: Prometheus Books, 1985), and T. J. Jackson Lears, *No Place of Grace*, p. 14.

24. Cited in Kevin Mumford, "Lost Manhood Found: Sexual Impotence and the Contradictions of Victorian Culture," in Fout, J. C. and Tantillo, M. S. (eds), *American Sexual Politics* (Chicago: University of Chicago Press, 1993), p. 96.

25. Jarvis cited in Barker-Benfield, *The Horrors of the Half-Known Life*, p. 29; Bryce cited in John Starrett Hughes, "The Madness of Separate Spheres: Insanity and Masculinity in Victorian Alabama" in Carnes, M. and Griffen, C. (eds), *Meanings for Manhood: Constructions of Masculinity in Victorian America* (Chicago: University of Chicago Press, 1991), p. 60.

26. George Beard, *American Nervousness* (1881), p. 138; see also Tom Lutz, *American Nervousness, 1903: An Anecdotal History* (Ithaca: Cornell University Press, 1991); and Edward Wakefield, "Nervousness: The National Disease of America," *McClure's Magazine*, 2 (February 1894).

27. S. Weir Mitchell, *Wear and Tear: Hints for the Overworked* (Philadelphia: J. Lippincott, 1891), pp. 28, 29, 67.

28. See E. Anthony Rotundo, "Body and Soul," 28; Leon Fink *Workingmen's Democracy: The Knights of Labor and American Politics* (Urbana: University of Illinois Press, 1983), 9; Delaware and cited in Kenneth Jackson, *Crabgrass Frontier* (New York: Oxford University Press, 1985), 138; John Muir cited in David Shi, *The Simple Life: Plain Thinking and High Thinking in American Culture* (New York: Oxford University Press, 1985), 197; George Evans, "The Wilderness," in *Overland Monthly* 43 (January 1904), 33.

29. Roosevelt and Grinnell, 1893, 14-15; Kent is cited in Roderick Nash, *Wilderness and the American Mind* (New Haven: Yale University Press, 1967), 153.

30. Woods Hutchinson, *Instinct and Health* (New York: Dodd and Mead, 1909). See also Martin Holbrook, *Eating for Strength; or, Food and Diet and their Relationship to Health and Work* (New York: Holbrook, 1888).

31. Sargent, cited in Joe Dubbert, *A Man's Place: Masculinity in Transition* (Englewood Cliffs: Prentice-Hall, 1979), 169. Fiske is cited in Donald Mrozek, *Sports and American Mentality* (Knoxville: University of Tennessee Press, 1983), 207. British paper cited in Melvin Adelman, *A Sporting Time: New York City and the Rise of Modern Athletics, 1820-1870* (Urbana: University of Illinois Press, 1986), 284.

32. Walker and Wesleyan Bulletin cited in Louise Knight, "'The Quails': The History of Wesleyan University's First Period of Coeducation, 1872-1912," BA honors thesis, Wesleyan University, 1972. I am grateful to Ms. Knight for sharing her work with me. New York newspapers cited in Melvin Adelman, *A Sporting Time*, 277. See also George Frank Lydston, *Diseases of Society and Degeneracy* (The Vice and Crime Problem) (Philadelphia: J. Lippincott, 1904), 582.

33. Thorstein Veblen, *The Theory of the Leisure Class* (New York: Modern Library, 1964), 208.

34. Cited in Michael C. Adams, *The Great Adventure*, 41.

35. Elliot Gorn, *The Manly Art*, 138.

36. Elliot Gorn, *The Manly Art*, 247.

37. Marshall, cited in Albert Spalding, *America's National Game* (New York: American Sports Publishing Co., 1911), 534. William McKeever, *Training the Boy* (New York: Macmillan, 1913), 91. Zane Grey, "Inside Baseball," in *Baseball Magazine*, 3; 4, 1909. Much of the material in this section is condensed from my "Baseball and the Reconstitution of American Masculinity, 1880-1920" in *Baseball History*, 3, 1990.

38. A.J. Spalding, *America's National Game*, 4. Cited in Melvin Adelman, *A Sporting Time*, 173.

39. Thorstein Veblen, *The Theory of the Leisure Class*, 204. Veblen was one of many who were less sanguine about sports' curative potential. His blistering critique of the nascent consumer culture suggests that organized sports are an illusory panacea. For the individual man, athletics are no sign of virtue, since "the temperament which inclines men to [sports] is essentially a boyish temperament. The addiction to sports therefore in a peculiar degree marks an

arrested development of the man's moral nature." And culturally, sports may be an evolutionary throwback, as they "afford an exercise for dexterity and for the emulative ferocity and astuteness characteristic of predatory life." Veblen, *The Theory of the Leisure Class*, 200, 203. Boy Scout leader Ernest Thompson Seton thought that watching would lead to "spectatoritis," and turn manly men into "mollycoddles of the bleachers." "The Dangers of Athletic Training," *American Medicine* 13, 1907, 500.

40. Rev. Roland D. Sawyer, "The Larger Side of Baseball" in *Baseball Magazine*, 1; 6, 1908, 31-2; Zane Grey, "Inside Baseball,"12.
41. Peter Filene, *Him/Her Self: Sex Roles in America* (Baltimore: The Johns Hopkins University Press, 1986), 139.

Chapter 4

Men, Bodies and Identities

VICTOR JELENIEWSKI SEIDLER

Men's bodies, men's minds

Within an Enlightenment vision of modernity there was a critical reorganization of the relationships between men's minds and men's bodies. With Descartes there was a crucial distinction to be drawn between minds and bodies and an insistence that it was reason, identified with the mind and with consciousness, that was the marker of human identity. It was reason that separated human beings from animals and that helped redefine "being human" in terms of being a "rational" animal. So it was that reason became a mark of superiority in relation to "animal," and also a mark of male superiority in relation to women. As I have argued it in *Unreasonable Men*, it was a dominant, white, heterosexual masculinity which alone could take its reason for granted. In this context it was a particular masculinity which set the universal terms for what it meant "to be human." Men alone could take their humanity for granted.[1]

So we could argue that the "modern" was defined in terms of the male mind being "human" whilst the male body remained "animal." As modernity insisted upon a radical separation between nature and culture, so this was reflected in the categorical split between body and mind. Modern philosophy and social theory learnt to disdain the body as "animal" as it give a secular form to the dominant Christian notion which had identified the body with sexuality and the "sins of the flesh." The body was traditionally deemed to be the site of sin, temptation and transgression. Human beings were caught in a struggle against the body as enemy, for the desires of the body remained as threats to dominant Christian notions of "what it means to be human." We had to learn to ignore the impulses of the body as the work of the devil and so had to engage in a struggle between the forces of good and the forces of evil. This duality became central in the iconography of the West. The body came to be identified with a sinful sexuality and was deemed to be intrinsically "animal."[2]

This fostered a re-evaluation of the notion of love, which along with notions of knowledge came to be disembodied. Pure love became a love that was not tainted by emotion or sexuality. For a dominant Christianity there was a constant task, as Foucault has explored in *The Uses of Pleasure*, to subordinate and regulate bodily desire. A war was declared against the body and its desires, which had to be constantly policed since they served as a threat to a sense of self. Not only was the self defined as disembodied, but it was part of a Christian ethics that identified ethics with selflessness, with learning to renounce your own selfish desires. The body was to be feared because of the temptations which rested there and we were to learn to be constantly vigilant in relation to the body, for you could never be sure when its "animal" desires would begin to stir. Within Catholicism this was linked to the institution of confession.

Confession kept open the possibilities of a new beginning, of starting again in your quest for goodness. With will and determination you could show a new vigilance. The body was to be constantly watched and it could never be left unguarded. Within Catholic cultures this leaves its mark upon dominant masculinities and the ordering of gender relations of power. It can influence the way men learn to think of their sexualities as "animal" and the guilt they learn to carry in relation to their bodily desires. It is as if their sexualities are deemed to have a life of their own, beyond the control of men. But it also influences the pervasive distinction drawn between women as "virgins" or "whores." This not only reflects ways in which men learn to see women, but also the uneasy ways men learn to relate to their own bodily sexual desires.[3] This also reflects itself in the conversation that takes place between men, who seek to prove their male identities through the negative and demeaning ways they use to talk about women. Often this helps to shape the contact that men have with each other and helps them to control their own fears of intimacy in cultures that remain strongly homophobic. Men seek to prove their male identities and place their heterosexuality beyond question, in the sexist ways they learn to talk of women from a very early age.

As Max Weber talks about the crucial relationships between Protestantism and the capitalist ethic, he is aware of the different ways men can learn to discipline their bodies in a culture that no longer allows for confession. The sense of guilt has a different intensity in a culture that casts human natures as irredeemably evil. There is a different ethics of self-rejection within a Protestant culture, which puts greater emphasis upon men being independent and self-sufficient. This creates a different kind of unease in the relationships men can have with each other, for the relationships remain competitive.[4] It can mean that men are more isolated and lonely, finding it harder to draw upon the support of other men without being left feeling that they have somehow failed. Within a Latin culture there might be more bodily contact between men and more emotional support offered in male friendships, though they remain circumscribed in different ways because the fear of homosexuality has to be policed differently.

The ways that men learn to mediate the relationships between mind and body have to be carefully traced within different cultures. Often the secular terms in which modernity has been cast make it difficult to re/member the theological sources that continue to resonate within modernity. The ascendancy of a dominant Protestantism within modernity allows for a particular forgetfulness, for it has the power to refuse to acknowledge its continuing hegemony. Rather we learn to take for granted the silencing of the body, which has been refused a voice within the dominant rationalist traditions. If the body is to be rediscovered within postmodernity, it is often only as a space upon which cultural meanings are to be inscribed. We learn to read off cultural meanings from the body and it remains a space for cultural representations.[5]

Within modernity men learn to live in the mind. As Kant has it, learning from Descartes, men must learn to "rise above" their animal natures. Learning to feel uneasy about their bodies, they learn to ascend into their minds. They develop an inner relationship with their reason and mind, which becomes the source of freedom and autonomy, and an external relationship with their body, which becomes a site of unfreedom and determination. This split is reflected in the iconography of the body, where it seems as if nature begins at the point where the neck joins the body. The head is separated from the rest of the body and is the space of mind and thought. But as Freud recognizes, there is a radical split between thinking and feeling, since emotions and feelings are sited in the body. The body is cast as part of the world of nature to be explained according to the scientific laws of the natural world. The body comes to be appropriated as an object of medical knowledge and it is the doctor who comes to have authority in relation to bodies. At some level our bodies come to be appropriated and they no longer exist as "part of" our identities as rational selves.

Men's bodies and emotions

At some level men can feel that they do not have emotions, they only have thoughts. While within a Latin culture it might be possible for men to acknowledge their sadness, even as this works as a form of power within gender relations, within the Protestant West it can seem as if sadness is a sign of weakness. A dominant masculinity would often suppress signs of sadness because they so easily could reflect badly in their male identities. Rather it is women who have emotions, and sadness might be described as a "feminine" emotion. To acknowledge sadness can be to acknowledge vulnerability and emotional need. Often mean learn to discount their emotional needs, especially in public. So it is that men often learn to suppress their emotions, and since emotions are sited in the body, they are "controlled" as men learn to exercise self-control.

As men learn to be independent and self-sufficient they learn that they should be able to survive without the love and support of others. They might appreciate the care that others have to offer, but at some level they know they can survive without it. This creates imbalance within heterosexual relationships, for it often means that men learn to support their partners, while at some level feeling that they do not need support from others. They learn to be "strong" for others, as if they do not have any emotional needs themselves. They learn to pride themselves in their strength, which becomes a mark of their superiority in relation to women. Women prove their supposed inferiority through their emotional needs for support, while men learn to prove that they are "man enough" though discounting whatever needs they might have. As Weber recognizes, men have to constantly prove themselves because they can be haunted by a sense of failure, of not being "good enough." This can give a compulsive quality to their activities, for they can feel that whatever they achieve, it is not enough. Within a corporate culture you can feel that you are only as good as your last deal and that your masculinity is constantly at stake.[6]

So it is that men often learn to be hard on themselves. With working-class men this can mean proving that they can handle whatever indignities that world throws at them. They learn to endure pain as a mark of their manhood. They learn not to complain but to keep their emotions to themselves. They constantly test themselves against the limits which their bodies might otherwise set. They do not want to talk about what they have been through, because expression is deemed to be a sign of weakness. But they also learn to impose pain on others as a way of proving themselves. At any moment they have to be ready to defend their male identities, for masculinities can never be taken for granted. Men learn that they have to be constantly "on guard" for they cannot afford to loose face in front of others. Nor can they afford to feel the fear they might experience, for this would already serve to diminish them in their own eyes.

But at some level men learn to carry their pain in their bodies. Sometimes it is carried as a psychic pain that they want to forget. They might have grown up in a family where there was a great deal of violence, sometimes precipitated by alcohol. They might have felt that their fathers were never really there for them, but not really expected anything different because fathers were not really supposed to engage with their children. In many families this is women's work and boys often grow up not knowing what it is like to have emotional support from another man. Rather boys learn early that they have to be able to survive on their own. They learn to harden their bodies against need. They learn not to reach out, but rather to contain any emotional needs they might feel. Sometimes it is difficult when you have witnessed your father beating your mother up and feeling powerless to intervene because you know this would only bring your father's wrath and violence onto yourself. Often there is a moment when you are strong enough to intervene and this becomes a powerful marker. You can learn that it is through strength that you win esteem and respect. But you rarely learn to communicate your own emotional needs, rather you can remain dependent upon women to interpret these needs for you. But in a man's world you learn to live by different rules.

As men learn to exercise self-control in relation to their bodies, it can be difficult to learn that the body carries its own memories. Sometimes these memories are experienced as a threat and as they begin to surface they are suppressed. Often men do not want to acknowledge their emotional need and dependency, for that threatens their sense of male identities. An earlier generation were often dependent on alcohol as a way of blotting out memory and silencing vulnerability. Sometimes they would automatically resort to violence which served to affirm their male identities rather than allow for a vulnerability which could only threaten it. For it could seem that being able to affirm male identities was paramount over other identifications. You could feel that to be a "weak" man was to be no man at all. To be "no man at all" was a fate that could seen worse than death. So it could seem that emotions had to be curbed at any cost and that the body had to be armored, in Reich's language, against feeling.[7]

But as Freud has it, emotions cannot be suppressed out of existence. This insight serves as a crucial challenge to Weber, who assumed that men were free to assign whatever meanings they wished to their experience. In this crucial sense modernity remained a fundamentally masculine project, for it assumed that with the disenchantment of nature comes the disenchantment of experience. The natural world becomes bereft of meanings, as does the social world. It is human beings alone who can assign meanings to their experience. There can be no communication with nature once nature has been dis/enchanted. Within modernity progress lies with the control and domination of nature. It is for men to assign meanings to their experience, for supposedly there is no tension between language and experience. But Freud and Wittgenstein knew different. They refused to accept that we could only come to experience through language and that experience was always discursive.[8] Feminism also came to recognize the tensions between language and experience, between what people felt and what they were ready to speak. Women knew what it meant to be rendered invisible within the prevailing discourses and learned to draw upon the support they needed within consciousness-raising groups to find their own voices.

Men, bodies and language

Often men learn to speak in the impersonal and universal language of reason. Being able to take their rationality for granted, men often learn to speak for others before they have really learnt to speak for themselves. Rather there is often a pervasive fear of the personal within modernity. Men learn to legislate what is good for others, for they can do this through reason alone. They do not have to communicate with others in order to legislate what would be good for them. As Rousseau has it, women's sexualities are a threat to male reason. For Rousseau, women were to be identified with their bodies and sexualities.[9] So it seemed proper for men to be suspicious of women, for they were deemed to be a threat. Their language was to be devalued within their own eyes as "personal" and "emotional." Men learnt to speak a different language. It was to be a language of the mind, not the body.

Within modernity women were cast as a threat to masculine identities, so men learnt to be wary of their contacts with women, often feeling that they needed to be in control. Sometimes control was sustained through physical strength while at other times it had more to do with intellectual superiority. Often men needed to feel that they somehow possessed a monopoly of truth within a relationship, even though they might not admit to it. Traditionally women were to be identified with their bodies and sexualities. This explained how their language was disfigured because, unlike men, they could never take their rationality for granted. Deemed to be "closer to nature," they could not escape the influence of their instinctual natures. But an Enlightenment vision of modernity also cast the body as part of nature. At some level this could mean that the body itself was "feminized," which goes some way to accounting for the struggle for control that men have with their bodies. It is as if the body represents an "enemy" within. Men often learn to silence their bodies, as they assume a form of self-control that involves a relation of dominance over their own bodies.

As men learn to identify with their minds they literally come to live in their heads. They becomes observers of their own bodily experience, because the body is deemed to be part of a disenchanted nature. The language of the body comes to be depersonalized, for bodies come to be treated as men's property. Within modernity men come to assume an instrumental relationship with their bodies. As progress lies in the control and domination of nature, so men learn that they have to exert control over their bodies. Since bodies are deemed to be part of nature within a Cartesian framework, they need to be constantly curtailed and controlled. They cannot to be trusted, for you never know when they might let you down. They are linked to emotions which are themselves defined as "unmasculine," so as a man, you have to be constantly vigilant lest you show yourself to be vulnerable in any way.

Men within different masculinities are constantly testing themselves against the limits of their bodies. Rather than respecting limits of tiredness or hunger, these become challenges that have be met. The body is not to be listened too, for it so often betrays and allows unwanted emotions to surface. Often there is a flight from the body into the mind, as men learn to sustain an external vigilance in relation to their bodies. Sex can so easily become a matter of performance and men can recognize themselves as disembodied observers watching their own experience from a safe distance. Men can learn to think of sex as a bodily need that comes to them from outside, as Kant has it in his understanding of emotions and feelings as externally influencing behavior.[10] It is a force that comes from outside, that men cannot really be held responsible for. Rather women are often to be blamed, for example "if she had not worn such a short skirt, he would not have been aroused." Rather than learning *how* to take responsibility for their own sexualities, men learn to displace this responsibility onto women. With the rise of feminism this has become much harder to do, and men are learning to develop more of an inner relationship with their own sexualities.

The dis/counting of sexuality has a long history within a dominant Christian culture that learnt to treat sexuality as "animal." It was not part of identities as spiritual beings and therefore not connected to self-identities. Rather the self was defined very much in contrast to embodiment. The body was deemed to be part of an "animal nature" that the spirit or the soul had to escape from at death. Supposedly it was the body which died while the soul lived on. So it was that embodiment was thought of as a necessary evil that was part of the condition of earthly life. Since the "earthly" was set in sharp contrast with the "spiritual," it was the realm that human beings had to escape from. This could make it very difficult for people to feel "at home" in their bodies; rather within a dominant Christian tradition it was through the suffering of the body, through self-flagellation, that the purity of the soul was to achieved. The temptations of the flesh were to be resisted and men were to punish themselves because of their sexual thoughts.

As a dominant Christian tradition learnt to displace the body and sexuality it became a dominant part of the narrative of Christian anti-Semitism that identified Judaism with "carnal Israel," as Daniel Boyarin has explored it.[11] The connection to the body and sexuality was somehow used to prove the inferiority of Judaism and the need to supersede its earthly character through the spiritualization of Christianity. This became part of the systematic denial of the Jewishness of Jesus, of the denial of Christianity's own roots. Within the dominant iconography Jews in their identification with the body and sexuality came to be identified with the devil. They had to be marked out in their difference, because they represented a threat to the purity of Christianity. So it was that the body was not only "feminized," but was also racialized. It was linked to the "dark forces within," that needed to be curbed and controlled.

Freud provided a critique of an Enlightenment modernity through his recognition of the misery and suffering that was created by the repression of sexuality. Possibly drawing upon Jewish sources, he insisted that the body and sexuality were not to be cast as "animal," but were to be acknowledged as expressions of our humanity. This is part of a Jewish postmodernism, which insists that the body is a source of knowledge and that emotions and feelings are not irrational in themselves, but are "part of" a redefined vision of humanity. This also resonates with the feminist critique of modernity, which refused to distinguish between reason and emotion, thought and feeling, and which insisted in the notion "our bodies, ourselves," that knowledge needed to be embodied and connected to experience. Feminism helped women to validate different ways of knowing and encouraged women to speak out of their intuition and sensitivity. It helped to open up a space in which men could also learn to reclaim aspects of their experience that had been devalued and silenced within a rationalist culture.

Within the context of men's consciousness-raising groups men learnt to speak about themselves in different ways. Learning to draw on the support of other men, they found that they could share aspects of their experience they would rarely have dared to talk about in front of other men out of a fear of being put down or losing face. Having learnt to put their emotional histories behind them, it was difficult to acknowledge how much emotional history men still carried. Having learnt to pride themselves in their independence, it could be difficult to recognize just how dependent they were on alcohol and drugs, in order to contain difficult emotions which were beginning to surface. Their substance abuse became a form of self-medication, a way of exerting control over emotions they did not want to feel. But as they learnt that other men also carried such emotions and feelings, they could learn to accept them more easily. Sometimes they became less judgmental and hard on themselves, as they learnt to share more of their experience without feeling that their male identities were being threatened. As they learnt to explore more embodied ways of thinking and feeling about themselves, they formed connections with aspects of their experience they would have automatically suppressed.

Bodies, risk and evil

If we carry the unconscious message that the body is a site of sin and temptation, it is easy to be trapped in an ethics of self-rejection. This is what Nietzsche challenged in Christian notions of renunciation and selflessness. He sought to suggest an ethics of self-affirmation in which the body and sexuality would be given meaningful expressions.[12] He refused to think of the body as evil. Rather he offered a critique of the dominant rationalist philosophical tradition. As Franz Rosenzweig expresses it in *The Star of Redemption*: "the mind enjoyed its independence from the instinctual murkiness in which the mindless spend their days; philosophy was the cool height to which the thinker escaped from the foggy plain. For Nietzsche this division into height and plain within one's self did not exist; he went his way intact, soul and intellect, man and thinker, an integer to the very last." (Quoted in Franz Rosenzweig [1953] *His Lie and Thought*, presented by Nahuman Glatzer, New York: Schoken Books, p.188.) As he goes on to express it in a later piece titled "The New Thinking": "where traditional philosophy comes to the end of its way of thinking, is the beginning of philosophy based on experience [*erfahrende Philosophie*]."[13]

Rosenzweig helps us grasp the ways traditional Western philosophy has been constructed on Christian foundations, especially in relation to thinking about body and soul. Philosophy works to deny our terrestrial anxieties, such as the fear of death, while never being able fully to dissolve this fear which is always with us. As Rosenzweig has it, "It lifts us above the tomb which yawns under our feet at every step. It abandons the body to the abyss, but the free soul soars above. What does philosophy care that the fear of death knows nothing of this division into body and soul, that it bellows 'I, I, I,' and refuses to acknowledge this relegating of fear to a mere 'body' ?" Since death only has to do with the "mere body" it should be of little concern, for we know that the soul lives on. But this is part of the flight from the body which is so familiar to men. As Rosenzweig puts it, "Man shall not shake off the anguish of earthly life; he shall *remain* in the fear of death." Though not written in gender terms, we can think about whether men find this "remaining" particularly difficult within modernity. Weber has it that men have to constantly move into action, as a way of assuaging their feelings of guilt and inadequacy. Within the Protestant ethic men can feel that they constantly have to prove themselves and that whatever they do is "not good enough."

So it is that young men often feel obliged to take risks with themselves, as if tempting fate and testing themselves against the limits of their bodies. Risk becomes a way of affirming male identities and proving yourself against the fates. At some level this can help to ward off feelings of inadequacy and lack of self-worth, but it means, for example, that many young men are often fatally injured in accidents. This can also touch the unease that so many young men can feel with themselves. It becomes difficult to "take time" for reflecting or simply to "remain" with the self. Often there is a fear of emotions that might begin to surface in ways that threaten male identities. This produces an acceleration in postmodern experience, whereby men are constantly trapped into testing themselves against time. There never seems to be "enough time" and there are also tasks that remain undone. But there is also the attraction of excitement and risk that is externally induced. Since men learn to suppress so much of their inner emotional lives, they can feel quite "unreal" and "flat" in relation to their lived experience. Within a corporate culture they can feel they are constantly measuring themselves against external targets, trapped into feeling that they could always achieve more.

But it is not easy for men to "rest" with themselves, for there is an abiding fear of what emotions might begin to emerge. It can be difficult for men to reach out for support from other men, especially when they feel low or depressed. It is easier to pick up the telephone when they are feeling good because they are less likely to loose face. This is the kind of risk men often will not take with themselves. They can feel ashamed of their inner emotions, especially since they serve to threaten the image they seek to sustain in public. Even when they know that their friends would be there to support them, they can find it too difficult to reach out. Rather they are more likely to turn their depressive feelings in on themselves and this links to the high rate of suicide among young males that are reported in different parts of the world. This can also reflect a broad cultural unease about how to redefine masculinity, especially in relation to feminism. Men can be left feeling unsure about their male identities, especially within postmodern cultures where the traditional social supports for masculinity have largely disappeared with the decline of traditional industries.

Postmodern masculinities

As men learn to relate to their bodies in instrumental ways, sometimes they are encouraged to imagine their relationship with their bodies as being akin to their relationship with their cars. Men learn to depend on their bodies as they learn to relate to their cars. Every so often they think that a check-up is in order, but they can feel angry and disappointed when they get ill, as if their body has let them down. They can feel that their bodies deserve to be punished. Having learnt to treat the body as being separate from their identities as rational selves, there is often a link between the stressful ways men live their everyday lives and the kinds of illnesses they get. The notion of stress is so threatening because it serves to question the autonomous space in which they body exists. But it can still be difficult for men to make sense of the notion of "listening to their bodies," for traditionally the body has been there to receive orders and instructions. It is the mind which supposedly rules over matter.

As long as men continue to conceive of the body as a machine that serves to carry our heads around, it will be difficult for men to rethink relations between mind and body, thoughts and emotions, spirit and flesh. It will also be difficult to acknowledge the emotional life of the body and the ways that particular forms of hypermasculinity can make you ill. There is a resistance to "new thinking" that could help men to learn from their experience and appreciate the embodied nature of their experience. It has taken time for men to acknowledge the gendered character of their own experience, having readily assumed that gender is the concern of women alone. But in the 1990s men have begun to engage more critically with the inherited masculinities of their fathers. There is the beginning of a widespread movement to re-vision masculinities, especially so that young fathers can be more involved with their children than their fathers were with them. Often there is a sense of emotional distance from fathers, that links specific cultures with the distancing of bodies. Men often cannot remember being hugged by their fathers or seeing their fathers cry. Sometimes they can remember being told to leave the room, as if tears had to be shameful.

Within a postmodern culture there is often the desire for immediate solutions. Sometimes this goes along with the promise that men can create their own identities and so sustain control over their own experience. But again this makes it difficult for men to "rest" with themselves and to take the time to learn from their experience. This does not mean that experience is given, but acknowledges that there are different levels of experience. As men learn to honor their own emotional learning they also learn to question the cultural values they have inherited. Sometimes this means re-valuing the importance of relationships within men's lives, both with partners and with children. But it can also mean that men recognize the need for more time and space with themselves so that they can grow into a deeper contact with themselves, finding a different sense of balance with different parts of their lives.

But this learning will not takes place if men learn to treat illness as if they were equivalent to the breakdown of a car. Often men resist going to visit doctors because they imagine that if their "illness" has come from nowhere then it might as well leave them. This can resonate with a rationalist postmodernism that suggests that men can choose to invent their own experience. Research shows that some men with testicular cancer have resisted going to see their doctors and often have gone only when pressured by their wives. Often this has meant that they have reported for treatment when the condition is more advanced, which also means they are more likely to be hospitalized. At some level men seem to prefer "not to know" because they can then get on with their lives. They would very much prefer to have a pill that would almost magically make the symptoms disappear. So when men are depressed, they prefer to take a pill "to make things better" rather than to dwell upon what is going on for them in their lives. Often they are used to putting a "good face on things" because to acknowledge that you might benefit from help is already to threaten your male identity. If you "put up with things" yourself then you can at least use your illness as some kind of proving ground.

Often it is as men take flight from their embodied experience, that they get drawn into idealized fantasies. Their dreams become disconnected from their everyday lives and often this means that they find it difficult to value what they have in their lives. Often utopian dreams grew out of a dissatisfaction with and rejection of the present. Men dreamed of "being different," as if they could transform their human condition once and for all. As long as these dreams were built upon an ethics of self-rejection, they could not be grounded in lived experience. Possibly we need a different kind of utopianism that is not scared of dreams and fantasies, but is at the same time much more grounded in embodied experience. This makes freedom and justice no less urgent, but it gives us a different kind of basis from which to critique the present. At one level this is to appreciate the ways that postmodernism remains in crucial respects a project of a dominant masculinity. It insists that men, in particular, can re-invent their lives according to their own image.[14] Life is conceived in individualistic term, as a project of invention, but if often fails to appreciate the importance of connection and relation. As men learn to value their relationships with other men, they can also learn to live differently embodied masculinities. Rather than treating the body as a machine, it can be consulted as a guide as we learn to listen and respect its needs and desires. This is not to forsake control, but it is to learn a form of control that grows out of reflection on our own lived experience. Rather than the body being treated as something separate, we learn ways of respecting bodies as "part of" who we are. In learning to honor the lived experience of the body, we learn to imagine an embodied postmodernism that helps men to come to terms with their emotional histories, to imagine different futures for themselves, their partners and children.

Notes

1. If it was a dominant masculinity which could alone take its reason for granted, this served to define reason as an independent faculty radically separated from a nature which had been dis/enchanted. This served to define 'others' through what they lacked, through being deemed 'closer to nature'. This helps to establish modernity in crucial respects, as a project of a dominant Christian, heterosexual, white masculinity. For some helpful reflections see also,

Genevieve Lloyd: "The Man of Reason: 'Male' and 'Female' in Western Philosophy" (Routledge, London 1993) and Evelyn Fox Keller: "Reflections on Gender and Science" (Yale University Press, New Haven, 1985).

2. The way in which dominant traditions of Christianity have been historically identified with the disdain of the body has been explored by Peter Brown in "The Body and Society: Men, Women and Sexual Renunciation in Early Christianity" (Faber, London 1989). It is also a central theme in Foucault's later work, particularly in "The Uses of Pleasure" (Penguin, London 1984).

3. The ways that a dominant masculinity instructs men in the denial of the relationship with an embodied nature as they learn to identify with culture, is a central theme in Susan Griffin: "Pornography and Silence" (Women's Press, London 1980). She makes crucial connections between misogyny, homophobia, racism and anti-semitism which are often missed, though sometimes her notion of the 'pornographic mind' can seem too generalised historically.

4. In "The Protestant Ethic and the Spirit of Capitalism" (Allen and Unwin, London, 1930) Max Weber draws crucial connections between the spirit of capitalism and the forging of a dominant masculinity within a Protestant culture. Though it is not framed in explicitly gendered terms, it shows how a dominant masculinity defines itself as 'independent' and 'self-sufficient'. The ways that this is tied to an ethics of self-denial is a central theme in Victor J. Seidler: "Recreating Sexual Politics: Men, Feminism and Politics" (Routlege, London 1991).

5. For some helpful discussions that have helped to open up the discussions of the body within sociological theory, see, for instance Bryan Turner: "The Body and Society" (2nd edition, Sage, London 1996) and Chris Shilling (Sage, London 1991).

6. I have explored the ways in which men can rarely take their masculinity for granted within modernity, so constantly have to prove themselves. Since male identities are sustained within the public realm of work, there is often a fear of 'losing face' in front of other men. This can make it difficult for men to value personal life and intimate relationships, even if they readily pay lip service to these relationships. These themes are developed in "Man Enough: Embodying Masculinities" (Sage, London 1997).

7. Though there has been a recovery of the body within social theory, there has yet to be re-evaluation of Reich's work that has been so tightly associated with 'biologism' within a post-sructuralist critique. For a helpful sense of the context of Reich's work that gives more sense of complexity see Myron Sharaf: "Fury on Earth: A Biography of Wilhelm Reich" (Macmillan, London, 1985).

8. For an exploration of some crucial resonances between feminist work and insights drawn from the work of the later Wittgenstein see the discussion of language in Victor J. Seidler: "Rediscovering Masculinity: Reason, Language and Sexuality" (Routledge, London 1989). There is a shared sense of the

difficulties of articulating different levels of experience and the importance of context for allowing people to share more of themselves.

9.   A helpful discussion of the sexual politics which informs Rousseau's diverse writings is given in Suan Moller Okin: "Women in Western Political Thought" (Virago, London, 1980) Since women are deemed to be 'closer to nature' they require a different kind of education. They also remain a threat to male reason which serves to legitimate the control men often assume.

10. I have explained the ways in which emotions, feelings and desires are deemed as 'inclinations' to be forms of unfreedom and determination within Kantian ethics in "Kant, Respect and Injustice: The Limits of Liberal Moral Theory" (Routledge, London, 1986). For Kant it is only a dominant masculinity which can take an inner relationship with reason for granted.

11. Daniel Boyarin argues that Israel came to be associated with the body and sexuality within dominant Christain eyes in "Carnal Israel: Reading Sex in Talmudic Culture" (University of California Press, Berkeley, 1993) Associating the body with 'the sins of the flesh' came to be a marker for a lack of spirituality for within Christianity it became difficult to imagine a spirituality of the body. Rather the body was identified with 'flesh' and came to be radically split from the 'spirit'.

12. For some useful discussions of Nietzsche that help to place his critiques of Christian ethics see, for instance, "Nietzsche, Feminism and Political Theory ed., Paul Preston (Routledge, London, 1993) and "Nietzsche and Jewish Culture" ed., Jacob Golomb (Routledge, London, 1997).

13. An insightful discussion of Rosensweig's work which explores some of his central concerns in an illuminating way is Richard A. Cohen Elevations: The Height of the Good in Rosenzweig and Levinas, The University of Chicago Press, Chicago, 1994.

14. A helpful exploration of some of the issues raised within a postmodern critique is provided by Zygmunt Bauman in "Intimations of Postmodernity" (Routledge, London, 1991). See also his "Modernity and Ambivalence" (Polity Press, Cambridge, 1991).

Chapter 5

What's Behind the Mask? Bodybuilding and Masculinity

THOMAS JOHANSSON

The masques of masculinity and femininity

Images of men and women are changing in contemporary society. The feminist critique of traditional and modern ways of conceptualizing sex and gender has problematized our whole way of understanding the construction of gender identities. Nowadays the words "masculinity" and "femininity" are often put in quotation marks, as are so many other central words in social science. When most people are asked which traits distinguishes men and women, they either fall back on essentialism and talk about "real men and women," or become confused and embarrassed when all their attempts to come up with distinguishing traits fail.

According to Judith Butler (1990, p. 139), we should consider gender as a matter of corporeal styles, or as she expresses it: "Styles of the flesh." The body is not a "being," but a variable boundary, a surface which is politically regulated and a signifying practice which should be understood within a cultural field of gender hierarchies. The various acts of gender also create the idea of gender. If we take away these acts, then we end up with no gender at all. Gender is thus a construction which regularily conceals its genesis. The very notions of an essential sex and a true masculinity or femininity should be understood as strategies which conceal the performative character of gender.

If we agree with Butler's view on gender, there are no limits to how far it is possible to change the gender order and to discover new ways of performing gender outside the restricting frames of hegemonic masculinity and the norms of heterosexuality. One way of changing gender would be through subversive bodies. In *Bodies that Matter* (1993), Butler continues her search for such bodies. These bodies can be regarded as a critical resource in the struggle to re-articulate gender.

Today it is easy to find bodies at the discursive limits of "sex." Through plastic surgery and body techniques it is possible to change the body in almost any direction. A good example of this plasticity is the famous French artist Orlans' experiments with her own body, making it into a piece of art. At the same time as she puts her face under the surgeon's knife, she reads aloud from a text of Lacan and the whole operation is recorded and shown for audiences as a "happening." The body is no longer sacred, no longer merely "natural," but a mouldable and aestheticized form which is used to express different styles of the flesh.

Nowhere are these cultural changes more obvious than when we enter into the world of the gym. Through their sculptured bodies, male and female bodybuilders are good examples of "bodies that matter." Looking into the gym culture gives us an opportunity to study transformations in contemporary gender identities.

Female bodybuilders are often interpreted in terms of subversive bodies. These bodies offer a form of resistance to hegemonic masculinity, but at the same time they submit to the project of femininity in terms of hyper-feminine ornamentation, posture and demeanor required for competition (St Martin & Gavey, 1996; Aoki, 1996). They thus represent a contradictory practice and a way of performing gender which both contest and confirm the existing gender system. Male bodybuilders may be interpreted in a similar way. On the one hand, they represent hyper-masculinity, but on the other, their desire to display their bodies in public, becoming objects of the gaze of the Other, signifies a feminization of the male body.

There seems to be a common tendency within male and female bodybuilding. Where does this masculinization of the female body and the femininization of the male body lead us? In order to find out it is necessary to look behind the physical appearance of the bodybuilder, and to study the regimes of discipline leading to the development of more and more androgenic bodies. The body techniques used in contemporary gym culture were originally constructed within a historical framework of hegemonic masculinity. These techniques and the lifestyle developed within this exclusively male culture subsequently attracted a much wider audience of both men and women.[1] In order to analyze the development of contemporary fitness culture I will, however, first concentrate upon three different paradoxes inherent in the male subculture and then return to the question of contemporary developments within gym and fitness culture. I will introduce the three paradoxes of gym culture by beginning with a case study from my recent book *The Sculptured Body* (Johansson, 1997) to illustrate some of the features of the construction of masculinity within gym culture.

On the mind of a bodybuilder

The body techniques developed within the bodybuilding subculture are used by people who want to sculpture their bodies into perfection, but not necessarily into the image of the bulky, hard and huge male body. Today we meet a new kind of bodybuilder, who is more into fitness and hardbodies and who also represents a more complex masculinity.

Steve is 30 years old. He has no steady job, but has nevertheless managed to get along studying at the university and playing in a band. He has studied both philosophy and psychology. Steve has a great interest in Eastern philosophy, he has read Reich and Lacan, and he goes to a psychoanalyst regularly. He spends a lot of his time in the gym trying to develop the perfect body. As a complement to his bodybuilding he also attends an Aikido class three or sometimes even four times a week. He finds the Western discipline of the body in the gym and the Eastern philosophy-inspired body technique of Aikido to be excellent complements to one another. Through these techniques he achieves perfect control over his body.

Steve is attracted to the possibilities of body perfection offered in the gym. He is quite satisfied with his own looks, and as long as he keeps his body fit and hard he enjoys life. But then there is always the possibility of becoming even more perfect. He says:

> The way you look and your self-image is the same thing. ... I am really satisfied with the way I look. It really makes it easier to get in contact with girls. And I can even improve more, and become more attractive. It gives me a positive feeling.

Steve is fascinated by the discipline and the aesthetics involved in the gym culture. He admires perfect bodies and he also enjoys the discipline he submits himself to in order to achieve his goals – the sculptured hardbody. As Steve puts it: "If you wanna look good, then you have to put a lot of effort into your physical training. You will have to sacrifice something to win a perfect body. If you feel you can't do that, you always have a choice, but then you won't have a nice looking body." In Steve's world there are people who discipline their bodies and develop the body beautiful, and there are those who are not prepared to do that. The technique is available so it is up to yourself how you want to look. According to Steve, there are also people who are objectively ugly, and they should develop other capacities and skills in order to live a good life.

Steve is not a bodybuilder in the ordinary sense of the word, that is, he does not want to develop a body like Arnold Schwarzenegger's, but he has internalized the same techniques as Schwarzenegger and he obviously shows the same kind of devotion to the art of bodybuilding. Steve is caught in the imaginary world of perfect bodies. As he says: "I'm even prepared to talk to a boring girl a whole evening, that is, if she is good looking." As many other people in the fitness industry today, Steve has got stuck in the mirror, admiring the image of his own body and spending all his energy trying to hold on to this imaginary picture of himself.

As we will see in the following analysis of the bodybuilding subculture, Steve's mind is not working all that differently from the minds of the "real" bodybuilders. Bodybuilding is no longer just a matter of huge bodies and the development of a particular subculture, but a body technique and a particular discipline. The reason why this particular body technique or lifestyle attracts so many people today is to be found in three major paradoxical features; the dynamics of *empowerment/disempowerment, discipline/desire* and *narcissism/ fragmentation*. Even though I will primarily focus on the male subculture of bodybuilding, I want to argue that these mechanisms are also to be regarded as more general features of late modernity. After presenting and discussing the three analytical categories mentioned above, I will return to the question of the androgenic character of contemporary gym and fitness culture.

Power and addiction

When a young man enters into the world of bodybuilding, he becomes a member of a specific lifestyle, with its own initiatory rituals and stages of membership. He starts wearing certain clothes, reading bodybuilding magazines, buying low-calorie drinks, eating lots of bananas, pasta and so on. He spends more and more time in the gym and starts to show an almost obsessive interest in his own body. The effects of this lifestyle-change is an improved self-image and better self-confidence. Many of the men I interviewed told me that they found it easier to attract girls' attention, and that they even became more popular among girls. They also found it easier to impress their friends and other people. All in all they became more self-assured. So, the new lifestyle actually strengthened the young person's identity and consequently led to an empowerment. But there were also some effects linked to the obsessive aspect of this lifestyle.

In order to build perfect bodies it is often necessary to sacrifice an ordinary life, which means: no career, no family, and no social life. Sometimes these people also sacrificed their bodies; dieting, drugs and hard physical training made them physically exhausted and sometimes even destroyed their physical health. Consequently, participation in the lifestyle of bodybuilders sometimes led to the development of an addictive behaviour.[2] I will distinguish between three different types of unintended consequences of this addictive lifestyle: social, physical and cultural.

The young man involved in bodybuilding becomes increasingly drawn into this all-consuming lifestyle. The larger part of his time is invested in activities in the gym. He becomes less interested in ordinary social life, that is, girlfriends, hobbies and friends. His identity is increasingly tied to the gym. Some of my interviewees expressed a great regret over what they called "the lost years." The "family" of the gym increasingly became more important than other people and other things in life. A man described this process of withdrawal the following way:

> Many men would certainly sacrifice their girlfriends if they had to. At that time I told my girlfriend that she had to accept that my physical training was more important to me than she was. However, I do regret this today. (Tom, 30 years old)

Although the aim of physical training is to achieve a healthier lifestyle and healthier body, disciplined training combined with an extensive use of drugs sometimes leads to deteriorating health. In the literature dealing with masculinity, it is often emphasized that men tend to treat their bodies badly. At the time when I did the ethnographic field work for the gym study, I once encountered a man in the dressing room who had a bandage around one of his legs. He was talking to another man, saying: "Well I know I should be at home in bed, playing computer games, but I really had to go here. I can still move my arms and one of my legs, so here we go." In some male sports, injuries become a normal career expectation. The body is assaulted in the name of masculinity and achievement. An empirical study shows that ex-athletes often live with damaged bodies and chronic pain. They also often die at an early age. These are the prices to be paid for the ideals created within the framework of hegemonic masculinity (Connell, 1995, p. 58).

The lifestyle of bodybuilding and fitness often involves a specific cultural identity and lifestyle. This identity is characterized, among other things, by a prolonged social moratorium, a common characteristic of many of today's lifestyles. The young man is not tempted by the adult lifestyle. He wants to stay young, fit and free. This lifestyle mixes badly with family life and other kinds of adult responsibilities. In a certain sense it would be appropriate to talk about the Peter Pan syndrome, that is, the young man who does not want to grow up and become an adult. One of my interviewees expressed his ambivalence in this way:

I do not regret the birth of my daughter. However, if I would have had the choice, I would certainly have waited a few more years before becoming a father. I have heard that the best years for a man are between 20-30. It seems t fit in for me. I do not regret having my daughter, but if I could have waited f /e more years, it would have been better. (Mick, 27 years old)

On the one hand, the young man idealizes and looks for typical male qualities, such as autonomy, will-power, strength, self-respect and maturity. On the other hand, he develops an identity which seems to be self-destructive and immature. He becomes addicted to bodybuilding, obsessed with his preoccupation, and thus loses some of his capacity to reflect upon and act in life. In this case, bodybuilding leads to a disempowerment. The addictive behaviour is counterpoised to the reflexivity inherent in modernity and the unintended consequences of bodybuilding thus lead to a loss of the feeling of masculinity (Giddens, 1992).

The pattern of *empowerment/disempowerment* is a central feature of the male bodybuilding subculture, but it is also of significance when describing the more general culture of bodybuilding and fitness. When physical training turns into an addictive behaviour it reinforces some of the more narcissistic qualities in contemporary identity. The young man or woman get caught in the imaginary of the global cult of the body beautiful. The hardbody becomes not merely a means, but a goal in itself.

Discipline and hardbodies

In his book *Muscle: Confessions of an Unlikely Bodybuilder*, Sam Fussell presents the three Ds of bodybuilding: *Dedication, Determination* and *Discipline*. In order to become a bodybuilder it is necessary to submit one's body to a high degree of discipline. This regime of discipline involves hard physical training, dieting, and a "healthy" and ascetic lifestyle, that is, no alchohol or tobacco. The young bodybuilder must become dedicated to his work with the body, he must be determined to develop a certain lifestyle and to make sacrifices. The discipline involved in bodybuilding is directed not only toward the body and the flesh, but also to the education of the minds of the bodybuilder.[3]

The aim of all this discipline is to form a hardbody; to reduce fat, to build muscles and to *define* the body. The hard and well-defined body becomes the ideal; it is set up as a norm and regarded as the desired body. In a changing world this kind of body gives a feeling of ontological security and of masculinity. Sam Fussell interprets his own devotion to bodybuilding in terms of insecurity and a lack of identity. He writes:

It also explained my presence in the gym. The threat wasn't just from without, it also came from within. The fright I'd felt on the streets of New York I also felt deep within myself. Who was this man who cried not just at graduations and weddings but during beer and credit-card commercials ... There wasn't enough pomade, mouthwash, deodorant and talc in this world to eradicate my sins, but what if I created a shell to suppress them? What if my armor not only kept the world out, but kept me in?[4]

Fussell's study of his own career as a bodybuilder is also a study of masculinity. Masculinity is often defined in terms of characteristics and traits which are *not feminine* (Chodorow, 1978). The hard muscular body is first and foremost a male body, a body which is threatened by soft bodies and by ambiguities. Historically these bodies have belonged to warriors or patriarchs – men who had to defend their families and countries (Theweleit, 1978). Today these bodies are primarily aesthetic objects of desire. Muscles are still closely linked to masculinity, but the muscular body has also become a floating signifier and is consequently also frequently tied to femininity.

More generally, the hardbody may be understood as a symbolic expression of the fight against ambivalence and ambiguity inherent in modernity. The discipline of the body also involves the making of a certain identity, an identity which is clearly opposed to the fat, slimy, badly defined softbody. Some of the people I have interviewed show an open contempt for the softbody. One of my interviewees declares that:

It's a lot about attitude. There are many people who don't respect themselves. I mean, your body is your only real possession. ... You see people all the time who are dirty, unclean, have filthy clothes. These people never go to the gym, because they lack discipline. ... Hopefully they have other interests. But as I mentioned earlier, your body is all you have got and if you don't take care of it, you are in big trouble. (John, 35 years old)

Bodybuilding is a highly disciplined activity, but it also involves some pleasure. Bodybuilders are often fascinated by their own bodies and by how their muscles actually grow and develop. The sometimes quite rapid growth of muscles is concrete evidence of a changing identity. These obvious changes in the body are often followed by changes in identity. Bodybuilders are sometimes absorbed by the mirror image of themselves. They like to watch while their muscles develop. Therefore, the thing called *pump* – that is, the reaction achieved when overstraining your muscles, the feeling of blood pumping in your arms – is very popular among bodybuilders. This reaction is often described in terms of an orgiastic experience.

Thomas: How about this thing called pump. Do you really enjoy pain?
Mel: Well, maybe it's a way of punishing yourself, no I am only kidding. You certainly feel your muscle pumping up while you're at it. That is what you really want, to get in contact with your muscles, to feel them. Then it also hurts. To a certain extent I enjoy pain, yes. (Mel, 30 years old)

Bodybuilders want to achieve a narcissistic feeling of wholeness and perfection. But instead of achieving this goal, they often get stuck in front of the mirror – caught in the regimes of discipline and narcissism. The mixture of pain and pleasure achieved when pumping muscles gives a good picture of the delicate balance between discipline and enjoyment involved in bodybuilding and fitness. The mental *discipline* and inner control developed is often opposed to the striving for *pleasure* and enjoyment in life.

Narcissism and fragmentation

When Lacan writes about narcissism, he focuses primarily on the mirror-stage and the frozen identity achieved through the gaze in the mirror. Gym culture encourages this type of identity; both young men and women tend to get stuck in front of the mirrors in the gym, admiring the image of their own bodies. In one gym I saw a young man who was touching, caressing and obviously admiring his body while looking at the mirror. He seemed all-consumed by this activity, lost in an imaginary world of beautiful bodies.

This kind of cult of the image is often regarded as a female passive position – where there are male spectators desiring and defining the female body – but nowadays men also are turned into, or rather are turning themselves into, objects of desire. This is obvious when one regards advertising, but maybe even more so in bodybuilding competitions where male bodies are displayed on a stage. [5] Male bodies are made into aesthetic objects, but does this necessarily signify a more passive "female" position? The narcissistic qualities in bodybuilding are mixed with the image of the powerful and dominant male body. We have a highly contradictory image here, or as Yvonne Tasker puts it: "Rather than understanding the muscular male hero as either a reassertion, or a parodic enactment of masculine values, we can examine the ways in which he represents both, as well as being produced by the ongoing and unsteady relationship between these, and other images of masculinity." [6]

Men are drawn into the aestheticization of everyday life; they use their bodies to attract attention from women and they feed their narcissism through the admiring gazes of both women and men. As one of my interviewees puts it:

> In the beginning I wanted to make an impression on the girls. I went down to
> the beach ... They really looked at me. I also wanted to be looked at. It made
> me feel good and it gave me a better self-confidence. (Tom, 30 years old)

The male hardbody is used to attract attention and it seeks for confirmation
and respect. The "new man" is often described as inward-looking, sensitive
and narcissistic. Many of the men in my study of the gym also fit into this
description – mixing traditionally male and female traits – but they also show
typically "male" characteristics, such as competitiveness, autonomy and a
technical rationality. This new negotiated position not only embodies a "new
masculinity," but is also an attempt to rescue traditional masculinity.

The hunt for the perfect body is linked to a fight against ambivalence. In
a more general sense, the hardbody signifies an intolerance to everything
which threatens its status; the old, fat and not so perfect body is regarded as
the Other, as something which poses a threat to perfection and youth.[7] This is
the other side of narcissism – which signals the fragmentation and
dissolution of identity. In the future we will be sent to the gym when looking
too old or too fat. As this young man said:

> My girlfriend's closest friend has a boyfriend who goes to the gym. So, she
> thought that I could go as well. I got a membership card as a Christmas
> present. She finds me really sloppy. I am getting more and more fat. I have to
> exercise if I want to become a policeman or a fireman. (Bengt, 23 years old)

There is always the other side to narcissism. The narcissism of contemporary
young men can be interpreted as a sign of a new masculinity – a more soft
and sensitive masculinity – but it may also be a sign of a threatened
masculinity, building an aestheticized hardbody in order to defend itself from
the threat of the failure of the masculine project. The bodybuilding culture is
built on a paradox: at the same time as it strengthens a certain masculine
identity, it also leads to a dissolution of traditional masculinity, and in the
worst cases even to shrinking testicles and a dysfunctional body.

Subversive bodies or a backlash?

There are clearly many different ways of approaching the phenomenon of
bodybuilding. Bodybuilding may be analyzed, for example, in terms of a
masculine subculture promoting hypermasculine ideals and bodies. But today
when gyms attract women as well as men it is increasingly difficult to hold
on to this type of analysis. Both male and female bodybuilders resist different

attempts to analyze the phenomenon of bodybuilding either as a confirmation of archetypical gender roles or as a transgression of traditional ideals and identities. So, is bodybuilding an example of subversive bodies or are we approaching a new example of the current reactionary backlash? In order to answer this question we have to study the historical development of gym and fitness culture in Western society.

In the middle of the nineteenth century a movement called "Muscular Christianity" developed in the northeastern United States, among middle-class and wealthy Americans.[8] This movement originated in England during the first half of the nineteenth century, but turned into a mass movement in the United States. Americans seemed particularly taken with "Muscular Christianity." Physical culture and morality were linked and the perfection of the body became an essential part of the Christian lifestyle. Muscles were regarded as a sign of a moral lifestyle and individual salvation. The body was not simply a container, but a form which could be altered and perfected – an expression of a solid character.[9]

The "Muscular Christianity" movement was probably the first example of a body technique and lifestyle which contained the seeds of modern bodybuilding. This movement coincided with a more general development toward stereotypical gender identities in Western society. According to George Mosse: "The building blocks of modern masculinity existed, but they were systematized, formed into a stereotype, only at the start of the modern age."[10] In the nineteenth century, masculinity was formed into a normative ideal of masculine beauty that symbolized virtue and character; this ideal spread through society and came to be regarded as the engine that drove the nation and society at large. The cultivated male body was thought to symbolize society's need for order and progress as well as middle-class virtues such as self-control, discipline and character. Although these ideals were frequently called into question, they became the prevailing stereotypical and normative ideal of manliness during modernity.

Although the movement of "Muscular Christianity" contained some seeds of modern bodybuilding, the technique and lifestyle of bodybuilding were prefected within the subcultural settings of the 1970s' and 1980s' bodybuilding culture. The ideals of masculinity and the bodies cultivated in these environments took stereotypical masculinity to its utmost limits. The discipline of the body, the ascetic ideals and the technical rationality developed within these subcultures were strongly informed by the cult of the masculine "body beautiful" developed in late modern times. Bodybuilding magazines and books often contained pictures of Greek and Roman statues, and these bodies, characterized by their noble proportions and lack of fat, were turned into ideals also for bodybuilders.

In the 1970s bodybuilding developed from a subculture into a more general physical culture, although the more innovative part of this culture was still located within the subculture. This process also involved women. The body ideals originally cultivated within a masculine sphere, and the techniques used to develop these bodies, were suddenly used by women as well as by men. So, the ideals of stereotypical or hegemonic masculinity were generalized and attracted young people in general. The ideal of the Greek sculptured body – a body which expressed will-power, narcissism and discipline – played a significant role in the development of the contemporary physical culture and fitness movement (Frank, 1991). Consequently, the stereotypical masculine ideal body was turned into an ideal for bodybuilders regardless of their sex. This kind of body was cultivated into perfection within bodybuilding and fitness training. Modern body technique has made it possible to sculpture the body in almost any direction, and the ideal body is no longer merely an ideal – it has become achievable possibility.

In order to understand the phenomenon of bodybuilding we have to look behind the mask of the bodybuilder. When entering a gym we see different bodies. Some are really huge and muscular, others are more slim and hard and so on. When studying the mask of the male and female bodybuilder or looking at the other hardbodies in the gym, we become confused. Are these bodies to be interpreted as totally different phenomena or are they aspects of the same underlying lifestyle? I have argued that these bodies are the result of a historical process involving the development and defense of a stereotypical male body ideal. The hardbody and the body techniques used in bodybuilding today are strongly linked to the disciplinary regimes developed in gymnastics and physical culture in the nineteenth century. The three aspects of modern bodybuilding which I have focused on in this article – discipline, power and narcissism – are also central aspects of masculinity in contemporary culture.

The dynamics of *discipline/desire, empowerment/disempowerment* and *narcissism/fragmentation* are all central to Western culture. When looking into the bodybuilding and fitness industry, we are therefore also studying aspects central to modernity/postmodernity. When young women are drawn into gym culture, forming their bodies into hardbodies and cultivating muscular bodies, they are also taking part in the formation of a particular body ideal. However, at the same time as they reinforce an old stereotypical masculine ideal, they also contribute to the dissolution of the links between this kind of hardbody and masculinity. So the convergence and growing similarity between male and female bodybuilders and male and female hardbodies must be understood as an effect of a more general process of civilization and discipline. In one sense this development may be interpreted as a form of strengthening hegemonic masculinity and consequently a particular type of rationality, but in another sense it calls into question traditional gender hierarchies and body ideals. This contradictory character of the bodybuilding and fitness industry makes it difficult to tell whether physical culture is a subversive phenomenon or just a sign of the current reactionary backlash. But although it is as yet impossible to say in what direction gym culture will take us, it is possible and necessary to discuss the body ideals cultivated within this physical culture.

Notes

1. I will use empirical material from a study of gym culture in Sweden in order to highlight some of the characteristics of the male bodybuilding culture, see Johansson (1998) Den skulpterade kroppen: Gymkultur, friskvård och estetik (The Sculptured Body: Gym Culture, Health and Aesthetics), Stockholm: Carlssons.
2. See also the discussion of neo-tribes, for example, Maffesoli (1996).
3. One of the more thorough studies of bodybuilding as a subculture is presented in Klein (1990, 1993a, 1993b).
4. Fussell (1991, p. 48); see also Wacquant (1995).
5. The femininization of the male body is discussed in Wernick (1991) and Neale (1983/1993).
6. Tasker (1993); see also Silverman (1992) and Cohan and Hark (1993).
7. In another article I develop the discussion of the abject body, particularly in relation to female bodybuilders (Johansson, 1995); see also Kristeva (1982).
8. The body has often been used as a mark of distinction. See, for example, Bourdieu (1984).
9. This movement is described by Harvey Green, Fit for America (1986).
10. Mosse (1996, p. 5); within men's studies Victor Seidler has developed this discussion of the relation between modernity and masculinity (Seidler, 1989, 1994).

References

Aoki, D. (1996) "Sex and Muscle: The Female Bodybuilder Meets Lacan," *Body & Society*, 4, pp. 59-74.

Bourdieu, P. (1984) *Distinction: A Social Critique of the Judgement of Taste.* London: Routledge & Kegan Paul.

Butler, J. (1990) *Gender Trouble: Feminism and the Subversion of Identity.* London: Routledge.

Butler, J. (1993) *Bodies that Matter. On the Discursive Limits of "Sex."* London: Routledge.

Chodorow, N. (1978) *The Reproduction of Mothering. Psychoanalysis and the Sociology of Gender.* Berkeley: California University Press.

Cohan, S. and Hark, I. R. (eds) (1993) *Screening the Male: Exploring Masculinities in Hollywood Cinema.* London: Routledge.

Connell, R. W. (1995) *Masculinities.* Cambridge: Polity Press.

Featherstone, M. (1991) "The Body in Consumer Culture," in Featherstone, M., Hepworth, M. and Turner, B. S. (eds), *The Body: Social Process and Cultural Theory.* London: Sage.

Frank, A. (1991) "An Analytic Review," in Featherstone, M. *et al.* (eds) *The Body: Social Process and Cultural Theory.* London: Sage.

Fussel, S. (1991) *Muscle: Confessions of an Unlikely Bodybuilder.* London: Scribners.

Giddens, A. (1992) *The Transformation of Intimacy.* Cambridge: Polity Press.

Green, H. (1986) *Fit for America. Health, Fitness, Sport and American Society.* Baltimore: Johns Hopkins University Press.

Jackson, D. (1990) *Unmasking Masculinity. A Critical Autobiography.* London: Unwin Hyman.

Johansson, T. (1995) "Främlingskap och det främmande: Bodybuilding, kön och identitet," *Kulturella perspektiv*, 4, pp. 19-33.

Johansson, T. (1996) "Gendered Spaces: The Gym Culture and the Construction of Gender," *Young*, 3, pp. 32-47.

Johansson, T. (1997) *Den skulpterade kroppen: Gymkultur, friskvård och estetik.* Stockholm: Carlssons förlag.

Keen, S. (1991) *Fire in the Belly. On Being a Man.* New York: Bantham Books.

Kipnis, A. R. (1991) *Knights Without Armor: A Practical Guide for Men in Quest for Masculine Soul.* Los Angeles: Jeremy P. Tarcher, Inc.

Klein, A. M. (1990) "Little Big Man: Hustling, Gender Narcissism, and Bodybuilding Subculture," in Messner, M.A & Sabo, D. F. (eds), *Sport, Men, and the Gender Order. Critical Feminist Perspectives.* Champaign A Ill.: Human Kinetic Books.

Klein, A. M. (1993a) *Little Big Men. Bodybuilding, Subculture and Gender Construction.* New York: State University of New York Press.

Klein, A. M. (1993b) "Of Muscle and Men," *The Sciences*, November/December.

Kristeva, J. (1982) *Powers of Horror: An Essay on Abjection.* New York: Columbia University Press.

Lloyd, M. (1996) "Feminism, Aerobics and the Politics of the Body," *Body & Society*, 2, pp. 79-98.

Maffesoli, M. (1996) *The Time of the Tribes.* London: Sage.

Middleton, P. (1992) *The Inward Gaze. Masculinity and Subjectivity in Modern Culture.* London: Routledge.

Mosse, G. (1996) *The Image of Man: The Creation of Modern Masculinity.* New York: Oxford University Press.

Neale, S. (1993) "Masculinity as Spectacle: Reflections on Men and Mainstream Cinema," in Cohan, S. and Hark, I. R. (eds) *Screening the Male: Exploring Masculinities in Hollywood Cinema*. London: Routledge.

Segal, L. (1990) *Slow Motion: Changing Masculinites, Changing Men*. London: Virago Press.

Seidler, V. (1989) *Rediscovering Masculinity: Reason, Language and Sexuality*. London: Routledge.

Seidler, V. (1994) *Unreasonable Men: Masculinity and Social Theory*. London: Routledge.

Silverman, K. (1992) *Male Subjectivity at the Margins*. New York: Routledge.

St. Martin, L. and Gavey, N. (1996) "Women's Bodybuilding: Feminist Resistance and/or Femininity's Recuperation?" *Body & Society*, 4, pp. 45-57.

Tasker, Y. (1993) *Spectacular Bodies. Gender, Genre and the Action Cinema*. London: Routledge.

Theweleit, K. (1978) *Male Fantasies*. Cambridge: Polity Press.

Wacquant, J. D. L. (1995) "Why Men Desires Muscles," *Body & Society*.

Wernick, A. (1991) *Promotional Culture. Advertising, Ideology and Symbolic Expression*. London: Sage.

Chapter 6

Putting on Make-up with Red Gloves: Masculine Aesthetics in an Exclusive Male Culture

GEIR A. ØYGARDEN

Each decade gets the heavy-weight champion it deserves. The progressive 1960s got Muhammad Ali, the cold war of the 1950s got Marciano, Roosevelt and his 'New Deal' got Joe Louis and so on. The regressive 1980s got Mike Tyson. (Säfve, 1995)

If we take Torbjörn Säfve's word seriously and accept the boxer as a metaphor of his time, then the question will be: Who is the boxer of the 1990s? What does he symbolize? What attitudes, knowledges and values does he express?

And does it really make a difference? What I mean is this: in spite of the poems of Muhammad Ali or Tyson's dream of knocking the nasal bone into the brain of his opponent, the craft is the same as it ever was:[1] the boxer of the 1990s will make it his purpose to knock out the front teeth of his opponent – as his colleagues of the 1950s, 1960s, 1970s and 1980s did – and we will be fascinated and slightly nauseated by that very same act.[2] In short: whatever mentalities a boxer may express in his capacity as a historical metaphor, they will have hardly any effect on his trade.

It is notable that this arena has been kept relatively intact and untouched by the widespread values and knowledges of our time, and despite ethical and medical condemnation. Boxing may be one of the few areas today where men are left to themselves, where the classic relationship – the manly love between mentor and disciple in a Greek understanding – is maintained to this day in the relation between the trainer and his trainee. Boxing offers a male space where the body is invested with a knowledge that may turn a left hook into a normative expression. In this essay, that knowledge will be treated as a *tacit knowledge of masculinity*.

Most branches of sport have been highly professionalized. The field of athletics today attracts the attention of all kinds of specialists, from natural scientists and psychologists to physiotherapists. These actors possess a professional knowledge that is – contrary to tacit knowledge – characterized by its reflexivity. This reflexivity is undoubtedly the specialist's most important commodity.

Today the athlete is part of both a network of professional knowledge and a network of economic interests. In 1969 professional boxing was outlawed in Sweden. When money went out of boxing, so did its interest in the public eye.[3] What was left was a small and almost forgotten arena, dominated by indigenous working-class and later by immigrant youth. This prohibition may well have had a preserving effect: since the accepted amateur boxing inherited neither the audience nor the ethos of professional boxing, the arena was plunged into a slumbering existence.

My main point is that amateur boxing may have eluded the professional and economic networks that mark the development of other sports today. As a social phenomenon, this field of sport has been too disrespected, peripheral and unrewarding to attract specialist interest. Boxing may also have evaded another form of reflexivity so characteristic of our time. Boxing, existing in a male space, seems to have remained intact to a relatively high degree. Obviously, bastions of manhood have been collapsing one after another lately, and women have received or taken the license to entry. Undoubtedly, these changes have affected previously highly sheltered male cultures, whose rites and norms are now put on open display. Female priests, paratroopers, professors, police officers – by their very existence they compromise male exclusiveness. Boxing, on the other hand, still offers a space where men are left to themselves. The advantages of placing a study of masculine culture in the field of boxing are obvious. Here is an exclusively male space that may be explored.[4]

If amateur boxing has escaped the kind of critical and reflexive attentions mentioned above, then it could be expected that certain traces of knowledge have been preserved. This perspective leads to a number of interesting questions: In which way is this tacit knowledge expressed? What can we learn from it? What does it embody?

> Without doubt, [boxing] is our most dramatically 'masculine' sport, and our most dramatically 'self-destructive' sport. In this, for some of us, its abiding interest lies. (Oates, 1995, Introduction)

Ordinarily speaking, *the masculine* is somehow taken to be a natural quality in men. It is simply their nature. This common-sense understanding forms the basis of this study, as well as its central problematic. The masculine will be understood as a myth. Its components, scene of representation and symbolic meaning have to be investigated, but at this point the focus will be on the myth as a form of language. According to Roland Barthes:

> Myths are nothing but this ceaseless, untiring solicitation, this insidious and inflexible demand that all men recognize themselves in this image, eternal yet bearing a date, which was built of them one day as if for all time. For the Nature, in which they are locked up under the pretext of being eternalized, is nothing but an Usage. (1987, p. 155)

The quintessence is: if we accept the masculine as man's nature, then we also renounce history. The masculine turns into a harmonious essence, an expression of eternal man. According to Barthes, what you find in the heart of every myth is a process of transformation. The actual world is changed into an image of the world, history is changed into nature. Within this perspective the myth can be blamed for emptying the masculine of praxis. In other words, the masculine has lost both its sense of origin and its historical attributes. What is left is masculine nature – "from which all soiling trace of origin or choice has been removed" (*ibid.*, p. 151).[5]

What will be treated here is what I call *external masculinity* or, more precisely, masculine *form*. The aesthetic principles of masculinity will be discussed in reference to the cultures of body-building and boxing, with emphasis on muscle expansion and scars. However, I will also touch upon something that could be labelled *internal masculinity*. In my interpretation, this signifies the expenses a boxer has in the ring, as a result of putting his body at risk. Concepts like self-discipline and physical courage, perhaps even a lack of visible reaction, may be seen as expressions of this *risk capital*. My main theoretical assumption is that the masculine is charged with meaning in a process whereby a practitioner internalizes a tacit knowledge which forms masculinity. This is achieved by the performance of a standardized set of actions. These standard actions may also be interpreted as model actions, or, with another word, as *exempla*. They are instrumental in constituting the masculine as a meaningful category, which otherwise would be difficult to communicate. In other words, these *exempla* give a concrete form to abstract qualities by displaying the masculine in live pictures – the body-builder or the boxer in the flesh. These standard actions can also be said to bring a *surplus value* to the body in the form of a tacit knowledge which forms the abstract concept of masculinity.

The masculine body language

One can ask whether boxing in our time should be understood as part of a consumer culture, or as representing an anti-culture. The manifestations of late modern culture – characterized by the project of approaching life aesthetically, the celebration of the artist as hero and the stylization of life into a work of art – has opened up a new layer in modern culture (Featherstone, 1991, p. 35). The constant thirst for new products and experiences characterizes the state of late modern life – a desire that has brought with it a multiplication of aesthetic choices, but also a need for guidance in consumer lifestyles and consumer aesthetics. "The new tastemakers, constantly on the look-out for new cultural goods and experiences, are also engaged in the production of popular pedagogies and guides to living and lifestyle" (*ibid.*).[6] In this perspective the construction of the body seems to be a stylistic project – where the choice of body is closely intertwined with lifestyle, identity development and social affiliation.

It may be fruitful to interpret the body-builder as an aesthetic provocation and the boxer as an ethical provocation. We can, consequently, separate between an external and an internal masculinity. The body-builder is concerned with visual constructs: the contours of the surface determine his work. However, the visual has a marginal utility that, when not respected, will easily turn a Henry V into a Richard III. The boxer, on the other hand, exposes an internal quality through a pattern of physical movements. One can only assume that the body-builder and the boxer end up with two essentially different concepts of the body. But despite the fact that the boxer and the body-builder are motivated by different interests in a way that seems to make the purpose and meaning of their physical labor incompatible, they are nevertheless united in the same negation: both cultures challenge, through their aesthetic or ethical deviation, good taste.[7]

Whether one is drawn to boxing for reasons of poverty or for want of experiences, one is submitted to the same discipline. In an article by L. J. D. Wacquant, "Pugs at Work: Bodily Capital and Bodily Labour Among Professional Boxers," the relational network of information and co-operation that surrounds the boxer (trainers, managers, colleagues, friends, and so on) is understood as a disciplinary mechanism. The object of this *quasi-panoptical apparatus* is to guarantee a maximum accumulation of *bodily capital* (Wacquant, 1995, p. 81). This means that the boxer is perceived as a contractor in bodily capital and the boxing gym as a social factory, where human bodies are transformed into virtual "fighting machines." It is a social machinery designed to convert abstract bodily capital into so-called *pugilistic capital*. The boxer's body is to be equipped with a set of "abilities and tendencies liable to produce value in the field of professional boxing" (*ibid.*, p. 66).

The economic perspective of Wacquant – or, more correctly, Bourdieu – may also prove useful for the theme of this essay. Why not introduce the concept of *masculine capital* as a third value next to that of bodily capital and pugilistic capital? Perhaps this third form of capital could be understood as the interest on the other two? The investment in bodily capital and pugilistic capital may even be said to produce a profit in the form of *masculine solvency*.

Why is boxing in our culture attached to masculine values? Female boxers do in fact exist, but compared to body-building, boxing is significantly dominated by men. There is, however, one exception: boxercise. This form of boxing includes all the traditional elements – co-ordination practice, skipping-rope, sack, and so on – except sparring and actual matches. In my opinion, this trend is nothing but kitsch, in terms of Trond Berg Eriksen's definition of the concept: "A possibility to enjoy imitations of virtue and seriousness with minimal intellectual expenses" (1992, p. 93). Boxercise is a way of simulating authenticity without personal effort. It is a parasite living on the genuineness of traditional boxing. Berg Eriksen finds those who use kitsch to be "more satisfied with the imitation than they would have been with the authentic. The genuine is beyond their reach anyway, and seems more threatening and strange than actually attracting" (*ibid.*). In a way, boxercise also sponges off the masculine, since there is a simulation of a behavior pattern that in boxing symbolizes what Torbjörn Säfve (1995) calls "the masculine psyche's single pride: personal courage." Boxercise equals boxing minus the masculine.

What is masculinity in this understanding? And why is boxercise not masculine? Personal courage as an exclusive male quality can obviously be disputed. But a broken nose, cauliflower ears, scars, and other fractures are undoubtedly aspects of a masculine make-up culture. The experiences of a man should be written on the body.

> For the body of every fighter is like a living 'fieldnote' on his entire career: it bears the visible traces of his pugilistic trajectory in the form of scar tissues and cuts, marks, welts, hematomas, and bone fractures. Is it not said of a fighter who gets hit at will during a bout that he is 'getting tattooed'? (Wacquant, 1995, p. 73)

It is reasonable to assume that the value of visible bodily experiences in a culture of production remains in a consumer culture, but that these attributes now should be understood as ornaments on the body. This idea can perhaps be linked to the project of approaching life aesthetically, celebrating the artist as hero and stylizing life as a work of art. Late modern man seeks experiences, and the ornamentation of the body renders cultural experiences visible. This applies to both men and women, even if the means differ.[8]

A key concept in masculine aesthetics is the fracture. For example: a crushed nose that breaks up the profile, a scar that marks the smooth surface of the skin like a scratch on the painting of a car, an ear in the shape of a not altogether perfect marzipan rose. The meaning of this masculine make-up art is that experiences are written on the body in a style that opposes its symmetry. Women's make-up, on the contrary, is designed to conceal symmetrical flaws, that is, to even out all edges and surfaces into a smooth whole. Female experiences in our culture are best kept hidden or invisible. Female culture constantly seeks to improve nature, by making it symmetrical. Charles Baudelaire expresses the following views on make-up:

> anyone can see that the use of rice-powder, so stupidly anathematized by our Arcadian philosophers, is successfully designed to rid the complexion of those blemishes that Nature has outrageously strewn there, and thus to create an abstract unity in the color and texture of the skin, a unity, which, like that produced by the tights of a dancer, immediately approximates the human being to the statue, that is to something superior and divine. As for the artificial black with which the eye is outlined, and the rouge with which the upper part of the cheek is painted, although their use derives from the same principle, the need to surpass Nature ... (1964, p. 33)

Scars, a broken nose, cauliflower ears, bruises and other physical marks – stretch-marks or sagging breasts and stomach due to child-birth included – are hardly looked upon as flattering ornamentation when found on a female body. On the contrary, everything that threatens the unity of the whole should remain a dark continent beneath segmented layers of opaque powder. Men, on the other hand, may see the deforming of nature as an aesthetic expression, or as a way of communicating masculinity: "One look at the Pazman's mashed and crooked nose tells the whole story."[9]

The wordlessness of boxing creates a space for symbolic interaction. The ring turns into an anatomical theatre, where bodily fluids, fractures and swellings are the symbols that give the idea of the masculine its guts.

Daniel Zaragoza – What makes him so exciting: Blood and guts. The game Mexican 122-pound champion has more scar tissue than the Frankenstein monster. Instead of a cutman he should use a sewing machine in his corner.[10]

Boxing differs from boxercise in the contingency that characterizes the creation of the masculine imagery; the broken nose, the crumpled ear, the swollen eye, the split chin, the skin sweating blood and water.

This is why the body-builder is an unsatisfactory example of masculinity. His sport turns into kitsch: he enjoys imitations of virtue and seriousness without personal effort. The body-builder constructs his body into a visualization of mythological manhood: Hercules, Goliath, Agamemnon, Ulysses, Tor and Golem. But the masculinity of body-building is artificial and it will never be put to the test. Body-building is one-sided since it revolves around an aesthetical dimension, a dimension that borders upon vanity. The problem is obviously that with a purely aesthetic objective, the body-builder comes across as anything but masculine. Andy Warhol's comment on his own art sums up the dilemma of the body-builder: "Just look at the surface of my paintings and films and me, and there I am. There's nothing behind it" (quoted in Honour and Fleming, 1982, p. 614).

The ornaments of a boxer's body are valuable because they are not products of an aesthetically defined goal. As proofs of the boxer's efforts and expenses, the marks on his body create an impression of authenticity. "I used to get a cut or a black eye, and that was my badge of honor."[11] Hearing Emile Griffith's revelation, one is reminded of Jean Genet's character who made a similar statement about the semen on a sailor's blue pants: "He wears those stains with a glorious impudence: they are his medals" (1993, p. 171).

Boxercise and body-building, on the other hand, simulate authenticity, the former by imitating a pattern of action that has been removed from its context – a man and a chair do not make a lion-tamer – the latter by pumping up a body that only mimics masculine qualities. For example, in a Swedish amateur porno film, that happened to take place in a motor-car repair shop, a body-builder features. Why? If a body is sculptured into a form that creates superhuman expectations and fantasies, an aesthetical piece of work that indicates a bestial potency, then one can also expect increased demands on the performance. In short, the body-builder constructs an overexposed image of the masculine, and risks a dissonance between the actual size of the body and its implied promises: the ideal is beyond his powers. This is obviously not a problem as long as the sculpture accepts that he is a sculpture, and realizes that losing his trousers means losing all optical illusions.

Figuratively speaking, a boxer is always caught with his trousers down. In the ring he exposes himself to a powerful physical and psychological bombardment that displays his masculinity on an open stage. Never can he allow himself to express fear or pain. There is only one manly way out of the ring: knock-out, or being saved by the merciful towel.

Perhaps we can say that the body-builder overcommunicates his masculinity. But is not this overcommunication a strategy usually associated with a feminine position – coquetry, make-up, push-up bras, stiletto heels that accentuate the breasts and buttocks, and so on? A parallel could be drawn between a boxer and an exhibitionist. In ordinary life most people have a limited set of masks at their disposal. Or, more correctly, there is a selection of culturally approved masks. The purpose of an exhibitionist is to provoke a removal of the mask. He breaches the context by performing an act that is not included in the cultural repertoire of adequate behavior – then he awaits a reaction. If the mask is shed he has succeeded – if not, he may, at most, be in danger of catching a cold. But boxing is also a play with masks, where the actor's virtue – in spite of a brutal physical treatment – is never to allow himself other expressions than those befitting the context. The young Mike Tyson liked to brag about how his opponents expressed pain in the ring: "Actually, he was crying in there, making women's gestures (imitates crying)" – that is, he let the mask fall.[12] In the same way that a woman, in front of an exhibitionist's open coat, knows that she is obliging him by letting go of the mask, and still is caught by surprise, the opponent of Mike Tyson knows that he is not supposed to reveal his reactions. The main point is that the park, the railway station, the underground and the ring are ruled by a set of *tacit conventions*, that have to be violated in order to be noticed. A glove in the face or a saluting prick may just do the trick. Another possibility is to think of the body-builder as an aesthetic *abject* and the boxer as an ethical *abject*. The fascinated disgust that Thomas Johansson (1995) has treated in relation to the body-builder's body, can also be applied to the boxer's physical behavior. Our relationship to this sport is highly ambivalent.[13] Like the body-builder, the boxer balances on the verge of the socially accepted. The oversized body challenges the tasteful, while the fighting body challenges decency. In either case, the norms of the superego are challenged and constructed through negation.[14]

The masculine example

I have discussed how the boxer and the body-builder express an internal versus an external masculinity. By embodying masculine qualities, they give a concrete form to the idea of the masculine. Therefore it is possible to interpret the boxer and the body-builder as *exempla*. In classic rhetoric, the role of the *exemplum* was to illustrate matter that would be too abstract and therefore not suited to convince an audience. The exemplum may be defined as "a true or fictive event or a living character that is included in the speech in order to give a concrete form to something abstract and serve as proof drawn from the historical past or the orator's personal experiences" (Johannesson, 1990, p. 228). Aristotle described the use of the *exemplum* as a sort of rhetorical induction – a method for deriving general statements or rules from observations of specific events and thereby supporting one's arguments and theses (*ibid.*, p. 96). I propose the use of a perspective that I choose to call *critical rhetorical induction*. Assuming that the masculine is an abstract term for real qualities in men, rather than seeking after a general meaning of the concept, one can uncover an empirical content by studying the *exempla* that carry the concept. Thus, the method is to study the concept of the masculine, by analyzing the *exempla* that illustrate, simplify and give definite meaning to its constructions.

Perhaps the relation between *exempla*, concept and general structure is made clearer by using an analogy. In Thomas Kuhn's (1970) model of a scientific paradigm, the scientist goes through a great number of standard problems and standard elaborations, and thereby he or she acquires a "tacit knowledge." This knowledge is difficult to analyze, since it is maintained by what could be called *the law of the innocence of small actions*. Standard elaborations and problems are understood as a routine, an institutionalized repetition of fixed motions, and a disciplining of the problematic. By these, the metaphorical components or the symbolic generalizations in a paradigm can be illustrated. The object is to internalize a common horizon of understanding that otherwise is difficult to verbalize or summarise in statements.

The scientific paradigm is maintained by tacit knowledge, inculcated by standard actions – *exemplars* in Kuhn's terminology. My point is that the masculine is constructed in a similar way, that is, by a process whereby knowledge is diffused or reproduced by standard actions. Within this knowledge standardized role interpretations function as *exemplars*. These help to legitimize and consolidate an understanding of the masculine, even though this knowledge remains tacit. Since there is no clear understanding of the fact that these standard actions are conditional, they will not be subjected to criticism. All actions are treated as axioms. They are, in the words of Roland Barthes, being *naturalized*. They seem natural to us, rather than resulting from an active choice. The reality of history, or praxis, is being suppressed to create a stable and implacable image of the masculine.

One starting-point, as I have already stated, is to consider the masculine as a *surplus value* of the body. I assume that physical labor bestows this quality on to the body. By physical labor a surplus value is conferred on the material – the body – which men assimilate as masculinity. It is reasonable to believe that the symbolic meaning of physical labor in a culture of production was closely associated with the masculine. The question is whether these associations have remained with the conception of the masculine, even during the transition to a less and less physical society.

In any case, it is important to stress that I understand the masculine to be a changeable category that constantly needs to be reconsidered, although the category is constantly being transformed into a transcendental one through the construction of myths. In this respect, it is the form that naturalizes the content. That is, the very moment a quality is seen as masculine, it is freeze-framed into an image of reality, since it is given the status of nature.

Having stated that the idea of the masculine is upheld by a chain of actions that generate a tacit knowledge, one natural but delicate question comes to mind: Can this tacit knowledge talk? The point is obviously that we tend to look upon the reproduction of masculinity as a natural, necessary, innocent, neutral, and harmless process. It seems to be motivated only by common sense, the general opinion, and by what is normal. These *exemplars* resemble Erich Fromm's *anonymous authorities* (1994, p. 166) or the previously mentioned *myths* of Barthes (1987, p. 109).

First, I assume that in boxing there exists a transference of masculine experience, of a knowledge that is tacit, not reflexive. Secondly, I think that the concept of the masculine is invested with meaning when the boxer acquires this tacit knowledge by performing standard actions. Thus, the boxer – interpreted as an *exemplum* – is an embodiment of the masculine essence.[15] But by interpreting individuals as *exempla*, they turn into something larger than themselves. They fill up a frame of meaning that has both historical dimensions and future relevance.

Masculine basement phenomena

There are two paths that lead down to Hades in Stockholm, two activities that lure you down under the ground. To find either a peep-show or a boxing gym you have to descend into a world of basements. In other words, it may seem as though one has to break through the surface to find the exclusive male rooms.

Boxing and sex can perhaps be defined as a play with intimacy and humiliation, a game where the stakes for a man are semen or blood. Roland Barthes theorizes that actors cry or sweat on stage becuase the middle-class audience reduces each quality to a quantity: "I give my money to the theatre, in return for which I demand a clearly visible, almost computable passion ..." (1988, p. 75). This principle also concerns pornography: semen is ejected on the face, semen is ejected into the mouth, semen is smeared on the breasts and other body parts. That is, ejaculation on the external body gives value for money.[16] Or in Barthes' words: "Combustion's great advantage is of an economic order: my spectator's money has a verifiable yield at last" (*ibid.*, p. 76). Pornography and boxing have two things in common: blood as well as semen is sprinkled on the face, blood drips into the open mouth, blood is smeared on the chest and other body parts.

Blood and semen both serve the same function: they are visual adjectives. Adjectives describe or emphasize specific characteristics and qualities in a noun. But

> the adjective (or the adverb) often plays a curiously ambiguous role: it seems to proceed from an anxiety, from the sentiment that the substantives used, despite their notorious character, have undergone a wear and tear which cannot be entirely concealed; whence the necessity to reinvigorate them: independence becomes *true*, aspirations *authentic*, destinies *indissolubly* linked. Here the adjective aims at clearing the noun of its past disappointments, presenting it in a new, innocent, credible state. (Barthes, 1988, p. 109)

If we trust Barthes, the purpose of the adjectival ornamentation is to give nothingness a character of being. In this perspective, both boxing and pornography seem to remind us of existence. Blood, as well as semen, as well as scarring, remind us of reality. Boxercise, or body-building, offers neither blood nor semen, just sweat. But sweat does not seem to have what it takes to create reality. That is why boxercise, like most kitsch phenomena, is a longing for reality.

Perhaps we are experiencing just that – a loss of reality. A deficit we try to balance by producing models. At any rate, Baudrillard thinks that we are facing a transformation of reality into a model, that we are living in a space of simulation, or in a hyper-reality that ends reality as a reference system by turning it into a model (Baudrillard, 1983). Earlier, I compared boxercise and body-building with kitsch or simulated phenomena. But I would like to add another simulator of reality: Karaoke. If Baudrillard is right in thinking that reality and the model of reality are mixed in the space of simulation, then we can also be said to live in a Karaoke show. A Japanese man can be Elvis Presley for 15 minutes. Halfway through "(Let Me be Your) Teddy Bear" he begins to suspect that he cannot possibly be Elvis. And yet he is Elvis, since – if I remember rightly – in the words of Beckett: All is alike, almost alike. But the question is, does this schizophrenic mix-up create a longing for experiences that cannot be constructed?

Roland Barthes thought that the quality of the simile was to imitate – with as little costs as possible – the most rare substances (1987, p. 98). In our time, reality – in a genuine, authentic rather than constructed sense – may be such a substance. Mike Featherstone has written that postmodernism "reflects a loss of confidence on the part of Western intellectuals in the superiority of their project, in their authority and capacity to establish universal standards of truth, morality, and taste, toward which mankind will progress" (1991, p. 40). But if our intellectual constructions have lost their ability to create meaning, while we suspect we are living in an aesthetic hallucination, where, then, do we seek our "new" reality? As Jean Starobinski notes:

> Everywhere there is talk about the body as if it had been recovered after years of oblivion: exercise, body language, bodily feelings and the liberation of the body are turned into catchwords. This also concerns the historian who is now so interested in how earlier cultures other than our own related to the body. He studies tattoos, mutilations, celebration, and rituals connected with the functions of the body. (1992, p. 5)[17]

The question is whether this interest in the body is built upon the suspicion that surface is everything, as in the case of Andy Warhol, that it is constructed, as in the case of the hallucination of the Japanese Elvis, that it represents the bankruptcy of the intellectual universe and the breakdown of the grand narratives, and therefore leads us to search for a reality beyond all aesthetical constructions.

The very surface of the body has to be penetrated to become meaningful, since blood or semen brings us as close to reality as we can get without feeling cheated. This may also be the reason why scars – never constructed, always incidental – are seen as valuable. In his book *Zeichen auf der Haut: Die Geschichte der Tätowierung in Europa*, Stephen Oettermann (1979) mentions five forms of body painting: cosmetics, masks, tattoos, scarifications and brands,[18] all characterized by being constructed. This is not the case with the scars won in a duel, where form and size always are created at random. An interesting question is then whether *unconstructable constructions are valued simply because they cannot be constructed?* The quality a boxer is supposed to show in the ring is "guts." "Show your guts," they urge. Metaphorically, the quality they ask for is placed beneath the skin, that is, below the surface.

It can be argued that one of the characteristics of postmodernism is the transformation of reality into pictures. However, the picture has one flaw. It may lie. Therefore, those representations of guts – like sweat as a quantitative guarantee for quality – may be our only proof that the picture is telling the truth. In this sense boxing can be interpreted as a ritual for creating reality, or as a kind of invocation. According to Mircea Eliade, the purpose of the invocation is to create signs. "When no sign manifests itself, it is *provoked*" (1959, p. 27). Two people enter a square – called a ring with corners – to conjure up, in three-minute intervals, the sight of blood as a sign of reality:

> It is not red cowberry jam that drips out of the boxer's nose. It is real blood. This is the reason why boxing is both hard reality and representative theatre. (Säfve, 1990, p. 7)

The product of pain

In this essay we have explored an exclusively male room with particular reference to those rites, norms and values signifying masculinity. We have discussed how bodily symbolic actions function as *exempla*, a perspective which has been illustrated by empirical examples from the field of boxing, body-building and boxercise. Scar tissues, cuts and fractures – earned in boxing – have been understood as part of a masculine ethics, and in their consequences as expressions of reality. However, this ethics exposes itself through an aesthetical form.

Let us recapitulate the two forms of masculinity that have been under consideration: 1) "internal masculinity" that manifests itself through accidental fractures that break up the surface and is opposed to symmetry, and 2) "external masculinity" which maintains, or improves if necessary, the symmetrical in an expanded form. The former is acquired on stage, in a process of facing the reality of pain and the possibility of death, where the aesthetical emphasis embodies internal qualities like self-discipline and physical courage. The latter is created through physical labor, that of course demands self-discipline, but never courage.

How can we understand this in relation to history? Do these forms of masculinity signalize stagnation or alteration? According to Cicero:

> *Virtus* has got its name from *vir* (man); that which characterizes a man is fortitude and the two most important features of fortitude are contempt of death and contempt of pain. (quoted in Wistrand, 1992, p. 119)

The boxer's broken nose becomes a manifestation of fortitude. Interpreted as an *exemplum* of *virtus*, it also turns out to be *archaic*: it transcends the contemporary, the individual, the particular by embodying and exemplifying masculine essence. But the broken nose creates nothing new; it does not violate the frozen structures of the past. Quite the reverse: a broken nose is a broken nose whether it belongs to Milo from Kroton, Joe Louis, or Evander Holyfield. The body-builder, on the other hand, is weaved from the same material as modernity. His construction is a product of physiological and mechanical *know-how* that is closely linked with the twentieth century.

The *beefcake* evaluates his body in accordance with what is usually considered to be a female comprehension of symmetry. It is not uncommon in body-building cultures for a man to remove the hair under the arms or on the chest. His construction, in this sense, becomes an attempt – even if the investment in muscles does not necessarily give the same profit in a consumer culture as in a culture of production – to fit contemporary norms of equality between the sexes. The body – male or female – is perceived with one contemporary gaze: the equality between the eyes. The boxer's body becomes conceivably an anachronism. The nose bone is beyond modernity; pain and death are beyond modernity. External masculinity can signify internal masculinity, but it is not. The scar *is virtus*, the oversized body *signifies virtus*. A boxer without marks on his body is a suspicious character:

> De La Hoya acknowledges that people are slow to accept him as the successor to Roberto Duran and Chavez because he lacks the scars of a warrior on his face. Chavez has them. Chavez merely needs to win, and if he must win ugly, it does not matter. [19]

Perhaps it would be possible to express the difference between internal and external masculinity as follows: Internal masculinity is a demonstration of willpower at the expense of symmetry – the body as a hammer – while external masculinity is the cultivation of symmetry – the body as an icon.

> By the finish he was cut over both eyes, had a bloody nose and a cut lower lip, his blood splashing on to Chavez's chest and shoulder. But Gamache went out fighting. …, he leaves the game with his head high.[20]

Internal masculinity produces snapshots of reality. These glimpses arise when the surface is penetrated and a wound, a ruin of flesh, is made visible – a traumatic point, that Lacan might have conceptualized as the *tuché* (the Greek *trauma* means "wound") and Barthes the *punctum*.[21] Hal Foster notes:

> the *punctum* breaks through the screen and allows the real to poke through. The real, Lacan puns, is *trou*matic, and I noted that the tear in *Ambulance Disaster* [Andy Warhol, 1963] is such a hole (*trou*) for me … Through these pokes or pops we seem almost to touch the real … (1997, p. 136)

The boxer cuts through the skin like a tin opener, which leaves a *trou*, an open wound behind, while the *beefcake* joins the *cheesecake* in homage to the surface, the symmetry, the immortality, yes, the powder …

A special thanks to M. Franzén, E. Lundgren, P. Engholm, T. Kumlin, P. Ekegren, E. Savoca, P. Fahlström.

Notes

1. Cf. "I try to catch him right on the tip of the nose, because I try to push the bone into the brain." Mike Tyson quoted in The Ring (1996), "Tyson Extra," 2 (1), p. 14.
2. Even among boxing aficionados it seems rather common to express one's feelings towards the sport in contradictory terms: "It was a brutal fight. It was also a beautiful fight" and "in the wonderful, terrible world of boxing," The Ring (1996), 75 (6), p. 71; and 75 (10), p. 27.
3. On November 26,1969, the Swedish Parliament decided to outlaw professional boxing in Sweden.
4. Despite its increasing popularity, female boxing is still a marginal phenomenon.
5. I am aware of the fact that "the later" Barthes viewed his theory of myth

critically. I am also familiar with his term idiolect (1989, p. 67).

6. Cf. the "new cultural intermediaries" (Bourdieu, 1992).
7. On the body-builder's body as deviation, see Johansson, 1995. On the "moral impeachment" of boxing, see Wacquant, 1995, p. 83 and footnote 15.
8. In the film "Tokyo Fist", boxing is associated with ornamentation of the body. Images of a woman getting tattooed and pierced are cross-cut with images of a man who is acquiring visible marks in the ring. These bodily expressions are interpreted as external manifestations of inner states. Tsukamoto (Director) 1995.
9. The Ring (1996), 75 (11), p. 23.
10. Ibid., p. 25.
11. The former welterweight champion Emile Griffith, quoted in The Ring (1996), 75 (4), p. 61.
12. Tyson's comment after his KO over Tyrell Biggs (October 16, 1987) Kopple (Producer and Director) 1993.
13. Cf. Note 3.
14. Cf. "To each ego its object, to each superego its abject" (Kristeva, 1982, p. 2).
15. Cf. "the intuition of general 'essences'" (Alvesson and Sköldberg, 1991, p. 97).
16. Cf. money shot – the term for a visible ejaculation.
17. The author's translation from the Norwegian edition.
18. Cf. Polhemus and Randall, 1996, for an up-to-date discussion, which also includes: Piercing, Body Sculpting, Gender Transformation, and so on.
19. International Boxing Digest (1996), XXXVIII (4), p. 13.
20. Boxing Monthly (1996), 11, p. 20. Cf. "less than a week later, he [Saad Muhammad] would be shedding blood for the amusement of the high-rollers in the Superstar Theatre, as well as for millions of boxing aficionados across the nation," The Ring (1996), 75 (12), p. 69.
21. Cf. Barthes, 1997, pp. 94-7; Lacan, 1981, pp. 53-64; and Foster, 1997, pp. 126-68.

References

Alvesson, M. and Sköldberg, K. (1991) *Tolkning och Reflektion: Veten-skapsfilosofi och Kvalitativ Metod*I [Interpretation and Reflection: Philosophy of Science and Qualitative Method]. Lund: Studentlitteratur.

Barthes, R. (1987) [1957] *Mythologies.* London: Paladin Grafton Books.

Barthes, R. (1988) [1979] *The Eiffel Tower and Other Mythologies.* New York: The Noonday Press.

Barthes, R. (1989) "Mythology Today," in *The Rustle of Language.* Berkeley & Los Angeles: University of California Press.

Barthes, R. (1997) [1980] *Camera Lucida: Reflections on Photography.* New York: Hill and Wang.

Baudelaire, C. (1964) [1863] "In Praise of Cosmetics," in *The Painter of Modern Life and other Essays.* London: Phaidon Press.

Baudrillard, J. (1983) *In the Shadow of the Silent Majorities.* New York: Semiotext(s).

Berg Eriksen, T. (1992) [1989] *Nietzsche og det Moderne* [Nietzsche and the Modern]. Oslo: Universitetsforlaget.

Bourdieu, P. (1992) [1979] *Distinction. A Social Critique of the Judgement of Taste.* London: Routledge.

Boxing Monthly (1996).

Eliade, M. (1959) [1957] *The Sacred and the Profane: The Nature of Religion.* New York: Harcourt, Brace and Company.

Featherstone, M. (1991) *Consumer Culture and Postmodernism.* London: Sage.

Foster, H. (1997) *The Return of the Real.* Cambridge and London: The MIT Press.

Fromm, E. (1994) [1941] *Escape From Freedom.* New York: Henry Holt.

Genet, J. (1993) "Querelle," in Edmund White (ed.), *The Selected Writings of Jean Genet.* New Jersey: The Ecco Press.

Honour, H. and Fleming, J. (1982) *A World History of Art.* London and Basingstoke: Macmillan Publishers.

International Boxing Digest (1996).

Johannesson, K. (1990) *Retorik eller Konsten att Övertyga* [Rhetoric or the Art of Persuasion]. Stockholm: Norstedts.

Johansson, T. (1995) "Främlingskap och det främmande: Bodybuilding, kön och identitet" [Estrangement and the Strange: Bodybuilding, Gender and Identity], *Kulturella Perspektiv,* 4 (4).

Kopple, B. (1993) *Fallen Champ: The Untold Story of Mike Tyson.* USA: ETC Productions, Inc.

Kristeva, J (1982) *Powers of Horror. An Essay on Abjection.* New York: Columbia University Press.

Kuhn, T. S. (1970) *The Structure of Scientific Revolutions.* Chicago and London: University of Chicago Press.

Lacan, J. (1981) [1973] *The Four Fundamental Concepts of Psycho-Analysis.* New York/London: W. W. Norton & Company.

Oates, J. C. (1995) [1987] *On Boxing.* New Jersey: The Ecco Press.

Oettermann, S. (1979) *Zeichen auf der Haut. Die Geschichte der Tätowierung in Europa.* Frankfurt am Main: Syndikat.

Polhemus, T. and Randall, H. (1996) *The Customized Body.* London and New York: Serpent's Tail.

The Ring (1996).

Starobinski, J. (1992) *Fra Kroppsfølelsens Historie/Kleine Geschichte des Körpergefühls.* Oslo: Cappelen.

Säfve, T. (1990) *En Gentleman Äntrar Ringen: Tio Berättelser om Boxning* [A Gentleman Enters the Ring: Ten Stories About Boxing]. Stockholm: Bokförlaget Prisma.

Säfve, T. (1995) "Vem vill ha en hatisk slugger?" [Who Needs a Slugger Full of Hatred?], *Aftonbladet*, 19 August.

Tsukamoto, S. (1995) *Tokyo Fist.* Japan: Kaijyu Theatre Co.

Wacquant, L.J.D. (1995) "Pugs at Work: Bodily Capital and Bodily Labour Among Professional Boxers," *Body & Society*, 1 (1).

Wistrand, M. (1992) *Entertainment and Violence in Ancient Rome: The attitudes of Roman writers of the first century A.D.* Göteborg: Acta Universitatis Gothoburgensis, Institute of Classical Studies of the University of Göteborg.

Chapter 7

When Boys Become Men: The Martial Arts as Young People's Revolt against the Youth Rebellion

HANS BONDE

In much of the present-day educationalist debate and research, female dominance is emphasized when discussing the education of modern boys. It is asserted, not without some truth, that modern family structure and children's institutions do not always offer the boys opportunities for finding masculine figures of identification within their immediate surroundings (Kryger, 1988 and Zlotnik, 1984). It is easily overlooked that throughout our century movements like sports and the Boy Scouts have offered important means for the teaching of masculine behavior (Kiselberg, 1979 and Bonde, 1991). With the breakthrough of industrialization and capitalism around the turn of the century the middle class in particular established a new division of labor according to sex: Mother was at home and Father was away. It is therefore tempting to see the socialization of children as occurring within a purely feminine sphere. This way it is easily ignored that throughout the century, side by side with the establishment of the female dominated family, special forums have been established where men have taught what it means to be a man. The forums in question were large areas in the sector of voluntary education, such as sports and the Boy Scouts movement. For older children in particular, instruction in masculine qualities may not have been in as short a supply as one might have expected.

During the initial stages of the breakthrough of modern competitive sport around the turn of the century we find explicit arguments why sport should be an introduction to masculine codes. At a time otherwise regarded as being characterized by degeneration, young men might preserve a "masculine" body and a firm character through sport. The great threat was the feminized, soft-muscled, weak man gradually coming into existence in the wake of the growth of the modern, white-collar workers' movement (Bonde, 1991). From its tender start down to our own time, sport has become Denmark's greatest popular movement, with both women and men participating. Yet it is still men in particular who seek out the hard competitive sports and new "hazardous sports," such as mountain climbing, triathlon and mountain biking.

The Oriental martial arts seem to have a particular attraction for young males. Below I shall attempt to show that the martial arts have become a modern voluntary introduction to masculine codes, a kind of manhood test. Characterized by rituals and authority, the martial arts may be seen as young people's rebellion against the youth rebellion, and also against the paucity of sensuous experience and the cultivation of literary and verbal-abstract abilities in our modern society. Nonetheless, the martial arts also develop elements of the youth rebellion, such as an interest in the Far East and in meditation.

This article seeks to show that, not least in a highly technological welfare society like our own, young people have a great need to experience the limits of the body, the importance of pain and ecstasy and the total absorption in the present. This is what makes life rich and worth living. But this also makes it even more important that within the framework of the ritual should be found people who have themselves experienced this fascination and who still preserve a humanistic perspective.

In a society characterized by paucity of sensuous experience and lack of social bearings the martial arts offer close bodily contact and rituals. The fascination of young people with the masters of the martial arts may certainly be seen in connection with the loss of apprenticeship and the overall undermining of craftsmanlike mastery. What may not be attained at your job might be attained in your spare time at the judo club.

The spreading of the martial arts

Whereas during the 1960s the market for the Oriental martial arts was dominated by judo, in the course of the 1970s karate became a serious competitor. While in judo you chiefly throw your opponent on his back, in karate you principally use blows. That is to say, in many kinds of karate you do not strike through, but only indicate the blows. In the course of the 1980s karate was challenged by the Korean martial art taekwondo, where you kick at specified protected parts of the body. Today there are approximately 10,000 people who practice judo, jiu-jitsu or ju-jutsu. Another 10,000 practice karate, while about 10,000 go in for taekwondo.

In the course of time judo has become an international competitive sport with millions of practitioners inside and outside Japan, and since 1964 it has been included on the Olympic program. In Danish judo clubs the technical terminology is still Japanese and the rituals remain intact, but the sporadic exotic elements have been almost entirely replaced by competitions, points and the pursuit of medals. To a certain extent this is also the case with taekwondo and karate, both of which, however, have shown greater power of resistance to the tendency toward becoming a competitive sport. Martial arts like the Japanese aikido and the Chinese tai chi have remained almost entirely clear of the sportification process and may almost be described as meditation in movement. They attract the gentle male types and quite a number of women.

A large element of fashion is involved in people's choice of the Oriental martial arts. All the time it is the new and unknown that attract people. At the present moment the so-called ninjutsuka, a Japanese shadow warrior, is gaining ground. The most popularized version of this phenomenon is found in the "Teenage mutant hero turtles" – cartoons that roll across the screen, bringing great pleasure to younger children.

Masculine fantasies

The cowboy and the ninja attract us by means of the same effects: the excitement, the night atmosphere, the man-to-man combat and the danger of sudden death. The cowboy of my boyhood was the great hero – today he has been replaced by new idols like the ninja, the Japanese shadow warrior who, wearing a dark suit and using incredibly sophisticated weapons, appears out of nowhere to carry out secret assignments, vanishing again into thin air. The boys' idols have moved east to the country of the rising sun.

To the modern boy the samurai becomes the exotic yet recognizable hero. He is untouchable and prepared to defend his honor. For that he is willing to die. The samurai is alone, but strong. He is a survival machine who, shielded by his armor and with sword in hand, is capable of defending himself in all situations. The samurai controls life and death. He is the law and everybody has to comply with his will. If we compare the life of a Danish school boy to that of the son of a Japanese samurai of the seventeenth century, we find distinct differences. At a ceremony at the age of five the warrior boy had his first little sword handed over to him, and at school he received just as many lessons in battle skills as in academic subjects. Among other things the samurai boys were taught archery, swordplay, jiu-jitsu and to swim while wearing armor.

The answer as to why modern boys dream about the samurai must be found inside ourselves. What we miss in our modern, busy lives, we dream about in tales of faraway countries and distant times. The lives we live today are characterized by academic drudgery in the classroom, at the machine or behind a desk. The most nerve-racking highlight of our day is getting safely across the pedestrian crossing.

Young Western men and boys direct their attention to at least two subjects within the Oriental martial arts. Many of them are attracted to the samurai, as noted above. In addition, some of them are spellbound by some deeper philosophical layers to which they are only gradually introduced. These layers date back to Japanese Zen Buddhist monks who from about the year 1600 contributed to making the martial arts a path to mental development. Whereas before the year 1600 the essential thing was killing an external enemy, it now became increasingly important to kill the restricting, aggressive and self-centered forces within oneself. Socially this development was reflected in the fact that from about the year 1600 the many civil wars in Japan were followed by a long period of peace.

When a student of the traditionally practiced Japanese martial arts (*budo*) has perceived that the fight depends on the momentary melting together of the two combatants, the next step of his development must follow directly. He is now expected to acquire a broader sense of the unity of man with his fellow men, the plants, the earth, the sea, indeed the entire cosmos.

The concept *mushin* (emptiness) should not be understood in the ordinary Danish sense of the word, as a feeling of indifference and lack of meaning. It is precisely when one stops the grinding stream of thoughts that one can experience a sense of meaningfulness. Many Westerners are afraid of emptiness and fill their heads with messages and pictures from newspapers, television, video and cartoons.

If the Japanese martial arts are perceived as a means to the development of the body and soul, the aim, at first, is not to make an external conquest, but to create a transformation in the heart of man. The focus is more upon the process than the result. "It is not the peak of the mountain which gives life, it is its sides and slopes. That is where things grow." Or, to put it differently, it is through the judo fight itself that man may develop mentally, not through clinging to external pats on the shoulder like medals, records and championships.

It is important to stress that the description of Japanese martial arts is romanticized and based on its self-conception. During the 1930s, in spite of all the beautiful pacifist declarations, the martial arts were used in the

Fascist mobilization. Nevertheless this does not detract from the beauty and appeal of the philosophy at the abstract level. The Oriental martial arts are like a sharp-edged axe. Used constructively they may cleave wood. Used egatively they may kill people. In themselves neither the axe nor the martia. arts contains any moral. In order to conduct the strong energies into constructive channels the moral must be added.

The master as a father figure

> A great master must also be a great teacher. With us the two things quite naturally go together. If he had started by teaching breathing exercises he would never have been able to convince you that these exercises are of vital importance to you. You would have to fail in your own attempts before you were ready to catch the life buoy he threw you. Believe me, I know from my own experience that the master knows you and his other pupils better than we know ourselves. He reads more in his pupils' souls than they themselves are willing to admit. (Herrigel, 1971, p. 32)

With the breakthrough of modern society the father was separated from the family. In pre-modern society the father was present, for better or for worse, since production and family were combined under one roof (Gillis, 1992). Modern society has been termed "the fatherless society" (Mitscherlich, 1973), and although throughout the century fathers have had more and more spare time, the modern father is often busy and hurried, the divorce ratios are high and the children's connection to the divorced father is often very weak. The Oriental martial arts offer a father figure whose authority cannot be mistaken. He is present and demanding. Perhaps this accounts in part for young men's acceptance of the authority to be found in the martial arts' hall.

By including an imitation of and perhaps even an identification with the teacher as part of the education, the learning form resembles traditional Western apprenticeship (Jespersen, 1993). Precisely throughout the last decades when apprenticeship with its cultivation of a paternal, patriarchal learning form has decreased, we notice young men willingly submitting themselves to the least hint of the master and cultivating "craftsmanlike" learning forms. The young men who practice the martial arts may thus acquire the visual and bodily abilities otherwise about to vanish entirely from our academic, highly educated society.

The best authority on the special pedagogy of the Oriental martial arts is *Bueskydning og Zen*, a book written by the German professor of philosophy Eugen Herrigel. Here Herrigel has given us an evocative portrait of the Japanese master archer Kenzo Awa, as a kind of authoritarian father figure who nonetheless has the development of his pupil as his absolute goal. Herrigel's text is rather romanticizing, but still central, being a rare example of the introduction of a Westerner to the more esoteric part of the Japanese martial arts during the inter-war period.

A teacher at the Tohoku-university of Sendia, Herrigel stayed in Japan throughout the years 1929-48. Herrigel has described in a convincing manner the shock he had when studying archery in 1930s Japan. From the very beginning he expected that the primary goal was to hit the target with the arrow, and he suffered one defeat after another. In the end he realized that the deeper aim of Japanese archery was not hitting the target as precisely as possible, but working toward self-insight and self-denial through concentrating on the activity. If one reaches this concentration the arrow will also hit the target perfectly. Not until he had penetrated deeply into the technique of archery was he allowed to forget about the arrow. He felt that he could not measure his advances, but his teacher sensed well enough his stage of development. Only when he was mentally ready for it was he allowed to practice the next step. His description of his learning process is a description of years of persistent training, crises and frustration before he seriously started to catch a glimpse of the master's idea.

As is the case with Western apprenticeship, traditionally practiced Japanese martial arts also use imitation and copying as the two central pedagogical mechanisms. Herrigel describes the imitation model thus:

> At the beginning nothing is demanded of the student beyond conscientous imitation of whatever his teacher shows him. The latter being against endless explanations and justifications, these are limited to brief instructions, and the student is not expected to ask questions. The teacher kindly follows the fumbling efforts without expecting independence and initiative. (Herrigel, 1971, pp. 47f)

I prefer the word "imitation" to "copying." The latter indicates a totally unconscious and mechanical copying which is far from the idea of the Japanese martial arts. We lack research on the wonderful process that makes human beings capable of studying other people's movements and repeating them. This is not merely a copy of other people's movements, but an entirely new body expression created by another individual. It is probably important to distinguish between different stages of the development. At first a relatively mechanical copying takes place. Later the movements begin to be "felt." In the end they become a perfectly natural part of the performer. At this point it is no longer an imitation, but a new, valid expression which at its point of departure has modelled itself on another person. Within the Japanese martial arts one talks about "living" and "dead" movements (Leggett, 1960 and 1978) distinguish between the insipid copy where the mind forces the body into patterns of movement and the process where the division between body and mind has been dissolved and only the action remains.

The quotation from Herrigel illustrates the relationship between traditional apprenticeship and the Oriental martial arts in their lack of language: too many explanations and rationalistic reasonings destroy the concentration and create an illusion that true mastery may be grasped intellectually, which blocks comprehension. Instead of rationalistic reasons the Zen masters use images (and riddles) as gateways to perceiving the incomprehensible. For example, the master describes the archer's lack of purpose by comparing him to a bamboo leaf that, weighed down with snow, suddenly throws off the snow and draws itself up.

Identification with the teacher also furthers the development of the student. In Herrigel's words:

> The road to mastery is steep. Often the only thing which keeps the student going is his belief in the teacher from whose hand he now expects to receive mastery: For the student the teacher appears as a living model of the inner work and seems convincing solely by his very presence. (*Ibid.*, p. 53)

Here, however, we see the inherent weakness of the martial arts as well as of apprenticeship. An almost submissive attitude is demanded from the student who recognizes his teacher's true mastery. This may be extremely dangerous if an authoritarian teacher makes use of his pupils' devotion for immoral purposes. Herrigel was lucky. His teacher understood that after the phase of identification came that of liberation. In Herrigel's own words:

> The teacher and master is not concerned with how far his student gets. As soon as he has shown him the right way he lets him walk on alone. Only one thing remains for him to do so that the student may pass the test of loneliness: He releases the student from himself, from the master, heartily enjoining him to get on on his own and to "mount the master's shoulders." (*ibid.*)

The student must carry on the tradition, but in true mastery he must express what he has learnt his own way.

The process of de-ritualizing

If we turn again to the Danish reality the basic question is: Why are boys and young men attracted to the Oriental martial arts? The pieces of this mosaic take the shape of the need to seek the mystical (the monk) and the omnipotent (the samurai) in a society which often offers only powerlessness and a paucity of sensuous experience. A third piece may be found in the wake of the youth rebellion and anti-pedagogy. The youth rebellion broke down the rituals of authoritarian society. School children should now be brought up to become citizens of a democratic society. They were allowed to call their school teacher by her Christian name. The right to use corporeal punishment disappeared, and the pupils no longer had to stand in a line when they arrived at school. Outside school many of the traditional rites of the Christian Church in connection with birth, marriage and death were done away with or weakened. The divorce rate rose, free love flourished. The lack of clear limits and rules encouraged many children to search for limits to a degree that nearly drove themselves and their parents crazy.

The youth rebellion was an extremely important part of the struggle to break down old, rigid authoritarian rituals. Putting other rituals in their place turned out to be more difficult. Rituals in themselves were subjected to hatred. The baby was thrown out with the bath water. Still, new rituals sporadically came into being, for example within the rock culture where an audience numbering thousands bathed in the sound of electrical guitars and paid homage to charismatic rock idols. All the same, for a large group of young people searching for more heavy-handed rituals all this took place – and still does – in a manner altogether too undisciplined and chaotic.

The youth rebellion should not be held entirely responsible for de-ritualization. Long ago the Reformation started to demolish many of the rituals of Catholicism so that Protestantism tended toward becoming a dried-out religion of words and myths without meaningful actions. The process of secularization that has taken place at great speed during the last hundred years contributed to driving back even this de-ritualized Protestant religion. Thus the role of the traditional religion as the focus of identity and creator of fellow-feeling, meaning and security through lofty and unassailable dogmas and ethical rules of conduct for the individual life disappears. Confirmation itself, that central Protestant initiation ceremony that marks the transition from childhood to grown-up life, is degenerating into a downright gift-shop. I am not going to lament the passing of the bourgeois, narrow-minded version of Christianity, but the "rational," calculating way of life that has taken its place is not a commendable alternative.

Some people might be of the opinion that to want rituals to cling to is a sign of immaturity and authoritarian tendencies. Nonetheless anthropology teaches us that many different societies create rituals which in condensed and dramatized form give the participants a key to handling difficult phases of human life. The transition from boyhood to manhood is of particular interest. Rituals make for security and a feeling that a chaotic and strange world is meaningful, recognizable and structured. Without rituals, many people feel empty and lonely; to be able to develop their identity in safety they need fixed points in their lives.

Re-ritualizing

The anthology *Sport in the Socio-Cultural Process* (Hart, 1972) presents many interesting analyses of modern sport from an anthropological point of view. That is to say that instead of taking as their starting point the self-understanding expressed by the athletes and the leaders, the researchers try to analyze sports from the outside like a "strange culture."

Anthropologist Shirley Fiske (1972) has analyzed rugby at American universities as a masculine initiation ceremony that takes the young men into the ranks of the grown-ups. Taking as her point of departure Van Gennep's classic from 1909, *Les Rites de Passage*, she states that the change from childhood to grown-up life is the most central stage of transformation of our social lives because at this point the rational and emotional training for the values of grown-up life is intensified. She continues in Van Gennep's spirit by stating that in every society ways of acquiring the norms of grown-up life in dramatized form must be developed.

Whereas Van Gennep primarily sees the initiation as a staging of changes of identity through the passage from the secular to the sacred world, the anthropologist Young (1965) first and foremost sees the initiation as a rite of transition that stresses the development of sexual identity. Whiting (1958) puts forward four requirements, one of which at least should be met in order to talk about a manhood ceremony: (1) painful operations performed by grown-up men, (2) surgical operations on the genitals, (3) isolation from women, and (4) manhood tests. Fiske then transferred these requirements to modern American rugby and found that apart from point 2 all requirements were met.

Without going into detail I think this also applies to quite a large extent to the modern Oriental martial arts as practiced in the Western world. The role of the trainer as whip and absolute authority can be seen as elements of point 1. As an illustration of point 3 the sexes are kept separate during the performance of most martial arts and during almost all competitions. Finally the tougher aspects of the spectrum of martial arts may be seen as a manhood test (point 4) which may lead to expulsion or self-contempt if one is perceived to be weak, womanly, childish or gay.

Frank Young emphasized that in an actual rite of transition the social importance of masculine solidarity will be so dramatic that the experience will become very intense and almost unforgettable. Transferred to modern Danish conditions one might add that "sport stories" have in fact nearly the same great significance for the masculine creation of identity as the memories of another male fellowship, the soldier stories. Among other elements of a modern sports initiation mentioned by Fiske, which to a certain extent recur within present-day Danish conditions, may be mentioned the stigmatization of those who leave the masculine cult world in the middle of the season, taboos during the training period such as prohibitions against alcohol and special diets, the use of uniform clothes, tough and exhausting physical activity, being lifted into a special sphere over or beside your everyday life and the transformation of your everyday identity.

In "The American Seasonal Masculinity Rites," an equally anthropologically oriented article, Arnold Beisser has put forward important viewpoints on sport as an initiation rite. Many men, he says, live only from one sports event to the next so that sport becomes the most important thing in their lives. According to Beisser, women make up a dominant part of the social contact environment of modern boys. The coach is one of the first male figures that boys who have very little contact with their father may adopt as their ideal. Through sport, boys may leave the female sphere of influence and enter a cult of manliness headed by older men. According to Beisser, in some indigenous cultures a youth initiation is accomplished in one brief ceremony, a manhood ceremony, which may consist, for example, of having a tooth knocked out. To the initiated this signals that he is able to say, "Today I have become a man."

Pain, death and purification

If we follow the ideas of the American researchers we might say that in spite of the overall process of de-ritualization, rituals are nevertheless preserved and flourish in the world of sports. In my opinion this is correct. If that is the case, then people might argue that surely there is no reason to practice Oriental martial arts because, after all, we do have our football. But in all fairness it must be said that the ritual elements in modern sports are somewhat faded compared to a traditional tribal initiation into manhood. Actually the introduction of the Eastern martial arts to the Western world testifies to the anaemic character of sports rituals. There are marked differences between football and karate, and most of the Oriental martial arts are much more heavily ritualized than football.

The martial arts mark off in their own sphere the separation which sharply distinguishes them from the rest of our social lives. The room where the martial arts are practiced is called "dojo," which means "sacred room" or the place where you study the road. In order to enter this room you have to be clean and dressed in a white suit as a symbol of this purity. The shift from the outside world to "the inner world" is marked by a bow at the threshold of the room. Still you have not entered into the training ceremony proper yet. In order to get there a purification of the mind through meditation is demanded. Consciousness must be emptied of all the thoughts and troubles of everyday life in order to mark a future total absorption in the martial art. Then follows the students' bow to the "sensei" (the teacher) and his to them. Perhaps one also bows to the extremely important symbols: the Japanese flag and the karate symbol (the open hand). Only then does the teaching start. The same rituals are performed in reverse order when the performers leave the sphere of the martial art.

Within many tribal cultures young men at their passage from boyhood to manhood are brought to a condition close to death, where they experience great pain and finally ecstasy. Women have such a transitional ritual in the shape of their capacity to give birth, but many men feel a need to seek out these extremes. Normally we regard pain as something to be avoided, and the awareness of our own mortality is something we try to forget. But does not the awareness that we are to die give life meaning? Our mortality throws the unique character of life into relief. Each minute becomes precious and potentially meaningful. Is not pain a part of human life? Without wanting to argue in favor of barbaric manhood rites I would like to ask: is not the experience of pain just as much a part of human life as the experience of love? Is it not better to meet pain half-way instead of repressing it? That is not to say one should deliberately seek out pain, but to practice a physical activity at the risk of feeling pain is not in itself negative. Opening oneself to love may also mean exposing oneself to pain if the love is not returned. That is the risk one has to run if one wants to acquire something. The secret, of course, is to practice a challenging activity without getting hurt.

The pains and threat of death open up people so that the current experience becomes a milestone and is stored deep within the personality. Perhaps this opening takes place because pain and the pressure of death make people try to leave their own bodies and psyche. They are at the limit of their normal protective armor. To a certain extent they leave their previous self because the person who emerges from the extreme experience is not the same person as the one who entered it. If the experience is negative it leaves a trauma, a mental wound. On the other hand, a positive experience may contribute to a basic feeling of clarity and meaningfulness. Through passing his manhood test, the individual gets his membership of the group confirmed, and the feeling of knowing from his own experience what it means to be a man is strengthened.

Within the traditionally practiced Oriental martial arts the initiation takes the form of a prolonged progress. The goal moves from a state of strong self-centerdness to a feeling of being connected to the entire universe. When one has reached this stage one has advanced from student to master. Externally this transition is indicated by the acqusition of the black belt, but before one reaches that stage one must have worked his way through a succession of different belt degrees and colours.

Japanese martial arts do not allow us to forget our own mortality. In the strangulations of judo and the make-believe blows of karate against throat and temples the presence of death is stressed as a fact of life. It is precisely this fact that creates the optimum concentration which distinguishes the Oriental martial arts, and which may make every Danish educationist turn green with envy. When a fist is on its way toward the upper part of your mouth there is no time for wavering. Unless you move away you might just as well get yourself a set of false teeth. When young men feel the pull of the Oriental martial arts it is because of the fact that in the fight you have to be 100 percent present. The imagination may travel out the window during a geography lesson, but inattention during a kung fu lesson may be fatal. And boys in particular have always sought the closeness of the battle, on the lawn or in the schoolyard. The job of the martial arts is to school this diffuse aggressive instinct in a constructive direction, toward self-development, attention and respect toward one's opponents. Obviously a certain amount of discipline is demanded in a room where people work with such highly explosive techniques. Uncontrolled aggression between agents using such weapons may be fatal.

The feeling of ecstasy may arise from hyperventilation, that is fast and deep breathing. Karate and taekwondo make use of powerful sounds (*kiai*), which are repeated together with specific movements by everybody at the same time. This way an atmosphere may be created that resembles the ecstasy built up in tribal dances by continuously making one particular sound together in a group.

Unlike football, the martial arts are based on direct, man-to-man, physical combat. Some people might think that this is increasingly true of football, but that is not the idea of the game. The physical closeness, the touches, the feeling and smell of a body close to you, of sweat, perhaps blood, and a pumping breath, help to give martial arts their particular aura. In a society characterized by a paucity of physical contact the martial arts will always arouse fascination and outrage. The flow of body liquids helps to give the agent a feeling of transformation. The movements are new, the muscles are changing and the new identity which one is trying to build up also involve another energy (*ki*) and a new bodily and mental center (*hara*). As is the case with any effective initiation ceremony, it is the entire identity one seeks to change.

The preoccupation of young men and boys with the Oriental martial arts should not in itself be seen as a critical sign. At least four groups are spellbound by the martial arts. Timid young people wish to learn self-defence and acquire self-confidence through the martial arts; this group also includes quite a few girls. In addition to this are the experimenting young people who wish to pave the way for other perceptions of reality and who wish to work with alternative body perceptions and patterns of movement. Here it must be remembered that within the philosophical tradition of Oriental martial arts lies an exciting challenge to Western rationalism. Then there is a group of young people who are particularly interested in the sportified martial arts, which are organized like other competitive sports where the concern with medals and entering a higher division plays an important part.

Finally there is the group which social educationists particularly get into contact with. It consists of the boys and young men who are confused and rootless. Often they have difficulties adapting to the rules of conduct at home and at school. These youngsters voluntarily submit themselves to the strict discipline of karate, whereas at school they are conspicious by their total lack of discipline. Through their engagement in the martial arts, these boys signal that they want limits, but these limits must enclose a fascinating activity. Their language is primarily the language of the body and the fight, and if the educationist is capable of interpreting and speaking

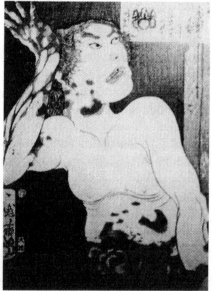

Figure 1: Total commitment and fusion in a judo bout at the Danish championships in 1976 (photo: Karl Sørensen).

Figure 2: The boy's romantisizing of the mysterious samurai is rar confronted with the bloody reality. From Turnbull, S.: "The Book of the Samurai" London, 1986.

this language he gets a key to the boys' fantasies and dreams, aspects of life which mean everything to them. Some boys need to seek out great challenges and go through tough manhood tests in order to feel that they are alive and are masculine creatures. The job of the educationist is not to prevent this, but to make sure that they do it of their own free will and without hurting themselves and others.

Perhaps the educationist may even help the boys to develop an ethic and a critical attitude toward authority in connection with their martial arts. Or even, after he has won their confidence, open their eyes to the fascination of other languages: those of science, art and oral expression. Perhaps the educationist should not do it for the boys' sake, but for his own. Imagination, dreams and excitement seem largely to have vanished from our busy, intellectual, grown-up life. What happened to our boyhood dreams? What has the ninja got to offer us?

References

Beisser, A. R. (1972) "The American Seasonal Masculinity Rites," in Hart, M. M. *et al.* (1972) *Sport in the Socio-cultural Context*. Dubuque, Iowa.

Bonde, H. (1991) *Mandighed og sport*. Odense.

Fiske, S. (1972) "Pigskin Review: An American Initiation," in Hart, M. M. *et al.* (1972) *Sport in the Socio-cultural Context*. Dubuque, Iowa.

Gennep, A. van (1960) *The Rites of Passage*. Chicago.

Gillis, J. (1992) *Bringing up father. Den Jydske Historiker*.

Hart, M. M. *et al.* (1972) *Sport in the Socio-cultural Context*. Dubuque, Iowa.

Herrigel, E. (1971) *Bueskydning og zen*. Haslev.

Jespersen, E. (1993) "Fra krop til krop. Gensyn med idraetsmesterlæren," *Dansk Pædagogisk Tidsskrift*, 1, pp. 26-31.

Kiselberg, S. (1979) *To og et halvt kapitel af mændenes historie*. Copenhagen.

Kryger, N. (1988) *De skrappe drenge*. Copenhagen.

Leggett, T. (1960) *A First Zen Reader*. Tokyo.

Leggett, T. (1978) *Zen and the Ways*. London.

Mitscherlich, A. (1973) *Auf dem Weg zur Vaterlosen Gesellschaft*. München.

Whiting, J. M. (1958) "The Functioning of Male Initiation Ceremonies at Puberty," in Whiting *et al.*, *Readings in Social Psychology*. New York.

Young, F. W. (1965) *Initiation Ceremonies*. New York.

Zlotnik, G. (1984) *De stakkels drenge. Konsforskelle i barndommen*. Copenhagen.

Further reading:

Bonde, H. (1989) *Judo den milde vej*. Copenhagen.

Bonde, H. (1993) *Sport en moderne kult*. Aarhus.

Chapter 8

Sylvester Stallone's Body: "A Peculiar, Not To Say Pathological, Interest"

MARTTI LAHTI

> Everything I am and everything I have boils down to Rocky Balboa. I didn't create Rocky. He created me. (Sylvester Stallone)[1]

> I have dialogue just at the beginning and end. The rest of time I speak with my body. (Sylvester Stallone) [2]

> For Stallone, pain isn't pain, it's an opportunity.[3]

Historically, it has frequently been noted that narrative cinema tends to construct woman as body and reduces her to the visible, a spectacle "to-be-looked-at." As Kaja Silverman demonstrates in *The Acoustic Mirror*, this tendency is reinforced by those narrative strategies which join the female voice and body while disembodying the male voice. According to Silverman, male subjectivity is most fully realized when it moves out of the regime of the visible: "[T]he male subject finds his most ideal realization when he is heard but not seen; when the body ... drops away, leaving the phallus in unchallenged possession of the scene."[4] Masculinity and the body do not, however, always reject each other, not even in the ideal representations of masculinity. In fact, a long list of male body genres[5] (for example Biblical epics, porn films, musicals, action cinema, Westerns, horror movies) are built on the presence of the male body and specifically emphasize the connection between masculinity and the regime of the visible. Excessive corporeality in the films of stars like Arnold Schwarzenegger and Sylvester Stallone exemplify Yvonne Tasker's "muscular cinema," where there is "a significant silence of the heroes" and "the primacy of the body over the voice."[6] This *over*presence of the body also frequently marks the representations of marginalized social groups, exemplified in the regular construction of gay and black masculinity through corporeal tropes.

These examples suggest that although representations of masculinity often incorporate the fantasy of an omniscient and disembodied male subjectivity, we should not ignore the cases in which masculinity is constructed specifically in and through the body. This paper explores how Sylvester Stallone's star image has evolved during the last two and a half decades, in response to Rosalind Coward's provocative comment that, "In spite of the ideology that would have us believe that women's sexuality is an enigma, it is in reality men's bodies, men's sexuality which is the true 'dark continent' of this society."[7] As I shall demonstrate, this relatively unscrutinized male body has provided a privileged representational space for the articulation of tensions between fantasies of power and powerlessness. I argue that it is "the ordering of social hierarchy"[8] that both regulates and functions through discourses on and images of Stallone's body. This idea becomes especially evident in the late 1980s, when, for example, Stallone's publicity started to shift his bodily alliance away from the working class to a new middle class. Indeed, as Mary Douglas has convincingly argued, "we are prepared to see in the body a symbol of society ... and powers and dangers credited to social structure reproduced in small on the human body."[9] The surface of the body is where various oppositions defining identity collide, negotiating an image and politics of self: "Our skin and its extensions are not only a literary boundary between ourselves and others but they are also symbolic of the psychological, social and political boundaries between us."[10]

My investigation begins with the *Rocky* and *Rambo* films which clearly still dominate Stallone's star image and form the basis against which publicity of the late 1980s and 1990s attempts to reformulate his persona and appeal. The core of my paper, however, concentrates on Stallone's later career and its representation of the male body, constructed in both his movies and various discourses circulating around these movies. I read these bodily representations as a meeting point and a site of struggle between various cultural narratives which define hierarchies between popular and high culture, body and voice, and accompanying forms of masculinity.

The surface of the body also forms a material base for the inscription of a star image, itself a central category for our reception of films. The meaning of the star system and the privileged position of stars in the signification of films is evident from their prominence in the everyday discourse of fans and the popular press, for example. According to Christine Gledhill, stars are actors whose "off-screen lifestyles and personalities equal or surpass acting ability in importance."[11] For John Ellis a star is "a performer in a particular medium whose figure enters into subsidiary forms of circulation, and then feeds back into future performance."[12] Anne Friedberg arrives at a similar definition, except that she calls special attention to the importance of a star as a commodity and as a medium of exchange of meaning and economic value: "The star is ... a particular commoditised human whose body, name and face have been routed through system of signs with exchange value."[13] It is also worth noticing that historically, according to Richard deCordova, the emergence of star discourse is tied to audiences' interest in the private life of a star as the truth of his/her identity.[14]

All of these definitions share the idea that there is a tension between a star's screen appearances and the discourses concerning her/his life off screen. Furthermore, they emphasize the intertextuality of star images, constructed across diverse media by texts such as the films themselves, trailers, posters, publicity photos, reviews, interviews, profiles, and candid newspaper photos. Thus what we see of the star in the films themselves are "the traces of an identity that is constituted elsewhere, in the discourses 'outside' of the film," as deCordova has argued.[15] When analyzing star images it is thus important to move beyond the form of individual films and to explore how categories and discourses "outside" films contextualize and frame the meaning given to that form (in this case, via stardom).

One of the problems associated with studying the intertextuality of star images "is the sheer wealth and diversity of material [that] resists any easy categorization."[16] This is not only a practical but also a theoretical problem. Most students of star images acknowledge the polysemic, contradictory, and fragmented nature of star images. Nevertheless star images are often seen as *images*, as complete and readily available entities (although contradictory and fragmented), whose meanings can be extrapolated by interpreting their constituent images and texts in sum. But as Judith Mayne warns, "the very nature of the texts one has to analyze in the case of stars makes it impossible to come to any homogenizing conclusions."[17] This is further complicated by the ambiguous activities and variable textual resources available to specific audiences. Star theories assume (yet paradoxically often ignore) that star images are constructed by a reader who must link and contrast various texts, images, and other materials (past and present) concerning a star. However, taking into account the role of the reader problematizes the idea of one homogenous and complete star image that can be extrapolated from texts circulating around a star. As Tony Bennett has forcefully argued, "Meaning is a transitive phenomenon. It is not a *thing* that texts can *have*, but is something that can only be produced, and always differently, within the reading formations that regulate the encounters between texts and readers."[18] Bennett's idea reminds us that a star image is defined differently according a context of reception that "regulates the encounters between texts and readers."

Sylvester Stallone's attempt to reformulate dominant meanings of his star image in the late 1980s and 1990s illustrates this point well. His publicity produced manifold texts and images that emphasized his "sophisticated" hobbies (art collecting, polo, golf, painting, poetry) in contrast to the image of him created by the *Rocky* and *Rambo* films. But it is difficult to assess the impact of this new publicity, and certainly misguided to attribute any wholesale revision of his existing image to these attempts, since these texts were often circulated in publications (for example *Vogue*, *GQ*, *Esquire*, and, more recently, *Cigar Aficionado*, *Architectural Digest*) that might have only limited circulation among "traditional" Stallone fans. That is, existing "reading formations" may have prevented most Stallone fans from encountering this aspect of his new image, as I shall elaborate below. Readers of these magazines may have formed a radically different perception of Stallone compared to those who never encountered such new publicity attempting to modify Stallone's public image. Nevertheless, and with or without a coherent, stable, or universally available star image attributable to Stallone, there is much to be learned from the *attempts* (successful or not) to reconfigure the social place and function of the spectacularly visible male body in contemporary culture.

"Stallone has always acted more expressively with his muscles than his mouth"[19]

As Yvonne Tasker suggests, "The phenomenon of stardom provides a useful starting point for thinking about the performative aspects of masculinity in the cinema, perhaps because spectacle, performance, and acting all function as both constitutive components of stardom and significant terms in those writings concerned with the sexual politics of representation."[20] Furthermore, Tasker continues, "the territory of the star image is also the territory of identity, the process of the forging and reforging of ways of 'being human'."[21] In the case of Stallone this territory of identity was constructed around his body from the beginning of his career. At the core of the *Rocky* series resides the heroic male body which renders the social mobility of the hero (and the actor) possible. In Stallone's films the body functions regularly as an instrument for gaining some noble, higher or sublime ends. It is an instrument, as Arjen Mulder suggests, for the pursuit of "classical values such as friendship, patriotism, brotherhood, family, and other historical determinants."[22] *Rocky* films, in a slightly nostalgic fashion, uphold the work ethic, friendship, the importance of family, and the possibility of overcoming hardship with strength of will. They are structured around stories in which the genuine, true identity of the hero is revealed beneath the surface of the body, and are tied to an attempt to prove the superiority of the hero's race, class and/or nationality. In this sense, the thematic movement of these films is from surface (mere appearances) to beneath the surface (inner truth). On the other hand, the narrative of *Rocky* films moves inexorably toward the spectacle of bodily surface, as the narration works to prepare the viewer for the final boxing contest between Rocky and his opponent. All of the *Rocky* films end with this spectacle and invite the audience to center their generic pleasures on the male body and its display. Thus on the level of "character psychology" the movement is from surface to depth; but, paradoxically, on the level of narrative culmination and visual spectacle, it is toward bodily surface as a final testimony to inner masculinity.

As a boxing film, *Rocky* (1976) relied heavily on the display of the male body in action. The film, as suggested by Kangasniemi and Lahti, also introduced one of the recurrent themes of Stallone's films, the opposition between technology and the naturalness of the body of the male hero.[23] The naturalness of Rocky's body is emphasized in the sequences where he prepares for the match with the heavy-weight champion, the black fighter named Apollo Creed (Carl Weathers). Particularly telling are those scenes in which Rocky practices in the slaughter-house punching carcasses, which associates the male body with nature. This contrasts with a traditional construction of the white male body being more distanced from nature than a primitive black male body.

In an analogous way in *Rocky III* (1982) it is Rocky's soft, effeminate body marked by consumption and luxury that is defined as being too civilized, too much influenced by culture. It is not until Rocky renounces his luxurious, easy living that he is able to beat his (black) opponent (Mr. T), in this case defined as being closer to nature and as being more primitive than Rocky. In *Rocky IV* (1985) the opposition between Stallone's/Rocky's natural body and technology is worked through in the most explicit way in the framework of a nationalistic ideology. Rocky has to fight with the Russian boxer, a genuine fighting machine named Ivan Drago (Dolph Lundgren). Training by Drago and Rocky is contrasted in a parallel editing sequence using fast cuts in time to rock music, a formal strategy typical of Stallone films. Rocky is shown strengthening his body through natural means against a Siberian landscape. He uses natural food for nourishment and exploits everything that his residence on a farm has to offer: he jogs through the snow, through forests, and up and down mountains; he chops wood and draws an ox-drawn cart. In contrast, Ivan Drago trains in a highly controlled gym, using technological equipment of exercise, diets, and drugs. He is also monitored by a group of scientists using computers. Drago subjugates his body to technology and the men controlling that technology, and in turn, it and they produce his body for him. Indeed, whereas Drago's unnatural, technology-made body is fabricated for him, Rocky's body is acquired through individual effort, producing a self-made and natural body. At the same time the sequence constructs the United States as being closer to nature in opposition to the unnatural, hyper-technological Soviet Union. And when the two men fight each other it is, of course, the natural body that wins out over the unnatural one in the end.

These training sequences are typical of all the *Rocky* films as well as Stallone films such as *Over the Top* (1986), *Lock Up* (1989), and *The Specialist* (1994). Together with the *Rambo* series and *Cliffhanger* (1993), which both exploit the male body tested against nature, these films underline the idea of the muscular male body "as the sign of power – natural, achieved, phallic."[24] The star body in these films is self-gained. Thus it is also always in a state of becoming, a "body in motion."[25] Correspondingly, masculinity, tied to the construction of the male body, appears as an unsettled and unfinished process, to be attained in the course of an unfolding narrative. Furthermore, as something to be gained and proved, masculinity requires a witnessing eye, which becomes the guarantor of male spectacle, but also the source of an underlying anxiety about masculine performance.

At the borderline of civilization and wilderness

The same opposition between technology and the body is later reworked in three *Rambo* films: *First Blood* (1982), *Rambo: First Blood, Part II* (1985), and *Rambo III* (1988). In *First Blood*, Rambo and his masculinity are defined in relation to nature (woods) – which is in turn defined as the space of Rambo – and civilization (town) constructed as its opposite. And in both *First Blood* and *Rambo*, woods or jungle function as an arena for the hero's performance and a stage for proving his masculinity. In *First Blood* Rambo demonstrates his superiority to the National Guard (who are unable to catch or kill him despite their greater numbers and fire power) by being able to manage in the woods without the help of technology or firearms and by exploiting what nature has to offer.

In a revealing scene in *Rambo*, in which the Russian soldiers are pursuing Rambo, neither the Russians nor the spectators know where Rambo's body is (behind the tree, in the mud, behind the waterfall) until he suddenly reveals himself from under camouflage. Susan Jeffords sees this scene as an example of Rambo's body as an extension of technology. For her, *Rambo: First Blood, Part II* "offers both the spectacle of technology and its 'pure' link to the body."[26] However, it can more easily be read as an example of the way the film defines Rambo's body through a rejection of technology or as its opposite. The scene associates Rambo's body with nature to such an extent that it becomes impossible to differentiate between the two. Furthermore, Rambo is stripped of technology and the useless clothes provided for him in the beginning of the film (both in *Rambo* and *Rambo III*), leaving him semi-naked and armed only with his big knife and a bow, again accentuating the half-Native American hero's closeness to nature and his distance from civilization and its technology.

Rambo takes great pleasure in destroying technology (computers and other devices belonging to the representatives of federal government). Thus at the same time that these movies display a certain fascination with technology, as Jeffords argues, they also take an intense interest in the destruction of that technology and in the display of the stripped-down – even primitive – male body taking its place and triumphing over it. One might speculate that this ambiguous relationship to technology is linked to the idea that "the values of masculine physicality are harder to maintain straightfacedly and unproblematically in the age of microchips,"[27] thus explaining the great pleasure and fascination that the spectacle of the destruction of technology holds for action cinema.

These films are also characterized by a tendency to construct the male body as the last resort or final solid basis for action in an otherwise untrustworthy reality-dominated technology. This notion is taken up in texts circulating around Stallone's films. Stallone's interviews and biographies regularly blur the difference between his film roles and his off screen persona. For example, Marsha Daly writes in a biography:

Sylvester Stallone's path to the pinnacle of the movie kingdom has been every bit as rocky as his film hero Rocky's road was to the heavyweight title. ... For Stallone, who rode to fame on the blood, sweat, and tears of his famous creation, Rocky Balboa, overcame the same kind of hardships in his off screen life as Rocky did on film.[28]

Adrian Wright's Stallone biography captures in its title, *Sylvester Stallone: A Life on Film,* the same idea of an equivalence between Stallone's life and his films. The impression is reinforced by text on the book jacket which reads, "[Wright] makes a careful reevaluation of his films and reveals parallels with the actor's real life."

The truth and reliability of the male body is evoked particularly in stories of how Stallone prepares physically for his roles. According to Wright's biography, "The physical preparation for *Rocky II* was even more grueling than that for *Rocky,* for Stallone knew the final sequence – the rematch with Creed – had to top everything that the original had offered as the most important set-piece of the movie."[29] This citation not only blurs the difference between off screen and on screen reality by pitting Sylvester Stallone against Rocky's *on screen* opponent Apollo Creed (thus confusing Stallone and Rocky), but also asserts the truthfulness of his body. This and numerous other accounts of Stallone's physical preparation for his films suggest that although everything else on the screen would be fiction (illusion), the spectator can still trust in the realness and truthfulness of Stallone's body. This embodiment of authenticity approaches a pornographic aesthetic discourse, which also underlines the "truthfulness" of the male body and its reactions, captured on film.[30]

This same idea of the male body bridging the difference between "real" and "illusion" is echoed in stories about Stallone doing most of his stunts as well as those concerning the harsh conditions in which his films were shot. In an interview by Bart Mills (*Houston Post,* November 14, 1982) Stallone recounts having to deal with rats and contaminated water while shooting *First Blood.* In a *Los Angeles Times* (June 2, 1993) article, the writer again celebrates Stallone's "real" performance: "Movie crew members who were climbers were impressed with Stallone's effort to learn techniques and to do the climbing himself up to the point where the doubles had to take over. Stallone actually did hang suspended from his left hand gripping a ledge that overhung thin air." These stories about *real* tests of masculinity are offered as alternatives or necessary supplements to on screen performances of masculinity. In either case, they heighten the reader's impression of Stallone's masculinity, but also simultaneously point up an anxiety which fractures and undercuts his macho image – that what viewers see on the screen is only a spectacle, a representation, and a masquerade of masculinity.

"Nothing much below"

As mentioned above, the centrality of the body to Stallone's star image is also recognized in the popular reception of the *Rocky* and *Rambo* films. The importance of bodily display is regularly defined in these texts in relation to the movement between the surface and depth. In most cases this takes the form of first invoking the opposition between depth and surface and then criticizing *Rocky* films for lacking depth: "The problem is that the characterization has such a busy surface one inevitably suspects there's nothing much below" (*New York Times*, December 12, 1976). However, pleasure derived from the spectacle itself, from a "busy surface," came to define much of the critical and popular reception of Stallone's films: for example, "For much of [*First Blood*], Stallone has only to demonstrate that he's in fine physical shape from all that training for his 'Rocky' movies" (*Des Moines Register*, October 28, 1982); and "'First Blood' is the sort of bloodpumping action movie that's more exciting to watch than it is to think about afterward" (*Los Angeles Herald Examiner*, October 22, 1982). The same kind of delight in surface spectacle is initially echoed by the *New York Post* (October 22, 1982) review of *First Blood*, which at first seems to acknowledge the generic pleasures offered by the movie: "[t]here are thrills galore." However, the reviewer immediately calls these thrills into question by going on to remark that "the whole thing is so ultimately pointless that I'm not sure the agony is worth the trouble," ultimately concluding that, "still, it's a perfect movie role for Stallone because it calls for lots of brawn and almost no dialogue."

These reviews exemplify not only the intertextual construction of Stallone's body as the main site of filmic spectacle, but also a simultaneous tendency to both acknowledge and disparage the pleasures provided by male bodily display in action cinema. In the popular press these pleasures are constructed as illegitimate ones to be suppressed. Thus, reviewers negotiate for themselves a space where they can both acknowledge the spectacularity and generic pleasures of many Stallone films and at the same time keep a distance from those pleasures and films. One way of doing this is by invoking what Ien Ang calls ironically the "ideology of mass culture":

In [the ideology of mass culture] some cultural forms – mostly very popular cultural products and practices cast in an American mould – are *tout court* labelled "bad mass culture." "Mass culture" is a denigrating term, which arouses definitely negative associations. In opposition to "bad mass culture" implicitly or explicitly something like "good culture" is set up.[31]

In this ideology, categories such as stereotypical and commercial "are not used in the descriptive sense but invested with moral status and emotional charge."[32] They serve as readily available and compressed explanations for a writer's dislike of popular products such as Stallone films. In the case of Stallone, this opposition between his films and art or "good culture" resonates with the opposed values of surface and depth used by the reviewers cited above, and is further "mapped onto an opposition between the mind and the body," as argued by Yvonne Tasker.[33] This is then translated into an opposition between voice and body, as exemplified by numerous references to Stallone's verbal abilities (or lack thereof):

Stallone has an unfortunate habit of swallowing words when he raises his voice. As a result, about half of what he is supposed to convey [in the end of *First Blood*] is incomprehensible. (*Houston Post*, October 27, 1982)

Stallone, who in any case can barely deliver a line, gets by with his smoldering, heavy-lidded stare, his sleepy, primal-man beauty. (*New York*, November 15, 1982)

Given that Sylvester Stallone has always acted more expressively with his muscles than his mouth, one has to admire the near wordless dispatch with which those who contrived *First Blood* set him to maiming and killing a multitude of people in a multitude of imaginative ways. (*Time*, November 11, 1982)

Sly Stallone is the jerk she [Dolly Parton] chooses [in *Rhinestone*] ... Stallone is defeated by the simplest lines, even when he writes them himself. It's all he can do to keep his eyes open. (*New York Post*, June 22, 1984)

"Rocky IV" has big problems. Like dialogue. There isn't any. (*San Francisco Chronicle*, November 28, 1985)

Stallone's script is basic dese-dem-doze stuff, uttered in the actor's customary hot-potato-in-the-mouth delivery. (*Des Moines Register*, December 1, 1985)

This commentary on Stallone and his films as lacking in linguistic expressivity, implicitly constructs (as an absent but desirable reference point) a cinema that privileges verbal mastery over visible corporeality. This inclination speaks to Pierre Bourdieu's suggestion that there are "homologies between the relation to the body and the relation to language that are characteristic of a class or class fraction."[34] Indeed, following Bourdieu, I would argue that this tendency in the critical reception of Stallone's films is "part of the larger field of struggles over the definition of the *legitimate body* and the *legitimate use of the body*," where one class or group of people (the middle class) "struggles for the monopolistic power to impose the legitimate definition of a particular *class* of body uses."[35] In this sense the opposition between depth and surface, art and commerce, or the verbal and the visible characterizing the critical reception of Stallone's films functions as a way of privileging a certain type of masculinity – defined against the overpresence of the body – which corresponds with the construction of a middle-class masculinity as bodiless, pure mind. That is, in lamenting the embarrassing visual centrality of Stallone's body, these critics implicitly express a class-based desire for the realization of (or normative return to?) the disembodied cinematic masculinity described and critiqued by Silverman.

"A combination of action and intellect"

According to star theory, the private life of an actor is constituted as a place of knowledge and truth which defines the star image. However, in the case of Sylvester Stallone this relationship between his private life, his films, and other discourses making up his star image is more ambiguous and complicated because only part of the knowledge concerning his private life has been regularly incorporated. Throughout Stallone's career he has been trying to change his star image, dominated by *Rocky* and *Rambo* films, by making more serious films or comedies, such as *F.I.S.T.* (1978) and *Rhinestone* (1984) respectively. Indeed, his career is characterized by a back and forth movement between *Rambo* and *Rocky* films and the rest of his movies, which include both action movies (for example *Nighthawks* [1981], *Cobra* [1986], *Over the Top* [1986]) and frequent attempts to break away from this generic formula (for example *F.I.S.T.*, *Victory* [1981], *Staying Alive* [1983], *Oscar* [1991]).

Stallone's desire to refurbish his public image is particularly prominent in his films of the late 1980s and early 1990s, such as *Tango and Cash* (1988), *Oscar* (1991), *Rocky V* (1990), and *Stop! Or My Mom Will Shoot* (1992). With the exception of the final *Rocky*, these films inaugurated a remodeled Sylvester Stallone who was no longer dominated by his physicality and display of the body. In these films Stallone's body is covered by expensive suits, he wears designer spectacles, and significantly his performances privilege the verbal over the corporeal.[36] In *Tango and Cash* the Stallone character is even called the "Armani with a badge." Working in tandem with this downplaying of bodily display is an emphasis on dialogue, underscored by verbal humor, and supplemented by an ironic and self-conscious relation to Stallone's star image and his previous films. For example, Tango, played by Stallone, even states that "Rambo is a pussy!" This kind of self-conscious bragging not only acknowledges the importance of *Rambo* films to Stallone's public image, but also plays with it while exploiting that image to emphasize the masculinity of a new Stallone character. Atypical of Stallone's earlier movies, in *Oscar* and *Stop! Or My Mom Will Shoot,* his character is not in control of the situation he is in. Instead, he is controlled by women, by his daughter and his mother respectively. The only time we see the body of Stallone displayed in either one of these comedies is when his character is taking a shower in *Stop! Or My Mom Will Shoot.* The purpose of this scene is not to put a hard male body on display. On the contrary, the audience is shown Stallone's softer body, "out of shape," and without the clearly carved muscles that define his earlier image as well as bodily masculinity itself. It is as though the emphasis on voice requires an attendant de-emphasizing of the hard body, otherwise so central and important to most Stallone films.

The attempt to reformulate Stallone's image in his films was paralleled by surrounding publicity. This intertextual effort centered on new information concerning Stallone's private life which was circulated in interviews and numerous articles designed to familiarize readers with his new image. One of the most often cited[37] examples of this is an interview with Sylvester Stallone by Cameron Stauth in *American Film* (January 1990). As Yvonne Tasker notes, there is a distinct tendency in the interview "away from the physical" and "into the verbal."[38] Stallone explicitly distances himself from his earlier action films: "*I'm* not a rightwing, jingoistic human being. *Rambo* is. He's psychotic, in many ways." He adds that, "I know I've been playing these monosyllabic sides of beef ... but you get caught up in it. ... I always had it in the back of my mind that there would be a period when I'd feel I'd done my commercial tour of duty, and I could do something uncommercial and experimental. I just didn't think it would take so long." This desire to downplay the importance of his earlier action films to his star image is supported by a careful monitoring of his physical and intellectual image. The interviewer draws his and our attention to Stallone's physical appearance in contrast to his films: "Wearing glasses and his standard outfit of dress shirt and slacks, he was well-tailored, well-barbered and very smooth of face." This new image is reinforced by the space constructed around him, one marked by intellectual and economic rather than physical power: "Stallone sat in the office of his production company in Santa Monica. It was an ordinary office, except for the million-plus dollars in art scattered around: Remington and Rodin sculptures, paintings by Andy Warhol and Will Mentor, and some of Stallone's own paintings." However, the photos of Stallone accompanying the interview do not display this new, "more sophisticated" image. Instead, one illustration is a still photo from *Rocky IV* with Rocky wrapped in the American flag; and another is a still photo from the shooting of *Rambo III* in which Stallone sits relaxed, wearing a T-shirt and staring at the camera. A third photo is a production still from *Tango and Cash* showing Kurt Russell and Sylvester Stallone in the middle of action, wearing wet T-shirts and displaying their bodies for the gaze of an audience. None of these pictures supports Stallone's new image of "a combination of action and intellect" as the story caption would suggest. Rather, in the context of the text they leave space for readers to incorporate new knowledge into Stallone's existing action star image, or even to ignore it in the face of the photos, which emphasize the importance of his body and most famous roles.

"Not your everyday muscle head"

During the same period, however, there appeared in popular magazines a series of more interesting interviews with and articles on Stallone that effectively underlined a new image. In February 1989, *Esquire* ran a cover story on Stallone showing him "well-barbered and very smooth of face," looking straight at the camera with a kind of soft expression, and wearing a white pullover and brown leather gloves. The caption next to him asks, "Him? Stallone Without Fists, Tanks, Bows, Arrows, Cudgels, Sabers, Flags, or Commies," creating an opposition between his previous image and the image presented by *Esquire*. This is explicitly a new Stallone who has left behind a hyperbolic list of the accouterments of masculine bodily power and the action film. This Stallone has "progressed" – as stated in the title of the profile, "Sly's Progress." And where he has progressed to is, apparently, the middle-class chic of *Esquire*'s world.

The impression formed by the cover and caption is reinforced by a heading in the article, "He collects art, he plays polo, he feels pain. He's not your everyday muscle head." These statements again underline the difference between the image and the "real" Stallone, who is now being held up as an affective ideal to the upper middle class – unlike his many working-class screen selves – with his expensive hobbies, sensitivity ("feels pain"), and a dissociation from a body marked as subordinate ("muscle head"). This new image is consolidated by pictures accompanying the interview by Elizabeth Kaye which draw attention to Stallone's "sophisticated" pastimes. In the first, Stallone is shown in his studio painting a portrait of a nude woman, seen in the background of the picture; another is of Stallone in a stable, dressed in his polo apparel and carrying a saddle.

The text portrays Stallone as a kind of double figure, caught between muscles and mind: "He's like two people. One is muscular and easy to see. The other expresses himself in poetic phrases and is a person those muscles belie. That person tends to be overlooked. Even he overlooks him at times." The citation invokes an opposition between the obvious, self-evident, and unproblematic body, that is "easy to see" (like his films according to this logic) and the mind that is belied by the overpresence of the body. This publicity constructs his body as a masquerade that covers the real identity of Stallone, again defined by his collection of art works (Rodin, Warhol, Francis Bacon, Monet and so on), by poetry, and emotions: "'The irony,' he says, 'is that emotional pain is what I've always understood best. And had the most experience in.' "The underlying idea of the whole feature-interview is sensitivity and style, which characterize Stallone's dress, speech, hobbies, and the space he works in: "His private office is vast, sparsely furnished with a few chairs covered in the finest black leather, a massive concrete and glass desk. Any place Stallone designs and inhabits is minimalist and maximalist simultaneously."

Around the same time, *Vogue* (December 1991) ran an interview with Stallone and a series of pictures of him. Again the interviewer draws readers' attention to Stallone's art collection, his other hobbies (painting, polo, golf), and the difference between his "real self" and his public image. According to the interviewer, "Stallone is smarter, taller, and funnier than most people give him credit." About his 1991 film, *Oscar*, Stallone says, "I wanted to be verbal. I really wanted to do a film where I couldn't physically use any attributes other than my mouth, my gestures." The interview is further accompanied (and contextualized) with a series of pictures that display his wardrobe and associate Stallone with high fashion.

In these interviews Stallone's new image is defined in relation to a new class alliance (upper middle class instead of working class), and to overlapping oppositions between the body and voice, between surface and depth, and popular culture (action cinema) and high art. This last point is illuminated by a July 1988 issue of *Ladies' Home Journal* that ran an interview with Stallone. Already the title of the interview, "The Unknown Stallone," suggests an opposition between a misleading surface and a hidden interiority to be revealed by the interview. This concept is reinforced by a caption in boldface, "Don't take him at face value – there's a lot more to Sly than meets the eye." And what doesn't usually meet the eye is again his art collection, his intelligence, and his emotionality: "Stallone not only buys [art], he can discourse very knowledgeably on the subject. ... [H]e is a sentimental softy." The construction of depth is crucial for the new image of Stallone, since his star image was dominated by discourses that define popular culture as self-evident, unproblematic, predictable, simplistic, and shallow. And these adjectives had a tendency to leak from the characterizations of his films to characterizations of him himself.

Yvonne Tasker sees aspects of Stallone's new image as "distinctly feminizing."[39] However, I would instead argue that the centrality of the voice (over the body), intellectuality, emotion, art, and style are markers that the new middle class uses to define its masculinity against that of the working class. Indeed, one could appropriate Tasker's criticism of Steve Neale's article, "Masculinity as Spectacle,"[40] and turn it against her own claims. Tasker rightly criticizes Neale for setting up a "stable gender binary" where only women can be objects of an erotic look. When a man (in Neale's case, Rock Hudson) is presented as an object of erotic looking, Neale is forced by his own schema to argue that his body is feminized. Thus, as Tasker points out, Neale falls into a circular logic, and furthermore equates the feminine "with women in a rather unproblematic fashion."[41] But in the same vein, one could call into question Tasker's unproblematic ascription of femininity to Stallone's new image and argue that she, too, has set up a "stable gender binary."

Stallone's attempt to redefine his star image can also be seen as symptomatic of a larger "crisis" of masculinity. According to Victor J. Seidler, the cultural demand to prove one's masculinity easily creates feelings of insecurity for men.[42] Masculinity is therefore in a state of continuous crisis, or is at least constantly prone to it. It may be then, that the crises of masculinity that were existent, for example, at the beginning of the century or in the 1950s are not states of emergency but simply more prominent manifestations of a permanent element of constituent instability that defines masculinity. Furthermore, as Richard Dyer suggests, "Stars are involved in making themselves into commodities: they are both labor and the thing that labor produces."[43] Stars are thus actively involved in the creation of their star image and attempt to control the "extensive, multimedia, intertextual"[44] field – unstable and uncontrollable discourses – which their image consists of. Taking into account these two suggestions and the radical instability of any star phenomenon, it can be argued that the dynamics of stardom inherently inscribe an additional layer of anxiety onto the instabilities of cultural representations of masculinity. From this close relationship between masculinity and crisis it follows that the representation of an idealized or stabilized masculinity functions to repress or work out anxieties regarding flux and change in the male role. Indeed, as Tania Modleski has argued, the crisis of masculinity is due to the fact that men try to hold on to their social power across new circumstances: "[H]owever much male subjectivity may currently be 'in crisis,' as certain optimistic feminists are now declaring, we need to consider the extent to which male power is actually consolidated through cycles of crisis and resolution, whereby men ultimately deal with the threat of female power by incorporating it."[45]

Modleski's analysis is similar to comments made by Maurizia Boscagli, Sasha Torres and Susan Jeffords.[46] They suggest that since the 1980s, masculinity has been emotionalized and linked to family values. In the case of Stallone, this tendency has been evident from the beginning of his career. According to Susan Jeffords even action movies now devote more time to male psychology, ethical problems and emotional traumas[47] – although I would argue that those have always been staples of action cinema. Male media displays of emotion work to convince the audience of a larger change in men. As Maurizia Boscagli has written, "The vision of men barely repressing tears, 'confessing,' reminiscing about their personal past, and exploring their inferiority has taken the stage and convinced the audience that a new generation of sensitive men has come of age."[48] Like Modleski, Boscagli sees "emotional masculinity" as self-defense against the developments of past decades which have seen the weakening of men's traditional status and privileges, if only in relation to limited areas of public discourse. According to Boscagli, these male tears should be seen "as a particular formation of power and as a symptom of male anxiety in a period of crisis."[49] Thus the attempt to incorporate emotions, sensitivity, and intellectuality into Stallone's star persona should be seen as yet another example of on-going redefinitions of masculinity to suit contemporary relations between genders, without relinquishing male power related to it.

High fashion star

The attempt to shift the focus away from the surface of Stallone's body into the interior is paradoxical in a sense that discourses appropriated for that purpose concentrate on the body's surface. Stallone and his publicity machine tried to redefine his image and masculinity through style and fashion. This was a logical move because, as suggested by Kaja Silverman, "clothing is a necessary condition of subjectivity. ... In articulating the body, it simultaneously articulates the psyche."[50] Jennifer Craik, drawing from Martin Pumphrey, argues that "definitions of masculinity are coded through clothes and the associated politics of style."[51] Style, as suggested by Pumphrey, "does offer heterosexual men new ways of conceptualizing and acting out masculinity."[52] Nevertheless, style in itself also underwrites the idea of masculine spectacle used for redefining Stallone's image. In this sense, the publicity constructed around Stallone in the late 1980s and early 1990s replaced one surface (the muscled body) with another (fashion), thus broaching Holmlund's notion of masculinity as "multiple masquerade."[53]

The danger connected to masquerade – "that under the mask there is *nothing*" or "that the costume hides *something*"[54] – was voiced in the critical reception of Stallone's films of this period. Stallone was characterized in a review of *Tango and Cash* (*Daily News*, December 25, 1989) as "almost, but not quite convincing as a white-collar cop; the clothes and glasses just aren't enough to make the man." The *San Francisco Examiner* titled its review, "Rambo's Desperate Tango: Hungry for Credibility, Stallone Resorts to Smiling" and went on to assert that, "In 'Tango and Cash,' [Stallone] makes his most desperate and pathetic lunge yet for credibility as a performer. He Smiles. ... Actually he doesn't dress like a banker. In pearl-gray wing tips, gold chains and sharkskin suits, he looks more like a pimp. The refinement is as false as the smile." This sentiment was echoed in a *New York Post* review (December 22, 1989): "'Tango and Cash' is Sylvester Stallone's latest and most desperate bid to lighten up his image. ... In this 'buddy movie' Stallone is 'the smart one'." This reluctance to accept Stallone's new image is also manifest in the unfavorable critical reception of *Rocky V* (1991) and *Stop! Or My Mom Will Shoot* (1992) and in the mixed reviews of *Oscar* (1991).

Regardless of this new knowledge about Stallone's private life, his overall star image did not shift accordingly, at least concerning the context in which his films were received. As far as can be inferred from both the negative critical reception and poor box-office returns of the above-mentioned films, Stallone's new star image was never really accepted by his established audience. Neither did new knowledge concerning Stallone's private life transmute his persona to such an extent that it could attract an entirely new audience for his films (to compensate for the loss of some of his earlier fans) during this period. As a result, Stallone had to return to a more traditional action role in *Cliffhanger* to satisfy the expectations created by his earlier (and still lingering) star image. In this sense Stallone's star image can be seen as a site of negotiation among competing discourses that limit what kind of knowledge and changes can be viably incorporated into an existing construct of masculinity. Interestingly, in the context of popular cinema, knowledge "excluded" is that concerning high art and intellectual achievements. Despite this resistant reception of changes in Stallone's movie image, however, the very fact that magazines like *Vogue*, *Esquire*, and *Gentleman's Quarterly* began to feature Stallone in cover articles and serious interviews is an important indication of a broadening (intertextual) audience for his stardom. And as I suggested above, the star image of Stallone constructed by these new audiences may differ from those constructed by his other fans.

In this context it is interesting to consider trends that characterize Sylvester Stallone's continuing career in the mid-1990s. First, we should notice that with *Cliffhanger* and *Demolition Man* Stallone "muscled back into action." But at the same time, *Vanity Fair* (November 1993) featured a cover with Stallone sitting nude on a rock (the "Thinker" pose) – an image which neatly harmonizes previously incongruent elements of his changing star image. That is, while insisting on the spectacle of Stallone's muscled body, the photograph also reconfigures his body's appeal as high art. The pose's pensiveness and reference to neoclassical sculpture also points to Stallone's more recently acknowledged intellectuality as well as his extensive art collection; but here he remains the object to be consumed, rather than being positioned as the consumer of art objects. The article itself, accompanied by more pictures of Stallone by Annie Leibovitz, also blends a celebration of Stallone's body with his intellectual interests and an acknowledgment that he is getting old for an action star. In a sense the *Vanity Fair* article indicates that Stallone has succeeded in meshing body (low culture) and intellect (high culture) in his star discourse.

The cover of the November 1994 *Details* adds a playfulness into this image: Stallone is pictured wearing black sunglasses and a golden, glittering leather jacket. He strikes an excessively stylized pose, playing with his own persona as a tough guy and inviting the viewer to enjoy the campiness of the image. A part of his forehead is covered with block letters forming one of the most valuable brand names in the film industry, "STALLONE." Below his name a caption reads, "This Time It's Personal," referring playfully to both the magazine's interview with Sylvester Stallone and to the revenge story so typical of action cinema. The *Details* cover is indeed symptomatic of the present phase of Sylvester Stallone's career. In it collides two different strands of his films – comedies like *Rhinestone, Oscar, Stop! Or My Mom Will Shoot*, and more spectacular action films like the *Rocky* and *Rambo* series, *Cobra, Cliffhanger, The Specialist* (1994), *Assassins* (1995), and *Daylight* (1996). These strands come together, for example, in the self-conscious Stallone characters of *Demolition Man* (1993) and *Judge Dredd* (1995), who allow the actor to poke fun at himself in such a way that viewers can either read the film as camp or bracket this possibility and just enjoy the action and spectacularity of the film – or even do both. Indeed, this level of irony, campiness, and self-consciousness seemingly inscribed in the star's cool pose in the *Details* cover suggests that Stallone is able to address and interest both his faithful fans and a newer audience, interested in men's fashion and men's magazines, who are often constructed as being more "sophisticated."

This new appeal was finally consolidated with Stallone's well-publicized choice to take a pay cut in order to appear in the "small" independent film, *Cop Land* (1997), among a cast of stars who made their names in "serious" (read: Scorsese) films and who remain primarily identified with discourses of "great acting": for example Harvey Keitel, Robert De Niro, and Cathy Moriarty. Indeed, as a sign of his newly gained status as a more "respectable" actor and an ideal of more contemporary – less sheerly bodily – masculinity, Stallone was recently featured in cover articles by prestigious magazines such as *Cigar Aficionado*[55] and *Architectural Digest*.[56] The former frames Stallone from the shoulders up, showing only his face and a hand with a cigar. The latter cover pictures Stallone, his daughter on one arm, in his atelier painting, linking Stallone to both artistic and familial discourses. *Architectural Digest* goes on to showcase Stallone's Miami estate, decorated in a style that reflects what its owner wanted: "warmth, boldness, pageantry and over-the-top myth." The article describes not only Stallone's house but also its various art objects, ranging from canvases by Bouguereau and Francis Bacon to Andy Warhol's portrait of Stallone, LeRoy Neiman's portrait of Rocky, and "dark and moody abstract canvases by the actor." *Cigar Aficionado's* interview with Stallone is illustrated with stills from Stallone's movies and photos of him surrounded by the accouterments of a masculinized economic power. In addition to the prominence of cigars, we see Stallone seated in a large leather armchair in a corner of his study, which is adorned by various trophies, an ornate chess set, and mahogany bookshelves displaying neat rows of handsome, leather-bound volumes. These rich visual details draw our attention to the importance of relations of power in framing the star's body. In Stallone's case (in particular as his star image is produced in the mainstream press), we can discern a shift toward a decentered and less spectacular embodiment, which corresponds more closely with a middle-class ideal of masculinity. In fact, it was not until Stallone was clearly associated with this style of masculinity in public narratives (exemplified by *Cigar Aficionado* and *Architectural Digest*) that he was also, and not coincidentally, more widely accepted and celebrated as both a serious actor and a worthy (dis)embodiment of contemporary changes in men's gender position.

Conclusion: A "de-Ramboed" Stallone?

Cop Land, Stallone's most recent film, represents the logical culmination of the star's move toward a less spectacular masculinity, disengaged from the display of a muscled body. Stallone's "de-Ramboed"[57] role in *Cop Land* was widely heralded as a welcome and productive career move. The film's immense critical success suggests that the farther Stallone moves from "body genres," the more closely he becomes identified with the middle-class values of the mainstream press. *Rolling Stone* (September 4, 1997) writes: "Nearly down for the count in the movie ring, Stallone isn't just back in the fight. He's a winner." A caption in a *Time* article by Richard Corliss (August 11, 1997) also contrasts *Cop Land* favorably with Stallone's earlier movies: "*Rocky, Rambo, Rhinestone* – Sly Stallone did all that; now, at last, he gets to be an actor." Corliss further underscores this shift when asserting that *Cop Land*'s star is battling "his own rep as a stolid, vaguely comic, pre-Modernist hunk-lunk."

Praise for Stallone's achievements typically focuses on two interconnected elements of his image in this film: Stallone's weight gain (or the loss of the hard body) and his acting style (an emergence of talent from the discarded, hard body). Janet Maslin of the *New York Times* (August 15, 1997) maintains in her review, "Forty well-publicized pounds on Sylvester Stallone make for a highly symbolic weight gain, since they usher him into a peer group of heavy acting talent." Indeed, Stallone's unpumping "his body to Budweiser blubber" (*Newsweek*, August 25, 1997) underlines the importance of corporeality to the role (marking it as similar to his past body-dominated roles), yet simultaneously lures (critical) attention away from his body to his acting. Stallone's voluntarily gained fat (instead of muscles) is seen as preparation for his (acting) role, in the tradition of, say, method acting or Robert De Niro's bodily transformations for *Raging Bull*. In this sense, fat becomes a sign of artistic commitment and the measure of an actor's identification with his role. Stallone's body paradoxically disappears behind his overweight body which now functions as an abstract symbol of "great acting." Or, in accordance with the contemporary ascendence of cultural narratives in the United States which construct white masculinity as being threatened by women and ethnic minorities, this flabby, disabled, and vulnerable body corresponds to the redefinition of a victimized yet virtuous, and ultimately triumphant, male body.

Indeed, the poignant diction used in numerous descriptions of Stallone's acting in mainstream reviews suggests a strong degree of identification with the damaged and downtrodden masculinity portrayed in the film:

> With eyes downcast, an awkward gait and a physical anti-swagger, Stallone speaks volumes about the man's hopelessness and passivity. (*New York Times*, August 15, 1997)

> The sweet sadness in his eyes reveals something rare in modern films: how much pain and insult a decent man with zero self-esteem can endure. (*Time*, August 11, 1997)

> There's no flab in his portrayal of a deaf, dull-witted lawman – Freddy is a sweet slug – who discovers his moral conscience. Branching out in a *bold new direction*, Stallone is quietly devastating. (*Rolling Stone*, September 4, 1997; emphasis mine)

What is most interesting and significant about these descriptions, however, is how easily they could apply to Stallone's earlier films, in particular the *Rocky* series. In *Cop Land*, Stallone plays a local boy who has failed to make it big, but who eventually rediscovers his moral conscience, beats the

Goliath enemy against all odds, achieves heroism and gets the girl – a scenario that faithfully replicates *Rocky*'s underlying structure. What makes this formula for masculine accomplishment so attractive now, is precis ly a renewed cultural resonance for its portrayal of an initially tired and beleaguered male victim-hero, who both needs and upholds the possibility of resuscitating masculine power.

Indeed, by exploring Stallone's star image over the last two decades we can see how the crisis of male identity has worked through the body. If we look at the reconfiguration of Stallone's body from his early films to *Cop Land*, we can discern a gradual movement from a fully embodied machoness (the boxing and fighting body), through a body associated with economic power and (upper middle) class position (polo, golf, fashion, art consumption), toward the vulnerable and lacking body of *Cop Land* which functions as an iconic disavowal of masculine power, only thinly disguising a very traditional narrative and ideological outcome borrowed from the likes of *Rocky* or *Rambo*.

Stallone's changing star discourse draws our attention to the centrality of the male body as a site of struggle over legitimate forms of masculinity. It also stands as evidence against the cultural belief that only (representations of) women are fraught with the overpresence of the body, corporeally defined and bound, and the corresponding notion that men's power and identity can be easily separated, or remain aloof, from bodily constructions. Indeed, by tracing masculinity's articulation through Stallone's stardom, this paper underscores the idea that the changing formulation of Stallone's body (in his movies and in popular narratives) is closely linked to shifts in his audience, class alliances, and United States culture's uneasy affective investments in slowly changing (or frighteningly changeable) versions of manhood. Stallone's many and various embodiments of masculinity demonstrate how intimately the gendered body as representational construct corresponds with larger social structures. This close relationship between visions of corporeality and social structure also explains why and how bodily representations are so deftly mapped onto cultural anxieties concerning the perceived dismantling of the traditional male position. If, as Mary Douglas argues, "we are prepared to see in the body a symbol of society,"[58] it is little wonder, then, that we, through the camera, "have developed a peculiar, not to say pathological, interest in Sylvester Stallone's body."[59]

Acknowledgements

I would like to thank Leo Charney and Samantha Holland for their comments on an earlier version of this paper. My deepest gratitude goes to Melanie Nash whose insightful and generous suggestions and criticism helped considerably to focus my argument.

The Filmography of Sylvester Stallone (born 6.7.1946, New York)

1970 A Party at Kitty and Studs/The Italian Stallion (dir. Morton Lewis)
1971 Bananas (Woody Allen)
1974 No Place to Hide/Rebel (Robert Allen Schnitzer)
1974 The Lords of Flatbush (Stephen Verona and Martin Davidson)
1975 The Prisoner of Second Avenue (Melvin Frank)
1975 Farewell My Lovely (Dick Richards)
1975 Capone (Steve Carver)
1975 Death Race 2000 (Paul Bartel)
1976 Cannonball/Carquake (Paul Bartel)
1976 Rocky (John G. Avildsen; sp. Stallone)
1978 F.I.S.T. (Norman Jewison; co-sp. Stallone)
1978 Paradise Alley (Stallone; sp. Stallone)
1979 Rocky II (Stallone; sp. Stallone)
1981 Nighthawks (Bruce Malmuth)
1981 Victory/Escape to Victory (John Huston)
1982 First Blood (Ted Kotcheff; co-sp. Stallone)
1982 Rocky III (Stallone; sp. Stallone)
1983 Staying Alive (Stallone; co-sp. Stallone)
1984 Rhinestone (Bob Clark; co-sp. Stallone)
1985 Rambo: First Blood, Part II (George P. Cosmatos; co-sp. Stallone)
1985 Rocky IV (Stallone; sp. Stallone)
1986 Cobra (George P. Cosmatos; sp. Stallone)
1986 Over the Top (Menahem Golan; co-sp. Stallone)
1988 Rambo III (Peter MacDonald; co-sp. Stallone)
1989 Lock Up (John Flynn)
1989 Tango and Cash (Andrei Konchalovsky)
1990 Rocky V (John G. Avildsen; sp. Stallone)
1991 Oscar (John Landis)
1992 Stop! Or My Mom Will Shoot (Roger Spottiswood)
1993 Cliffhanger (Renny Harlin; co-sp. Stallone)
1993 Demolition Man (Marko Brambilla)
1994 The Specialist (Luis Llosa)
1995 Judge Dredd (Danny Cannon)

1995 Assassins (Richard Donner)
1996 Daylight (Rob Cohen)
1997 Cop Land (James Mangold)

Biographies of Sylvester Stallone

Daly, Marsha, *Sylvester Stallone*. New York: St. Martin's Press, 1986.
Wright, Adrian, *Sylvester Stallone: A Life on Film*. London: Robert Hale, 1991.

Reviews, columns and interviews in newspapers and popular magazines
(alphabetized according to the name of the publication)

Stauth, Cameron, "Requiem for a Heavyweight," *American Film*, 15 (4) (January 1990) (interview with Sylvester Stallone).
Thurman, Judith, "Architectural Digest Visits Sylvester Stallone: Life on the Grand Scale for the Actor in Miami," *Architectural Digest*, November 1997.
Mott, Gordon, "Stallone II," *Cigar Aficionado*, April 1988 (interview).
Arar, Yardena, "'Tango and Cash': Two Left Feet and Bankrupt," *Daily News* (Los Angeles), December 25, 1989 (review).
Anon, "Powerful Screen Play Draws 'First Blood' with Bold Strokes," *Des Moines Register* (IA), October 28, 1982.
Bunke, Joan, "Stallone's a Sly One: Delivers New Punch," *Des Moines Register* (IA), December 1, 1985 (review of *Rocky IV*).
Heath, Chris, "Rough Trade," *Details*, November 1994 (interview with Stallone).
Kaye, Elizabeth, "Sly's Progress: Profile," *Esquire*, February 1989 (interview with Stallone).
Leydon, Joe, "Film: 'First Blood'," *Houston Post* (Texas), October 27, 1982 (review).
Mills, Bart, "Stallone vs. Adversity," *Houston Post* (Texas), October 14, 1982 (interview).
Goodwin, Jan, "The Unknown Stallone: The World's No. 1 Superstar," *Ladies' Home Journal*, July 1988 (interview).
Rainer, Peter, "'First Blood': It's Rocky vs. the World," *Los Angeles Herald Examiner*, October 22, 1982 (review).
Stall, Bill, "Making a Movie Out of a Mountain: Climbers Give High Marks to 'Cliffhanger's Realistic High-Altitude Action Sequences," *Los Angeles Times*, June 2, 1993.
Denby, David, Review of *First Blood*, *New York*, November 15, 1982.
Denby, David, "Blood Simple," *New York*, June 3, 1985 (review of *Rambo: First Blood, Part II*).
Reed, Rex, "Violence & Gore Galore as Sly draws 'First Blood'," *New York Post*, October 22, 1982 (review).

Reed, Rex, Review of *Rhinestone, New York Post*, June 22, 1984.

Bernard, Jam, "Sly Cashes in on Class," *New York Post*, December 22, 1989 (review of *Tango and Cash*).

Canby, Vincent, "In Films Acting Is Behavior," *New York Times*, December 12, 1976 (column "Film View").

Maslin, Janet, "'Copland': Sly Holds His Own," *New York Times*, August 15, 1997 (review).

Kroll, Jack, "Survival of the Fittest," *Newsweek*, August 25, 1997 (review of *Cop Land* [and *G.I. Jane*]).

Travers, Peter, "Comebacks for Two Fallen Stars," *Rolling Stone*, September 4, 1997 (review of *Cop Land* [and *G.I. Jane*]).

LaSalle, Mick, "Rocky Is Losing His Stuff," *San Francisco Chronicle*, November 28, 1985 (review of *Rocky IV*).

Mills, Bart, "Rats and Blood on Rambo's Mountain," *San Francisco Examiner*, October 17, 1982 (interview with Stallone).

Shulgasser, Barbara, "Rambo's Desperate Tango: Hungry for Credibility, Stallone Resorts to Smiling," *San Francisco Examiner*, December 22, 1989 (review of *Tango and Cash*).

Schickel, Richard, Review of *First Blood, Time*, November 11, 1982.

Corliss, Richard, "Sly's Next Move," *Time*, August 11, 1997.

Heller, Zoë, "Sly's Body of Art," *Vanity Fair*, November 1993 (interview with Stallone).

Carter, Graydon, "Stallone on the Range," *Vogue*, December 1991 (interview).

Notes

1. Marsha Daly, *Sylvester Stallone* (New York: St. Martin's Press, 1986), p. 120.

2. Sylvester Stallone *on First Blood* in Adrian Wright, *Sylvester Stallone: A Life on Film* (London: Robert Hale, 1991), p. 111.

3. Bart Mills, "Rats and Blood on Rambo's Mountain," *San Francisco Examiner*, October 17, 1982.

4. Kaja Silverman, *The Acoustic Mirror: The Female Voice in Psychoanalysis and Cinema* (Bloomington: Indiana University Press, 1988), p. 134.

5. I use this term to designate genres that prominently showcase the male body as spectacle. Linda Williams uses the term "body genres" in a somewhat different way, referring to those genres (specifically porn, melodrama, and horror) designed to elicit a certain corporeal effect in their audience (arousal, empathy, and fear, respectively). See Linda Williams, "Film Bodies: Gender, Genre, and Excess," *Film Quarterly*, 44 (4) (Summer 1991), pp. 2-13.

6. Yvonne Tasker, *Spectacular Bodies: Gender, Genre and the Action Cinema* (London: Routledge, 1993), p. 6.

7. Rosalind Coward, *Female Desires: How They Are Sought, Bought, and Packaged* (New York: Grove Press, 1985), p. 227.
8. Mary Douglas, *Purity and Danger: An Analysis of the Concepts of Pollution and Taboo* (London and New York: Ark Paperbacks, 1989), p. 125.
9. Douglas, *Purity and Danger*, p. 115.
10. David Curry, "Decorating the Body Politic," *New Formations*, 19 (Spring 1993), p. 69.
11. Christine Gledhill, Introduction, *Stardom: Industry of Desire*, ed. Christine Gledhill (London: Routledge, 1991), p. xiv.
12. John Ellis, *Visible Fictions: Cinema/Television/Video* (London: Routledge,Ke-gan, and Paul, 1985), p. 91.
13. Anne Friedberg, "Identification and the Star," *Star Signs: Papers from a Weekend Workshop* (London: BFI Education, 1982), p. 51.
14. Richard deCordova, *Picture Personalities: The Emergence of the Star System in America* (Urbana: University of Illinois Press, 1990).
15. deCordova, *Picture Personalities*, p. 19.
16. Judith Mayne, *Cinema and Spectatorship* (London: Routledge, 1993), p. 128.
17. Mayne, *Cinema and Spectatorship*, pp. 128-9.
18. Tony Bennett, "Texts, Readers, Reading Formations," *Midwest Modern Language Association* (Spring 1983), p. 8.
19. Richard Schickel, review of *First Blood*, *Time*, November 11, 1982.
20. Yvonne Tasker, "Dumb Movies for Dumb People: Masculinity, the Body, and the Voice in Contemporary Action Cinema," in Steven Cohan and Ina Rae Hark (eds), *Screening the Male: Exploring Masculinities in Hollywood Cinema*, (London: Routledge, 1993), p. 233.
21. Tasker, "Dumb Movies for Dumb People," p. 233.
22. Arjen Mulder, "Body Conspiracy," *Mediamatic*, 4 (3) (Voorjaar/Spring 1990), p. 123.
23. Hanna Kangasniemi and Martti Lahti, "Lihasten ja vallan symbioosit: Stallone, Schwarzenegger ja ruumiillistettu kuva," in Erkki Huhtamo and Martti Lahti (eds), *Elävän kuvan vuosikirja 1992* (Helsinki: VAPK-kustannus and Suomen elokuvasäätiö, 1992).
24. Richard Dyer, "Don't Look Now," in Angela McRobbie (ed.), *Zoot Suit and Second-Hand Dresses: An Anthology of Fashion and Music* (Basingstoke: Macmillan, 1989), p. 205.
25. Margaret Morse, "Sport on Television: Replay and Display," in E. Ann Kaplan (ed.), *Regarding Television: Critical Approaches. An Anthology*, The Ameri-can Film Institute Monograph Series, Volume 2 (Los Angeles: The American Film Institute and University Publication of America, 1983).
26. Susan Jeffords, *The Remasculinization of America: Gender and the Vietnam War* (Bloomington: Indiana University Press, 1989) 11.
27. Richard Dyer, *Heavenly Bodies: Film Stars and Society* (London: Macmillan, 1987), p. 12.

28. Daly, *Sylvester Stallone*, pp. 2-3.
29. Wright, *Sylvester Stallone: A Life on Film*, p. 81.
30. It is only the *male* body that functions in this visibly authenticating capacity in pornography, since female orgasm (and the female body) has had no clear cinematic reality index attributed to it.
31. Ien Ang, "*Dallas* and the Ideology of Mass Culture," in Simon During (ed.), *The Cultural Studies Reader* (London: Routledge, 1993), p. 407.
32. Ang, "*Dallas* and the Ideology of Mass Culture," p. 405.
33. Tasker, *Spectacular Bodies*, p. 85.
34. Pierre Bourdieu, "Sports and Social Class," in Chandra Mukerji and Michael Schudson (eds), *Rethinking Popular Culture: Contemporary Perspectives in Cultural Studies* (Oxford: University of California Press, 1991), p. 367.
35. Bourdieu, "Sport and Social Class," pp. 361-2.
36. Kangasniemi and Lahti, "Lihasten ja vallan symbioosit," p. 58. The same argument is made by Yvonne Tasker and Chris Holmlund: Tasker, "Dumb Movies for Dumb People," pp. 234-6; Chris Holmlund, "Masculinity as Multiple Masquerade: The 'Mature' Stallone and the Stallone Clone," in Cohanand Hark (eds), *Screening the Male*, p. 222.
37. This interview is cited by both Chris Holmlund and Yvonne Tasker in their treatments of Stallone: Holmlund, "Masculinity as Multiple Masquerade"; Tasker, "Dumb Movies for Dumb People"; Tasker, *Spectacular Bodies*.
38. Tasker, "Dumb Movies for Dumb People," p. 234.
39. *Ibid.*
40. Steve Neale, "Masculinity as Spectacle: Reflections on Men and Mainstream Cinema," *Screen*, 24 (6) (November-December 1983).
41. Tasker, *Spectacular Bodies*, p. 115. A similar argument is made by Paul Smith in "Action Movie Hysteria, or Eastwood Bound," *differences*, 1 (3) (1989).
42. Victor J. Seidler, "Reason, desire and male sexuality," in Pat Caplan (ed.), *The Cultural Construction of Sexuality* (London: Tavistock Publications, 1987).
43. Dyer, *Heavenly Bodies*, p. 5.
44. *Ibid.*, p. 3.
45. Tania Modleski, *Feminism Without Women: Culture and Criticism in a "Postfeminist" Age* (New York and London: Routledge, 1991), p. 7.
46. Maurizia Boscagli, "A Moving Story: Masculine Tears and the Humanity of Televised Emotions," *Discourse*, 15 (2) (Winter 1992-93); Susan Jeffords, "Can Masculinity Be Terminated?" in Cohan and Hark (eds), *Screening the Male*; Susan Jeffords, *Hard Bodies: Hollywood Masculinity in the Reagan Era* (New Brunswick and New Jersey: Rutgers University Press, 1994); Sasha Torres, "Melodrama, Masculinity and the Family: *thirtysomething* as Therapy," *Camera Obscura*, 19 (1989).
47. Jeffords, "Can Masculinity Be Terminated?", p. 245.
48. Boscagli, "A Moving Story: Masculine Tears," p. 64.

49. *Ibid.*, p. 67.
50. Kaja Silverman, "Fragments of Fashionable Discourse," in Kaja Silverman (ed.), *Studies in Entertainment: Critical Approaches to Mass Culture* (Bloomington: Indiana University Press, 1986), p. 147.
51. Jennifer Craik, *The Face of Fashion: Cultural Studies in Fashion* (London: Routledge, 1994), p. 179.
52. Martin Pumphrey, "Why Do Cowboys Wear Hats in the Bath? Style politics for Older Men," *Critical Quarterly*, 31 (3) (Autumn 1989), p. 97. Cited by Craik, *The Face of Fashion*, p. 179.
53. Holmlund, "Masculinity as Multiple Masquerade."
54. *Ibid.*, p. 218.
55. Gordon Mott, "Stallone II," *Cigar Aficionado*, April 1988, pp. 132-63.
56. Judith Thurman, "Architectural Digest Visits Sylvester Stallone: Life on the Grand Scale for the Actor in Miami," *Architectural Digest*, November 1997, pp. 212ff.
57. Jack Kroll, "Survival of the Fittest," *Newsweek*, August 25, 1997, p. 74.
58. Douglas, *Purity and Danger*, p. 115.
59. David Denby, "Blood Simple," *New York*, June 3, 1985; cited by David Savran, *Taking It Like a Man: White Masculinity, Masochism, and Contemporary American Culture* (Princeton, NJ: Princeton University Press, 1998), p. 199.

References

Ang, Ien, "*Dallas* and the Ideology of Mass Culture," in Simon During (ed.), *The Cultural Studies Reader*. London: Routledge, 1993.

Bennett, Tony, "Texts, Readers, Reading Formations," *Midwest Modern Language Association*, Spring 1983.

Boscagli, Maurizia, "A Moving Story: Masculine Tears and the Humanity of Televi-sed Emotions," *Discourse*, 15 (2) (1992-93).

Bourdieu, Pierre, "Sport and Social Class," in Chandra Mukerji and Michael Schudson (eds), *Rethinking Popular Culture: Contemporary Perspectives in Cultural Studies*. Oxford: University of California Press, 1991.

Coward, Rosalind, *Female Desires: How They Are Sought, Bought, and Packaged*. New York: Grove Press, 1985.

Craik, Jennifer, *The Face of Fashion: Cultural Studies in Fashion*. London: Routledge, 1994.

Curry, David, "Decorating the Body Politic," *New Formations*, 19 (1993).

deCordova, Richard, *Picture Personalities: The Emergence of the Star System in America*. Urbana: University of Illinois Press, 1990.

Douglas, Mary, *Purity and Danger: An Analysis of the Concepts of Pollution and Taboo*. London: Ark Paperbacks, 1989 (1966).

Dyer, Richard, "Don't Look Now," in Angela McRobbie (ed.), *Zoot Suit and Second-Hand Dresses: An Anthology of Fashion and Music*. Basingstoke: Macmillan, 1989 (1983).

Dyer, Richard, *Heavenly Bodies: Film Stars and Society*. Basingstoke: Macmillan, 1987.

Ellis, John, *Visible Fictions: Cinema/Television/Video*. London: Routledge, Kegan, and Paul, 1985 (1982).

Friedberg, Anne, "Identification and the Star," *Star Signs: Papers from a Weekend Workshop*. London: BFI Education, 1982.

Gledhill, Christine, Introduction, in Christine Gledhill (ed.), *Stardom: Industry of Desire*. London: Routledge, 1991.

Holmlund, Chris, "Masculinity as Multiple Masquerade: The 'Mature' Stallone and the Stallone Clone," in Steven Cohan and Ina Rae Hark (eds), *Screening the Male: Exploring Masculinities in Hollywood Cinema*. London: Routledge, 1993.

Jeffords, Susan, *The Remasculinization of America: Gender and the Vietnam War*. Bloomington: Indiana University Press, 1989.

Jeffords, Susan, "Can Masculinity Be Terminated?" in Steven Cohan and Ina Rae Hark (eds), *Screening the Male: Exploring Masculinities in Hollywood Cinema*. London: Routledge, 1993.

Jeffords, Susan, *Hard Bodies: Hollywood Masculinity in the Reagan Era*. New Brunswick: Rutgers University Press, 1994.

Kangasniemi, Hanna, and Lahti, Martti, "Lihasten ja vallan symbioosit: Stallone, Schwarzenegger ja ruumiillistettu kuva," in Erkki Huhtamo and Martti Lahti (eds), *Elävän kuvan vuosikirja 1992*. Helsinki: VAPK-kustannus and Suomen eelokuvasäätiö, 1992.

Mayne, Judith, *Cinema and Spectatorship*. London: Routledge, 1993.

Modleski, Tania, *Feminism Without Women: Culture and Criticism in a "Postfeminist" Age*. New York: Routledge, 1991.

Morse, Margaret, "Sport on Television: Replay and Display," in E. Ann Kaplan (ed.), *Regarding Television: Critical Approaches. An Anthology*. The American Film Institute Monograph Series, Volume 2. Los Angeles: The American Film Institute and University Publication of America, 1983.

Mulder, Arjen, "Body Conspiracy," *Mediamatic*, 4 (3) (Voorjaar/Spring 1990).

Neale, Steve, "Masculinity as Spectacle: Reflections on Men and Mainstream Cinema," *Screen*, 24 (6) (November-December 1983).

Pumphrey, Martin, "Why Do Cowboys Wear Hats in the Bath? Style politics for Older Men," *Critical Quarterly*, 31 (3) (Autumn 1989).

Savran, David, *Taking It Like a Man: White Masculinity, Masochism, and Contemporary American Culture*. Princeton, NJ: Princeton University Press, 1998.

Seidler, Victor J., "Reason, desire and male sexuality," in Pat Caplan (ed.), *The Cultural Construction of Sexuality*. London: Tavistock Publications, 1987.

Silverman, Kaja, "Fragments of Fashionable Discourse," in Kaja Silverman (ed.), *Studies in Entertainment: Critical Approaches to Mass Culture*. Bloomington: Indiana University Press, 1986.

Silverman, Kaja, *The Acoustic Mirror: The Female Voice in Psychoanalysis and Cinema*. Bloomington: Indiana University Press, 1988.

Smith, Paul, "Action Movie Hysteria, or Eastwood Bound," *Differences*, 1 (3) (1989).

Tasker, Yvonne, "Dumb Movies for Dumb People: Masculinity, the Body, and the Voice in Contemporary Action Cinema," in Steven Cohan and Ina Rae Hark (eds), *Screening the Male: Exploring Masculinities in Hollywood Cinema*. London: Routledge, 1993.

Tasker, Yvonne, *Spectacular Bodies: Gender, Genre and the Action Cinema*. London: Routledge, 1993.

Torres, Sasha, "Melodrama, Masculinity and the Family: *thirtysomething* as Therapy," *Camera Obscura*, 19 (1989).

Williams, Linda, "Film Bodies: Gender, Genre, and Excess," *Film Quarterly*, 44 (4) (Summer 1991).

Chapter 9

Searching for the Body: Making Connections between Health, Bodies and Men's Violence[1]

JEFF HEARN

Recent debates on the body have moved beyond the opposition between biology versus social constructionism, and toward a concern with embodiment and embodied and embodying practices and processes. Mapped onto these more general questions are more specific analyses of men's bodies. There are, for example, a number of contradictions in dominant social constructions of men's bodies – between on the one hand, men and masculinities as embodied, as present bodies, even simply as the body; and on the other, as disembodied, or as separate minds and bodies. The practices, processes and indeed contradictions of embodiment/disembodiment pervade the public discussion of men's bodies, including this chapter.

My particular focus here is on health, bodies and men's violence, and the connections between them, which have often been left unstated. Following an initial discussion of definitions of violence, the first section focuses on the relative lack of separation of the study of health, illness and the body, and the study of violence, especially men's violence. This is followed by an examination of some of the ways in which men's violence bears on health, illness and bodies – of men, women, young people and children. The impacts of men's violence are both short-term/ immediate/psychological and long-term/less immediate/indirect. The practice and the threat of men's interpersonal and other violence are major causes of physical and psychological pain, stress, distress, and ill health. Violence is antithetic to health. The doing of violence involves action on the body of others, and it also involves the making of the body of the violator, in this context the bodies of men.

The final section explores these themes in terms of men's violences to known women, drawing on research on men's accounts of their own violence, and the responses of agencies, friends and family.[2]

As such, it has necessarily been concerned with the interrelations of health, bodies, both men's and women's, and violence. In examining these questions it is necessary to place men's actions and experiences, including those involving violence, in the context of men's social relations, both structural and interpersonal, with women, and especially the effects of men and men's violence on women. In bringing together health, bodies and men's violence, this chapter is cast in the intermediate zone[3] between the study of health, illness, and the body, and the study of violence.

What is violence?

While I do not think there is any one simple definition of violence, it may be useful to consider the following perspectives on violence:

> that which is or involves the use of force, physical or otherwise, by a violator or violators; that which is experienced by the violated as violation; those acts, activities or events designated as "violent" by a third party, for example, doctors, police, court officials.

All these three perspectives are themselves historically and culturally specific. Rather than seeking an absolute definition of violence, it is more accurate to see what is defined as violence as being itself the product of complex processes of debate and negotiation between these perspectives.[4] In particular, an important part of this is that what is *not* named as violence in one situation or time may become named as violent elsewhere or subsequently. This in turn may make possible the naming of other violences. This is clear, for example, in the naming of certain kinds of sexual-social relations as "sexual harassment." This is clearer still when what are at one time named as "consensual" sexual-social relations are renamed as power relations, exploitation, abuse or harassment. Indeed the historical process of naming violence is a fundamental part of the politics of opposition to violence.

Furthermore, violence is both interpersonal and structural. While interpersonal violence refers to direct violence from one person to another in an identifiable situation, what is meant by structural violence is more variable. There are several related meanings of the term structural violence, as follows:

- structural violence as the structural pattern of individual and interpersonal violence, such as the societal patterns of men's violence

to women in the home;
- structural violence as the acts and effects of social institutions such as the state, which might be more accurately referred to as institutional violence;
- structural violence as the violent effects of inequalities, including those on a world scale, such as the distribution of famine;
- structural violence as the violent effects of warfare and inter-nation and inter-community violence;
- structural violence as the social structural relations of institutions when and where those social relations have historically been violent or have underwritten violence, for example, the social relations of fatherhood or capitalism.[5]

Making the connections more obvious

Violence is bad for your health. Yet it still seems that for many men, health and violence remain rather unconnected social issues and arenas. In the first case, health is misconstrued through the invisibility of caring and the neglect of the body; in the second, violence is misconstrued through denial and even glorification, thus directly serving men's interests. And yet, the connection of health and violence may be clear in the experience of many who experience violence, for example, women who are abused and violated by men.

Similarly, if one goes to the casualty department of any large hospital, especially late evenings on Fridays or Saturdays, it would be difficult to doubt the connection of violence and health, or lack of it.[6] These facts may be known at one level by most doctors and other health professionals, though it is only relatively recently that the full policy and practice implications of working against violence have been taken up in the health sector. Yet our television screens are full of graphic indications of how violence destroys health. Such connections may appear to men most obviously in wartime, when certain groups of men are then being threatened, violated and killed. But while men participate more than women in formal military institutions, women and children may in fact be the greatest casualties of war.

The opposition of violence and health is clearest in death and the destruction of people. Death is the end of health. The scale of manmade (*sic*) death is difficult to appreciate. Writing in 1972, Gil Elliot calculates that in the twentieth century alone there had been 110 million manmade deaths, including 62 million by various forms of privation (death camps, slave labor, forced marches, imprisonment), 46 million from guns and bombs, and 2 million from chemicals (Elliot, 1972).[7] A rather different approach to violence, health and death has been put forward by Amartya Sen in "More than 100 million women are missing" (Sen, 1990) and elsewhere. Patterns of female mortality in many parts of the world suggest that pervasive discrimination against women (and especially girls) deprives them of both adequate food and basic health care (Nussbaum, 1992, p. 43).

The separation of problems and the separation of sociologies

The frequent relative separation of health and violence is not just a matter of everyday, "commonsense" perceptions (or lack of them); it is also reproduced within the ways that health and violence are studied, conceptualized and understood. This is illustrated by the contrast between the sociologies of health, illness and the body, on one hand, and the sociology of violence, on the other. While the sociology of health and illness, and specifically medical sociology, are well established sub-disciplines within sociology[8] the "sociology of violence" is not a coherent or strongly recognized sub-discipline. Indeed in some senses it could be argued, if controversially, that the sociology of violence does not exist as a sub-discipline at all.[9] Instead there are a number of ways in which the sociology of violence has been conceptualized, including military sociology, violence against women, the sociology of deviance, criminology, police studies and so on. The fact that the sociology of violence is not a term in common use in sociology is part of the problem of sociology, just as the absence of equivalent terms constitutes a similar problem in many other disciplines.

The sociology of the body is a rather different institutional development, with its increasing recognition and yet profound fragmentation. Strong influences have come from feminist scholarship; gay, lesbian, queer and other critical work on sexuality; psychoanalysis; post-structuralism, particularly through the impact of the work of Michel Foucault; and postmodernism, much influenced by the changing forms of representation of the body in media and cyberspace. In recent years, the rapidly spreading experience and sociology of HIV/AIDS has brought a further focus on the body, paradoxically through its potential destruction. The sociology of the body and the sociologies of health, illness and medicine have developed in a close relationship verging on reciprocity. For example, Arthur Frank's (1990) review of scholarship on the body emphasizes the significance of the study of "the medicalized body." Other important connections with health and illness include the focus on "the disciplined body" and the history of diet.

One of the major concepts within the sociology of the body is fragmentation. Both sociologically and psychologically, the body is not one "thing." Bryan Turner (1984) constructs a framework for understanding how bodies confront social organization: reproduction of populations in time, regulation of bodies in space, restraint of the "interior" body through disciplines, and representation of the external body in social space. Bodies are both collective (populations) and individual; and they exist in time and space; and they are "interior" and "exterior." Put this way, there are eight rather than four major sets of processes. More specific descriptions of the representations on/of the exterior surface of the body are provided by Gilles Deleuze (1981) and Felix Guattari (1977). Scott Lash (1984) summarizes these as follows: as figures recorded on the surface of bodies, corresponding to part objects of desiring-machines; figures recorded from the outside world on the body; phantasms, such as "desire"; the "language" of bodies; and sense organs themselves. In this view even the exterior surfaces of bodies are fragmented and fractured.[10] While this kind of approach may be analytically and even experientially appealing in some respects, it may not grapple with the specific experiences of doing or receiving violence.

Why is the relationship between health/the body and violence so underdeveloped? I think there are a number of not always consistent reasons for this. First, I have already noted many men's relative disconnection from the recognition of both health and violence. The invisibility of caring, the neglect of the body, and the denial of violence apply not just to many men "in society," but to men in sociology. Sociology has its own social structure, which has reproduced to some extent the invisibility of caring, the neglect of the body, and the denial of violence. Such features can be related to various forms of masculinity, just as some men may show themselves as men by showing off their body, "building it up," or refusing to show it to doctors (Briscoe, 1989).

Second, there is the question of the often subtle and indirect impacts of other knowledges, particularly professional knowledges, on sociology – most obviously, medicine in the case of the sociologies of health, illness and the body, and law in the incipient sociology of violence. Medical knowledge is constituted very differently from legal knowledge. The former is framed in terms of surveillance of the body, diagnosis of its aberrations (it not being a "complete" body), and intervention in/on the body. The latter is framed in terms of the occurrences of the event, evidence of its occurrence, and precedential and subsequent legal proceedings and argument, both in and out of courts. Medicine is itself related to anatomy and physiology; law to procedure and jurisprudence. Medical and legal discourses are founded on different assumptions about the body: in the first case, as an "organic machine," a physical construction; in the second, as evidences (traces) of perpetrated social actions and events.

The sociologies of health and the body, and of violence, examine these different social objects, sometimes critically and deconstructively. In doing so, they have different emphases and traditions, which in part are reactions to those social objects and their social constructions. Yet both health/medicine and violence/law specialize in the body. Both are mediations (or mediations of mediations) of the body and bodily experience. Such bodily experience is mediated by medicine and law, and their associated professional knowledges and statistical and other official evidences respectively. In both the sociologies of health and the body and of violence, there have been major attempts, notably from feminist work, to step outside these implicit "professionalizations." This is the clearest in attempts to return to women's experiences of illness/health and of threat/damage/ violation rather than a reliance on medical, criminal or similar statistics (see for example Hanmer and Saunders, 1984; Kelly, 1988).

Men, health and bodies

These issues of health, the body, and violence have figured very differently and unevenly in recent studies on men and masculinities. In the first case, the connection of men and health has proceeded, partly through an emphasis on the "hazards of being male" (sometimes from a male liberationist stance), in terms of men's relatively high mortality and morbidity rates.[11] Not only do boys and men have lower life expectancies in virtually all nations, but men are prone to particular diseases, illnesses, occupational hazards, and accidents at relatively higher rates than girls and women. It is important to note also that the question of men's health has taken on an additional urgency in the former Soviet bloc, especially Russia, with dramatic reductions in men's life expectancy since the collapse of the state apparatus, including the state health system (Deacon, 1997). In the UK and many other European countries the question of men's health has attracted a great deal of attention from a very wide range of political perspectives and institutional sectors, including government, business and trade unions, as well as health professionals (see Hearn, forthcoming). It has almost appeared to act as a focus of consensus in talking about men.

There are, however, several problems with a narrow approach to men's health:

- gender differences between men's and women's health need to be placed in their historical context (Ehrenreich, 1983);
- there is a danger of overstating gender differences;
- there is a danger of equating quantity (for example, life expectancy) and quality (of life);
- gender differences need to be placed in the context of power and privilege, and specifically the dispensability of individual men co-existing with the maintenance or enhancement of the collective power of men (Hearn, 1987, pp. 95-8);
- relations between women and men, including men's violence to women and children, should not be neglected;
- the extent of men's, particularly young men's, risk-taking social actions needs to be understood as contributing to men's health;
- more specific questions, such as the way in which the cultural meanings of certain illnesses, notably heart disease, may be used as a means of prioritizing some health issues over others.[12]

Recent sociological work on men and the body has, however, tended to address a rather different set of concerns. First, there has been the recognition of the frequent denial of men's bodies, and the associated undertheorizing of men's bodies: the ideological construction of men as absent bodies (Coward, 1984; Lehman, 1988). Second, there is more explicit understanding of men and masculinities as embodied, as present bodies, as the body (Connell, 1983, 1987, 1995). Third, there are attempts to interrogate the representation of men and masculinity as separate minds and bodies, such as when "minds" use "bodies" (Brittan, 1989). Fourth, there are more specific, critical analyses of men's pursuit of "body projects" and "body activities," most obviously sport (Messner, 1995) and bodybuilding itself (Klein, 1993). Fifth, there is also an emerging tendency which attempts to "talk the body," to talk more directly from/on the body. In this, following post-structuralist feminisms, the body fractures, as a metaphor for a fracturing of masculinity (Jackson, 1990). Together this constitutes a significant body of work. Developing a sociology of men's bodies involves consideration of all these issues. In particular, it is necessary to locate the material unities of men's collective power as bodies and the diversity of men's bodies within patriarchies, and to place the question of men's violence and potential violence at the center of analysis of men's bodies.

Men, violence and bodies

The connections between men and violence have of course been a major theme in feminist work, both in general and specifically on violence. Even until recently men's academic response to feminism had relatively rarely focused on the problem of men's violence – indeed it could be said to have often been avoided by men. One possible reason for this is that much of men's anti-sexist activity outside the academy has not been based primarily against violence. However, since the late 1970s, some men have addressed the problem of violence through a variety of programs that aim to reduce or abolish men's violence to women. There are major debates about the appropriate resourcing, philosophies, methods and effectiveness of such programmes (for example Gondolf and Russell, 1986; Horley, 1990; Dankwort, 1992-93). The problem of men's violence is rather slowly being addressed in critical studies of men by men. Yet it is remarkable how men can still be interested in the critical study of men without attending to the problem of violence.

As emphasized in feminist work, the crucial questions seem to include the amazing preponderance of men's violence; men's domination of criminal violence as reported in criminal statistics; men's domination of the institutions of violence; discussion of the nature of violence; explanation and theories of men's violence (Gondolf, 1985, Hearn, 1998). Increasingly, the interrelationships of "normal masculinity" and violence (Hearn, 1993), and "hegemonic masculinity" (Carrigan, Connell and Lee, 1985), are being acknowledged. Certain dominant forms of masculinity and everyday forms of masculinity both often carry associations, assumptions or practices of violence. Having said that, there are powerful forms of masculinity, especially those that command organizational, managerial and intellectual resources that may appear to be unassociated with violence. These may be directly violent (see for example Ramazanoglu, 1987), and they may be violent in other arenas, for example, at home or in sport.

While men collectively dominate violence and women and children collectively experience the violation of men, it is important to consider the social variations in men's violence to each other.[13] Some powerful men are able to dominate resources without the direct use of violence. Also the maintenance and enhancement of the collective power of men can continue alongside the dispensability of individual men, whether through illness, disease, occupational hazards, accidents, suicides, or violence of men against men. This is a further link between health and violence. Men's violence against other men can be particularly significant for the experience of less powerful men; this can apply in terms of both violence between men and violence from more powerful men upon these less powerful men. Such violence can be interrelated with all other kinds of oppression, for example, by age, class, "race"/ethnicity. The dispensability, even decimation, of, say, black men in a society dominated by white men can reinforce men's power (Franklin, 1987). Indeed class, gender, race and other oppressions and exploitations are themselves ways of producing, reproducing and indeed destroying bodies. In a related way, boys and young men may be violated as part of their becoming men. Boys may be taught to be violent to other boys, and this instruction is itself a form of violence. Furthermore, all these violences/masculinities are themselves embodied: they involve the body, in the very extent, tensing and exercise of muscle and flesh. They are not mechanical processes, but   rather structural, multi-faceted, fractured, inconsistent and contradictory.

Men's violence would also seem to necessitate a minimum of health; this seems to be especially so in direct physical violence. Health may affect the ability to be violent; indeed the ability to be physically violent may be seen as an indication of health. This would appear to apply much less to emotional violence, technological violence or violence through the command of others, resources and others' violence. On the other hand, men's violence may also be interpreted as illness – of both violated and the violator. Illness may also affect the practice of violence, as, for example, a reassertion of power, in the face of declining authority.

Men's violence can also take many forms: it includes physical violence, sexual violence, psychological violence, emotional violence, destruction of property and pets (Ganley, 1981). It also includes linguistic violence, violence in the form of neglect, for example child neglect (Hearn, 1988), cognitive violence, visual and representational violence, economic violence, technological violence, and environmental violence. Men's violence can be interpersonal or institutional, agentic or structural. It may be toward women, other men, the self, babies, children, young people, as well as animals and other non-human existences ("environmental terrorism" is not a new phenomenon).

Violence, like politics, occurs not only in space, it is also in time. Violence is not only against others in the present; violence is also and more profoundly against people in time. Violence is not just a series of actions in the present, it is in the future and the past: violence is an attack on future existence and a reaffirmation of past historical violences, an attack against existence and time.[14]

There are some dangers in seeing interpersonal violence as the paradigm case of violence.[15] As noted, violence also persists in structured relations. Violence is a fundamental, if negative, form of reproduction.

Human beings have the capacity for destruction of each other and indeed ourselves – that is violent labor power. This is socially structured in definite and differential ways between women and men, both interpersonally and institutionally. Relevant institutions include hierarchic heterosexuality, fatherhood, the professions and the state, each of which is clearly and historically structured between women and men. Within such (violent) structured relations, violence is a routine way in which men relate, agentically, to women, though this is in no way determined. In other words, men do have agency to maintain or reject violence.

Within these structural contexts there are many different ways in which men may relate to violence. Men may be publicly employed to be violent or potentially so (for example as soldiers), or be their managers (for example as officers); men may be violent in private (for example as child abusers), in the street (for example as "muggers"), in sport (for example as boxers). Different types of men engage in different violences, be they physical, emotional, technological. Other men may be rarely violent, or active against violence. These categories are not mutually exclusive. And they in no way diminish the general structured relations of violence, and the general association of masculinities and violence.

The impact of men's violence can be direct and/or shorter term in the act of violence itself, producing physical hurt, pain and damage; sexual hurt, pain and damage; psychological and emotional hurt, pain and damage; neglect; cognitive hurt, pain and damage; linguistic and visual hurt, pain and damage. The effects of men's violence can also be indirect and/or longer term including all of the above. Seen in that way, violence is not just the "immediate act" but includes the indirect effects as a process, such as subsequent physical and psychological pain, disability and recurrent illness. Brende and Parson (1985) state that of the 3,780,000 men who served in the Vietnam War, at least 800,000 were subsequently in need of counselling – for post-traumatic stress syndrome/"battle fatigue"/"shellshock" (Sayce, 1991).

A review of U.S. research on the direct and indirect effects of domestic violence and sexual abuse of children has been provided by Richard Gelles and Jon Conte (1990). The effects of violence toward women noted include "a high incidence of depression and anxiety ... higher levels of moderate and severe psychological distress." The impacts of sexual abuse (virtually always by men) upon children noted include "... higher scores ... on ... dimensions (of) concentration problems, aggressive, withdrawn, somatic complaints, character personality style (for example, ... too anxious to please), irrational behaviour, nervous/emotional, depression, behavioral regression, body image/self-esteem problems, fear, and symptoms of post-traumatic stress" and "symptoms of muscle tension, gastrointestinal and genito-urinary difficulties, emotional reactions, runaway behaviour and other behaviour problems." Although there are some methodological and other problems with some of these kinds of studies (for example, psychological labelling, assumption of "trauma"), they do point to the dire effects of violence and abuse upon the lives, bodies and minds of others.

The exact way in which violence and abuse are related to the effects of violence and abuse is contested (see Dobash and Dobash, 1992, pp. 221-35). In some cases the effects of men's violence may lead to women, children and other men affected being brought into contact with institutions and agencies that may have their own institutional violent practices. For example, entry into the mental health system may lead to further violences to the body through the use of tranquillizers and physical restraint.

It is important to reiterate that the exact form of the social processes around men's violence, health and bodies varies greatly with different kinds of violence. Indeed it is partly for this reason that it is more accurate to speak of violences rather than violence. This is clear if we compare, say, the impacts of pornography with the impacts of dangerous driving. With pornography, violence is in visual or other cultural form, often using bodies in its production; with dangerous driving, violence may be present for the driver, other road users and pedestrians. Alternatively we may compare physical attack causing direct pain and damage with technological violence, which employs technology which causes pain and damage, or with, say, environmental violence, which may also produce direct or indirect violence to people. For example, during the Gulf War it was reported that the burning oil wells of Kuwait released into the atmosphere sulphuric dioxide, sulphuric acid, nitrates and other chemicals, which are likely to produce chest, bronchial and asthmatic problems, as well as hydrocarbons which may lead to cancer and leukaemia. Both the threat of men's violence and the threat to health remain.

Men's violence to known women, health and bodies

The patterns outlined in the previous sections indicate some of the broad connections between men's violence, bodies and health. These rather generalized connections do not, however, address very directly the specifics of individual men's use of violence to known women, and the responses to that violence. First, we need to consider the social and historical context in which such violence takes place. Social structures, social sentiments, governmental laws, policies and practices all contribute to the constructions of the body in and around men's violence to women.

They all impact upon what is and is not acceptable in the doing and receiving of violence, and so also upon the bodies of those concerned, actually and, significantly, potentially. In the UK there has been a dreadful history of non-intervention against such violence. The Matrimonial Causes Act of 1878 which allowed women to cite cruelty as grounds for divorce only followed on after the Cruelty to Animals Act of 1876. Prior to 1878, the "rule of thumb" had operated whereby husbands were permitted to beat wives with a stick that was not thicker than a thumb. It was only in the late 1980s that police forces began to issue force orders requiring officers to deal with violence to known women as they would with other violent crime.

Then there is the set of institutional arrangements that exist around men and women. Of special importance are the extent of provision of income support to women, independent from men; the policies and practices of the criminal justice system; the availability of both short-term and permanent housing for women and children free from men, including especially refuges and shelters; and the responsiveness of doctors, health professionals and health agencies. The actions of these institutions and agencies, amongst others, materially affect and produce the bodies of both men and women. In some cases, by their action or inaction, they materially determine whether men continue using violence or women continue to live; these are literally matters of life and death.

Particular acts of violence by men do not usually occur in isolation; more likely there are several interrelated violences and abuses. Men's violence to women is not just a cause of problems or of stressful situations; it *is* the problem (Hanmer, Hearn and Bruce, 1992, p. 42; Hanmer and Hearn, 1998). Violence is not just a stressful social variable; it pervades, infuses and reproduces bodies, gendered bodies. Violence is not a thing that is affected or even determined by gender; rather it is the very constructions of both violence and gender that are formed in relation to each other. Men's doing of violence involves actions on and to the body of the person receiving the violence, in this case the woman or women. In that way the man contributes to the shaping of the woman's body and the women's health – sometimes in producing specific damage and alteration to the body, more or less lasting; sometimes by affecting how the woman holds her body or presents herself or is more or less comfortable or confident in her body. The woman may thus modify her own body in responding, perhaps pre-emptively, to the man's violence. This is not just a matter of how violence is coped with, but the very construction of bodies through the impact of other bodies, including through violence. Coping with violence does not mean accepting violence; it refers to what people do, including action to reduce the likelihood of the reoccurrence of the problem, through, say, changing the appearance of their body or removing themselves from the situation. Thus while violence can be understood as disrupting or challenging what is considered to be the "normal body," it also simultaneously and none too subtly forms the bodies.

At the same time, in men's embodied use of violence the man constitutes himself and his body. Men's bodies become a form of capital, part physical, part cultural, in their performance or potential performance of violence. Interestingly, while men's violence is clearly bad for women's health in the form of social, psychological and physical damage, in a very different way it is also not good for men's well-being. Men who use violence to known women are likely to be more depressed, less assertive and less happy (Hotaling and Sugarman, 1986; Mauiro *et al.*, 1988). A man's use of violence is also partly a matter of his sense of self, of who he is, of what he can or is able to do, his identity. However, it is also something more material still in the very construction, reproduction and elaboration of a particular kind of body, that is called "male" or "masculine."

Men's accountings for and recognitions of particular actions as violence and non-recognition of others as such are themselves part of the reproduction (or not) of such actions, and thus themselves as particular kinds of men – they are in effect material, bodily discourses. For example, men who use violence to women generally use a very limited definition of what is counted as violence in the first place. Their understanding of their own "violence to women" is usually restricted to physical violence that leads to visible or lasting damage, or that is delivered by the arm, elbow, hand, head, knee or leg and that involves pronounced force (and so often excludes pushing, shoving, blocking, holding, even throwing), or that leads to arrest.   Such definitions are embodied and themselves create bodily effects, through denial, minimization, avoidance and so on.

Additionally, "sexual (sexual) violence"[16] and violence to children are rarely talked about by men as violence to known women. Men generally separate violence from sex/sexuality. For most men, what is usually called "sexual violence," including pornography, is not included in accounts of violence to known women. Apart from legal rape following arrest and charging, men rarely define coercive sex and pressurized sex as violence. While some men do acknowledge that children witnessing violence to women, usually the children's mothers, is relevant, men do not usually see this as part of their violence. Violence to women and violence to children seem generally to be seen by men as unconnected. This may be reinforced by the way agency responses to child abuse are separated, through the child protection system, from those to violence to women. No men described their violence to children and young people as a form of violence to women.

Sometimes definitions and ways of talking about violence involve very complicated, contorted logic on the man's part. For example, one man explained:

> I wasn't violent, but she used to do my head in that much. I picked her up twice and threw her against the wall, and said "Just leave it." That's the only violence I've put towards her. I've never struck a woman, never, and I never will. ... When I held her I did bruise her somewhere on the shoulder, and she tried making out that I'd punched her, but I never did. I never to this day touched a woman.

Thus in this account, "throwing against a wall," "holding," "bruising" do not appear to be constructed as violence; while "striking," "punching" and "touching" do. Men's generally narrower definitions of violence are partly a product of men's generally structurally dominant social position and partly a consequence of the particular form of the particular social relationship with the woman in question. Namings and definitions of violence are themselves a social rather than a natural process that in turn contributes to the making of both men's and women's bodies in definite material ways. Men's definitions of violence thus implicate the bodies of the man and the woman in different ways.

Similar points can be made on the forms of accounting that men give for their violence to women. In some accounts, violence is denied or almost denied; the violence may be described as "just happening" or as "50/50" or as having almost a life of its own without any clear reference to the bodies involved. The body figures more clearly in two other common kinds of accounts: first, excuses that present the violence as lying "in wait" *within* the body of the man, and, second, justifications that present the violence as being enacted *by* the man's body *on* the woman's in order to "correct" her behavior. In the first case, men speak of their bodies as containers of violence or potential violence that then cease to contain "it." This is expressed in such terms as:

> I seem to explode.

> It all boils up like a volcano, it's waiting.

> It's like somebody else what's inside me controlling me to do them things, and it hurts, you know. And I keep saying no, and I keep pressing it down, saying, "no, I don't want it to come out in me." Or "leave me alone." You

> know, like as though they were bad dreams and that, and I still think about a lot to do with my childhood. You know, it's like haunting me and I can't get rid of it.

The cause of the violence in these schemes is located elsewhere, in the past, in the actions of others, in drink, drugs, psychiatric illness; the body retains the violence; and that which is elsewhere provides the excuse for the violence. The man accepts the blame but not the responsibility for the violence.

Justifications have the opposite structure: the man accepts responsibility but places blame elsewhere, usually with the woman. With justifications, violence is accounted for by the man in terms of him using a part of his body on the woman to "correct" her behavior, punish her or achieve some other particular end. In this kind of account the man recognizes at least to some extent his agency and also usually explains his violence in the context of the "legitimacy" of his correction of the woman. The man uses (part of) his body to continue (what is to his mind) his "legitimated" control and ownership of the woman and indeed her health and welfare. This kind of accounting thus conforms closely to the practical enactment of patriarchy and patriarchal relations. It is the putting into effect and the reproducing of social and societal structures. It is the doing of patriarchy through the doing of bodies.

The most obvious example of this kind of account is when men refer to women's "infidelity," known, assumed or alleged, as justification of their violence to them. "Sex" and "sexuality" figure strongly in men's accounts of violence to women, usually as a "justification" for their violence (Hearn, 1996). However, men also justify violence by referring back to all manner of apparently trivial actions, such as not turning the television off. In addition, excuses and justifications can sometimes be used side by side with each other despite their different "logics."

A few men gave confessional accounts of their violence, explaining in some detail their clear intention to harm and taking full responsibility and blame. For example, one man accepted that his violence was not justified, explaining quite precisely:

> So, basically, I grabbed hold of her and thumped her one. But it's like the thing was, I thumped her hard enough to hurt her, but not hard enough to knock her down, because I didn't want to hurt the baby. I knew what I was doing.

However, even with such accounts, what remains rare is attention to the body and health of the woman, beyond her being constructed as the receiver of the man's violence. Moreover, by no means all confessions were remorseful. Some men were able to articulate their intention to dominate without remorse:

> I've always liked to dominate, get everything my own way.

> I think *basically, it's power.* I have had enough of this argument, I have had enough of this argument, I want to stop it now.

In practice, many accounts are of course much more complex and contradictory: they may include a combination of different kinds of "explanation," sometimes quite inconsistently; they may involve violences to more than one woman or by more than one man; and men who have a long history of violence may in particular develop a greater range, a larger "menu," of possible accounts.

Some idea of the complexity of some men's accounts may be conveyed by the following example from a man who had attended a men's programme and was able to both give "explanations" of his violence, as he had previously seen it, and reflect on those explanations. In his account the body figures in multiple ways, ranging across possession, love, social space, insecurity, oppression, loss, alcohol, jealousy, ownership and control; it provides one particular commentary on the brutality yet subtlety of the relation of health, bodies and men's violences:

> Q. You said you felt you owned her, felt you were in charge.
>
> A. No, I think that is the reason why I felt violent towards her, because I felt that she were a possession of mine, that I owned her. That's why I felt motivated to be violent towards her and not to anyone, because I didn't care about anyone else as much as I cared about her. Like sort of, I love you so much, I'm going to smother you, you know what I mean. That's what it were. And then I were motivated to hit her because I were frightened of her leaving. Through all that period of time, but eventually I were pushing her that much she obviously were going to leave. ...
> My constant promptings instead of just letting her get on with her life. I smothered her. Because I cared that much about her. I know it's a stupid thing to say, but I did. I tried to protect her yet I smothered her. I wouldn't let her have any space of her own, you know. I strangled her. I think that's why I don't feel

violence towards anyone else, I didn't care that much for anyone else.

Q. When you were doing it, was that the way you felt?

A. I felt insecure about things. I know now looking back that the reasons I were doing it were yes, because I were frightened that she were going to run off. But at the time I think I was more possessive of her, you know what I mean. I think it were like a jealousy type of thing. But I were frightened that she were going to go.

Q. So before she did leave you didn't really have anything to base that on?

A. No. Very irrational, oppressed her that much over t'years and I realize that it were my fault, that part of it. ... She did say that, in that last fight we had, she said, "I do love you but I can't stand to be hit any more. I must go." And then she were off. ... I can believe that she were that frightened. ... I mean that night, I were really fired up. I were really motivated – I could have killed her the state I were in.

Q. You can't remember what brought you down from that?

A. No, I can't remember what stopped it. Probably the fact that I were hurting her. I don't know. But I did use alcohol as an excuse, like a vehicle, so that I could do it. To give me an excuse in my own head, saying, "Oh, I've had a drink." But it were an excuse for me to do it that's all. ... But I think it were that sort of raging jealousy like when I'd had alcohol let me motivate meself to do these things. I'm quite convinced, I know it sounds daft, but the reason that I hit her was because I cared more about her than anyone else. And I were frightened of losing her, but I wanted to possess and control her you know in a strange kind of way.

Q. You wanted to be in charge.

A. Yes, not love at all. Well I loved her, but I wanted to own her, you know. I were that worried that she were going to leave me. It was like a self-fulfilling prophecy, if you tell someone often enough they'll do it anyway, because if they're getting blamed for it they might as well do it.

Finally, the ways men talk of violence often interconnect closely with those used by the agency staff with whom they have had the closest contact.

Interestingly, both men and agency personnel may see the men as exceptional to some supposed "other men" who are violent to women. For example, men with their prime contact with the probation service tend to define themselves as criminals, and as such are felt to be different from men who "beat up women"; often the probation officers who work with them also do not focus primarily on their violence to women but on other problems. For men in men's programmes, their sense of individual intention is often much greater. This matches to some extent the constructions of men and men's violence promoted by the leaders of such programmes. For them the violence is both endemic and liable to be changed if attended to seriously enough. Definitions of what counts as violence and how violence is explained and understood are equally important for agency policy development, and this in turn produces options for women and men, including their bodily health, livelihood and survival. After all, the agencies in contact with men are themselves generally dominated by men, and their understandings of violence are themselves also highly gendered.

Conclusion

In this chapter I have analyzed some of the connections between health, bodies, and men's violence. Despite their neglect, the connections are many and various, obvious and subtle. This is a way of reappraising often separated analyses, political, academic or policy-oriented, and of recognizing the interconnectedness of experiences through time. While some of this discussion may apply to violence in general, the focus on men and violence is important, partly because of the vast scale of men's violence from local to world arenas, partly because of men's occupational and cultural specialization in violence, and partly because of the intense associations of men, masculinities (including "normal" and "hegemonic" masculinities) and violences, albeit in diverse and fractured embodiments.

Relations of health and violence are embodied; they operate through bodies; and they act in and through bodies. Violence is enacted by bodies, upon bodies, and in so doing, reproduces those gendered bodies, gendering, and arguably gender itself. Gender is formed, at least in part, through violence. The approach outlined here is not only theoretical and empirical; it is also personal and political. As such, it is premised on changing men, opposing violence, and reformulating the ways in which violence is researched, analyzed, opposed and ended.

Notes

1. This chapter began life as the paper, "Recent developments in critical studies on men and men's bodies – or trying to talk men's bodies," presented at Kropp og Kjønn, Norges råd for anvendt samfunnsforskning (NORAS), Oslo, June 1990. A further version was given at the British Sociological Association Annual Conference "Health and Society," University of Manchester, March 1991 (see Hearn, 1992). Following empirical research on men's violence to known women (see note 2), a further presentation on these themes was "Men's violence to known women: questions of history, methodology, the body, theory," Nordic Summer University Masculinity Group Seminar, Helsinki University, January 1997. I am grateful to all those who have commented on these papers.

2. ESRC Research Project No. L206 25 2003, "Violence, Abuse and the Stress-coping Process, No. 2" (1991-94) examined 60 men who had been violent to known women (Hearn, 1998). Project No. 1 was a linked but separate project on women's experiences of violence from known men, and was directed by Jalna Hanmer.

3. The term "intermediate zone" is used by Margaret Stacey and Celia Davies (1983) to refer to the social and spatial zone that is ambiguously between or overlapping with the public and private domains. Here the term is used in parallel to refer to overlaps between academic domains.

4. For further discussion of the definition of violence, see Hearn, 1994, 1998.

5. For a discussion of structural violence in relation to men's abuse of children, see Hearn, 1993, and in relation to men's violence to known women, see Hearn, 1998.

6. Ronald Frankenberg (1986, 1988) makes the point that this is a re-neologism, having been used earlier by John Ruskin, Sir Oliver Lodge, and George Bernard Shaw in the late nineteenth century "as the reverse of health in the sense of well-being."

7. Elliot, 1972 is cited in Sjöö and Mor, 1991, p. 421. They also cite (p. 475) *New Perspectives: Journal of the World Peace Council*, 1985 that 20 million people had been killed directly in 150 wars since the end of World War II.

8. The relationship between the sociology of health and illness and medical sociology is complex, itself drawing on the distinction between "the body" and "inter-vention on the body."

9. This is not to diminish the major research and scholarship on violence, but rather to note the lack of recognition within sociology, including in the teaching of sociology.

10. Because of these kinds of conclusions, it may be helpful to distinguish frag mentations of material bases and social practices, including those in and of patriarchies, and men, masculinities, and types of men; and fracturings in/of experience (Hearn, 1992, p. 22).

11. The "classic" text from the male liberationist stance is Hal Goldberg's (1976)

The Hazards of Being Male. A more recent and informative contribution is from Harrison, Chin and Ficarrotto (1989).

12. I am thinking of the diverse focus on the heart from male liberationist perpectives, government preventative health policy, and employers' schemes. For those interested in the individualistic political implications of some of these approaches see the U.S. magazine *Men's Health.* This magazine is now published in several European editions, including those in Finland and the U.K. The theme of men's health is also prominent in consumerist men's magazine's, such as *Gentleman's Quarterly (GQ)* and *Arena.*

13. More general discussion of unities and differences between men and between masculinities are to be found in Hearn and Collinson, 1993.

14. See Paul Virilio's discussion on "chrono-politics and the distribution of time" (Virilio and Lotringer, 1984, pp. 116-17, cited in Sjöö and Mor, 1991, p. 22).

15. This is in no way whatsoever to diminish the importance of direct physical violence; it is to argue that violence is a more widespread set of phenomena than that.

16. The term "sexual violence" is conventionally used to refer to violence that is sexualized or is sexual in meaning to at least one of the parties or is directed against parts of the body that are defined as sexual. However, Kelly (1988) argues that the term is more appropriately used as a general term to cover all forms of abuse, coercion and force that women experience from men. Following this approach, the term "sexual (sexual) violence" refers to those forms or aspects of sexual violence that are overtly sexualized.

References

Brende, Joel and Parson, Erwin (1985) *Vietnam Veterans: The Road to Recovery.* Plenum: New York.

Briscoe, M. E. (1989) "Sex differences in mental health," *Update,* 1 November, pp. 834-9.

Brittan, Arthur (1989) *Masculinity and Power.* Oxford: Blackwell.

Carrigan, Tim, Connell, R. W. and Lee, John (1985) "Toward a new sociology of masculinity," *Theory and Society,* 14 (5), pp. 551-604.

Connell, R. W. (1983) *Which Way is Up?* Sydney: Allen and Unwin.

Connell, R. W. (1987) *Gender and Power.* Cambridge: Polity Press.

Connell, R. W. (1995) *Masculinities.* Cambridge: Polity Press.

Coward, Rosalind (1984) *Female Desire.* London: Collins/Paladin.

Dankwort, Jürgen (1992-93) "Violence against women: varying perceptions and intervention practices with woman abusers," *Intervention* (Quebec), No. 92, pp. 34-49.

Deacon, Alan, with Hulse, Michelle and Stubbs, Paul (1997) *Global Social Policy.* London: Sage.

Deleuze, Gilles (1981) *Francis Bacon, Logique de la Sensation.* Paris: Eds. de les difference.

Dobash, Rebecca Emerson and Dobash, Russell (1992) *Women, Violence and Social Change.* London: Routledge.

Ehrenreich, Barbara (1983) *The Hearts of Men.* London: Pluto Press.

Elliot, Gil (1972) *The 20th Century Book of the Dead.* New York: Charles Schribner's & Sons.

Frank, Arthur M. (1990) "Bringing bodies back in: a decade review," *Theory, Culture and Society,* 7, pp. 131-62.

Frankenberg, Ronald (1986) "Sickness as cultural performance: drama, trajectory, and pilgrimage. Root metaphors and the making of social disease," *International Journal of Health Services,* 16 (4), pp. 603-26.

Frankenberg, Ronald (1988) "'Your time or mine?' An anthropological view of the tragic temporal contradictions of biomedical practice," *International Journal of Health Services,* 18 (1), pp. 11-34.

Franklin, Clyde, II (1987) "The institutional decimation of black men," in Brod, Harry (ed.), *The Making of Masculinities, The New Men's Studies.* London: Allen and Unwin.

Ganley, Anne (1981) *Court Mandated Counselling for Men who Batter.* Washington, D.C.: Centre for Women's Policy Studies.

Gelles, Richard J. and Conte, Jon R. (1990) "Domestic violence and sexual abuse of children: a review of research in the eighties," *Journal of Marriage and the Family,* 52, November, pp. 1045-58.

Goldberg, Hal (1976) *The Hazards of Being Male.* Plainview, New York: Nash.

Gondolf, Edward W. (1985) *Men who Batter.* Holmes Beach, FL: Learning Publications.

Gondolf, Edward W. and Russell, David (1986) "The case against anger control treatment programs for batterers," *Response,* 9 (3), pp. 2-5.

Hanmer, Jalna and Hearn, Jeff (1998) "Gender and Welfare Research," in Williams, Fiona, Popay, Jennie and Oakley, Ann (eds), *(Re-)Forming Welfare Research.* London: UCL Press.

Hanmer, Jalna and Saunders, Sheila (1984) *Well Founded Fear.* London: Hutchinson.

Hanmer, Jalna, Hearn, Jeff and Bruce, Errollyn (1992) *Gender and the Management of Personal Welfare,* produced for E.S.R.C. "Management of Personal Welfare," Gender Theme. Mimeo. University of Bradford, Bradford: Research Unit on Violence, Abuse and Gender.

Harrison, James, Chin, James and Ficarrotto, Thomas (1989) "Warning: masculinity may be dangerous to your health," in Kimmel, Michael and Messner, Michael (eds), *Men's Lives.* New York: Macmillan.

Hearn, Jeff (1987) *The Gender of Oppression. Men, Masculinity and the Critique of Marxism.* Brighton: Wheatsheaf; New York: St. Martin's.

Hearn, Jeff (1988) "Child abuse: violences and sexualities towards young people," *Sociology,* 23 (4), pp. 531-44.

Hearn, Jeff (1992) *Men in the Public Eye. The Construction and Deconstruction of Public Men and Public Patriarchies*. London and New York: Routledge.

Hearn, Jeff (1993) "'Child abuse' and men's violence," in the Violence Against Children Study Group, *Taking Child Abuse Seriously*. London: Routledge.

Hearn, Jeff (1994) "The organization(s) of violence," *Human Relations*, 47 (6), pp. 731-54.

Hearn, Jeff (1996) "Heteroseksuaalinen väkivalta lähipiirin naisia kohtaan. Sukupuolistunut väkivalta miesten kertomuksissa," *Janus* (Journal for Social Policy and Social Work Research) (Finland), 4 (1), pp. 39-55.

Hearn, Jeff (1998) *The Violences of Men*. London: Sage.

Hearn, Jeff (forthcoming) "A crisis in masculinity, or new agendas for men?," in Walby, Sylvia (ed.), *New Agendas for Women*. London: Macmillan.

Hearn, Jeff and Collinson, David (1993) "Unities and differences between men and between masculinities," in Brod, Harry and Kaufman, Michael (eds), *Theorizing Masculinities*. Newbury Park, CA: Sage.

Hearn, Jeff, and Parkin, Wendy (1995) *"Sex" at "Work." The Power and Paradox of Organisation Sexuality*. Hemel Hempstead: Harvester Wheatsheaf/Prentice Hall; New York: St. Martin's.

Horley, Sandra (1990) "Responding to male violence against women," *Probation Journal*, December, pp. 166-70.

Hotaling, G. T. and Sugarman, D. B. (1986) "An analysis of risk markers in husband to wife violence," *Violence and Victims*, 1, pp. 101-24.

Jackson, David (1990) *Unmasking Masculinity. A Critical Autobiography*. London and Boston: Unwin Hyman.

Kelly, Liz (1988) *Surviving Sexual Violence*. Cambridge: Polity Press.

Klein, Alan (1993) *Little Big Men*. New York: State University of New York Press.

Lash, Scott (1984) "Genealogy and the body: Foucault/Deleuze/Nietzsche," *Theory, Culture and Society*, 2 (2), pp. 1-18.

Lehman, Peter (1988) "In the realm of the senses: desire, power and the representation of the male body," *Genders*, 1 (2), pp. 91-110.

Mauiro, R. D., Cahn, T. S., Vitaliano, P. P., Wagner, B. C. and Zegree, J. B. (1988) "Anger, hostility and depression in domestically violent versus generally assaultive men and nonviolent control subjects," *Journal of Consulting and Clinical Psychology*, 56, pp. 17-23.

Messner, Michael (1995) *Power at Play*. Boston: Beacon.

New Perspectives: Journal of the World Peace Council, Helsinki (1985), 15 (4), p. 16.

Nussbaum, Martha (1992) "Justice for women!," *The New York Review of Books*, 8 October, pp. 43-8.

Ramazanoglu, Caroline (1987) "Sexual violence in academic life or you can keep a good woman down," in Hanmer, Jalna and Maynard, Mary (eds), *Women, Violence and Social Control*. London: Macmillan.

Sayce, Liz (1991) "Mental stress at the battle front," *The Times*, 1 February, p. 11.

Sen, Amartya (1990) "More than 100 million women are missing," *The New York Review of Books*, 29 December.

Sjöö, Monica and Mor, Barbara (1991) *The Great Cosmic Mother. Rediscovering the Religion of the Earth* (first published 1987). New York: Harper Collins.

Stacey, Margaret, and Davies, Celia (1983) *Division of Labour in Child Health Care. Final Report to the S.S.R.C.* Mimeo. Coventry: University of Warwick.

Turner, Bryan (1984) *The Body and Society. Explorations in Social Theory*. Oxford and New York: Blackwell.

Virilio, Paul and Lotringer, Sylvere (1984) *Pure War*, trans. Mark Polizotti. Semiotext(e), Foreign Agents Series. New York: Columbia University Press.

Chapter 10

Male Ways of Giving Birth

KLAUS THEWELEIT

The idea of changing humans into humans by changing working conditions into human conditions was the most influential idea about labor in the last 150 years. The capitalist "idea" of labor that makes people work to gain their livelihood (and lets somebody else gain some bigger profit out of that work he doesn't do by himself) was not so much an idea, as a very successful way of organizing working conditions. As an idea it was in a defensive position. In practical terms it was an aggressive war-winner of high supremacy.

I am talking about work, because to talk about war, means to talk about ways of working: productions, destructions, male ways of working, female ways of working, ways of constructing a reality, consuming a reality, destroying a reality.

Work has three major aspects of producing: it produces a product that can be sold and used; it produces the worker as a product (by the structure of the working conditions), and it produces social relations. The working place is (besides the dwelling place) the most important producer of social relations in a given society. Work produces "the reality," different ways of human realities.

This beautiful idea of work has seldom been criticized for being a male idea. The female production – giving birth to children and taking care of them, doing housework – appeared under the term of being "reproductions" when thinking about productivity. Even many feminist women use the term "reproduction" for the sort of labor their mothers did. The term "reproduction" is meant to be nearer to "natural processes": the human species is "reproducing" itself like the ants and plants do following the wise and unthinkable plans of The Creation. Though many mothers probably would love their work to be perceived like that, to others it is an act of deep injustice not to recognize human labor, acts of "producing human reality," in the daily productions of mothering.

The term "reproduction," so seemingly innocent, continues to maintain the gender gap, continues to deepen it. I wish it could be erased completely and left to the ants. But it is kept alive by trade unions, governments, house fathers, mothers themselves, and ahead of them all, the industries producing the "real" GDP. Mothering doesn't contribute to the GDP. That's how it is. But war does. War is more reasonable in terms of production than mothering.

The term "reproduction" is upheld even in a text which, above all others, offers a fundamental criticism of the terms of production and labor as they are used in the Western world. "My life has been shaped by a love-affair with reason," Sara Ruddick opens her book on *Maternal Thinking*.[1] She describes that love affair as an affair that had coupled her to a male being: studying philosophy became a love affair with Him. He, Reason, gave her strength to avoid the humdrum world of wives and mothers and to escape from her own world of haunted dreams and weird feelings, to escape from *herself* (= femininity), she says.

It didn't last, that love affair, as it could have lasted. She became a professor, but she also married a man and became a mother. Becoming a mother meant entering a different, new world, not ruled by *his* rules. That meant completely different forms of labor from those she was used to before. But she discovered that these forms of labor had to do with reason as well. She had to solve problems every single day. Not "philosophical" problems, but problems with the handling of the children; with neighbor's children, with child care places, doctors, schools. Chatting all day long with other women. What kind of talk was it? A reasonable one? What a surprise it was beginning to work as a mother: only mothers know that most of a mother's work is done publicly – in front of the controlling eyes of teachers, doctors, other officials, bank people, cashiers, neighbors, friends, policemen, passengers. "Housework"?

She realized the ambivalence of a mother's power: Her "powerful presence (for the child) becomes powerless in front of their father, a teacher, a welfare worker, doctor, judge, landlord – the world" (p. 36). What can a mother do to make this powerless power understandable, *acceptable* to her own children? Especially to daughters, who are forced into hatred against their mothers when they discover the powerlessness of their own sex in them?

Her plain answer to problems such as these was: "Certainly as a mother I had found myself thinking." That formed the title of her book, *Maternal Thinking*, with stress on thinking. *Mothers* must think.

But more than that, it's a book about labor. Sara Ruddick, thinking about mothering, finds definitions of human labor that are based neither on the philosophical abstraction of "human productivity" nor on the practice of industrial work/war in Western societies. Her term of labor has grown out of the conditions of women's daily ways of dealing with the things that have to be done. She calls that kind of labor caring labor. There are all kinds of work that mothers have to do in giving life, keeping someone alive, giving shelter, keeping things and people going and growing, in nourishing, helping, teaching, caring for the ability of children in matching an (often) hostile reality. The product of caring labor is not measured in money (though it has, in certain ways, to match market conditions). It is measured in abilities and competencies a human being acquires by a woman's work, when grown up: abilities of being alive, of perception, being able to listen, being efficient and clever in producing things like "peace," dealing with people and their problems without being destructive, inventing rooms and procedures for a caring life.

Sara Ruddick sees the basis of the special female ability for these kinds of labor in a woman's capacity of giving birth to a new human being. "Whatever the state of technology, a man engages in no activity that can match, in labor, a woman's pregnancy, with its anxieties, discomfort, intrusive testing, painful delivery, and unique excitements and pleasures." That is the basis of the ability for caring labor in the bodies of humans. But it is not its precondition, nor does one necessarily have to deliver a child-birth in order to enter the realm of "caring labor."

Out of that term a whole system of living and thinking is developed. A "system": in a way Sara Ruddick has continued her love affair with reason. That, by the way, is an important characteristic of "caring labor": you don't drop what you once loved. But you can change the relationship. She even changed the gender of her beloved *one* and made a sort of woman out of Reason: caring labor is a way of living, of thinking, a way of producing reality that (though it can be or perhaps even has to be militant) disconnects itself from making war, disconnects itself from the common male ways of destruction, disconnects itself from the common (male) way of linking labor to a sort of productivity that expresses its worth or worthlessness only in money relations of economic victory or defeat.

Everybody, women, children and men, are capable of maternal thinking and caring labor, when they do some work in that field. After a while they will have learned to distinguish between ways of making things and people grow, or making them die. You can add life to things and people and you can take it away from them. It's not a "natural gift" to make the things you touch flourish or wither. It's the sort of labor you do to them. It's a very far-reaching term, if you *want* to use it like that. It's not difficult at all, for example, to tell a caring architecture from a destroying architecture. Living conditions would change rapidly if they were put under the views and procedures of caring labor. And it's easy to see that no economy would have to suffer breakdowns by "caring labor" at work. Only the world of profit *distribution* would have to suffer.

It's a vivifying labor, producing labor feelings that transform the bodies of the women involved into states of being that can serve as models for men's works as well. There is a gender difference not just in terms of biology but in terms of doing different forms of *work*.

I feel that this is a radical new and revolutionary definition of labor. Labor giving life, caring for growth, labor fighting all forms of death-giving, torture, destruction. Sara Ruddick's minimal formula reads: "I aim to identify principles of maternal non-violence that I believe could contribute to collective, public understandings of peacemaking." This time it's not the public talk of war-makers about their being peaceful down to the bottoms of their hearts. It's like a formula modestly hiding what the book, what *maternal thinking*, really does contain.

Male reader, you are not convinced – how could you be? You will laugh: true utopian thinking seldom succeeds in talking you into something. Caring labor and maternal thinking include the knowledge that it is an experience to be practiced that leads to them, not simply believing in an "idea."

Sometimes it turns out to be a fundamental experience. Part of the self-knowledge of my body is the experience of the distance I had to maintain when looking at my wife giving birth to a child; sitting at her bedside, trying to give signs of help which in a way reached her and much more didn't reach her – because she was in a reality too far away and too alien for me to enter: she working, me watching, realizing a kind of labor that threatened to tear her body apart. I could see her body change her "nationality," beginning to live in a country I would never be living in the same way.

It's not difficult to realize that, witnessing a birth as a male. You're witnessing a transubstantiation: a female body, who tortures herself into this new life "child." I think women transform themselves through that labor into beings possessed by a deep-rooted unwillingness to take that life away again. Not only *that* life: a disgust at killing, at taking life away from anybody. I often realize it in women; not only women who had born a child. Call it mysticism; call it biology.

I hadn't realized it in my body before, because it probably hadn't been there with certainty: the feeling that it is profoundly evil to take lives away from anybody – war or no war – by any kind of violence. It began growing in that moment and continued growing in later moments related to work with children. That was a strange discovery for someone who had believed in the possibility of "just wars" up to then. The parts of my body armor that had "seen" the world as something you could "free" by the use of weapons in "the right way" began to fall.

In a man dealing with children or being engaged in a comparable form of labor, this unwillingness to take life away will take some time to grow and develop, maybe years, until he really can speak of a self-transformation. But it certainly happens. You can realize this change of the self in the growing distance from common male procedures of talking, walking and speech, to the tempo of decision-making, the gestures of hands, the change of that steadily shown wisdom smile, usually covering men's faces, in a changing attitude to male hierarchies (so very, very important to them). You will realize most men's badly developed capacity for listening compared with their wonderfully developed capacity for public talk or for talking things down that are not compatible with their systems: different kinds of labor of the tongues and ears. Hard work to change. The disconnection of "work" from "war" is one of the pre-conditions of this change.

You awake in the middle of the night and you don't know – was it the wheels of a car on the rainy street or the whimper of the baby in the room next door that took you out of your half-doze? You get up to watch, waking up the baby; having to bring a bottle now; learning to say: it's OK, stop complaining. It's food for you as well. You're feeding yourself. You're feeding your thinking.

During the last 18 years I made the strange (and horrifying) discovery that most of the men you meet haven't the slightest possibility of understanding what you are talking about, when talking about "caring labor," unless they have done some work in that field themselves. Not necessarily with a child – it can be with everything you foster and really care for (the clearly felt unwillingness for sharing any longer the pleasures of destruction). The kinds of labor one does really do change the self. The real gender differences, as we feel them to be at work in all our social relations (not only in our love affairs), are connected to the special kinds of labor that individuals do (want to do, are forced to do) in their daily lives.

Giving birth as a form of labor and living has been held in contempt throughout Western history. Sara Ruddick reviews the steps from Plato to today:

> Although we are a species that knows its fatality, in philosophical texts we are "thrown" into the universe somehow, appearing at the earliest when we can talk and read. ... in the dominant view of common sense and Western philosophy, birth is as troubling as sexuality and as psychologically provocative, if not as unhappy, as death. ... Birthing most likely provokes in non-birthing women as well as men envy, awe, and fear of the unknown. But

it is only men who learn that they were excluded at birth from birthing labor. (pp. 191-2)

Western males learned to minimize and fear birthing labor, which should "stand at the center of a maternal history of the flesh." In her great chapter "Histories of Human Flesh" Sara Ruddick develops the perception that men (unlike women) don't have a knowledge of this history and in many cases don't want to have one. In all Western philosophy the roles of natality, sexuality and mortality are diminished. The body was eliminated from philosophical and scientific discourse through practices that alienated bodies from their own feelings.[2] Minimizing women's birthing labor, men got used to claiming for themselves a higher creativity. "Accepting no presuppositions but those they stipulate, they sail away, disown what went before, begin anew as Fathers of themselves" (Ruddick, p. 192). Men are the products of their own labor (not wanting to be born by mothers: giving birth to themselves, from Plato to Goebbels, who called the way of being born by a mother "the wrong way").

Men "spiritually" produce things, which they feel belong to a higher order than the productions of the female body: "Everyone would prefer children such as these to children after the flesh," as Sara Ruddick quotes Plato about "productions of the (male) soul" from the *Symposium*. Men always led this war most aggressively: not hesitating to call their productions children and to place them in competition with the productions of women, giving themselves the crowns of being *the real creators*.

Not to put birth in the place it deserves, not to take it as the basic human labor, has become the fundamental distortion of Western culture and all other male-dominated societies. Disowning the mothers is the basic expropriation. To expropriate women of their labor, men are fighting the fact that it is not God who gives life, but women. To accept birthing labor as the basic labor would mean accepting women in the godly position of life-giving. Most men sternly refuse to do that. You would no longer need a god, if women were recognized in their position as creators. Where creation and reason walk "hand in hand" there is no need for any figures of transcendence. Men lead their wars with "God on their side." And He is War. The term "caring labor" includes the wisdom that human productions happen between at least two people. The *subject* in traditional philosophical discourse (it's a single; a male single) disappears in the lucidity of caring thinking. "I is another one," a relatively emancipated sentence from this discourse, is just halfway to the truth. "Me is the ways I connect with you," would take some steps further in the direction of understanding human persons as consisting of (at least) two. Me is the ways I make you grow.

Sara Ruddick suggests that within two people who are connected in caring labor, new *drives* will appear. To psychoanalysts (still suffering from their last invention in that field, the "death drive") she makes the case for a "drive for truth." This is truth not in a detective's sense, but caring, clearing the air of all those hurting lies, constructions, tricky making and doing, which is the most common form of leading the daily war against people you don't care for (people you give a damn for, a shit).

One of the opposites of care is crime. *Crime* against *care*. Crime doesn't pay, they say. "Crime does not pay in Chicago, especially for Loop parking offenders," Sara Paretsky ironically adds. But in all other respects, crime is the form of war that pays wonderfully. What doesn't pay (until now) is caring labor. Care is not paid for, and socially it is despised. It has no authority.

There is a difference between the mother's and the father's authority in the family, a difference we all know: the father's authority is not earned by caring, Sara Ruddick says. That means it's worth more. That makes it more powerful. It's closer to war. This is one of the bridges children cross for finding their mother's labors contemptible. It's a very seducing offer of male society to them. Children get used to dance across this bridge from one shore to the other, blaming the mother's work when having adventures on father's side (what else do they have two different parents for? Who could blame them?). Walking across this bridge too often means slipping into the common worship of war and crime as paying better than care does.

It *is* the basic crime between the genders to accept as a rule that you need not care for care.

So we have three main complexes of labor. First the sum of all that labor contributing to the GDP (in factories, on farms, in workshops, offices, universities, airports, film studios, and so on). Jean-Luc Godard suggested that it be separated into two great divisions: industries of day and industries of night; he wanted to add all the work that is done in connection with human pleasure and recreation, tourism, show business, prostitution and so on as "industries of night," to a definition of human industrial productivity.[3]

Second, there is the complex of wasting the economic wealth that is accumulated by all the working people of a community (wasting it in military expansions; in astro adventures; in wars; the grand destruction organized between nations to keep their own citizens poor, needy and greedy). It's very hard work, but regularly done in our history at certain intervals. All nations have special workers for that kind of work, simple soldiers, officers, scientists.

A third, definitely different sort of work is the one I have described with Sara Ruddick's words as caring labor, a new kind of human labor.

The first two ways of work are closely linked to wars and to male procedures for organizing life, especially to organizing forms of birth and rebirth that are independent from the bodies of women. Its basis is *the single (male) person* involved in a struggle for permanent increase of power.

The third way is linked to peaceful ways of production. It is fighting war as a means of human productivity. It can be done by women and men. Its basis is the connection of at least two people of whatever gender or age, caring for the growth and welfare of the other.

Many men, stating that *war* has been a major productive force for the development of our societies, are completely right. They don't evade it: they say yes! But they avoid answering the question whether it has to be wars that lead to new inventions, ventures, investments and so on. And they avoid counting the cost of destruction. Instead they look at human lives as something to be converted into the abstractions of victories or defeats, as something they have the right to *use* for their special productivity. Each of them feels himself to exist independently from other people, in powerful I-solation.

The military body is the perfect incarnation of traditional philosophical thought, of the "I." (Being right, Being unable to defeat. Being systematic. Being addicted to work. Being alone. Shining in a body armor suit. Bearing a head on the shoulders for seeing through and winning wars.)

The rocket as the most perfect representation of the military body is the perfect embodiment of Plato today (his contemporary reincarnation). The nuclear load in the rocket's top is a transformation of Plato's brains. The old boys' network of science and black magic never stopped spreading from the days of the Plato/Socrates male couple onward.

Peacemaking (as a form of labor) does not mean sitting there watching the sun rise and set; it is "to identify violence wherever it occurs – in boardrooms, bedrooms, factories, classrooms, and battlefields. Peacemaker: do not turn away from violence but ferret it out, asking in detail who is hurt and how" (Ruddick, p. 137). Diminishing pain is what caring labor is all about.

Some words about the rocket in my pocket

"We'll do the motherhood role – telemetry, tracking, and control – the maintenance," the control officer says. He's speaking about a new communications satellite system that would be resistant against the electromagnetic impulses set free by nuclear explosion. (Not knowing that he's quoting anybody, he is using a central term from Margret Mahler's psychoanalysis of psychotic children: "maintenance" for their hard struggle of finding a state of balance for their disturbed bodies.[4]) Carol Cohn, having spent some time among so-called *defense intellectuals*, learned a lot from them about the explosive abstraction of male birth-giving. From the makers of the first atomic bomb to now it has become usual to handle these weapons as "new-born" babies. The first atomic bomb was saluted as a newly born *boy* (and Edward Teller as the mother who carried the baby – not having needed to provide an egg, only a womb for that task). The bomb is taken as a male progeny. Males give birth to wonderful explosions.

You could take that for just a "code"; for example, when an American general cables his expressions of joy about the first successful testing of that atomic boy to the Secretary of War in the words "I could have heard his screams from here to my farm," and when that Secretary, Henry Stimson, hands that information to Winston Churchill at the Potsdam Conference with the words: "Baby is satisfactorily born." Quoting many similar sentences, Carol Cohn states: "The entire history of the bomb project, in fact, seems permeated with imagery that confounds man's overwhelming technological power to destroy nature with the power to create."[5] The fact itself is undeniable. But I doubt whether a "confounding" or an "imagery" is really operating here. I discover something worse.

I read Carol Cohn quoting William L. Laurence, who witnessed the Trinity test of the first atomic bomb:

> The big boom came about a hundred seconds after the great flash – the first cry of a new-born world ... They clapped their hands as they leaped from the ground – earthbound men symbolizing the birth of a new force." Watching "Fat Man" being assembled the day before it was dropped on Nagasaki, he described seeing the bomb as "being fashioned into a living thing.

Evidently when Laurence reports "the first cry" of the new-born bomb in obvious terms of birth, he is doing it on purpose, applying a provocative and torturing imagery. But looking at his description, we discover that the whole event parallels a real birth process as it factually happened in normal hospitals. "A big boom" and a "great flash" are the first two things a baby has to experience in the old, traditional form of birth: getting her or his head out into a world of noise, s/he was taken by the doctor, banged with a clap of his hand on the ass and the great flash of light outside the womb broke into the baby's eyes. The newly born child began crying and the doctor said everything is OK. Then some people who had been waiting outside (a father, grandparents, friends, relatives) receiving the news leaped from the ground, laughing with joy (like the men in the desert watching the explosion), beginning to admire the newborn world and to hail it: "It's a boy."

Laurence's description of the birth of the bomb contains every little trait of that traditional "real birth." He speaks out the truth of bodies that never really had the chance to experience the difference between being emotionally dead or alive. That doctor's clap on their asses has been followed by a series of treatments that have separated men from their bodily feelings as potentially enjoyable feelings: Laurence is speaking in the language of body-armored soldierly men; the military documents of the Western world consist not only of those of German soldiers, whose writings I have analyzed to some extent.

These are no metaphors. He writes down what he sees, and what he sees is not a bomb exploding. What he *sees* is the birth of a new world. So he salutes the explosion of the bomb in exactly those words and actions a doctor would use, holding the new born baby in his hands. Thousands of soldiers have written like that, describing their newly born being by the eruptions of a machine gun. A machine gun is only a somewhat weaker item to make that miraculous parthenogenesis really happen.

It's not his problem that other people would consider this to be a form of life that comes into living by giving death to everybody. It's a form of life *he* can connect with. A form of life that is not threatening, like the usual forms of life are to him. The form of death he felt himself connected to before it is handed over to all those who will be killed by the bomb. That starts life in the bomb thrower.

The soldiers' way of speaking about total destruction as birth, tells us that they are not sure (in terms of feelings) whether they (their "bodies") are dead or alive. Their real feeling of being converted into living persons by viewing the sensations of real destruction warns us against reading just "metaphors." *This* is the act their body experiences as real.

At the moment of the bomb's explosion in real war they hand their own death over to some hundred thousand (in this case) killed Japanese. It *makes* them feel alive. It's not language. It's not a way of talking: they try to be accurate in the description of *their* bodily transformation: the overwhelming feeling of becoming alive through powers of unthinkable energy: being born by a mother of the greatest strength ever. (By *nature herself.* By the controlled power of nuclear nature herself.) It makes them jump and cry.

"And the gods made love," the old mythologies and religions tell us: the heavens came tumbling down and melted with Mother Earth, and their children stood trembling, hoping for an end to that love before being killed by it. It's not the same here: they, the children, create the godly parents (not only in mythological writings, but really, physically, technically). They *let* this godly parent (it's only one) make love in an atomic mushroom 25 miles high. "Everything is under control now."

He who has the power of destroying everything, he who is *death* and *life* in person, really can claim to have created *himself*. The makers of the bomb are the first men who were really successful in bringing this oldest of male fantasies into material reality. They really proved themselves to have made themselves and to be *alive!* While all the "Living Dead" (we), crawling around in never ending intermingling, polluting the surface of the globe, disappear into the melting pot of that evolving mushroom. Only the *eye* that belongs to the witness of that process belongs to a person who really deserves living.

They, too, are transformed by the experience of witnessing a *birthing labor process*. They just manage to do it better without women. You don't need women when you are in the position of the *creator*. "It was as if we stood at the first day of Creation," Oppenheimer says (to the Taxi Driver).[6] The taxi driver doesn't answer. He is driving Godfather Death, the figure successfully surviving life. That demands some respect.

If the threat of the bomb's destructive power primarily lies in the bodily structure of the men handling it, it would be right to say that they are nuclear power "defense intellectuals" waiting for the moment of the button that will start Life. "The enormous destructive effects of nuclear weapons systems become extensions of the self, rather than threats to it," Carol Cohn states in a beautifully clear perception, using the term Marshall McLuhan used when he "understood" technical media as "extensions of the self."[7] Men are being extended, transformed, reborn through the use of new technical media. The bomb was a new medium, like television; it has become the ultimate medium of change through media: being (re)born without women.

Chatting on a telephone line with Friedrich Kittler,[8] I learn that Mr. Shockley, the famous inventor of the transistor, which revolutionized broadcasting and made us grow new ears, which opened the door to all the *portable* electronic machines we know, in the years following 1944, was the coordinator of the bombing of Japan in the American military staff. He *defense-intellectualized* the Japanese into becoming part of the Western industrial world; helping them raise kamikaze kids playing with kamikaze machines as adults. Adults, supplying the world with transistor radios and all these beautiful electronic machines that at this moment are busy taking over the task of educating the children of Western (and soon Eastern) parents.

Perhaps it's too impossible to imagine: that there are human beings for whom *real life* begins at the moment which for "us" would be the moment of the biggest thinkable (or "unthinkable") destruction. But probably there have been such moments, and "we" and "they" have been just the same or similar persons. We are living on that thin line every second of our lives. "Powder barrel" was the old term for it. But it's wrong to call it a powder barrel. We should call it a vivifying miracle machine. The bomb's womb will give life to a world that previously was dead.

Or previously was uneducated, childish, staggering toddler-like through the oriental universe, as we hear General Westmoreland eloquently speaking in his *Talking Vietnam Blues*: Life is cheap, life is not important in the "Orient," we hear him say. They are not really born down there. The Vietnam War somehow was dealing with a child, he says, a child crawling around, trying its first steps.[9] The general opened his mouth, a mouth with a cap on top – and He was War.

What was he doing there? Obviously he was caring for the later life, the life to come for those half-born Oriental people, while bombing as if they had living rooms.

Giving birth to *new realities* (transforming oneself from a child into an adult) by killing something is a standard beloved by war books, male biographies, movies, warrior diaries or interviews. We find a very sophisticated version in Tim O'Brien's Vietnam novel *What They Carried*. A group of people, carrying names from the PR-office of War Himself – Curt Lemon, Rat Kiley, Mitchell Sanders, Dave Jensen and so on – momentarily waiting at the Gates of Eden to bomb some Arabian baby countries into adulthood are busy searching for what O'Brien calls A True War Story. If you have found your True War Story, O'Brien suggests, you have taken an important step in not having lost your war. One of the True War Stories O'Brien tells is about Curt Lemon, who stepped on a booby-trapped 105 round, while he was playing catch with Rat Kiley. He is blown up into a tree. The trees are thick and it takes nearly an hour to get the parts of his body down to have him buried somehow. One of the men fishing for Curt Lemon's limbs had been singing *Lemon tree*. "A true war story, if truly told, makes the stomach believe."[10]

Male ways of giving birth always involve the stomach. What does your stomach say, listening to the Real Story that follows? "This one does it for me. I've told it before – many times, many versions – but here's what actually happened." Thus O'Brien begins, sticking the American proof of Truth to his story. The Dead Lemon Platoon, marching through the mountains, comes across a bay VC water buffalo. They get a rope around it and lead it along to a deserted village, where they sit up for the night.

After supper Rat Kiley went over and stroked its nose. He opened up a can of C rations, pork and beans, but the baby buffalo wasn't interested. Rat shrugged. He stepped back and shot it through the right front knee. The animal did not make a sound. It went down hard, then got up again, and Rat took careful aim [it's a great piece of careful labor we are going to get now] and shot off an ear. He shot it in the hind quarters and in the little hump at its back. He shot it twice in the flanks. It wasn't to kill; it was to hurt. He put the riffle muzzle up against the mouth and shot the mouth away. Nobody said much. The whole platoon stood there watching, feeling all kinds of things, but there wasn't a great deal of pity for the baby water buffalo. Curt Lemon was dead. Rat Kiley had lost his best friend in the world. Later in the week he would write a long personal letter to the guy's sister, who would not write back [see, who does the caring?], but for now it was a question of pain. He shot off the tail. He shot away chunks of meat below the ribs. All around us there was the smell of smoke and filth and deep greenery, and the evening was humid and very hot [... jungle fever ... trance-like state ... remember?]. Rat went to automatic. He shot randomly, almost casually, quick little spurts in the belly and butt. Then he reloaded, squatted down, and shot it in the left front knee. Again the animal fell hard and tried to get up, but this time it couldn't quite make it. It wobbled and went down sideways. Rat shot it in the nose. He bent forward and whispered something, as if talking to a pet, then he shot it in the throat. All the while the baby [the baby the baby the baby] buffalo was silent, or almost silent, just a light bubbling sound where the nose had been. It lay very still. Nothing moved except the eyes, which were enormous, the pupils shiny black and dumb.
Rat Kiley was crying. He tried to say something, but then cradled his rifle and went off by himself.

It's not necessary to say anything about the elaborated anti-femininity of this narration. O'Brien is too clever to have a woman killed openly (as it is done in comparable Nazi war literature). He's content with giving it to a "sister," who doesn't write back and a baby and a pet, then hugging his rifle and bringing it to its cradle – that's clear and ugly enough in all its well-done distortion.

The point still to make is the birth. The defense non-intellectuals have been standing there watching (the sun going down):

For a time no one spoke. We had witnessed something essential, something brand-new and profound, a piece of the world so startling there was not yet a name for it. Somebody kicked the baby buffalo. [Don't think it's a dream.]
It was still alive, though just barely, just in the eyes. "Amazing," Dave Jensen said. "My whole life, I never seen anything like it."
"Never?" "Not hardly. Not once."

Some of them dump the buffalo in the village well. Then they sit waiting for Rat to get himself together.

> "Amazing," Dave Jensen kept saying. "A new wrinkle. I never seen it before." Mitchell Sanders took out his yo-yo. "Well, that's Nam," he said. "Garden of Evil. Over here, man, every sin's real fresh and original."

They're men before The Fall, living in paradise, a life fresh and original. And we may leave the book, enriched by another True Version of the Creation Story. It says: Coming out and getting clear is done by pulling the trigger. The New Reality appears in a sea of blood when something beautiful dies.

> "When your heart's on fire, you must realize, Smoke gets in your Eyes," the transistor radio says. It had belonged to Curt Lemon and is still alive [but that's the version of an older war, long forgotten ... forget it]. "When a loving flame dies, you must realize ..."

The smoke of a male giving birth. Playing with the vivification buttons in these vivification games are *men*, not women. O'Brien makes an extra effort not to have that point mistaken. He invents a woman sometimes coming up to him when he has finished lecturing on publicity tours: "Usually it's an older woman of kindly temperament and humane politics." She doesn't like war stories, but this one she liked, she usually says.

> I won't say it but I'll think it. I'll picture Rat Kiley's face, his grief, and I'll think, You dumb cooze.
> Because she wasn't listening. It wasn't a war story. It was a love story.

So the "Make Love Not War" button ends its life in a True War Story: in Tim O'Brien's Vietnamerican male paradise it reads: Making War *Is* Love. ("A Desire named Rat," Baby.)

   "Women are not better than men, they are just different." OK, but even if millions of women would take their egalitarian rights in insisting on "not being better" than anything else under the sun, I would continue by saying: be as bad as you want to be; you will not manage to be half as dangerous as men have been in millions of moments in the past or present. Is it really worthwhile to become *just as good* as they are?

   The great event of giving birth to Death Himself – is this a thinkable aim for women? I would doubt that capacity in women. At least I never heard of or never read about a woman speaking like that. It's another form of *male genius* you will not find among non-males. The supremacy of the male gender in giving birth to Death is unmatched and will remain unmatched. There will be no female geniuses in that field – probably; but as predictions often turn out to be inaccurate, I better take that sentence back.

There is no limit for anybody in her struggle to become everything. We cannot really *hear* the sound of The Shape of Death To Come before that record has been recorded. (Under the subtitle of: Great White Music. Unknown to the Future). (Or well known to the future?) But I would sure doubt the band having a girl on drums just then.

Notes

1. Sara Ruddick, *Mütterliches Denken* (translation of *Maternal Thinking*) (Frankfurt a.M., 1993).
2. I tried to describe certain kinds of bodies in *Male Fantasies*, especially in Vol. two.
3. Jean-Luc Godard, Einführung in die wahre Geschichte des Kinos (München/Wien, 1981).
4. Margret S. Mahler, Fred Pine and Anni Bergman, *Die psychische Geburt des Menschen. Symbiose und Individuation* (Frankfurt a.M., 1978).
5. Carol Cohn, "Sex and Death in the Rational World of Defense Intellectuals," *Signs*, 12 (4) (1987).
6. Robert Oppenheimer.
7. Marshall McLuhan, *Die magischen Kanäle* (Düsseldorf/Wien, 1968) (translation of *Understanding Media. The extensions of man*, London, 1964); *The Medium is the Massage* (New York, 1967).
8. Friedrich Kittler, *Gramophone, Film, Typewriter* (*Aufschreibesysteme 1800/1900*, 1985) (München, 1986).
9. These are the words Westmoreland uses in *Hearts and Minds* ....
10. Tim O'Brien, *The things they carried. A work of fiction* (Boston, 1990).

Chapter 11

The Psychodynamics of Shame in the Autobiographies of Modern Finnish Men

JUHA SILTALA

Shame imbricated in cultural forms

This article is based upon my analysis of 55 autobiographies from a sample of 350 that were collected in the writing competition "Hurray for man!" held during 1993 by the Council for Equality in the Ministry of Social Affairs and Health (TANE).[1] The sample is not statistically representative, but it allows some observations on the cultural regulation of self-feeling that was common to almost all participants. In spite of the optimistic title of the competition, the resulting stories described a man's life mainly as a series of losses and anxieties and as a continual battle to maintain one's self-esteem.[2] It has been suggested that participants in an autobiographical competition will naturally be self-absorbed losers – healthy and lucky Finnish men do not bother entering them, because they are busy playing ice hockey or repairing their houses. But my view is that these autobiographies are descriptions of common men in crisis, not of uncommon anti-men.

This view may be seen as an insult by those who believe that people, especially men, are born ready-made and that life in general flows without frictions. But a psychoanalytically oriented researcher must recognize that the same mental processes are at work both in loosers and in winners – the difference is rather gradual, not qualitative. Everybody is shattered sooner or later, if they receive enough unpredictable blows. An adult living in a world populated by different personalities with their different interests can regress to earlier positions, where the world is conceived as totalizing, undifferentiated moods and dealt with by being split into good and bad parts.[3]

Old and young, educated and uneducated, employed and unemployed are ruled by shame in these autobiographies. Dependence fills the writers with overwhelming shame, because it reminds them of their position as a helpless child, a passive victim at the mercy of powers beyond their control. Apparently few men can trust in an accepting mutuality. Is this due to unresponsive child-rearing practices or economic struggle for survival – or both, fuelling each other?

The ethos of achievement is the dominant cultural model, which makes diffuse shame manageable. This agrarian ethos adapts itself to the competition between individuals in the labor market, where both social rise and social fall are accounted for by reference to individual characteristics.[4] Large social realities are passed over and replaced by personal traits. Social competence is transformed into inherited manhood. A man's honor is experienced as physical potency, as being an agent – not a victim. Shame, on the other hand, is equivalent to the loss of one's psychological borders and one's exposure to the eyes of others as a passive victim. Shame destroys self-esteem from within.

According to Sylvan Tomkins and Malcolm Pines, shame is experienced, phenomenologically, as a wish to sink beneath the earth and relinquish one's identity. Shame affects one's whole self, whereas guilt is connected just with certain deeds or thoughts. An ashamed man cannot reconcile his life to that of others. The Finnish psychoanalysts Eero Rechardt and Pentti Ikonen have interpreted shame as an auto-immune reaction fuelled by the death drive. Its purpose is to enable the person to retreat from contacts that do not affirm one's existence by accepting mutuality and "state sharing" (Daniel Stern's concept).[5]

The origins of narcissistic vulnerability

According to classical psychoanalysis the mother should affirm a boy's basic trust and the father should guarantee his access to the world outside dyadic relations. In the world of well-developed, individualized people "dyadic" closeness can be tolerated without fear of re-engulfment.

In our stories very few homes have fulfilled their duty in guaranteeing basic trust and a feeling of oneself as a separate, worthy personality. But the parents had hardly any other choice. A mother overburdened by work and too often left alone to care for children is obliged to be strong and is thus remembered as a phallic figure.[6] An emotionally isolated mother can use her son as her means of achieving independent life vicariously without separating him psychologically from her. Trapped in her own difficulties, she is unable to "vitalize" the world outside the dyadic relationship.[7] I do not judge the unlucky mother as guilty: she is simply transferring her own sensitivities onto the children, because she has no place for her own wishes.

Christopher Bollas defines the power of the early caretaker as the power of defining the quality of interaction and the image of the world as either accepting or rejecting. A mother who has only bad experiences cannot animate the world as being hopeful.[8]

Attachment patterns are inherited from generation to generation: can one trust others or expect caretaking? The outside world is experienced through these patterns, especially when one is shattered.[9] Very many men in my sample had been mired in the sufferings of their parents.[10] They had mentally retained their parents or violently broken their ties with the home. Both solutions can perpetuate early subject-object-affect configurations. Inner dialogues from childhood are repeated beneath the adult cover.

For example Ilari, a journalist in his forties, identified even with his mother's broken leg. The mother had been abandoned by her husband and filled the room with her groans. Her pain left no room for the growing boy's feelings. "My mother lies on the couch like a huge volcano of suffering. The abyss poured out the smoke of suffering ceaselessly. Sometimes the volcano erupted as crying and roaring." Ilari grasped at psychoanalysis to loosen his ties with his mother. Ilari himself had worried about everything in order to guarantee the mental presence of the worried mother.[11] The suffering shored up his sense of being.

Fathers in these stories are mentally absent: either they are workaholics or violent alcoholics. They show their best characteristics outside the home, their worst among their families. Such fathers cannot be used as male role models, especially if the mother and the boy have excluded him from their dual relationship.[12]

"You cannot be near such a father, or hug him. You cannot tell him about the great perch you have caught in the creek and given to the mother cat, who carried it into the attic of the cowshed. You eschew the bundle of clothes snoring in the bed, you don't want to awaken it into life," explains Vaikko, an engineer born in 1964, concerning his deficient relationship with his father. "The heavy smell of stale liquor irritated my nose. My mother chided the bundle: you drunkard! you adulterous bastard! you're not a man! Mother ceased to speak, went to the bedroom to her children and closed the door, excluding that animal from their lives, too." A six-year-old boy wondered why the father drank, although he knew that he would be sick and terrify the mother and the children. "If I were big, I would kill him." Veikko would not identify with the model of his father and built his life completely differently. He did not dare to unburden his feelings through alcohol, because he was afraid of his violent heritage. The abandoned father remained a part of his structure through this negative identification.[13]

Broken fathers offer another version of the same disturbance to positive self-structuring through identification. Marko (born in 1940), a waiter, would have needed his father's knowledge during his puberty, but sickness absorbed his father's attention. "However, he had himself been young once. He should know, how a young boy becomes a man. My heart cried, that he didn't know. He had never been allowed to know it. He lived at that time and never had a father." Now Marko had to cling to his elder brother, who became independent early.[14]

Outer borders shelter from overwhelming feelings

Mother-bound boys, who feel ashamed of their fathers, are sensitive to others' attitudes and become aware of themselves as separate individuals only when something is wrong.[15] The peer group inherits the symbiotic might of the dyadic mother in kindergarten, in the class and in the work-place. According to sociogist J. P. Roos, many a lively and active boy turns into a shy victim at school. The school period seems to be a formative factor, although the narrators of our stories mostly pass over it in silence.[16] The peer group offers no "second chance" to build up one's sense of self, but takes advantage of members' sensitivity: tough guys base their toughness on the fragility of nerds. In the male culture in the schoolyards there seems to be no room for various sources of self-esteem: everybody is measured by only one dimension, male ruthlessness.

Because closeness means exposure to the arbitrary violence of the abusive others, our typical narrator seeks distance and independence in order to stay alive. Through his work a Finnish man achieves control over a capricious life, at least temporarily. Through his work he earns some human rights and receives decent treatment from others.[17]

Metalworker Jussi (born in 1949) returned to the dockyard after having become fed up with the compulsory pace of work at the car factory. But his new peers would not introduce him to his task and they also refused to lend him the tackle and jack. His peers were "complacent little devils. They pretended to be tough but feared facing the bosses, so that they had a black circle around their assholes." Jussi's own projected hate devastated the environment further – there was no one to receive and hold him. Without proper tools Jussi was unable to bend the iron correctly. He felt that he was losing control over his life. "I raised hell. I shouted the bosses and all the workers to hell." The boss had to intervene in order for Jussi to get the tools he urgently needed. "So I achieved the speed of the others."

Jussi observed well enough how hot steel behaved. "With force it straightened out and stayed in the state it should." He remembered that he sometimes had seen other workers handle steel without tackles or jacks, too. "The iron was malleable, if you could handle it right. If you could not, you had to learn. Otherwise you had better forget the job. Many men had to leave it." In a few weeks Jussi learned the right method and was spared the tackle and jack. "Some began to wonder what the hell that kind of straightening was? The work went on quickly without too many tools. I began to enjoy working and sometimes earned the bosses' approval. In rush situations I was the first asked to do overtime. Actually I did not like overtime: you can get to your grave with less effort, too."

Jussi's story points up some ever-present features in Finnish male culture: others are psychologically and practically present only as a hindrance, enviers and malevolent critics. They do not teach and help the novice, but the novice tries to bend their attitudes more positively just as he bends the resistant iron. If one can make the physical environment predictable, one can manage the others, too. A man makes his own holding environment, as a competent adult, whereas a needy child/apprentice is determined to be victimized.

After a full day, Jussi read books and magazines in his room. Sometimes he went out to see other people: "They were the same as elsewhere. Full of themselves and too proud to address me. – They talked nonsense to each other and grinned at me behind my back. Some even came too close." Jussi's own eyes were as suspicious and malevolent as he supposed the others' eyes to be. Books were more reliable than humans, because they could be easily changed, unlike people. "A human being is also a book, but, unfortunately, I cannot turn its pages, at least not as I wish."[18] When a man reduces human beings to their information content, one can conclude that, for him, the emotional side of human contact is intolerable.

The myth-making Finnish project after the Second World War – "clear and build" – has meant that men must conquer and defend their territory at work and at home. The male self is boosted by comforting images of interaction, and a predictable environment can provide him with emotional nourishment; this is why a Finnish man tends to turn his human relationships into manageable exchange.[19] Doing things is reassuring, whereas exposure to emotional exchange (also in sexual relationships) is threatening.[20]

The tendency toward privacy should not be labelled pathological as such. Men seek a space for friendliness and spontaneity through their efforts to control their lives. The peace of home heals self-feeling after a wounding work life. There one can be psychologically born anew, sheltered from the evil eye of others. In the Winnicottian sense the room of one's own is like the state of primary narcissism, whence one can reach out toward the outer world after having retired under the heavy bombardment of external influences. Spontaneous life begins only when others do not interrupt the fantasies of the child.[21]

Paradoxically, the Finns have been subjugated even through their longing for freedom: they acquire their own flats or houses in order to minimize their dependence on the arbitrary others, but in doing so they have maximized their dependence upon banks and economic fluctuations.[22]

The skilled Finnish man, blue-collar or white-collar, seems to be diametrically opposite to the dyadic Japanese personality in spite of a similar mother-bound childhood. The Japanese are used to teamwork but suppress individual initiative because they see the firm as a continuance of the dyadic mother-relationship. They expect attention for their unarticulated needs. Finnish men, on the other hand, do not expect anyone to give attention to their needs, if they cannot control others' attention through their achievements. They are on guard at their fragile borders before the re-engulfing bad mother, while the Japanese *amae*-personalities live trustingly within the borders of the familial self.[23] This is why I would not recommend Japanese teamwork methods for Finnish firms.

If a Finnish man can make the rate of exchange work favorably for himself, he can repress the memory of a rejecting environment in childhood and at school. Little privileges or secret controls over the work process correspond to emotional nourishment, which welcomes the child into the world. If he can no longer set his own pace and loses his privileges – for example due to downsizing or increased efficiency control – he confronts the worst memories from his earliest childhood: this world does not exist for me, so I do not exist.[24]

Unbound shame and its projective identification onto scapegoats

If a man cannot bind his anguish through predictable exchange, shame and doubt threaten to render him completely worthless. If a Finnish man cannot force the world to handle him justly, he too easily identifies himself with the aggressor and denies his own right to exist. Christopher Bollas says that the structural ego can mishandle the experiencing self because it follows the pattern of early interaction and repeats the mother's relation to her own needs. Grandparents have faced a merciless world and this metaphor of life is perpetuated in their grandchildrens' self-relation through the slightly hidden anxiety of the parents.[25]

The man who has lost control over his life feels that he is not allowed to occupy the space he once occupied. The narratives of unemployed white-collar workers repeat the experience of losing one's space and being annihilated in front of others. "Don't stare open-mouthed! There are better men for your position! Get out of the way, you bastard!"[26] For example, an unemployed chief of production ceased to be a husband or a father in his own mind, because he could no longer care for his family: "I am not a father! If they learn to hate me ... Or, if they begin to despise me. They would handle me like some filthy shit. Dear God, if You exist, don't let this happen to my family. Take me rather away from here, so I don't have to bear this shame!"[27] The physical sense of filthiness is transmitted by texts in which a man depicts himself as "waste", set "aside to rot".[28] A senior clerk who had been laid off wondered if he would be degraded to the position of a lavatory cleaner.[29] If one does not produce surplus value, one has no human value.[30]

Object relations psychoanalysis teaches us that a man never becomes so autonomous that he would cease to build himself in relation to others. Individual activity presupposes that one can also find rest in accepting mutuality.[31] According to psychoanalyst Nikolaas Treuniert, one can mentally treat external objects only when the basic sense of continuity is guaranteed in one's mind by affirmative state sharing ("ein gemeinsam empfundenes Universum").[32]

By studying the dynamics of shame, we can see the history of the child repeated in the deeds and words of the adult who in many other respects has a mature sense of proportion. When the predictability of an adult life is shaken, the paranoid-schizoid core is activated. Splitting and projective identification can supersede more developed defense mechanisms.[33] We can expect violent reactions, because people can no longer use full-time employment and a middle-class standard of living as their ego boosters. The end of full employment in Western countries challenges social integration: basic values and male identity especially should be defined anew, or we can expect the growth of hate groups and ethnic purges as attempts to build up new psychological boundaries.[34]

The outcasts can themselves cast away the feeling of being a helpless victim when they experience themselves as active attackers. One cannot attack banks or international capital, but one is allowed to make scapegoats of more marginalized people. The victims should in some "natural" respect differ from the bulk of the population, so that the attackers can deny any human link with them. They deserve to be punished, because they bear one's own loathsome weakness and incompetence. Because they are different from birth, the incompetence is their problem, not mine.[35]

An illuminating example of a proto-skinhead or X-Generation attitude can be found in the story of Petri (born in 1967), a graduate of a commercial institute. He reminds us of the self-production of Brett Easton Ellis in *American Psycho* or the tough-guy dialogue in Humphrey Bogart movies, but through these genres and literary models we may make some observations of his psychodynamics. People use autobiographies to wrap their feelings in symbols, which refer to something that cannot be directly expressed. (If we do not accept this approach, we can drop psychoanalysis altogether and play with floating senseless signifiers as post-structuralists from the 1980s have done.)

Petri did not dream of changing a bad world. He was totally engaged in keeping himself up to date. His work as a car salesman was frustrating, because the material rewards were too small to compensate for its inner emptiness. "My attitude towards the expectations of the car firm and in fact towards the work as such were shit, and I could not even hide it." He felt himself to be a nobody in the wrong place, because the world did not fill him with good nourishment. After having been fired, he walked to the bus stop: "The smell of tobacco was mixed with the heavy stench of sweat and farting. At the bus stop a whole group of clerks like me, who are two a penny, were waiting for the bus in a blue mood." Petri felt that he was mingled with the loathsome mass through their secretions, sharing their physical unattractiveness.

His standard reaction was to annihilate the others in his mind. His religious roommate, for instance, was "a bloodsucker," whose habits made him "vomit" and whose face was like "a bloody asshole." "I wanted to tear that shit into tiny bits and scatter the bits among all the shit on the tip area." At the workplace he saw the bosses as empty shells; salesmen, "the studs," reached out their "slack pasty hands"; under the arms of the person who introduced him to his job Petri noticed "wet blotches," as she raised her "massive carcass" and "rolled on me to breathe her sweet smelling breath on my neck." On the way home "a stubble-haired idiot" nearly crushed him. The others are present as invaders of the sphere of the purified pleasure self.[36]

Strong feelings toward unknown people make us suspect that in Petri's mind the others are absorbed into the undifferentiated drive object from early childhood, which does not nourish Petri as he expected.[37]

> In front of the National Museum a lousy bum came to me, asked for a mark; his hand reached out and prevented me from going. I took his hand and threw

him to the road. He stared at me with a humble look on his face, so that I dug a five mark coin out of my pocket. "Here you are, you rat!"

The others are always losing their own features and are transformed into shit. This observation invests the other person with Petri's self-loathing.[38] Petri recommended that his religious roommate tear the blinkers away from his eyes, so that he could acknowledge his solitude on the earth. Petri did not care for his life, because nobody took care of him. This talented young man became an alcoholic. "Everything is lost. Faith, hope, love ... I was only about twenty, but had already seen everything that was worthy of seeing and found that it was only shit."[39] "Shit" is more than a metaphor in Petri's story, and many other stories. Petri changes others into shit. Many unemployed men feel themselves to be shit. Petri projects this feeling onto others by tearing them apart in his mind and text.

Shame is felt at the loss of active control over one's life and environment. This experience is so strong that it cannot be adequately symbolized, but is dealt with by projecting undigested experiences onto others and making them behave as if these were their problems. In common Finnish usage "homo" or "gay" means on the subconsicous level a loser who is a passive victim – a composite symbol of being an object rather than a subject.[40] The term "vitun homo" widely used by schoolboys condenses diffuse anxieties of incompetence and of being shit without personal boundaries. Simultaneously, it transfers these suspicions onto others, who have to submit themselves to witch hunts and show that they are not anti-men.

In Finnish, and perhaps also in the American context, the double signifying function of "homo," meaning both a sexual orientation and a bundle of unmanly qualities, gets its special cathexis from the fact that the boy must separate from the dyadic mother without the dyadic father, whose power he can experience as his own.[41] The model of being a real man is purely negative: you should not be like mother, like a baby, like girls, like nerds or faggots.[42] "The logic of masculinity is demanding – protect and maintain what you are intrinsically, or you could lose it, mutate, become something else," says Patrick D. Hopkins.[43] Because "real" boys and men cannot accept the homosexual dynamics of idealization or the merger with the self-object which is going on in them in any case, they lose the only opportunity for healing the wounds left by the absent father.[44] The special cathexis of "homo" and its ability to dehumanize are explained by the fact that our culture does not cater to the developmental needs of the boys, so they repress the areas which are most important for the development of healthy self-feeling. Self-feeling is replaced by hierarchical structures.[45]

Projective identification of one's weakness onto others and the use of scapegoats as poison containers are the reversal of male self-sufficiency, which our culture requires. According to Gerhard Härle, a defender of purity experiences anal-sadistic satisfacton when he projects weakness, effeminacy and filthiness onto homosexuals.[46]

For German skinheads, people belonging to other races are "vermin", and women are "toilet paper" for free use. Violence is sexualized, because it simultaneously means separation from filth and a pleasurable contact with the filth, with the forbidden wishes of unity with the rejecting mother-world. Sexuality as such is a dangerous reaching out, because it exposes oneself to the reaction of the others. It is safer to retire into the purified pleasure self and build up a holy nation untainted by frustrated expectations.[47] After the era of nationalism, such a male fiction could be attached to the European Union or other large alliances consisting of big letters and arrows and other hierarchical abstractions of male fantasy, which protect men from re-engulfing intimacy and let them rule over their mother-substitutes, distancing them from the filthy life of women and children.

Alternative ground for self-esteem

Luckily, this circle of projective identifications is only one scenario for the future. If men can experience personal continuity and response after their social fall and maintain contact with others and themselves, the social catastrophe can become a personal beginning.

Rauno (born in 1941) had been the model of a young achiever, a building engineer and chief of big projects throughout the world. He wept for the first time after having faced anaclitic deprivation, as his beloved wife met with an accident. He could not remain alone without feeling depersonalized. The male armor was broken down. After crying his panic aloud and grasping onto an old friend for support, Rauno reached his wife on an emotional level. She was now convalescing after severe brain hemorrhage. "I was in contact with Liisa and with all that existed." Feeling a part of this unity, Rauno began to tolerate his problems. "My goal would be achieved, if I was only ready to accept life in all forms and love it." Rauno knew that his goal was not to become rich or receive appreciation, not even to gain knowledge. The quality of life was no longer dependent on Rauno's capabilities.

Empathy with his helpless wife opened up new dimensions between the spouses after Liisa's recovery. Family ties became more solidly based.

"I am glad about the fact that I no longer require achievements from my boys as a precondition for love. They, too, have seen me in a new role as a caretaker." Rauno recognized the compulsive influence of his suffering mother and lacking father on his motivation for achievement. He now came to feel that his mother would accept his life without public acclaim and would let him choose what he wanted in his later years.[48] This kind of story may sound like therapy philosophy, at least in the ears of sociologists who have read Robert N. Bellah's treatment of expressive individualism as an ideology of our time.[49] But for Rauno and many other drop-outs in their middle age such words mean something: a contact with real feelings, which for the first time are as much a reality as external pressures.

The younger generation is no longer so closely attached to working life as the older. According to surveys, younger people see work merely as a means of self-actualization and they do not adore drudgery as such. One can also build one's identity on hobbies and relationships, not only on a linear upward movement, which in any case seems to be impossible in an age of diminishing expectations for the middle classes.[50]

The utterances of the X-Gen may sound cynical, cool or fragmented, but before explaining them away by theories of narcissism and multiple personality, we should listen to them. Are they really nihilists or are they protecting their values, balance of mind, close relationships and narrow commitments for a better world?[51]

"Life is for living, you cannot reject it. The life will revenge itself on you some time, if you refuse to take part in it now," concluded Mika, a student born in 1968. He failed in school, tried to become a writer, sought adventures in the world, and volunteered for a hospital in St. Petersburg and in an orthodox monastery. He was more worried about the possibility of missing a course in parachute jumping than a steady pension. He accepted humiliating experiences, too, as being part of a full life. "It depends on character, whether one has as his goal being pensioned after 30 years and getting a brownie cap filled with candies as recognition at the firm's Chistmas party, or if one seizes the day and moment, as if it were the last you were ever allowed to live."[52]

One can also define one's identity without comparing quantitative achievements and one can find quality of life in concrete, small things. Qualities do not compete with each other and do not need to destroy each other in order for one to achieve the feeling of wholeness. Lifestyle enclaves may be apolitical, but they do offer some firm ground by which one can distance oneself from the destructive mainstream and set life goals relatively independent of the world market. The greatest hindrance has already been removed: shame for one's inability to satisfy everyone's contradictory expectations. Both young and old retire among family, friends and hobbies in lifestyle enclaves, but perhaps the mainstream culture is also gradually being affected by such human rebirths after social deaths. People who have gone through sorrow and faced their incompetence can turn into the most competent subjects and defend their rights as human beings.

This is one possible narrative that can be extracted from these lives in the prevailing historical conditions. Hopefully other researchers will make more positive narratives and will rescue the heroic Finnish man from the disparaging definitions too often made by critics. The suffering beneath the tough surface of the prevailing male identity cannot be effaced by labelling the new field of male studies as unmanly or its practitioners as effeminate anti-men. The ideal of a self-sufficient, positive hero is too often based on a taboo against grief, which prevents one from acknowledging one's vulnerability and thus also one's ontological dependence on the others. Neither mature individuality nor ethical responsibility can begin with denial of the basic facts of the human condition.

Notes

1. Juha Siltala, Miehen kunnia. Modernin miehen taistelu häpeää vastaan A (Man's Honour: modern men fighting against shame) (Keuruu: Otava, 1994).
2. J. P. Roos, "Souffrance masculine dans les récits de vie," paper read at the Ecole des hautes études en sciences sociales, 8 June 1993.
3. Compare Thomas H. Ogden, The Matrix of the Mind. Object Relations and the Psychoanalytic Dialoque (Northvale, N. J. and London: Jason Aronson, 1993), pp. 41-65.
4. Matti Kortteinen, Kunnian kenttä. Suomalainen palkkatyö kulttuurisena muotona (Hämeenlinna: Hanki ja jää, 1992). See also S. Hutson and R. Jenkins, Taking the Strain: Families, Unemployment and the Transition to Adulthood (Milton Keynes: Open University, 1989); D. Walsgrowe, "Policing Yourself: Social Closure and the Internalization of Stigma," in G. Lee and R. Loveridge (eds), The Manufacture of Disadvantage: Stigma and Social Closure (Milton Keynes: Open University Press, 1987), pp. 45-57.
5. Eero Rechardt and Pentti Ikonen, "How to Interpret Death Drive?", Scandinavian Psychoanalytic Review, 2, 1993, pp. 84-99; Pentti Ikonen and Eero Rechardt, "The Origin of Shame and its Vicissitudes," Scandinavian Psychoanalytic Review, 2, 1993, pp. 100-124; Sylvan Tomkins, "Shame," in D. L. Nathanson (ed.), The Many Faces of Shame (New York: Guilford Press, 1987), pp. 133-61.
6. Satu Apo, the folklorist, explains the phallic mother imagery in Finnish tradition and literature by the real situation of most small farmer wives during

the nineteenth and twentieth centuries; see Satu Apo, Naisen väki. Tutkimuksia suomalaisten kansanomaisesta kulttuurista ja ajattelusta (Hämeenlinna: Hanki ja jää, 1995), pp. 50-129.

7. See R. Atkins, "Transitive Vitalization and Its Impact on Father Representation," Contemporary Psychoanalysis, 1984, pp. 663-776.

8. Christopher Bollas, "The Shadow of the Object: Psychoanalysis of the Unthought Known" (London: Free Association Books (1987), 1991), pp. 13-40.

9. See Peter Fonagy et al., "The Capacity for Understanding Mental States: The Reflective Self in Parent and Child and Its Significance for Security of Attachment," Infant Mental Health Journal, 12 (3), Fall 1991, pp. 201-18.

10. Compare W. R. D. Fairbairn, "Endopsychic structure considered in terms of object-relationships" (1944), Teoksessa: An Object-Relations Theory of the Personality (New York: Basic Books, 1952), pp. 84-117; Mathias Hirsch, "Das Fremde als unassimiliertes Introjekt," in Ulrich Streeck (ed.), Das Fremde in der Psychoanalyse. Erkundungen über das "Andere" in Seele, Körper und Kultur (München: J. Pfeiffer, 1993), pp. 213-24.

11. TANE/Autobiography No. 252, pp. 3-4, 7-13.

12. See Ralph R. Greenson, "The Struggle Against Identification," Journal of the American Psychoanalytic Association, 1954, pp. 200-17, and "Dis-Identifying from Mother: Its Special Importance for the Boy," International Journal of Psychoanalysis, 1968, pp. 370-74.

13. TANE/Autobiography No. 150, pp. 5-7.

14. TANE/Autobiography No. 317, pp. 30-31.

15. Melvin L. Lansky, Fathers Who Fail. Shame and Psychopathology in the Family System (Hillsdale, N. J. and London: The Analytic Press, 1992), pp. 37-41, 122-3.

16. Roos, "Souffrance masculine dans les récits de vie". See also Sirkku Aho, Oppilaiden moraalikehitystason, minäkäsityksen, sosiaalisen aseman ja kouluasenteiden muuttuminen peruskoulun ala-asteella. Seurantatutkimuksen loppuraportti. Turun yliopiston kasvatustieteiden tiedekunnan sarja (Turku, 1993), A, p. 167.

17. "Decent treatment" derives from Barrington Moore, who crystallized the expectations of the British working class in that concept; Barrington Moore, Injustice. The Social Bases of Obedience and Revolt (London: Macmillan, 1979).

18. TANE/Autobiography No. 253, pp. 14-18, 28.

19. Compare Kortteinen, Kunnian kenttä.

20. See Peter Middleton, "The Inward Gaze. Masculinity and Subjectivity in Modern Culture" (London and New York: Routledge, 1992), pp. 189-232; Larry May and Robert A. Strikwerda, "Fatherhood and Nurturance," in Larry May and Robert A. Strikwerda (eds), Rethinking Masculinity. Philosophical Explorations in Light of Feminism (Lanham: Rowman and Littlefield Publishers, 1992), pp. 75-92.

21. For the ideals of privacy at home see: Erja Lauronen, Unelma ja sen

toteuttajat. Tutkimus suomalaisista omakotirakentajista. Sosiaalipolitiikan lisensiaattityö (Helsingin yliopisto, 1991), pp. 67-8, 78-9, 88-94, 180-93; Hilkka Summa, Muuttoliike ja asunnonvaihdot pääkaupunkiseudulla. Kirjallisuuskatsaus. Pääkaupunkiseudun julkaisusarja (Helsinki, 1984), B: 3, pp. 29; Horelli-Kukkonen, Liisa: Asunto psykologisena ympäristönä. Asujan ja asunnon vuorovaikutusta koskeva tutkimus pientalojen itsesuunnittelukokeilun valossa. Teknillisen korkeakoulun arkkitehtiosaston tutkimuksia 1993/3 (Espoo, 1993), pp. 107, 139-57, 170-73. On the house as a restorative environment guaranteeing ontological safety, see also Clare Cooper, "The House as Symbol of the Self," in H. Prochansky, W. Ittelson and G. Rivlin (eds), Environmental Psychology, 2nd edn (New York: Holt, Rinehart and Winston, 1976), p. 447; Peter Saunders, A Nation of Home Owners (London: Unwin Hyman, 1990), p. 295; Barrington Moore, Barrington, Privacy. Studies in Social and Cultural History (New York: M. E. Sharpe, Inc., 1984), pp. 126-43. On transitional space, see D. W. Winnicott, Psychoanalytic Explorations, Clare Winnicott, Ray Shepherd and Madeleine Davis (eds) (Cambridge, Massachusetts: Harvard University Press, 1989), passim, esp. pp. 53-4, 205.

22. Compare Anneli Juntto, "Asuntokysymys Suomessa. Topeliuksesta tulopolitiik kaan," Sosiaalipoliittisen yhdistyksen julkaisu, 50 (Helsinki: VAPK, 1990).

23. See Takeo Doi, "The Concept of amae and its Psychoanalytic Implications," International Review of Psychoanalysis, 1989, pp. 349-54; Alan Roland, In Search of Self in India and Japan. Toward a Cross-Cultural Psychology (Oxford: Princeton University Press, 1989).

24. For emotional reception see D. W. Winnicott, Human nature (London: Free Association Books, 1988), pp. 112-13, On the difficulties of recognizing abandonment and abuse and on the tendency to maintain the illusion of care, see Klaus Theweleit, Buch der Könige. Band I: Orpheus and Eurydike (Frankfurt/M.: Stroemfeld/Roter Stern, 1988), pp. 251-66, 441-8, 736-67.

25. Bollas, The Shadow of the Object, pp. 41-63.

26. Työttömän tarina, Archives of the Finnish Literature Society (SKS), 5134-5.

27. Työttömän tarina, SKS, 443-444.

28. Työttömän tarina, SKS, 5133.

29. TANE/Autobiography No. 81, pp. 72-3.

30. TANE/Autobiography 69, pp. 3, 6, 90-91.

31. For example see Heinz Kohut, The Analysis of the Self. A Systematic Approach to the Psychoanalytic Treatment of Narcissistic Personality Disorders (New York: International Universities Press, 1971); Heinz Kohut, The Restoration of the Self (New York: International University Press, 1977); Jay R. Greenberg and Stephen A. Mitchell, Object Relations in Psychoanalytic Theory (Cambridge, Massachusetts and London: Harvard University Press, 1983). See also Siri Erika Gullestad, "A Contribution to the Psychoanalytic Concept of Autonomy," Scandinavian Psychoanalytic Review, 1, 1993, pp. 22-33; Klaus Theweleit, Männerphantasien. II:

Männerkörper – zur Psychoanalyse des weissen Terrors (Frankfurt/M.: Stroemfeld/Roter Stern, 1980), pp. 264-5.

32. Nikolaas Treuniert, "Was ist Psychoanalyse heute?", Psyche, 2, 1995, pp. 115-17, 132-3.

33. Ogden, The Matrix of the Mind.

34. See Howard S. Stein, "'The Eternal Jew': Resurgent Anti-Semitism in the Post-Cold War World," Journal of Psychohistory, 22 (1), 1994, pp. 39-57.

35. Annette Streeck-Fischer, "'Geil auf Gewalt'. Pscyhoanalytische Bemerkungen zu Adoleszenz und Rechtsextremismus", Psyche, 8, 1992, pp. 745-68; V. D. Volkan, The Need to Have Enemies and Allies. From Clinical Practice to Intenational Relationships (New York: Jason Aronson, 1988).

36. See Annette Streeck-Fischer, "'Ihr könnt uns nicht vernichten, denn wir sind ein Teil von Euch.' Über den 'deadly dance' eines jugendlichen Skinheads," Streeck (ed.), Das Fremde in der Psychoanalyse, p. 38.

37. See Klaus Theweleit, Männerphantasien. I: Frauen, Fluten, Körper, Geschichte (Frankfurt/M.: Stroemfeld/Roter Stern (1977), 1980), pp. 398ff; II: Männerkörper zur Psychoanalyse des weissen Terrors (Frankfurt/M.: Stroemfeld/Roter Stern, 1980), pp. 248ff.

38. See Theweleit, Männerphantasien. I: Frauen, Fluten, Körper, Geschichte, pp. 220-21.

39. TAN/Autobiography No. 10, pp. 1-6, 12-14, 20-22.

40. See Patrick D. Hopkins, "Gender Treachery: Homophobia, Masculinity, and Threatened Identities," in May and Strikwerda (eds), Rethinking Masculinity, pp. 111-31.

41. Peter Blos, Son and Father Before and Beyond the Oedipus Complex (New York: The Free Press, 1985), pp. 7-13, 16, 25, 33-6, 40, 48-51.

42. Elisabeth Badinter, De l'identité masculine (Paris: Éditions Odile Jacob, 1992).

43. Hopkins, "Gender Treachery," pp. 123-5.

44. On the self-object as a transitional object see Heinz Kohut, The Restoration of the Self (New York: International Universties Press, 1977), pp. 99-101; and Noel Ryce-Menuhin, The Self in Early Childhood (London: Free Association Books, 1988), pp. 118-19. For homosexual dynamics in heterosexual development see Peter Schellenbaum, Homosexualität im Mann. Eine tiefenpsychologische Studie (München: Kösel, 1991). Compare Guy Corneau, Père manquant, fils manqué (Quebec: Les éditions de l'homme, 1989), p. 34; and Samuel Osherson, Finding our Fathers (New York: The Free Press, 1986), pp. 44-5. On its tabooing see, for example, Robert A. Strikwerda and Larry May, "Male Friendship and Intimacy," in May and Strikwerda (eds), Rethinking Masculinity, pp. 95-110.

45. My aim is not to insult homosexuals by dealing with the fixation of the homosexual dynamics of heterosexuals. According to Peter Schellenbaum, Homosexualität im Mann, there are mother-fixated, self-seeking heterosexuals and homosexuals but also homosexuals and heterosexuals with freely developed homosexual dynamics and mature relationships. We must

distinguish between sexual object choice and the ability to relate to separate others despite the fact that becoming a man through sharing and identifications and becoming a self are so closely imbricated in men.

46. Gerhard Härle, Männerweiblichkeit. Zur Homosexualität bei Klaus und Thomas Mann (Frankfurt/M.: Athenäums Programm, 1993), pp. 91-113; Béla Grunberger, Vom Narzissmus zum Objekt (Frankfurt/M.: Suhrkamp (1971), 1982), p. 168. Compare Theweleit, Männerphantasien. II: Männerkörper, pp. 268-301, 434.

47. Hans-Jürgen Wirth, "Sich fühlen wie der letzte Dreck. Zur Sozialpsychologie der Skinheads," in M. Bock, M. Reimitz, H. E. Richter, W. Thiel and H. J. Wirth (eds), Zwischen Resignation und Gewalt. Jugendprotest in den Achtziger Jahren (Opladen: Budrich and Leske, 1989), p. 191. On the purified pleasure self in typical skinhead experience see Robert Heim, "Fremdenhass und Reinheit – die Aktualität einer Illusion. Sozialpsychologische und psychoanalytische Überlegungen," Psyche, 8, 1992, pp. 710-29. On purity and asexuality see also Theweleit, Männerphantasien. II: Männerkörper, pp. 436-40, "Cleanliness is next to godliness."

48. TANE/Autobiography No. 110, pp. 81-90.

49. Robert N. Bellah et al., Habits of the Heart. Individualism and Commitment in American Life (Berkeley, Los Angeles and London: University of California Press, 1985), pp. 14-26, 140-41, 177-92.

50. Lasse Siurala, Nuoriso-ongelmat modernisaatioperspektiivistä. Helsingin kaupungin tietokeskuksen tutkimuksia (Helsinki, 1994), p. 3.

51. In the surveys made by Helena Helve, the leading youth researcher in Finland, inner balance, close relationships and values other than external success were more important during the 1990s than during the 1980s. Personal communication.

52. TANE/Autobiography No. 54, pp. 1-6, 34-6, 43-5.

Chapter 12

Asthma: The Construction of the Masculine Body

ARTO TIIHONEN

The cough

My legs give way. Vision clouds. I head straight for the toilet. I hope no one noticed, especially the coach. Over the toilet bowl and hacking. Not just a hack, but a rasping cough that throws up green sputum down the front of my sports shirt. Tearing lungs, but the coughing won't stop. I lean against the toilet for support. I'm faint … .

When the coughing fit finally eases off, my shirt front is covered in green slime and my chest hurts. I'm amazed. This cough has bothered me for weeks, but I didn't think it was so bad. I'm scared, though I don't dare show it. I don't tell the coach.

The place is the Finnish sports college in Vierumäki, the camp for the candidates of the 1975 national under-16 football team. I had just finished the league test which consisted of stomach and back muscle training, jumping, press-ups and interval running. The test usually lasts from three-and-a-half to four minutes depending on your condition. This time it took me nearly four minutes, though I thought I was in good condition … and then this attack – maybe I should go and tell someone.

I don't go, though I know that I should. The game tunes you down. I don't dare to run flat out, because I'm scared of another attack.

The narrative of illness

After camp my cough worsened to become exercise-induced asthma, which led to my continuous use of medicine and made me take care of my health. I had been ill with asthma when I was very little, just two years old. In my memory is a tiny red medicine bottle that I asked my mother for whenever I felt an attack approaching. I was in any case a very weak little guy until the age of five. It was then that my inborn heart problem was operated on and my life changed from a careful, inward, somewhat misty existence to one of wild joy. As an active boy I became "the runner," as the neighbors called me.

My asthma stayed away for about ten years. At 13, when we had just got a puppy, the symptoms re-emerged. For the puppy's sake I tried at first to get over my breathing problem, to hide it, but it was pointless because afterwards late summer – when we had the puppy – was difficult for many years and anyhow we couldn't keep the dog. I had also been exposed to other irritants.

Following my time in Vierumäki my history of asthma proceeded changeably. Sometimes I felt splendid and only rarely did I have to rely on stronger tricks. Using drugs was awkward and embarrassing because they were inhalants, which you had to gasp down many times in rapid succession. I tried to keep my affliction to myself.

It was a long time before I realized the connection between my frame of mind and my asthma. I learnt to listen to the "inner voice" of my body. Colds and the beginnings of other minor illnesses were immediately perceptible from my breathing, but it was only occasionally, after hard exercise, that my breathing trouble caused wheezing. Otherwise I just felt a weariness, a "weight on my heart." I found that tension did not compound the problem as long as I stayed active and hopeful. Although the diagnosis was bronchial asthma, the tough burden of it did not, for the most part, cause me any problems. The main rule, as my doctor emphasized, was to "rush slowly," to warm-up the engine before accelerating and going for top speed.

I only noticed the psychosomatic character of my disease in the army, where the torment of "going through hell" was really rammed home. This was a surprise for me because I lived near the barracks and throughout my youth I had been there skiing, playing and visiting friends of my own age. I hadn't realized the kind of senselessness that is forced on young lads when they are "made men." The aspect which before had prompted such pleasant memories changed in a flash to something completely different: the company of Kafkaesque ranks, the organized and shackling regulations, in which familiar men became figures of authoritarian rule.

It was too much for my asthma. The problems began when I got flu during exercises and went to complain of coughing and sputum, which I knew indicated inflammation. Despite my protestations the medical orderly would not let me see the doctor because I did not have a temperature. "Back to your rank!" But by evening I was taken in because of chronic bronchitis.

Although I got over the bronchitis and my duties as a messenger were light, the asthma did not let up. It continued from the first to be as difficult from spring right through to autumn. Luckily, my general condition was good so I was able to exercise and play a little. When in the autumn I returned to civilian life my feeling improved almost immediately, though usually I find autumn to be the most difficult time for my asthma.

This experience led to some internal discussions with my bodily feelings. If they felt bad for some reason I left off from exercising. This worked. The stress decreased and I felt more healthy. I also reduced my use of medication.

Later, when I was studying in the faculty of sport sciences, the pressure was considerable. On top of seven hours of physical training and lectures there was also football practice. At the age of 23, however, I stopped using drugs altogether. I do not know which had proved most effective: my fit condition (it had not improved), my relationship with my body (I learnt new things about it), my frame of mind (contradictions continued), the natural development of the disease (the cause of the asthma may be as I have described), or perhaps falling deeply in love. Anyway, I could now describe myself as healthy.

Anxious corporeality

My sports history is colored by illnesses of which asthma overshadowed my most active years for nearly a decade. I cannot think of sport without thinking of asthma or of asthma without thinking of sport. In my mind they are linked with everything to do with corporeal capacity.

The main idea of competitive sport is to improve one's capacity. How to get the most out of yourself in the competition, how to succeed at recovering, or how to have experienced the ("none-scientific") trainers' ways to tell you how well you know yourself.

In addition to training methods, this idea also comprises psychology, sociology, philosophy and history. To learn the limits of your own ability is not just a matter of technique. The "myself" or "me" also contains its own internal constructions and genesis which can be analyzed and worked out. I look at the issue through the prism of asthma. My relationship to performing becomes compacted in it.[1] It puts the sporting imperative to improve in a new light. It was not a problem of the results being weaker – that did not happen. My ability got better all the time, and my career mainly continued to boom, though the asthma did hinder my training. My skills, power, speed and even endurance improved.[2] And yet I felt that the limits of my capability were continuously on trial, on the threshold of pain.

During training and competitions you have to deal with your pain tolerance (cf. Sabo and Panepinto, 1990). Usually there are no greater problems associated with this. When skiing or running, you of course experience pain when your condition is not up to going harder, and the skill of skiing fast is related in some way to endurance. If you are in bad condition, you do not "know" how to ski so fast that you would be on the limits of your capacity.

My asthma changed the situation. Earlier, the training which had felt easy might have become an impassable obstacle where breathing became constricted and my muscles did not get the oxygen they needed. This, however, is only the physiological side. What happened to my self-image as a man, a sportsman and a healthy human being was another question (cf. Morgan, 1992). I had to explain my changed situation, not only to myself but to all in the communities where I lived and did sports.

The instrumental body

After puberty I had become stuck in the culture where goodness was measured by physical ability. Was I a strong skier, fast runner and skilful goal scorer? Though I lived in a small village, I was soon defined according to the standards of society, the town, the district and, finally, according to people of my age throughout the whole country.

At the beginning of the 1970s the sports organizations started age-level competitions in which I belonged to the first wave that produced many young champions. Finnish sport came to be "total" (Heinilä, 1982). I compared my results to those of other athletes by reading about them in the newspapers. Even the teachers seemed to value sport over doing well at school. As a child I also had known the culture of backyard games – in which everyone was included in order for the game to begin. The elder members of the village appeared not to take any notice of sport, they had had enough of competing – in the fields, in the forest, in wars and in their ill health. Our family was an exception, and my father subscribed to *Helsingin Sanomat* (the national daily paper) for its sports coverage. I lived in a contradictory situation in which the older community, based on segmental ties (of village community and bartering) was giving way to a new form of community based on functional ties (division of labor, specialization, and money economy). Of course the transition had been going on for decades, if not centuries (cf. Dunning, 1986). Finland was then experiencing the fastest pace of change compared with any other West-European country.

The functionalism of age-level competitions pushed me to improve as a forward striker in the C, B and A juniors (under 14s, 16s, 18s), as a club and district five-kilometer skier and in other roles according to the type of event, level, age, area and venue. The future offered by the village community was nothing compared to this. Though the common games gave my childhood a certain rhythm, already by my teens I would have been stuck in the mud and in a world lacking alternatives, where the farmer gradually became the agricultural entrepreneur, part of one functionalist system.

I was probably about 13 when things changed and I secretly sneaked into the county athletic championships. I jogged six kilometers through the forest to reach the venue – I was really excited. I remember how at first I hesitated when I saw my competitors' fine spiked running shoes. I was wearing old basketball pumps. I decided to run barefoot. I won both the 100 and 1000 meter events, and walked proudly home with the glass trophies under each arm. After that there was the inevitable progression to inter-province competitions in cross-country running and football.

The segmental ties to the home village turned into functional ties, especially toward the trainers, who based their roles mainly on biological knowledge, simple command relationships, and stereotypical views. It was odd that the toughest and meanest coaches appeared the most "correct," though they were not liked. Their attitude represented the model of adult man, the kind that succeeds (cf. Carrigan, Connell and Lee, 1985).

The male body

Changing from a boy into a man is not the easiest task in Finnish culture. Suicides, the dangers of life, fear of the unknown, the pressure to succeed and the fear of failure are all too well known. We had learned these things already as young boys, whether we wanted to or not. With my change to manhood my orientation to sport was surely easier. I was appreciated outside the home and found my place among people my own age. I learnt to know my skills. But there was also a price to pay.

When I started sports at the club level, when I was 11, I came across masculinity – something I had not encountered earlier. I had spent my childhood among girls and now ran into attitudes such as the sense of superiority and self-sufficiency which the coach especially emphasized. I, too, wanted to be competent, but the feeling of being an outsider and alien soon became stronger, and I gave in. I do not know which affected me the most – my own failure or the attitude of the team. I was in goal in my first junior game against the other team of the town. I let in three goals in the first half and was replaced. It was enough for me. I was humiliated (cf. Messner, 1992).

The club I belonged to was a bourgeois club. Later, when I joined the town's working-class club, I noticed the difference in the players' attitudes. The working-class boys did not act superior toward each other, they were straightforward and cold when they felt like it. Their attitude toward girls was the same.

I learned that you should not be feminine, sentimental, over-friendly or talk too much about your own affairs. It was better to boast and brag a bit. The all-boys school taught me even more. I cannot remember that masculinity was defined at all, other than through denial – through what a man should not be. By rules, hidden fears and the insolent language of the gang – "homo," "wanker" – we became men.[3]

The other construction piece of identity was honesty or, even better, genuineness. The boys of my generation were taught to believe in the faultless "I" and the authentic self. Dispassionate masculinity, which is experienced negatively, had to stand unaffected by all the attacks directed at it.

The lives of the athlete

Nevertheless, I had the luck to live two or more lives within many different "frames" (Goffman, 1974). I worked relatively independently in different institutions – at home, at school, in the village community, in the football team and in skiing groups. They were separated from each other according to what we talked about and the ways in which we talked and acted (cf. Veijola, 1994).

At home there were two ways of talking: there was the patriarchal language used by my father where consensus was sustained and contradictions were avoided; and there were the women's discourses in which it was typical to talk about personal things, though there were also contradictions, arguments and displays of emotion. I cruised between the two. I often played a mediating role, to listen to different versions of events. With my father we played different games, often quite seriously, and we went fishing and to sports competitions. With my sisters we journeyed to school and did our homework, we cleaned, went to dances and chatted together.

All forms of play were important in our family, as in many others. We played cards when guests came. At coffee time we would exchange pleasantries, but it was in the game that social experience was concentrated. You could show your emotions in games, express yourself, exhibit distinction, enjoy your good luck and bemoan your losses.

There were also two ways of talking in the village community. One was totally agrarian – adult ways of speaking that were connected with the forest, the field, with ploughing and harvest and hunted quarry. This language was also used by the neighbors' boy, who was three years older than me, and with whom we went to the forest to train his dog, or went fishing or did farm work. We did not talk about anything other than practical matters. He was going to stay on the farm. On the other hand, there was also a newer language oriented to studying, paid work, and contradictory perspectives of the future. We pondered these various and concealed contradictions with my sisters and the local girls. It was with them that I learnt to speak about all possible things.

At school I learnt the discourse of a good pupil, which I took part in throughout my school days, though after secondary school I stopped being the teacher's pet. In this talk was an appreciation of knowledge and the consideration of different subjects and further education. In the football team the speech was manly and working-class in its signs of jesting and small talk. There were exceptions and I had "best friends," as did the girls, with whom I could talk deeply and purposefully.

Some girls also belonged to the skiing group, as well as some adults who came along to the events. Discussion with the girls was often as superficial as among the gangs of boys, but there was no shouting, embarrassment or cruelty. The skiers were also individuals and not members of a team, and I too behaved differently in this group. When I was about 16 or 17 I opted for football instead of skiing, in which, in addition to a greater chance of success, there was a higher appreciation of the identity of a footballer as a man (cf. Willis, 1984).

The ambivalent body

My asthma made it difficult for me to separate notions of the body and spirit, the physical and the psyche. My experience was a totality – the constricted breathing of asthma produces a very corporeal feeling. The subject is of course one of the main issues of Western philosophy. Are we divided into two parts: the spirit which intellectually and sovereignly guides the body, the machine? Or are we a totality which cannot be divided without violence?

The Western philosophic tradition offers two possibilities. The old Cartesian view divides us between soul and body, whereas more recent phenomenology supports the idea of totality. In this way one can talk of Husserl's notion of "lived experience" or of Merleau-Ponty's "lived body." According to the phenomenological view our body is always in relationship to itself, with others, with human space and time, and everything affects it in terms of how we experience ourselves and the world around us. According to phenomenologists, our experiences are not detached, and in them there is always the question of totalities (Schrag, 1988). As Klemola (1990) has stated, in addition to body and spirit there exists a "third" something – the way, happiness or life. But, as a Westerner, not even my yoga has helped me to really understand this.

Pursuing sports taught me to instrumentalize my body and separate it from reason to become an object of reason. Exercises for different limbs, for durability, power and acceleration taught me also the vocabulary for which this kind of dismemberment worked easily. In the game the dismembered parts had to be put back together "to put the parts in order."

These days this kind of language is familiar also to Finnish television viewers, when journalists and studio guests talk in everyday terms about "features," "factors," "field sectors," "strengths" and "weaknesses." The breaking up of the game performance into video stills has become the common language of the sports world; real knowledge of the body is knowledge of the robot.

However, asthma shattered that machine world. I no longer functioned like a nippy sports car but had to warm up with considerable use of the gas pedal. Breathing and relaxation exercises, as well as yoga, taught me to know my corporeality in different ways. I realized the meaning of slowing down, listening, relaxing – though the will to succeed still attracted me. I lived in a contradiction without knowing what would be sensible. The prolonged coughing attacks and constricted breathing made me depressed and caused me to question the meaning and sense of sport. A good game, a successful performance and the feeling of belonging prompted me to try again, although endangering my health. I knew that being in good condition helps prevent disease ... on the other hand health for me was not a thing in itself. There did not seem to be a simple answer.

Because of asthma, I had to consider the relationship to myself and my identity. My bodily experience had been devastating and did not follow any kind of pattern of the kind that can be learnt from books on biology or psychology. The one identity, the sportsman's, seemed to drift toward disaster. A solution had to be found to the crisis.

The alternatives were spread among those parts which different institutions (home, school, team), ways of speaking (of village, school friends, sportsmen) and my own body experiences (performances, illnesses) offered (Frank, 1990). "Forgotten" identities powerfully emerged in this crisis as I learned to behave as a single authentic "I." I did, as Thomas Ziehe (1992) would say, "identity work." Though I did not belong to the "pioneering generation" which was born in the 1970s, described by Ziehe, I had to do some kind of bodily identity work. Finland in the 1970s was still a unified culture, so the models of comparable groups and consumer youth culture were more limited than during the late 1980s, the period Ziehe analyzed.

Discussions with girls from my village, with sporting and class friends grew in importance. Their multi-level and various natures made an exception to a one-track "sportsman's identity."[4]

At first my learning of something other than a sportsman's identity was not conscious. The aim was still to "show the world that I'll become something" (cf. Messner, 1987). Through the eyes of a working-class boy sport seemed the best way to succeed in this. However, I no longer underestimated other alternatives, though among these sport was an exception as it gave an immediate and positive experience. With sport you did not have to study books for years on end or plan a common future in a couple relationship. The experiences of sport were not only bodily. The team spirit, the things done together and the appreciation of others also attracted me.

The disciplined body

The asthma kept up its unpredictability. Sometimes things went well, at other times there were great difficulties. I tried to understand the non-linear and non-continuous logic of the disease (Jackson, 1990), which was not easy, at least not for a man. I learnt to avoid getting colds or training when I had them, but the attacks brought on by stress were more difficult to anticipate. I had always been sensitive to contradictions between people, and in the team these existed as a matter of course. At worst, the other part was the trainer or the team leaders. Such taxing situations are rarely brought out into the open because the player is expected to back down, even though he may know he is right. Play, don't speculate!

Already before my military service I had noticed that external forces caused me stress. But I still thought I would survive, though I hated the army. I was wrong. My body was wiser than my speculations. It did not like control and force, and clearly rebelled against the involuntary drills, though because of my well practiced motor coordination I got through them easily. But acting like a machine, commanded and guided by others, did not attract my body, and it began to show the symptoms.

"The disciplined body" (Foucault, 1977) is the basis for the use of power, and especially so in the army. This kind of body finds it difficult to express and receive emotion, which is continually repressed by hazing. Due to sport, my body was certainly more controlled than would have been normal. Yet I was always self-motivated by the discipline of training, which I had always thought of as sensible. I could not take the military exercises, the only aim of which seemed to be to humiliate and to stretch your tolerance. Such exercises were carried out in a way that my asthma could not bear; we went at full pace with no pause for breath.

The released body?

For the most part I have enjoyed those situations in which I have felt "as one body" with someone else, such as when making love, or when I have done something for someone with my body, as in a football game, or by being united with other players and in front of the spectators.

Phenomenologists talk about the "lived body" in relation to other people, sociologists talk about the "mirroring body," and psychology speaks of narcissism. In each of us there exists the will to be seen, experienced and accepted. For me, at least, this aspect of corporeality was important: in playing football I was poised as a performing artist. Imagine the feeling when, as an object under hundreds if not thousands of pairs of eyes, you manage a good ball trick, a tackle, a pass, a goal. Even more important is the support you get from your own team, which following a goal exhibits strong physical emotions. Isn't that something in a culture which shies away from touching?

Mirroring corporeality, which is defined from the exterior, from fashion and from ideal images of the body, can at worst lead you to withdrawal, to narcissistic imbalance, or to anorexia. But the mirroring body is also a well of enjoyment that should not be blocked up, as with old-fashioned morality. The body that has built its world on denials can petrify like "human armor," which finds enjoyment in control, submission and destroying others.[5]

The denial of the body has been almost a central principle in Finnish culture. This is so especially concerning the enjoyment of sexuality, which in my youth could not even be mentioned. It was a matter for embarrassment, concealment, filthy but witty stories, full of threatening contradictions. Out of this folk wisdom we constructed our sexual fantasies, which were later fed by representations of the (female) body, offered mainly for male eyes by the mass (crotch) culture. This externalized and possibly limited our sensual experience.

The body was not, however, defined only by discourse; it was also affected by personal experiences that were exceptions to the cultural code, and that always, of course, interrelate with what is learned. The interpretation should not be determined in advance, but it is not totally free either. Nor should the interpreter fear contradictions when reality is itself non-homogeneous.

The body can be disciplined, mirroring, dominated, or communicative.[6] I discover all these in the story of my own body. From sport and the army I know what it means to be disciplined; as a mirroring body I played the ball under the eyes of the audience; for domination I learned through my sexual fantasies; for communication I learned through childhood games and in teams, and later through everyday intimate relationships.

Even identity is not stable or the same in different situations (cf. Weckroth, 1991). That which we experienced will remain marked in our body like a "map" of experiences. But in their deepest regions our bodies retain the project of the present and the future. We can change ourselves by envisaging and changing the idea of our own life history. That is what memory-work (Haug *et al.*, 1987) has meant for me.[7]

Asthma has felt like a burden, a deficiency and a shame. Maybe it prevented the life project of "becoming a top athlete." But it also helped the progress of my playing career when my body was changing to be mirroring from the body which used to be disciplined. After that the discipline became looser. Because I did not dare to invest in a long sporting career I tried to find more joy in the here and now.

In the case of memory-work asthma provides for me today a richness which I would not want to erase from my world of experiences. What form of corporeality would now dominate had I lived as a healthy, disciplined and self-satisfied young athlete?

Notes

1. The Olympic champion javelin thrower Miklos Nemeth, it is said, had to carefully consider his relationship to sport and to himself after finding himself lying in the street – he had been thrown out of a pub. This prompted his new beginning. The multiple Olympic winner in cross-country skiing, Marja-Liisa Hämäläinen's (now Kirvesniemi) failure in the 1978 world championships set the press against her: sending her to competitions abroad was deemed a waste of money. She had to decide, as she later explained, whether skiing was

enough fun in itself to be able to stand it, or whether to ski simply in the hope of succeeding. Both these sports personalities had to face the sorts of problems which were linked through the ability of "self." But these ponderings led to an improved self-knowledge, and through that to even greater success.

2. On the basis of present-day knowledge I know that the capacity of my lungs was hindered, but because of my improved condition I was able to manage with less oxygen. This is a problem which arises today, especially in cross-country skiing and in swimming, when the major part of the world's topics are "asthmatic." If the question is not that of the side effects of using asthma medicines, then where does one draw the line between health and sickness?

3. In my area of experience the working-class children were raised mainly in the spirit of "what is not allowed" (no crime, no violence), whereas the middle-class children were taught what they should do (get good grades, pursue hobbies). How have the older working-class generations known how to manage with their children who are oriented toward white-collar professions (cf. Willis, 1984)?

4. In the 1980s when I started "memory-work" I noticed immediately how I had forgotten many key things, for instance as described at the start of this article. To recall is a long and taxing process. I also noticed that history, one's personal history, is not a single thread, a rational story, but is full of irrational breaks.

5. The analysis carried out by Klaus Theweleit (1977 and 1980) is an extensive psychoanalytic research about "semi-birth," concerning the memorial of the German semi-military members of the main guard, which tells of the hardened, armored, bodies that deny everything experienced to be irrational, drifting and formless – such as women, Jews and communists. Their bodies were "dominated." "The war was a means to govern internal chaos and to confront emotion without destruction. Military men loved everything which protected them from love." As Siltala (1988) has written: "To feel one's body as total and functioning is the only way by which Theweleit overcomes the problem of semi-birth."

6. The dominated, mirroring and disciplined body exists concretely according to Frank (1990), but the communicative body is one kind of ideal situation. Eichberg (1990) also talks of this when he analyzes the idea of "det-krop" ("it-body," to have a body), "jeg-krop" ("me-body," to be a body) and "du-krop" ("you-body"). The latter is connected to communicating, to the socialized, reflexive and mystic.

7. To recall is individual and modern. As Eeva Jokinen (1989, p. 101) has formulated it: "When the human body draws up a biography for itself it is hard work: some events have to be highlighted as important, and others have to be forgotten. Memory work, however, goes in the other direction – in it one tries to unpack the logic of biography, to remember the forgotten, to shift the remembered to the margins. Thus it concentrates more on breaks than on continuities."

References

Carrigan, T., Connell, B. and Lee, J. (1985) "Toward a New Sociology of Masculinity," *Theory and Society*, 5 (14), pp. 551-604.

Dunning, E. (1986) "The Sociology of Sport in Europe and the United States: Critical Observations from an 'Eliasian' Perspective," in Rees, R. C. and Miracle, A. W. (eds), *Sport and Social Theory*. Champaign, IL: Human Kinetics Publications.

Eichberg, Henning (1990) "Krop, legeme - og hvad ellers? Overvejelser ov er den tredje krop," *Centring*, 25, pp. 24-40.

Foucault, M. (1977) *Discipline and Punish. The Birth of the Prison.* New York: Vintage Books.

Frank, A. W. (1990) "For a Sociology of the Body: an Analytical Review," in Featherstone, M., Hepworth, M. and Turner, B. S. (eds), *The Body. Social Process and Cultural Theory.* London: Sage Publications.

Goffman, Erving (1974) *Frame Analysis. An Essay on the Organization of Experience.* Boston: Northeastern University Press.

Haug, F. *et al.* (1987) *Female Sexualization. A Collective Work of Memory.* London: Verso.

Heinilä, K. (1982) "The Totalization Process in International Sport," *Sportwissenschaft*, 12.

Jackson, D. (1990) *Unmasking Masculinity. A critical autobiography.* London: Unwin Hyman.

Jokinen, E. (1989) "Muistelutyö" (Memory-work), *Sosiaalipolitiikka*, 14, p. 101.

Klemola, T. (1990) *Liikunta tienä kohti varsinaista itseä. Liikunnan projektien fenomenologinen tarkastelu (Sport as a way to the real self. Phenomenological analyses of different projects in sport).* Tampere: University of Tampere.

Laitinen, A. and Tiihonen, A. (1990) "Narratives of Men's Experiences in Sport," *International Review for the Sociology of Sport*, 3 (25), pp. 185-200.

Messner, M. (1987) "The Meaning of Success: The Athletic Experience and the Development of Male Identity," in Brod, H. (ed.), *The Making of Masculinities: The New Men Studies.* Boston: Allen and Unwin.

Messner, M. A. (1992) "Boyhood, Organized Sports, and the Construction of Masculinities," in Kimmel, M. S. and Messner, M. A. (eds), *Men's Lives.* New York: Macmillan.

Morgan, D. H. J. (1992) *Discovering Men.* London: Routledge.

Sabo, D. F. and Panepinto, J. (1990) "Football Ritual and the Social Reproduction of Masculinity," in Messner, M. A. and Sabo, D. F. (eds), *Sport, Men and the Gender Order: Critical Feminist Perspectives.* Champaign, IL: Human Kinetics Publications.

Schrag, C. O. (1988): "The Lived Body as a Phenomenological Datum," in Morgan, W. J. and Meier, K. V. (eds), *Philosophic Inquiry in Sport.* Champaign, IL: Human Kinetics Publications.

Siltala, J. (1988) "Symbioottisesta hallintapakosta suhteelliseen toimintavapauteen - psykohistorian ulottuvuus?" (From symbiotic imperative of domination to relative freedom of action – the possibility for psychohistory?), *Tiede and edistys* (*Science and Progress*) 2-3 (13), pp. 136-47, 232-44.

Theweleit, K. (1977 and 1980) *Männerphantasien.* Vols 1 and 2. Frankfurt/M.

Veijola, S. (1994) "Metaphors of Mixed Team Play," *International Review for the Sociology of Sport,* 1 (27).

Weckroth, K. (1991) *X voi olla kuka tahansa* (*X could be anyone*). Tampere: Hanki ja Jää.

Willis, P. (1984) *Koulun penkiltä palkkatyöhön. Miten työväenlu okan nuoret saavat työväenluokan työt* (*Learning to Labour. How Working Class Ki ds Get Working Class Jobs*). Jyväskylä: Vastapaino.

Ziehe, T. (1992) *Uusi nuoriso. Epätavanomaisen oppimisen puolustus* (*The new youth. In defence of unusual learning*). Jyväskylä: Vastapaino.

Chapter 13

Disabling Men: Masculinity and Disability in Al Davison's Graphic Autobiography *The Spiral Cage*

PAUL MCILVENNY

> While many progressive intellectuals have stepped forward to decry racism,
> sexism, and class bias, it has not occurred to most of them that the very
> foundations on which their information systems are built, their very practices
> of reading and writing, seeing and thinking, and moving are themselves laden
> with assumptions about hearing, deafness, blindness, normalcy, paraplegia,
> and ability and disability in general. (Davis, 1995, pp. 4-5)

Patriarchal societies in the West have assumed that to be human is to be a
man, to be a man is to be strong and able, and to be able is to have a
culturally "normal" yet impervious body. Feminists have assailed the first
two assumptions, but how does the disabled man fit into the remainder of
this ableist logic? For too long we have made discriminatory and
oppressive assumptions about the male body which many men cannot live
up to, for example, if they become chronically ill or are born with an
impairment (Sabo and Gordon, 1995, pp. 10-11). Davis (1995, p. 158)
argues that these assumptions of *normalcy* continue their hegemony even in
progressive areas such as cultural studies. Disabled bodies are not
permitted to participate in the erotics of power or in economies of
transgression. Thus, we need to investigate how a hegemonic notion of
masculinity informs and interacts with cultural notions of disability. With
such an understanding we may be better able to cope with men's dire
behavior when they are confronted with illness and a diseased body,
whether it is their own or another's.

My particular focus in this article is on the relations between men
when one or more is "disabled." Unfortunately, these relations are often
pervasively violent, insidious and subordinating, with the result that men
dis-able other men. In order to explore the everyday assumptions of male

ability in Western culture, which conceal dis/ability and the "failures" of masculinity, I examine one example of autobiographical comics, a "genre" in which comics creators tell their life narratives.[1] Autobiographical comics give insights into the cultural narratives and discourses which bound and limit the construction of the visible self. Written and oral life narratives have been used in men's studies research to document men's experiences and practices (for example, Jackson, 1990; Seidler, 1991 and Connell, 1995), as well as in disability research to bring forth the patient's perspective on illness and impairment (for example, Shakespeare *et al.*, 1996; Monks and Frankenberg, 1995; Gershick and Miller, 1995; Charmaz, 1995). A focus on representations of men and disability in autobiographical comics adds to these growing literatures. Autobiographical comics creators use a unique graphic medium (both visual and textual) to narrate and construct a life story. Although such creators are few in number,[2] there are several who have told of the effects of an impairment on their lives and their relations with others. One creator, Al Davison, is of particular interest because he narrates in subtle ways his fundamental search for identity and purpose – going against the grain of hegemonic masculinity – on the margins of an ableist, patriarchal society.[3]

Al Davison was born with severe spina bifida in 1960 in northern England, and his comic book called *The Spiral Cage* (*SC*) relates in a rich graphic style the trials and joys of growing up "disabled" in English society. It was first published in the USA in 1988 by Renegade Press.[4] I will mainly concentrate on the longer and less chronological second version published by Titan in 1990. The jacket copy of the 1990 edition reads:

> Doctors considered him a hopeless case, condemned for life to the inescapable 'spiral cage' of his own DNA. But they reckoned without the fighting spirit of Al and his parents, and this book movingly portrays in Al's own words and pictures his struggles to overcome his 'disability' and the prejudice that surrounds it. A true story of one man's coming to terms with his physical, artistic and spiritual potential, that will move you to laughter and tears.

In his sometimes distressing autobiography we have a chance to observe the self-representation and visualization of the fragmented and abject[5] male body in relation to other men and a dis-abling society and body politics.

Autobiography and masculinity

Middleton (1992) claims that there is a silence concerning men's self-reflections about their subjectivity and power as men. In fact, most men do not know they have a gender, and the inward gaze, when it occurs, is dispersed and deconstituted. In his insightful critical autobiography, Jackson (1990) finds that most traditional male autobiographies search for a true self, present a chronological, linear and ejaculatory narrative structure, support the myth of unified identity, split the personal from the social, and are falsely universal. The tradition of male autobiography unfolds with a major concern for the growth of the autobiographer's mind – for example, first influences, the realization of a capacity for self-determination, and an emergent sexual awareness. For most of his book, Jackson tells us of his upbringing and the impact of a life-threatening disease on his sense of body and self, a sense of falling apart and a challenge to the assumed qualities and values of growing up a "real man."

However, it is not possible, and Jackson acknowledges this, to consider autobiography without recognizing the impact of feminist critiques of the male norms of autobiographical writings and criticism (Järvelä, 1996). In her challenge to the male norms of autobiographical narrative, Mason (1980) proposes that the self of women's autobiography has often required the presence of another in order to represent itself in writing: identity is constructed "by way of alterity." Indeed, "the self-discovery of female identity seems to acknowledge the real presence and recognition of another consciousness, and the disclosure of female self is linked to the identification of some 'other'" (p. 210), which enables women to write openly about themselves. Friedman (1988) amends Mason's original formulation by arguing that female autobiographers tend to locate the self of their project in relation not only to a singular, chosen other, but also in relation to the collective experience of women as gendered subjects in a variety of social contexts. Women's autobiography is possible when the "individual does not feel *herself* to exist outside of others, and still less against others, but very much *with* others in an interdependent existence that asserts its rhythms everywhere in the community ... [where] lives are so thoroughly entangled that each of them has its center everywhere and its circumference nowhere. The important unit is thus never the isolated being" (p. 38). The naturalized illusion of individualism, a trait of male autobiographies, is a reflection of privilege. For instance, "a white man has the luxury of forgetting his skin color and sex. He can think of himself as an 'individual.' ... The cultural categories MAN, WHITE, CHRISTIAN, and HETEROSEXUAL in Western societies, for example, are *as significant for a man of the dominant group* as they are for a women at the margins of culture" (p. 39, my italics). We should add "ABLE-BODIED" to the (ever-expanding) list of cultural identity categories so as not to preclude analysis of Davison's untraditional graphic life narrative, which at times has a strong sense of standpoint and community.

In an interview Davison has said that he began his autobiographical project in 1984. The first published version comprises a chronological narrative of 40 pages, interspersed with dream sequences, childhood memories and a fairy tale embedded in an appended story. He substantially revised this version, added many new pages (a new total of 105) and organized it into five thematic sections for the publication in 1990 by Tundra.[6] Davison has claimed that "organizing the material thematically gives a clearer understanding of my life. Each section shows the improvement in different aspects of my life" (Thorpe, 1990, p. 37). The differences between the two versions are marked and noteworthy: not only do many new dimensions emerge with the addition of new pages and the organization of the autobiography into thematic narratives of transformation,[7] but the whole tone of the autobiography is altered by his post-1988 heterosexual relationship with Maggie Lawrence.

It is clear from the first pages that Davison's autobiography will qualify as a *Bildungsroman*, a "tale of progressive travelling of a life from troubled or stifled beginnings; in which obstacles are overcome and true self actualized or revealed" (Stanley, 1992, p. 11). Davison has made clear that he wanted to "challenge people's assumptions about disablement. One of my original ideas was for the book to be used in colleges and schools" (Thorpe, 1990, p. 35). Its use as an educational tool is undoubted, but when we compare the two published versions we can also see that Davison is engaged in reconstituting a sense of identity by re-creating the later version. For example, the tone of melancholic self-pity that characterizes his reflections in chapter three before he dramatically smashes the mobility "aids," is turned outwards into anger at the dis-abling, alienating "destructive," "hateful" comments of "normal" society. This is a process indicative of "coming out" as a dis-abled man, redefining disability as a political oppression (Shakespeare *et al.*, 1996, p. 58).

Dis/ability and masculinity

One only has to look in a dictionary or a thesaurus to get a sense of the moral evaluation of the term "able" and its antonyms. If one is "able" then one is capable, apt, fit, efficient, proper, skilful and clever. The opposite is to be incompetent, incapable, silly, weak, feeble and inept. People with disabilities have often been considered grotesque creatures of disorder. Stallybrass and White (1986) include in their list of the discursive norms of the grotesque: impurity, heterogeneity, protuberant distension, disproportion, decentered and eccentric arrangements, a focus on gaps, orifices and symbolic filth, physical needs and pleasures of the "lower bodily stratum." They argue that "the grotesque physical body is invoked both defensively and offensively because it is not simply a powerful image but fundamentally constitutive of the categorical sets through which we live and make sense of the world" (Stallybrass and White, 1986, p. 23). That is why we must pay close attention to cultural discourses of impairment, incompleteness, and the chaotic or "grotesque body."[8] In addition, Turner's (1996, p. 1) notion of the "somatic society," a society in which "major political and personal issues are both problematized in the body and expressed through it," gives further weight to any project to examine masculinity and disability in contemporary life narratives in which the body appears visibly and repeatedly.

But any analysis of disabled lives should not dwell on the personal or biomedical perspectives. The social model of disability has recently emerged as disabled people have begun to challenge the patriarchal institutions that control their lives.[9] The model rejects medical and constructionist perspectives because "it is not disabled people who have defined the experience, neither have they had control over either medical treatment or the social consequences of impairment. *Thus if disability is to be made sense of, it is the non-disabled society and its institutions which should be the subject of study*" (Morris, 1993, p. 87). From this empowering perspective, able society is the dis-abler, and therefore we need to reconceptualize the object-centered, passive terms "impairment" and "disabled."[10]

Zola (1984) has pointed out that people with disabilities are mostly born into "normal" families. Hence, they are socialized into an ableist culture and have to adopt their disabled identity. As a consequence, "we think of ourselves in the shadow of the external world. The very vocabulary we use to describe ourselves is borrowed from that society. We are *de*-formed, *dis*-eased, *dis*-abled, *dis*-ordered, *ab*-normal, and most telling of all *in*-valid" (p. 144). It is clear from his autobiography that Davison was born into a male-dominated society that is intent on regulating his body, its performance and his identity.

Insults and verbal hatred are the common currency of an ableist society. The naming, shaming and dehumanizing of the disabled body occur at various points in the narrative, for instance, when Davison is called or remembers being called "spacka," "scarecrow legs," "fuck face," "vegetable," among other insults. In one panel in chapter three a teasing phrase echoes across the frightened face of the boy Davison: "Cat got your tongue, Why don't you run ... Cat got your feet too ...." The expression "Cat got your tongue" is commonly used to admonish and shame children for failing to speak up when addressed by an adult. The second and third lines tie together with Davison's perceived lack of mobility and imply that he should be ashamed to lack such a "normal" ability (for an active boy) as running (cf. Sedgwick, 1993 for a discussion of shame).

What happens to men when their bodies fragment, fail or malfunction? How does a boy grow up to be a man when he has a physical impairment? In order to address these questions we should take note of historical changes in cultural notions of the male body in hegemonic masculinity. With the bourgeois ideals of "Christian manliness" in the nineteenth century (Segal, 1990, p. 288), we find stressed "spiritual, cerebral and moral precepts. As well as the dignity of labour and the importance of manly independence and autonomy" (p. 105). By the close of the nineteenth century, a competing "muscular masculinity" emphasized sport and physical labor as well as celebrating a Spartan athleticism and conformism (p. 106).

In comparison, contemporary hegemonic masculinity in relation to the male body[11] often emphasizes ability, superhuman strength and stamina, power, physical violence, unemotionality, hardness, imperviousness, independence, autonomy, potency, assertiveness, status, authority, and the shame of failure (Connell, 1995). In the late twentieth century, there has been a proliferation of contemporary media discourses and social inscriptions (in English) on and about the male body (Murphy, 1987; Simpson, 1994; Craig, 1992). In contemporary sport, there is a panoply of institutions and rules for the regulation of men's bodies on display, in contact, in competition and hierarchy, and which most often exclude women.[12] As a consequence, Connell (1995, p. 54) notes that "the constitution of masculinity through bodily performance means that gender is vulnerable when the performance cannot be sustained – for instance, as a result of physical disability [impairment]." Gershick and Miller (1995) have studied how North American men cope with a disabling accident or illness. They found that there were three types of response: one is to redouble efforts to meet the hegemonic standards (*reliance*); another is to *reformulate* the definition of masculinity, though still pursuing masculine themes such as independence and control; and a third response is to *reject* hegemonic masculinity as a package. Although Davison has lived with an impairment all of his life, and thus has no former "normal" masculine identity to reject, we can see in his behavior certain parallels with that of men who have become disabled later in life. In the next sections I focus on his reformulation and rejection of masculinity in and through his encounters with others.

Disabling men: Between men, masculinity and disability

Davison constructs graphic narratives of his encounters with other boys and men, at school, at home, in institutions and in comics. In many encounters he is infantilized and emasculated, yet he finds ways to overcome his subordination and marginalization and to express creatively alternative visions of a "failed" masculinity. Most shocking are the pernicious engagements he has with aggressive bullies, both boys and adult males, who take it upon themselves to circumscribe his impairment and dehumanize him in certain performances of masculinity. These violent acts and words are the outward manifestation of the threat to the sovereignty of hegemonic masculinity that is projected onto and consolidated in abject "others."

Childhood, boyhood, manhood

Does Davison's life narrative follow the typical Freudian trajectory of how the boy becomes a man? Does he separate both psychically and socially from his mother? Does he journey to pass some test in the "outside world" that will prove his autonomous identity? Indeed, he does leave the family home when his parents become infirm. He does feel complete when he settles down with Maggie. He does reject the "care" of institutions, which he sees as attempting to immobilize him and deny his break from the "mothering" body politic. Nevertheless, it is clear in his treatment by (male) medical doctors that he is to remain a "boy," in the care of his mother and under the protection of the state. "You, boy, have ideas above your station ... walk ... indeed!" and "You can't avoid your limitations, boy" are gendered injunctions that infantilize the aspirations of Davison.

Morris (1993) notes that for a disabled women there is a partial congruity between normative roles of being a woman and being disabled – for example, passivity and dependency – yet a disabled women may be unable to fulfil her "role" as homemaker, wife and mother, and as a physically attractive woman. In contrast, a disabled man fails to measure up to the dominant culture's definition of masculinity – as strength and autonomy – which means that the disabled man is often seen as dependent and emasculated. The wheelchair is the ultimate symbol of dependency and lack of autonomy.[13] In Davison's autobiography we only see his infant self in a wheelchair on two occasions, otherwise from an early age he was repeatedly rejecting the mobility "aids," and hence refusing to be intelligible as the "other Other."

As a child, Davison regularly appears in costume or he is active in role play; for instance, he appears as Gene Kelly in *Singing in the Rain* (with his sister supplying the legs), or he imagines himself as a pirate or adventurer scaling the bookshelf-ship to rescue (or steal) a book from the crew. On several occasions Davison appears in a Batman or Superman costume. The most ironic and playful moment occurs near the end of the first chapter when he takes his first public steps towards the viewer in his Batman-logo shirt and cape, beaming to those present at the clinic: "Look.. Mam! I can walk!" Equally poignant is the short reflection about the time he enters a telephone box, transformed from the mild-mannered Clark Kent into Superman, only to find the wheelchair is stuck. He calls the police station and reports that he, "supaman," is trapped in a telephone box and needs help.[14]

A conventional dismissal of superhero comics relevates the genre to the psychological mire of pre-adolescent power fantasy. In contrast, Middleton (1992) argues that superhero comic books are a substitute world, a fantasy that is a symptom of the social structures of desire and emotion produced by the general absence of continuity between men and children. In short, boys read superhero comics because they do not have close relationships with their fathers or access to their fathers' work environments. Other critics argue that superhero comics are less about unlimited and unbridled power, than about powerlessness. In his essay "The Myth of Superman," Eco (1981) suggests that in spite of all his powers, Superman is "a creature immersed in everyday life, in the present, apparently tied to our own conditions of life and death."

Although his father features rarely in the autobiography, there is nothing to suggest that Davison did not have a positive relationship with him. However, as a child Davison had little access to the environment of a "normal" boy; he lacked continuity between his cared-for world and the worlds of the active child and man – he was powerless, or more to the point, disempowered. Middleton's interpretation of the role of superheroes in boys' lives suggests that superhero comics would have provided Davison with a substitute fantasy world in which the ironic structure of much of the best of the genre matched his own sense of powerlessness.

Subordinated masculinity and crisis

Often Davison graphically represents himself unclothed, and many of the naked self-representations occur when Davison is almost helpless. Thus, we see graphically the male body paralyzed, in pain, prostrate, suffering or depressed. On one occasion, in chapter three, a psychological crisis point is reached as a consequence of his tortuous relationship to other schoolboys who bully him. In a four-by-two matrix of reminiscences of adolescent trauma, Davison uses the technique of parallel editing to cross-cut[15] between the external, public attitude towards him at school, and his internal, troubled thoughts. David Jackson's (1990) critical autobiography tells us much about the complicit relations between boys at school over everyday violence toward other vulnerable boys. He concludes that in his schooling (in the 1950s), violence was a central part of the process of masculine identification, and that bullying, daily beatings and psychological violence were institutionally naturalized and taken for granted by both teachers and pupils (see Mac an Ghaill, 1994 for a comprehensive discussion of the school as a masculinizing agency). At the age of eleven, Davison is bullied at a "mainstream" ("normal" in the first version) school for being different.[16] At home, naked and ill at ease in the "home" of his body, he reflects on the taunts at school: "They say I want to grow up to be like them, that not everyone grows up 'normal.' They call me 'scarecrow legs,' [next panel in "home" sequence] spacka … maybe … I … do … don't want to grow up … normal … maybe I don't … [next panel in sequence] don't want to grow up."

As with the young boy in Gunter Grass' *Tin Drum*, Davison almost refuses to grow up to see the world as "normal" adults do. In desperation at his abjectness, he contemplates suicide, hara-kiri style, with the help of a sharp-pointed knife. At school, he fights back against his male aggressors, and as they leave the scene in humiliation, one shouts back, "I'll see you dead! Spacka!" At this point, the young Davison, about to do the deed at home, drops the knife and replies "No … you won't!!" across the otherwise impermeable adjacent panel boundary of the checkerboard matrix. The connections between the dichotomies of the private/public, of the internal/external, of social oppression/psychological trauma, of blame/shame, are made and shattered. The autobiographer dramatically places great significance on this crisis event because it leads to his eventual rejection of the cultural regulation and inscription of his body and identity by "normal" society.

Who is disabled? Encounters with disabling men

The common understandings and applications of the terms "disabled" or "handicapped" are problematic. Davison demonstrates in his autobiography that the notions of being "differently abled" or "temporarily abled" may be more appropriate. He does this by challenging the ways that "able-bodied" men attempt to regulate the bodies of "other" men. For example, in chapter three, while outdoors at a party he is told by an "able-bodied" man to face up to the reality of his disability. Davison challenges him to prove his "ableness," and the man patronizingly accepts. Davison matches him for the first two physical tests: to snatch an apple from a tree and to run a race. Then, Davison chooses the third task, which the "able" man cannot perform, thereby embarrassing his competitor and reversing the original presumptive question, namely "How does it feel to be disabled?" In fact, the male partygoer has accepted a performative, "I dare you." Davison accomplishes the dare in front of a witnessing audience, and thus points to a potential crisis in every authority-wielding normative categorization – it may fail.

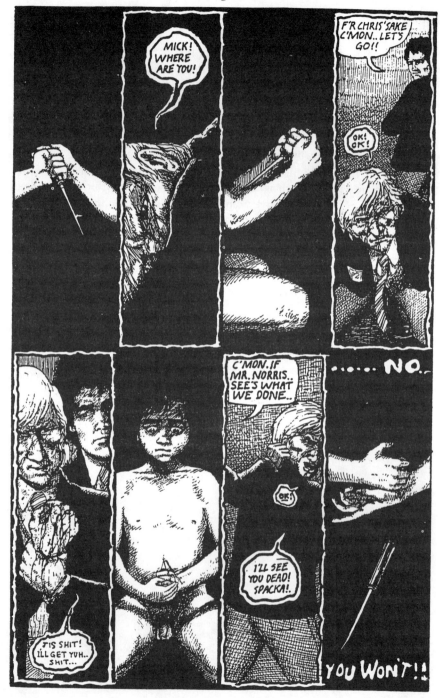

Figure 1

Figure 2

The consensual nature of the party-goer's presumptive categorization of Davison as "disabled" has been put under stress.[17] Hence, Davison has shown us that a person's abilities are multifarious, and that one should not be defined by an impairment. He destigmatizes the term "disabled" and points to the originating source of that stigmatization, the dis-abler.

Male violence toward "other" men

The thematic chapter three, titled "Push 'n' Shuv," recounts some of Davison's encounters with aggressive males who take it upon themselves to circumscribe his impairment in certain performances of masculinity. As a reader who has lived in a caring community in the North of England, I find this element of the autobiography the most shocking – in the book there are five instances of male violence and aggression toward Davison. One can interpret these violent acts and words as the outward manifestation of the threat to the sovereignty of masculinity that is projected onto and consolidated in abject "others." If a man must be invulnerable, indefatigable and vigorous, then the opposite is to be repelled from the male body and the body politic. A sign of weakness or a blatant disregard for the performative gestures and public display of masculinity invites harassment, teasing, and even aggression. Davison asks in exasperation, "Why would anyone ... want to attack me just because of the way I walk? And why are some people sacred of me?"

Overall, chapter three encourages us to see his growing spirituality and control as a means both to feel "at home" with his body and to deny the grounds on which masculinity is performed. In one encounter, we are shown in the first five panels how a bully attempts to play a humiliating stunt on Davison in front of his witnessing friends. Amazingly, the bully tries to repel the "helpless" objectified body[18] of Davison over the counter of an Indian takeaway, but Davison quickly retaliates, using his martial arts skills to kick the intruder to the ground. The gang back off, vowing vengeance. This is the first of four connected incidents layed out in corresponding horizontal panel sequences one above the other on the page. Across the sets of panels we see unfolding the deplorable but familiar tale of male violence and retribution.

Figure 3

The repeated attempts at revenge for the bully's shaming in public physical violence display a set of interpretations of prior actions. Just how the bully and his friends interpreted the previous encounters and their consequences for social identities and relations is made clear in Davison's framing of the four encounters over a period of two weeks. When the bullies return for the second time, ten days later, they approach Davison from one direction. After announcing, "Hi ya spacka! Remember me?," the one who was beaten in the first encounter (Chaz) throws a punch, but Davison winds him with one blow. Two others are defeated as well. Two days later, a group surround Davison, and encourage the twice-beaten one (Chaz) to fight once more. They no longer call him "spacka" and Chaz is unsure of doing battle. It appears that they no longer treat him as an easy target, and engage in a physical fight "man-to-man." Davison easily defeats Chaz once again. Two days later, Davison is approached in the street by a gang that includes Chaz. The leader performatively challenges Davison: "Think y'a real hard don't y' spacka ... Y've shown Chaz up once too of'n ... Let's see how hard y' really are ...." For the first time Davison is acknowledged in their eyes as the victor of the previous fights and that Chaz has been shamed, but this time Davison is invited to accept a challenge. However, Davison has learnt when to say "no" through his spiritual training, so, like David Carradine in the popular TV series *Kung Fu*, Davison refuses and walks away from the latest provocation, much to the bewilderment of his aggressors. He has finally been accepted on manly terms, interpellated by the performative verbal challenge. However, he refuses the performance now required by him on precisely those grounds, thereby implying that the behavior of the bullies is unworthy of men – a coup, indeed. In parallel with these narratives of vanquished masculinity, Davison represents himself chanting meditatively in a vertical panel sequence. A smile grows on his face as the coup reaches completion.

Relations to women

There is little space here to do justice to the complexity of Davison's relations to different women and of Davison's heterosexuality and femininity, but I will mention a few observations. Davison's relationship to his mother and other women is made more explicit than that between himself and his father (and other men). He puts much emphasis on his lack of early contact with his mother. In an interview, Davison (in Thorpe, 1990, p. 39) points out "how big an effect that the isolation period during my first two years, when I missed maternal bonding, had on my relationships later."

His early heterosexual impulses and infatuations are demonstrated when Davison portrays himself sitting in the classroom of middle school surrounded by his fellow pupils. Three girls are picked out for favorable comments in arrowed boxes: "Leslie," who was "the most beautiful girl in our school. I was madly in love with her"; "Louise," "the other most beautiful girl in the school. I was also madly in love with"; and "Golem," famous for her knowledge of the alternative rock musician Frank Zappa. Three boys are picked out in rather different ways: "The Brain" is the nickname of a boy with the brain of Einstein but physically incompetent; "Jam-Jar" is his "arch-nemesis"; and "Toad" needs no introduction.

As an adult male, Davison finds that women want to stay friends, possibly to care for him, but not to have sexual relations. On several occasions in the narrative, women reject his advances, and Davison is left puzzled and confused. Davison's bewilderment can be seen as a consequence of an anxiety that he cannot be loved or that he cannot narcissistically love himself. At the end of chapter five, while recalling to his lover Maggie his earlier relationships with women, he summarizes his attitude as: "Well. Like I was falling for any woman who showed me any affection." As is true for many men, Davison had to negotiate the regulated, normative boundary between friendship or affection and desire in a heterosexual relationship, but unlike most he also has to negotiate that between pity and friendship.

I have been considering Davison's narrative, a male autobiography, to be insightful with regard to relations between men and other men, as well as with women. However, Miller (1994, p. 18) advises that we need to examine how our interpretations of self and other, separateness and differentiation, autonomy and relatedness have depended on and promoted assumptions about autobiographical gender. She speculates that we need to ask "new questions about what and whose needs sustain the critical fiction of an isolated masculinity" (p. 5). Although Davison desperately searches for independence both spiritually and physically, his autobiography is also a tale of his maturing relationship with his heterosexual partner, a significant "other," without whom he is incomplete.

Conclusions

Davison's autobiography is pedagogic in its thematic structure. An able-bodied reader can learn from his struggles over his right to walk, his spiritual journey, his engagement with masculinity in its most brutal form, his channelling of creativity into an artistic vocation, and his learning to "polish his mirror" to reflect the love of a woman. Davison sites himself in antithetic relation to normative notions of the "damaged" masculine body. He must deal with the norm that if the life of a man in English working-class culture is one of toughness, struggle and dignified labor, then he is weak, dependent and impotent. Nevertheless, Davison resists the cultural inscription of the disabled body as "feminine." He refuses to be still, to be inactive, to lack mobility, to be confined by aids to mobility, and he refuses to be bullied by men who take it upon themselves to embarrass him, to man-handle him, to terrorize him in public places and institutions. He "writes/draws back" his own developing vision of masculinity through conflict, a successful transition from boy to heterosexual man.

Yet in Davison's autobiography we find competing tensions. On the one hand, he is constantly reminded of his impairment by institutions and other men in often violent and uncaring ways. This leads to his desperate search for independence both spiritually and physically. On the other hand, the autobiography is also the tale of his relationship with his heterosexual partner, a significant "other," without whom he is incomplete. Not only is Davison caught between oppressive discourses of disability and normative conceptions of heterosexual masculinity, he is torn between a masculine and a feminine mode of life narration. However, we must remember that his respect for bodily control and narrative closure, his rejection of dependency, and his consummation in a heterosexual relationship are all accomplished painfully. Davison struggles to perform, and yet ironize, the masquerade of hegemonic masculinity that "normal, able-bodied" men with privilege and power accomplish all too easily, often to the disadvantage of subordinated and marginalized men. We need to remind ourselves that Davison's metaphor of the "spiral cage" extends beyond the confining realm of the "disabled": "I've always felt that everyone has a disability in some way, whether they acknowledge it or not, and the best way of dealing with it is to use it, to challenge it, to overcome it" (Davison in Thorpe, 1990, p. 37).

Notes

1.   Since the 1960s, comics for older readers have slowly but surely developed into quite a feast of genres and styles, and autobiographical comics in particular provide a distinctive and rewarding domain for exploration from a critical gender perspective. In this article I assume that comics are a mature and sophisticated medium, a set of cultural signifying practices in which gender, masculinities and sexual difference can be interrogated by cartoonists and their adult readers.

2. There are approximately 50 male autobiographical comics creators altogether in my corpus, of whom twenty or so have devoted a substantial proportion of their effort to autobiography. In addition, I know of about 30 female autobiographical comics creators.

3. In her in-depth psychoanalytic examination of the male subject at the margins, Silverman (1992) proposes that images of the body in film tend to create a protective shield that insulates it against the possibilities of mutilation, fragmentation and castration. Davison gives us graphic images of his body without the comfort of protection.

4. A third publication, *The Minotaur's Tale* (*MT*), published in 1992, is not explicitly autobiographical but does rewrite ("write back") the Greek myth from the contemporary point of view of a disabled man whose life bears some resemblance to that of Davison's.

5. According to Julia Kristeva (1982, p. 4), the abject is that which "disturbs identity, system, order. What does not respect borders, positions, rules." The abject represents what human life and culture exclude in order to sustain themselves.

6. Much of the material for the thematic sections is drawn from Davison's daily comics diary, a graphic record of his life. Other pages are clearly memories of his childhood. Pages and panels are often dated and located geographically.

7. Charmaz (1995, p. 267) notes that adult men's experience of chronic illness can threaten already formed masculine identities; the resulting identity dilemmas can also be recurrent and chronic. From Davison's autobiography, we can see that this might also apply to men with disabilities from birth.

8. Stallybrass and White (1986, p. 193) reflect on an "unnoticed slide between two quite distinct kinds of 'grotesque,' the grotesque as the 'Other' of the defining group or self, and the grotesque as a boundary phenomenon of hybridization or inmixing, in which the self and other become enmeshed in an inclusive, heterogeneous, dangerously unstable zone." If we separate the two, it becomes possible "to see that a fundamental mechanism of identity formation *produces* the second, hybrid grotesque at the level of the political unconscious *by the very struggle to exclude the first grotesque*" (p. 193) – a "double-articulation."

9. Recently, the social model has come under critical attention from disabled women/feminists (cf. Crow, 1996) who desire to reinject in the social model a personal dimension to the experience of impairment.

10. Several disability rights organizations have officially proposed the following revised definitions: "*Impairment* is the lack of part or all of a limb, or having a defective limb, organ or mechanism of the body. *Disability* is the loss or limitation of opportunities that prevents people who have impairments from taking part in the normal life of that community on an equal level with others due to physical and social barriers" (Finkelstein and French, 1993, p. 28).

11. Connell (1995) notes that "true masculinity is almost always thought to proceed from men's bodies – to be inherent in a male body or to express something about a male body" (p. 45). Either the body drives and directs

action, or the body sets limits to action. However, he argues that neither social determinism nor biological determinism, nor a combination of both, will serve as the basis for an account of gender. Instead, Connell suggests that bodies in their own right as bodies, do matter. He goes on to say that "there is an irreducible bodily dimension in experience and practice; the sweat cannot be excluded .... The physical sense of maleness and femaleness is central to the cultural interpretations of gender. Masculine gender is (among other things) a certain feel to the skin, certain muscular shapes and tensions, certain postures and ways of moving, certain possibilities in sex" (pp. 51-2).

12. From personal experience with the illness asthma, Arto Tiihonen (1994) considers the construction of the masculine body and male identity in sport.

13. With regard to popular cinema, Morris (1993, p. 87) notes that "the association of disability with dependency and lack of autonomy has in fact been used by film-makers in recent years to explore an experience of vulnerability for men." For example, the wheelchair can be used as a metaphor of impotence for exploring the awfulness of dependency. According to Morris, these films tell us little about the actual experience of being a disabled man, but for a critical observer they can tell much about the non-disabled society's definitions of both masculinity and disability.

14. A double irony not foreseen by Davison is that Christopher Reeve, the star of the wholesome film versions of Superman in the 1970s and 1980s, recently became paralyzed from a horse riding fall.

15. Usually, panels relate directly to just prior panels in terms of the conventional reading of Western comics; that is, a viewer interprets a panel in relation to the panel conventionally just prior to the current one, and the interpretation process is called closure (McCloud, 1993). Davison often invokes delayed or deferred closure. Coherent sequences are juxtaposed in alternate panels within the matrix layout of the page, so the closure of one sequence is not immediate in the next panel. This technique is very similar to parallel cross-cutting in the cinema. Because of his extensive use of non-linear parallel cross-cutting, with delayed closure between panels, panels often amass into a checkerboard design on the page, a result not possible in temporal film.

16. See Kehily and Nayak (1997) for an empirical study of how masculinities are differentially regulated through comic routines and rituals in school.

17. One might argue that Davison has not effectively disrupted the masculine mode of the performative dare. He issues the challenge and proceeds to elaborate it in the same manner as would be expected between two men but without parody (though with a strong sense of irony). What he has disrupted in front of a witnessing audience is the presumption of physical superiority by the man whom he has challenged.

18. Following Butler (1990, p. 133), I suggest that the repudiation of bodies for their impairment is an "expulsion" followed by a "repulsion" that founds and consolidates culturally hegemonic identities. On this occasion, we see this process literalized.

References

Butler, J. (1990) *Gender Trouble: Feminism and the Subversion of Identity.* L ndon: Routledge.

Charm z, K. (1995) "Identity dilemmas of chronically ill men," in Sabo, D. and Gordon, D. F. (eds), *Men's Health and Illness: Gender, Power, and the Body.* London: Sage.

Connell, R. W. (1995) *Masculinities.* Cambridge: Polity Press.

Craig, S. (ed.) (1992) *Men, Masculinity and the Media.* London: Sage.

Crow, L. (1996) "Including all our lives: renewing the social model of disability," in Morris, J. (ed.) *Encounters with Strangers: Feminism and Disability.* London: Women's Press.

Davis, L. J. (1995) *Enforcing Normalcy: Disability, Deafness and the Body.* London: Verso.

Davison, A. (1988) *The Spiral Cage: Diary of an Astral Gypsy.* Long Beach, CA: Renegade Press.

Davison, A. (1990) *The Spiral Cage.* London: Titan Books.

Eco, U. (1981) "The myth of superman," in Eco, U. (ed.) *The Role of the Reader.* London: Hutchinson.

Finkelstein, V. and French, S. (1993) "Towards a psychology of disability," in Swain, J. *et al.* (eds), *Disabling Barriers – Enabling Environments.* London: Sage/Oxford University Press.

Friedman, S. S. (1988) "Women's autobiographical selves: theory and practice," in Benstock, S. (ed.) *The Private Self: Theory and Practice of Women's Autobiographical Writings.* Chapel Hill: University of North Carolina Press.

Gerschick, T. J. and Miller, A. S. (1995) "Coming to terms: masculinity and physical disability," In Sabo, D. and Gordon, D. F. (eds), *Men's Health and Illness: Gender, Power, and the Body.* London: Sage.

Hearn, J. (1996) "Is masculinity dead? A critique of the concept of masculinity/masculinities," in Mac an Ghaill, M. (ed.) *Understanding Masculinties: Social Relations and Cultural Arenas.* Buckingham: Open University Press.

Jackson, D. (1990) *Unmasking Masculinity: A Critical Autobiography.* London: Unwin Hyman.

Järvelä, M.-L. (1996) *"Why hath this lady writ her own life...?" Auto/biography from feminist perspectives.* Oulu: Northern Gender Studies 2, Universities of Oulu and Lapland.

Kehily, M. J. and Nayak, A. (forthcoming). "Another laugh? Repertoires of humour within the schooling cultures of young men," *Gender and Education,* Special Issue on Masculinities.

Kristeva, J. (1982) *Powers of Horror: Essays on Abjection.* New York: Columbia University Press.

Mac an Ghaill, M. (1994) *The Making of Men: Masculinities, Sexualities and Schooling.* Open University Press.

McCloud, S. (1993) *Understanding Comics.* Kitchen Sink Press.

Mason, M. G. (1980) "The other voice: autobiographies of women writers," in Olney, J. (ed.) *Autobiography: Essays Theoretical and Critical*. Princeton, NJ: Princeton University Press.

Middleton, P. (1992) *The Inward Gaze: Masculinity and Male Subjectivity in Modern Culture*. London: Routledge.

Miller, N. K. (1994) "Representing others: gender and the subjects of autobiography," *differences*, 6 (1), pp. 1-27.

Monks, J. and Frankenberg, R. (1995) "Being ill and being me: self, body, and time in multiple sclerosis narratives," in Ingstad, B. and Whyte, S. R. (eds), *Disability and Culture*. Berkeley, CA: University of California Press.

Morris, J. (1993) "Gender and disability," in Swain, J. *et al.* (eds), *Disabling Barriers – Enabling Environments*. London: Open University Press.

Murphy, R. (1987) *The Body Silent*. New York: Henry Holt.

Sabo, D. and Gordon, D. F.(eds) (1995) *Men's Health and Illness: Gender, Power, and the Body*. London: Sage.

Sedgwick, E. K. (1993) *Tendencies*. Durham: Duke University Press.

Segal, L. (1990) *Slow Motion: Changing Masculinities, Changing Men*. London: Virago.

Seidler, V. J. (ed.) (1991) *The Achilles Heel Reader: Men, Sexual Politics and Socialism*. London: Routledge.

Shakespeare, T., Gillespie-Sells, K. and Davies, D. (1996) *The Sexual Politics of Disability: Untold Desires*. London: Cassell.

Silverman, K. (1992) *Male Subjectivity at the Margins*. New York: Routledge.

Simpson, M. (1994) *Male Impersonators*. Chapman and Hall.

Stallybrass, P. and White, A. (1986) *The Politics and Poetics of Transgression*. London: Methuen.

Stanley, L. (1992) *The Auto/biographical I: The Theory and Practice of Feminist Auto/biography*. Manchester: Manchester University Press.

Thorpe, D. (1990) "Al Davison: breaking free," *Speakeasy*, 108, pp. 35-9.

Tiihonen, A. (1994) "Asthma – the construction of the masculine body," *International Review for Sociology of Sport*, 29, pp. 51-62.

Turner, B. S. (1996) *The Body and Society: Explorations in Social Theory*. Oxford: Sage.

Zola, I. K. (1984) "Communication barriers between 'the able-bodied' and 'the handicapped'," in Marinelli, R. P. and Orto, A. E. D. (eds), *Psychological and Social Impact of Physical Disability*. New York: Springer.

Chapter 14

Ethos of Sexual Liberation and the Masculine Other

In this article I will make a few remarks about a cluster of meanings and topics in moral and political discussions referred to as "sexual liberation." By culture of sexual liberation I mean the field of discourses (various figurations, categories and generalizations) and practices which enable modern, "liberal" Western men and women to articulate and evaluate our relation to our bodies and pleasures, and which make experiences expressible and communicable. Sexual liberation is essentially an ethos. It consists of ethical problematizations of proper sexual conduct in general and of individual ideals of the good sex life, and the relation to the sexual self, to a person's own desires, pleasures and experiences.[1] In addition, sexual liberation has political dimensions related to the questions of power relations and individual liberties and rights. In the following, I will focus on men, beginning with a brief excursus on the figurations and meanings of masculinity and the man in the ethos of sexual liberation.

The field of liberation

By sexual liberation I refer to the changes in Western culture and morality concerning carnal pleasures which gradually took place from the mid-1960s, and which has become established during the past three decades. There are three major strands of sexual liberation, which form the world of liberated sexuality, or the condition of "lust modernity."

Perhaps the most influential strand of sexual liberation in the 1960s and 1970s was an expansion of pornography. From the late 1960s pornography became legalized and legitimized, and the production and marketing of obscene and erotic pictures, films and other goods became a prosperous industry. A huge growth of the market for pornographic publications has formed the general condition for liberated sexual pleasures, the "free flow" of images of undressed human bodies in exciting and seductive positions. Images and bodies in the Flyntian and Hefnerian empire are mostly those of women, meant to attract "the man's eye" and to arouse his desires. The naked pin-up girls of *Playboy*, the whorish nudes of *Hustler*, Linda Lovelace's cunt and deep throat are staged and framed as objects of both visual and carnal penetration, for the excitement of the male viewer.

Although the pornographic marketplace forms a major condition for sexual liberation, there are two discourses and projects which are more important than pornography in terms of sexual politics and ethics. Since the late 1960s and the early 1970s "orgasmology" and radical feminism have most significantly formulated the contemporary "liberal" views of the nature, meaning, norms and practices of sexual pleasures. These two discourses have articulated in an elementary way the prevailing questions and problematizations concerning sexual subjectivity and individuality. In this sense orgasmology and radical feminism have formed the basis of sexual liberation's practical reason, its politics and ethics.

Orgasmology is based on William Masters' and Virginia Johnson's sex research and therapy.[2] Masters and Johnson were among the staunchest adovocates of sexual liberation at the end of the 1960s. Their orgasmology challenged psychoanalysis both as a theory of sexuality and as a practice of therapy. It became one of the most widespread and successful forms of critique of psychoanalysis, which grew especially in the US in the beginning of the 1960s. It also offered the backbone and model for various forms of sex therapy, and inspired the formation of a new profession of sex therapists. Masters and Johnson's conceptions and models of therapeutic treatment were also the most important point of reference to new popular sex manuals and therapeutic self-help guidebooks, the first of which were published at the beginning of the 1970s. The best known examples of this genre are Alex Comfort's *Joy of Sex* and *More Joy of Sex* and David Reuben's *All You Want Know about Sex*.

Masters and Johnson's research and sex therapy also influenced and paralleled the second major strand of sexual liberation, radical feminism. Kate Millet's, Germaine Greer's and Ann Oakley's analyses and political programs, among others, expounded the connection between women's oppressed social status and their personal experiences of sexual repression, and politicized the personal. In addition, various feminist guide-books, self-help groups and therapies were formed which aimed to empower women to rule their own bodies and pleasures and to teach them to find their own feminine sexuality.

The orgasmological and the feminist projects of liberation have major points of disagreement, but also common basic assumptions. Both of them conceive sexuality to be a natural phenomenon, a basic tenet of human beings or the biological force that is basically similar in both men and women. They also emphasize the essential particularity and individuality of sexual experience and of the "patterns" or "repertoire" of experience and habits of pleasure. They also give orgasm – in fact lack of orgasm, inability to experience orgasm – a focal position. In both orgasmology and radical feminism the natural and individual characters of sexual pleasure are united in orgasm, and in both versions of ethics sexual liberation defines the task of discovering the relation to one's sexual self, of "finding" one's own sexuality, in terms of "becoming orgasmic."

In addition, both orgasmology and radical feminism are based on problematics of difference between man and woman – considered as two sexes and/or genders. First, there is the question of the sexual relation of man and woman. In orgasmology, this is articulated in the figure of the sexual couple, while in feminist discourse it consists of the subordination of women to men. Secondly, there is the problematics of determining clear and definite difference between men and women. Orgasmology argues that feminine or masculine features of sexuality are natural, whereas feminists concentrate on the distinctiveness of female sexuality, that is feminine desire, experience and ways of pleasure.

The most significant affinity between these two discourses is the tendency to focus on women and to emphasize the feminine. The core issues in both orgasmology and radical feminism are connected to the nature, problems and liberation of women's sexuality, and their major concern tends to be women "becoming orgasmic." This tendency is clear in Masters and Johnson's texts, which I will focus on in order to clarify the figuration of this emphasis.

Women's Lib

Masters and Johnson do not present a theory of inner sexual drives or insticts, but an empirical picture of human sexual reponse. They describe the essence of sexuality as a kind of stimulus-response model, as a series of physiological reactions of excitement of the body, culminating in orgasm. They consider that psychical and social factors – "patterns" of behavior, experience, habits and values – can either facilitate or block the orgasmic reactions of the body. Compatible with this conception of sexuality, their sex therapy is founded on behaviorist psychology and techniques of reconditioning.

Masters and Johnson do not accept anatomical differences as the ground of difference between male and female sexuality. On the contrary, they emphasize repeatedly that basically, that is on the level of physiological reactions of excitement and orgasm, there is no essential difference between men and women.

Despite this, Masters and Johnson conceive both the orgasmic response of the human body and the disturbances, that is "dysfunctions," of normal reactions as being inseparable from biological and bodily differences between the two sexes. Sexual difference – the difference between man and woman and masculine and feminine, based on and caused by factual, biological difference in functions of body and life – is the basic framework of orgasmological knowledge and therapeutic practice. Therefore they name both response and dysfunctions as sexual (instead of orgasmic). In this framework, Masters and Johnson tend to focus on the female body and the sexuality of woman. This emphasis has three different contexts.

First, Masters and Johnson present the female body as the model of the orgasmic human body. Due to its orgasmic capacity – its ability for multiple orgasm – and complexity the female body becomes the paradigm of human sexual response. They stress that laboratory research has proved the fact that the female body has a greater capacity for orgasms than the male body:

> Women have the response potential of returning to another orgasmic experience from any point in the resolution phase if they submit to the reapplication of effective stimulation. This [is the] facility for multiple orgasmic expression ... For the man the resolution phase includes a superimposed refractory period ... Effective restimulation to the higher levels of sexual tension is possible only upon termination of this refractory period;[3] ... her physiological capacity for sexual response infinitely surpasses that of man.[4]

In sex manuals, this conception of woman's "endless" and superior ability of sexual pleasure is presented as a self-evident truth and a kind of model and measure for possibilities of orgasmic pleasures. In the world of orgasmic skills and techniques, woman is the embodiment of limitless natural human potential for increasing and expanding sexual satisfaction: "the female sexual equipment surpasses the male in every possible way – design, function, complexity, and endurance."[5]

The orgasmological gaze focuses on the clitoris as the locus and organizer of orgasmic reactions and capacities of the female body. Masters and Johnson argue that through the clitoris woman's potential for orgasmic pleasures are actualized, that she becomes orgasmic through the clitoris. In other words, the clitoris is a condensation of woman's superior power to experience sexual pleasure. Furthermore, the clitoris becomes the focal point of the sexual independence and self-sufficiency of woman. Masters and Johnson present results of laboratory observations, according to which the female body does not need the penis to "trigger" the orgasmic reaction, and it is in fact masturbation that effects the most intense orgasmic reactions of women – the "fact" that Kinsey earlier had called attention to. The orgasm of woman is no longer regarded as the consequence of male penetration and intercourse – that sexology and the advice books for "married love" from the 1920s to the early 1960s had presented as being normal and natural – but as an independent phenomenon. In Masters and Johnson's texts, this independence of female orgasmic pleasure is embodied and symbolically intensified in the clitoris.

This picture is congruent with the basic ontological premises of orgasmology. It defines the sexual human being as the essentially self-sufficient orgasmic monad. And since the woman is the model and embodiment of human sexual response, she with her clitoral body is the model of the self-sufficient – masturbatory – sexual subject.

The second context in which Masters and Johnson tend to center woman, is sexual politics. They state repeatedly that most sexual problems of women – "dysfunctions" is their term – are general symptoms of both social and personal repression of female sexuality. They suggest that the condition of woman, mainly originated by male-dominated culture and society, does not allow her to express her sexuality openly and to be sexually active. This belief is closely connected to their more general declarations to fight sexual repression and to progress sexual liberation. The feminine figure epitomizes the task of sexual politics: woman, female sexuality, is the most evident and exemplary victim of the repressive traits of Western culture, and thus it is she who is the actual subject of sexual, orgasmic liberation.

The third and the most important focus on women by Masters and Johnson is therapeutic. Their sex therapy is mainly concerned with "sexual dysfunctions," that is cases in which some psychosocial influences frustrate normal sexual response by blocking the series of bodily reactions leading to orgasm. Dysfunctions express "human sexual inadequacy" or lack, and the task of sex therapy is to analyze and cure this lack from which the individuals suffer. "Human sexual inadequacy," that is lack, is social – a "scourge of society" – and is caused by general hostility to and repression of sexuality in Western, "Judeo-Christian" culture. But it is even more an individual matter, a project of experiencing, facing and overcoming inhibitions and frustrations caused by a person's own particular course and situation in life.

It is within the practical context of sex therapy that the picture of the orgasmically reacting body becomes significant, and it is through the phenomenon of "human sexual inadequacy" that orgasmology articulates the issue of sexual subjectivity, that is, gives expression to the individuality of orgasmic response, to the particular forms of desire and experience of pleasure. In other words, lack (of pleasure) articulates sexuality as the matter of subjectivity, of the individual self.

For men the most common problems are impotence and premature ejaculation, and for women "orgasmic dysfunction," that is frigidity as renamed by Masters and Johnson. This difference is not, however, based on "biology." The different causes of dysfunctions and the contexts of influence have cultural origins:

> Over the centuries the single constant etiological source of all forms of male sexual dysfunction has been the level of cultural demand for effectiveness of male sexual performance. The cultural concept that the male partner must accept full responsibility for establishing successful coital connection has placed upon every man the psychological burden for the coital process and has released every woman from any suggestion of similar responsibility for its success.[6]

> Sociocultural influence more often than not places woman in a position in which she must adapt, sublimate, inhibit or even distort her natural capacity to function sexually in order to fulfill her genetically assigned role. *Herein lies a major source of woman's sexual dysfunction.*[7]

By this Masters and Johnson express the gendered nature of lack and the gender difference of sexual subjectivity. The core of this definition is the difference between manly and womanly patterns of psychical conditioning that causes the dysfunction. Behind the impotence of man lies the fear of sexual performance, whereas the orgasmic capacity of woman is distorted by repression of "all" sexual stimuli and reactions. The "psychological" dimension of typical male sexual dysfunction is conceived to be a damage of ability and action, a reaction of fear toward a certain act and situation. On the contrary, female orgasmic dysfunction concerns the whole of her personality and sexual self.

This difference between man and woman, as defined in the practical context of therapy, was considered as the most important by Masters and Johnson. Through lack – or experience of lack – orgasmology specifies the difference of sexual subjectivity. Manly, masculine lack consists in a fracture of sexual actor or performer, whereas in the case of feminine lack the whole of her sexual identity and self – that is the whole of her being a woman – is under the influence of lack. And the feminine form of human sexual inadequacy is considered to be the more severe and difficult: hers is lack proper. So, she is the actual subject of lack and of becoming therapeutically orgasmic.

Various projects for sexual liberation have accepted and adopted Masters and Johnson's emphasis on the women's cause and its picture of orgasmic woman. Sex therapies took it as their point of departure. The sex manuals which gave advice for enriching and expanding "the repertoire" of orgasmic satisfaction, tended to stress sexual liberation of women. There was also a connection between Masters and Johnson and those projects which conceived the liberation of women's personal pleasure to be the key point of feminist politics. Masters and Johnson's clitoralism and their "scientific proofs" of the sexual self-sufficiency of woman were compatible with Anne Koedt's declaration against the "myth of vaginal orgasm." The "facts" which orgasmology presented offered themselves as the picture of sexual reality, against which women could – collectively and individually – identify themselves as opressed, understand that their bodies, experiences and pleasures have been repressed, and demand their right to sexual satisfaction.

The focus on woman by the liberal views of sexuality could be summarized in the following way. Both orgasmology and radical feminism identify woman as the subject of sexuality through three aspects. She is clitoral, her sexual experience is complex, and her sexuality is repressed by male-dominated culture. Woman is the model for human orgasmic nature and potential, and she is self-sufficient in her experience of sexual satisfaction. In these respects, the feminine figure articulates the two essential characteristics of the "liberated" sexual subject: she is the subject of self-satisfaction and of choice. But, in addition, woman is also the embodiment of sexual inhibitions and frustrations, of lack: she is the victim of repression of sexuality par excellence, and "orgasmic dysfunction" and attempts to find her "own" sexuality, that is her "own" individual ways of orgasmic satisfaction and pleasure, concern the whole of her identity and personality.[8]

The politics and ethics of sexual liberation are formed between *choice* and *lack*. In demands for rights and security for individuals to pursue orgasmic satisfaction and to choose their manners of sexual pleasure and sexual relations, the personal and the political are intertwined. The figuration of relation to the self – ethics – is even more interesting. In the realm of sexual liberation, the basis for liberating one's own sexuality, of "becoming orgasmic," is the identification of one's own lack. The individual person has to clarify to herself her inadecuacy, inhibitions and represssed desire. Then, by understanding her own experience and the "traumatic," inhibiting events of her life, by overcoming the negative feelings concerning sexual activities and experiences, and by finding and experimenting with her own ways of satisfaction, the individual "becomes orgasmic." After this process, an individual person becomes capable of making sexual choices and of becoming sexually reponsive in an unrestrained way. The remarkable point is that both orgasmology and radical feminism stress that both in the political and ethical senses, sexual liberation concerns especially women. In other words, "one's own sexuality" is a feminine issue.

Masculine margins

In the feminized world of sexual liberation, man and the masculine become shadowed, even outcast. Whereas the picture and problematics of feminine sexuality touch the whole of woman's human condition, personality and self, the figuration of man and manliness is concentrated on the penis and its capabilities. The orgasmic essence of man is presented as being simple and focused on the "drama" of ejaculation. Impotence and premature ejaculation tend to be defined as problems of sexual act and performance. In addition, the advice to the "male partner" given by sex manuals is presented as a repertoire of techniques for the improvement of his sexual performance. Against the feminine model of "endless" orgasmic capacity and masturbatory self-sufficiency, the male body and man are depicted as a kind of sex machine and orgasmic supplement, a kind of tool for releasing excitement. This conception of man's role made it possible to make the following statement about the possibilities of feminine pleasure: "Vaginal penetration is very erotic with fingers, a dildo or a penis."[9]

Sexual liberation articulates two images of the masculine, as kinds of shadow men which follow the feminine focused ethics and politics of sexual liberation: the voyeur and the rapist. On the horizon of sexual liberation, the essential masculine attitude toward sexual excitement and pleasure and the basic manly approach to women are depicted as gazing and/or raping, that is taking women by force. These figures of man and the masculine form a kind of common battleground of orgasmological and radical feminist projects. Both of them "agree" on the fundamentals of man and the masculine, but they disagree about the practical consequences of this "fact."

First, man is the voyeur. He exposes woman and her body by his gaze which originates in his own desire and pleasure. This is a common depiction of man in orgasmological sex manuals. For example, Alex Comfort's *Joy of Sex* repeatedly refers to the "fact" that an essential feature of male sexuality is the "need" to look and the pleasure gained from looking. By appealing to "naturally a fetishistic character" of man's sexuality, Comfort presents the task and option for woman. She can and ought to position herself seductively, "in an erotic manner," she has to surrender herself to be the object of man's gaze and desire, and in that way – that is by appealing to his voyeuristic-fetishistic inclination – arouse his desire and excite him. In other words, woman has to adjust herself to the male gaze. For radical feminism this gaze epitomizes the subordination of women by men. The male gaze is objectifying and undressing, it denies and represses woman's desires and her sexual activity, it is ignorant of the feminine quality of sexuality. Thus man the voyeur is one of the main opponents of feminism, the embodiment of male-dominated culture.

There is also a kind of "agreement" that due to the aggression of man, he has an essential desire and tendency to take woman by force, that is to rape. The figure of the rapist represents the inevitable animality of manly sexual urges, deeds and desires. Masculinity has become equated with animality; man is defined as an aggressive animal both in his sexual essence and in his sexual expressions and deeds.

Orgasmological sex manuals present the animal aggression of man as a biological fact which, however, is altered to elements of erotic fantasy and play by civilizing forces of sexual conduct. When, for example, Alex Comfort brings forth "patterns of sexual behavior and urge" which are characteristic to men, he frequently appeals to etiological evidence and depicts masculine sexuality as being inherently aggressive and striving for "dominance." Like an ape, man enforces his sexual urges upon his mate. In other words, the orgasmic urge and behavior of man consists of the masculine element of raping – though in an imaginary form – and it properly belongs to normal love-making. Orgasmological manuals suggest that the sexual experimentation and the techniques of joyful sex can make use of the animal aggression of man. Woman has to be responsive to male aggression, to adjust herself to gain pleasure from it and even learn to use it for increasing her satisfaction. By this Comfort implicitly suggests that normally any woman is constantly ready "to be taken" by man.

Radical feminism takes the opposite view. It considers masculine animality to be the real threat to women's bodily and sexual integrity. Sexual activity by men toward women expresses the violent essence of masculinity, which culminates in the oppression of women by men. The radical feminist definition of man and the masculine implies that in every man there is a potential rapist and an impulse to rape – if not the beast, at least the brute inside him.[10]

Thus, as an outcome of the orgasmological and the feminist focus on women, the projects for sexual liberation articulate very poorly, or scarcely at all, masculine sexual individuality. Sex therapies do pay attention to sexual "dysfunctions" of men, and sex manuals do give advice to men for enriching their orgasmic experience. However, the relation to one's own sexuality, the questions of individual lack, choice and ways of orgasmic satisfaction, and the practices of becoming orgasmic are not articulated in terms of "the problems of man." The ethical space of sexual liberation between personal lack and choice is not depicted in terms of the masculine. Therefore, there is neither masculine self nor individuality, whereas the problematics of feminine sexual self and individuality are even excessive. Men and the masculine are not subjected to an interpretation of their own desire and lack, and man is not obliged to remember and work through the traumas of his sexual life and to search constantly for his orgasmic self. Consequently, man as the subject of sexual satisfaction is not characterized by individuality and own-ness, but by masculinity in general.

In other words, man's pleasure is not personal and his "own," but belongs to "the male" in general: it is pleasure of the other and for the other. The ethics of sexual liberation articulate poorly the masculine relation to one's own pleasures and experiences, and tends to regard sensitivity toward oneself as womanly and as belonging to women. In the world of liberating sexuality for each and all, masculine sexuality figures only in the general matter. And this general masculinity, the general other, is embodied in the two above-mentioned figures: the voyeur and the rapist.

Phallic imaginary and the feminine self

The visual form of man in general has a close affinity to the pornographic image. Man the voyeur is the counterpart to the "free flow" of undressed, arousing images. Pornographic objects and goods persuade and seduce the general masculinity, the male gaze, and reinforce that gaze and make it unrestained by letting it follow the endless stream of naked bodies, the continuous (ex)change of visual objects.

Altogether, sexual liberation gives "man" the position of the voyeur, and this male gaze entwines with the pornographic mode of representation. Another position of man, or the form of general masculinity, is biological determination, that is the popular and scientific conceptions of masculine sexuality – desires, deeds, experiences of men – as inborn animal instincts and essentially aggressive. This influential combination of voyeurism, pornography and animality which defines "liberated" masculinity can be considered as a continuation of the long phallic tradition of the West.

It could be said that for a century and a half Western culture and its morality of veneral pleasures have been characterized by the tension between the regime of the sexual and the phallic regime. The former is constituted by the mystery of the feminine, expressed for example in Freud's famous question "Was will das Weib?," whereas the latter is ordered around the symbols and rituals of masculine power and the superiority of men. In a sense, the world of sexual liberation preserves and transforms this duality. The projects of both orgasmology and radical feminism create the realm and practice of subjection of female sexuality characterized by feminine individuality that is overdetermined by searching for and harmonizing her own sexual self. In this sphere of political and ethical sexual liberation, man as a sexual subject and the masculine individuality are defined as being marginal, even supplementary figures. In tension and opposition with the domains of orgasmology and radical feminism is the realm and practice of male subjection characterized by general masculinity, that takes the form of unrestrained gaze and sexual aggression and lacks any relation to the self. In this sphere, most clearly epitomized and deployed by commercial pornography, woman – the female body, in fact – is restricted to the object of phallic excitation and urge.

The sexual and the phallic can be considered as two forms of subjectivization of desire, in other words, as forms of practicing "sexual liberty." Some aspects of the opposition and even incompatibility of the sexual and the phallic can be summarized in the scheme below.

The sexual	*The phallic*
* individualizing (self-sufficiency of the "feminine" self)	* generalizing (self-referential "masculinity")
* remembering, phantasy	* substitution

* touching and feeling oneself as embodied	* penetrating into the other's body
* inwardness	* striving toward outer objects
* repressed	* unrestrained .

What is characteristic to the subject of sexuality, is the effort to overcome the repression of sexual desires and urges. The practice of overcoming is compounded of reflecting, interpreting and working through particular, personal inner experiences. In contrast, the essential feature of the figurations of phallic subjectivity is the wish to "realize" urges and desires as if they were unrestrained. This leads to practices which are essentially a repetition of the striving toward exterior objects.

The most interesting aspect of this figuration is that there is no "real" man in the realm of sexuality: there is no reality principle articulated as being masculine. The feminine has connection to "real" sexual pleasures and experience – it is her individual reality, the real world of her own sexuality – through remembering which, according to both orgasmology and radical feminism, has a close relation to phantasies. This constitutes the form of an individual's "own" desire. In contrast, for the "common" man the object of orgasmic urges constitutes the world of pleasure. In the present condition of commercial obscenity, the pornographic picture is the paradigm case of the object of masculine pleasure: a substitute. For "liberated" common man the primary pleasure is provided by the hyperreality of images of the naked body, which is a plain surface, a pure object, the factuality of which captures desire and blocks any phantasy.[11]

Notes

1. By ethics I mean, following Foucault (1985, pp. 4-32), the practices of forming and transforming the self. The projects which try to formulate the meaning of sexual individuality and explicate the problematics of the person's relation to her/his "own" sexuality and give guidance in improving the personal life of carnal pleasures, are an essential part of sexual liberation.
2. André Béjin (1985a; 1985b) calls Alfred Kinsey's and William Masters and Virginia Johnson's sex research projects "orgasmology."
3. Masters and Johnson, 1966, p. 7.
4. Masters and Johnson, 1970, p. 219.
5. Reuben, 1971, p. 39.

6. Masters and Johnson, 1970, p. 159.
7. Masters and Johnson, 1970, p. 218.
8. According to Véronique Mottier's analysis (1995), the Hite Reports have similar "ontological" and political emphasis.
9. Dodson, 1983, p. 42.
10. For many radical feminist thinkers rape is the embodiment of oppression of women and reveals the violent character of male-dominated society and culture. As rape epitomizes the power of men over women, every man represents the act of masculine violence toward women, that is he is symbolically a rapist. From this argument Susan Brownmiller (1975) draws a conclusion that all women living in male-dominated Western society and culture are actually raped, because they have experienced the threat of becoming raped and the fears and anxieties caused by that male threat.
11. Cf. Falk, 1994, pp. 201-207.

References

Béjin, André (1985a) "The Decline of the Psycho-analyst and the Rise of the Sexologist," in Ariès, Philippe and Béjin, André (eds), *Western Sexuality*. Oxford: Basil Blackwell.

Béjin, André (1985b) "The Influence of the Sexologists and Sexual Democracy," in Ariès, Philippe and Béjin, André (eds), *Western Sexuality*. Oxford: Basil Blackwell.

Brownmiller, Susan (1975) *Against Our Will: Men, Women, and Rape*. London: Secker and Warburg.

Dodson, Betty (1983) *Selflove and Orgasm*. New York.

Falk, Pasi (1994) *The Consuming Body*. London: Sage.

Foucault, Michel (1985) *The Use of Pleasure. The History of Sexuality*, vol. II. New York: Pantheon.

Masters, William H. and Johnson, Virginia E. (1966) *Human Sexual Response*. Boston: Little, Brown and Co.

Masters, William H. and Johnson, Virginia E. (1970) *Human Sexual Inadequacy*. London: J. and A. Churchill.

Mottier, Véronique (1995) "The Politics of Sex: Truth Games and the Hite Reports," *Economy and Society*, 24 (4), pp. 520-39.

Reuben, David (1971) *Any Woman Can!* New York: David McKay.

Chapter 15

Coming Out to be Straight: Young Men's Constructions of Heterosexualities

STEPHAN W. CREMER[1]

Social norms about sexuality have changed dramatically over recent years in the Netherlands.[2] Clear rules and strictures concerning sexual interaction emerged in the course of the 1970s, developing in the direction of one hard and fast rule: "everything should be possible." This adage, however, has come under sharp criticism in the 1980s and 1990s, and in the end it has been modified. Feminism caused the quality of sexual contact to become a topic of discussion. This meant that more attention was given to the concerns of women in sexual matters. Feminism has successfully achieved the acceptance of a norm of "respect for another's boundaries" among broader layers of society. Moreover, the norm "everything must be possible" has also been undermined by warnings against AIDS and guidelines for "safer sex."

In line with these developments, the permissiveness of the 1970s has been modified today by a few rules that keep cropping up in sex education: only do things you feel comfortable with yourself, be considerate of your partner's boundaries, and keep "it" safe. The first two of these rules, to which I limit myself in this article, are especially unclear in relation to initial sexual contacts. They require "self-knowledge" ("What do I want?"), the ability to communicate one's boundaries and to observe those of the other. The new vague rules for sexual behavior demand rather a lot from our youngsters; already existing personal insecurity can gain yet another dimension.

Differences in sexual behavior between the sexes, as revealed by sexual research since the 1960s, are strongly diminishing: boys are no longer more experienced than girls, and girls take the initiative in making sexual contact just as often as boys. On the other hand, clear differences have been found in the setting of boundaries with lovemaking: approximately three times as many girls as boys are protective of their boundaries (Vogels and van der Vliet, 1990). The role of being able to refuse something is attributed more often to girls, by other girls as well as by boys (Buysse and van Oost, 1994, p. 140). Similarly, during sexual activities girls are more likely to indicate what they want (Brugman *et al.*, 1995, p. 47) and they guard the boundaries more often (Rademakers and Ravesloot, 1993). The pattern of child-rearing promotes this difference. Parents encourage their daughters to watch their boundaries, while their sons have to learn to have respect for their girlfriends (Ravesloot and te Poel, 1996).

Although the new behavioral codes are supposed to apply generally, they seem to be differentiated by gender: "Do only what you want" seems to be directed at girls, while boys are commanded to "respect the boundaries of the other." Prevention programs on sexual violence, Marneth (1991) concludes, aim to enable girls to defend themselves better, and to encourage boys to have more respect for the boundaries that girls set. That boys experience personal insecurities in initiating sexual contacts is often ignored.

Although such insecurity has been reported in research (Vennix *et al.*, 1993; Cremer *et al.*, 1994), the way boys handle it has not yet been explored. How do boys interpret the basic rules for sexual contact, and what frames of reference can they choose from? Do images about sexuality exist which can offer boys some form of security, and some direction in their search to overcome their insecurities, or which they can identify with? Are there images which a boy can share with other boys of his age, and which fulfil the (assumed) expectations of girls? How do boys relate images of masculine attributes to (hetero-) sexuality? How do they construct heterosexualities in different situations: being together with the girlfriend, or being in an all-male group? How do they combine these different constructions in a male heterosexual identity?

In this article I will try to answer these questions, on the basis of my research on images about sexuality amongst boys.[3] The accomplishments of feminism, the nuances of the slogan "everything should be possible," seem to have been integrated by the boys interviewed, into their images about sexuality. At first glance, the boys seem to do everything to enhance the quality of sexuality: "as long as the girl is happy" is their motto. The "ideal partner," which they like to see themselves as, puts the wishes of his partner before the satisfaction of his own desires. But when we look further, we see that the image of the "ideal male lover" has another side: he is not able to identify himself in a positive light with other boys about sexuality, and projects his own insecurities onto his partner.

I used various theories in this study. Social constructionism gives theoretical insight into the way images relate to each other, and how individual and social images influence each other (Shotter, 1984; Gergen, 1985). Connell's (1995) concept of hegemonic masculinity provides a framework for a power analysis of gender relations in different situations. To do justice to the gender-determined character of socialization, I make use of the insights of Chodorow (1978, 1994) and Dinnerstein (1983).

Biographical interviews were carried out with 15 boys.[4] This form of interview gives the boys room for "retrospective self-definitions": they can express their expectations and experiences in their own words, and describe images. The interviewer keeps the number of questions to a minimum, but encourages and draws on what the person interviewed has to say. It is quite possible that the boys interviewed have not talked about all of their experiences. Sexual encounters experienced up to the age of 12 are typically not mentioned. With this non-directive method, I focus on their images of sexuality, expressed in the way they talk about their experiences and expectations.

The average age of the boys interviewed was 17 years.[5] Given my line of inquiry, I did not interview homosexual boys. I recruited my first respondents through colleagues, hoping that the "grapevine mechanism" would begin to operate. In this I was not disappointed. In fact I had to put a stop to the grapevine, to avoid a lack of variation in my small group: too many boys with a high level of education, and living in the same cities. Establishing contact with three different schools soon solved this problem, resulting in greater variation in the level of education, though it is on the whole still quite high.[6] I tried to involve more than just Dutch boys in the research. Thus, one or both of the parents of four boys selected are non-Dutch.

Initially I had my doubts as to whether the boys would be willing to talk "face to face" about sexuality, and whether they would do that with a man. Earlier research with Childline (a telephone help service) had shown me that anonymity is very important for young male callers (Cremer *et al.*, 1994). Other interview-based research on sexuality involved female interviewers talking with boys (Vennix *et al.*, 1993). I was pleasantly surprised with the cooperation of the 15 boys. Most interviews lasted for one hour and forty minutes, some lasted longer (a maximum of three and a half hours) or shorter (a minimum of forty-five minutes). The respondents were informed about one of the goals of the project: improving sex education for boys.[7] For many of the boys, this provoked an association with research in AIDS prevention and condom use. Although nearly all the boys considered themselves to be well-informed, they considered it important to improve sex education for the benefit of other boys. (I will elaborate on this differentiation later.) This is why they were keen to cooperate with the research. At the beginning of the dialogue, most of the boys found it very exciting to talk about their sexuality. They seemed uncertain about what words were fitting for them to use in my presence. To avoid too much tension, I mentioned a few "four-letter words," and assured them they should feel free in talking about sexuality with me. In the course of conversation the tension disappeared.

The analysis is carried out according to the qualitative method of "grounded theory" (Glaser and Strauss, 1967; Strauss and Corbin, 1990). To make the boys' perceptions about sexuality visible, three groups of images were collected: images about their own sexuality, about the sexuality of other boys, and about the sexuality of girls. I then made a horizontal comparison of the images in terms of frequency and exception. In this way, I searched for the relevant images that can make a statement about the group of interviewed boys as a whole. Next, I investigated what function these images have for the boys, what meaning they draw from them, and whether and how they legitimize their behavior with them.

Well-informed and well-prepared

In most empirical research, sexual development is presented in a certain order of sexual activities: French kisses, stroking with clothes on, stroking with clothes off, sexual intercourse (Noordhoff, 1969; Kooy *et al.*, 1983; Vogels and van der Vliet, 1990; Brugman *et al.*, 1995). Full sexual intercourse (coitus) is certainly not the only form of mutual sexual gratification. Boys ask Childline counsellors more questions about oral and manual sexual gratification of the partner, than about coitus (Cremer *et al.*, 1994).

Sexual "freedom" has put the standard pattern of sexual behavior into perspective. Boys want to be well prepared for all possible sexual actions.[8] Most of the boys interviewed said they acquired a lot of information about the technical side of having sex from pornographic films. When they talk about these films, they detach themselves from the personalities presented and their forms of behavior:

> my opinion is that they are exaggerating. They really go so far as to do everything they can, but in reality when you are making love with someone you don't do such terrible things. ... In normal life you don't do that. How do the men get these girls? You enter a room, and a girl is standing there ready for you. I don't think you would ever really experience that in your life ... Really, these men that you see there, they're ... they're users, they use those girls. (Pedro)

Several boys explained that they watched films together with their friends.

> Yes, I have seen more of those pornographic films. With a whole group of
> friends, we went out one night and, just for a laugh, we went together to see a
> pornographic film. ... Usually at someone's home. We would double up from
> laughing so much. (Frits)

> Interviewer: Didn't you also find it arousing?

> Well, on the one hand yes, but then again no, because you're with your
> friends. So then you think, what would I want to be here for with a hard-on.
> So you really watch more for a lark than for the erotic aspect. (Frits)

Arousal is taboo in the presence of other boys. Together, the boys comment
on the actions of the actors. They find the scenes so grotesque that they
have to laugh about them – Pedro's detachment is typical. On the one hand,
the boys interviewed clearly put the realistic content of the pornographic
films into perspective, they find them overdone, and watch just for fun. On
the other hand, they said that they took advantage of the techniques shown.

> Because really, I find porn movies rather boring. I think it was all a bit
> exaggerated how that happened. ... Naturally we experimented later with food
> and so on. I had seen that in a film, with ice blocks. (Ruud)

> But I have "filmnet" and Isabel too. On Saturday night there are sex films.
> And then we watch them, the two of us. This gets you excited. And then for
> example we might copy what we saw. You learn from it. (Aad)

Some other boys were critical, and completely rejected pornography:

> [Films] do not show that every person is sexually unique, that sex is different
> with every person. A kind of sex is portrayed which is good for everybody ...
> but this is of course not true, I mean those kind of things, they are, they are
> things you should discover.

How pornography influences the boys can vary among them. It is clear,
however, that watching porn movies is not necessarily a solitary
occupation. To watch porn movies with peers, and have a laugh about the
sex on screen, seems to belong to the rituals of (heterosexual) masculinity:
a way of drowning out one's own insecurities.

The boys interviewed report the ideal image that making love comes
"naturally." They sketched a romantic scene, of perfect bodily contact and
physical harmony, where words are not necessary, and each person
instinctively feels what the other wants. This image offers some protection

against having to express anxieties and desires. On the other hand, this image is technical. Pornographic film produces the impression that everything happens naturally: everyone feels like having sex at every moment, the men are in control, and communication is superfluous. The boys interviewed were quick to explain that they found the pornographic picture to be "unrealistic." The unromantic image, and the fear of talking about their desires and feelings, remained. According to their ideal image, the transition from one action to another involves the silent consent of both parties.

> Yes, we instinctively knew what to do, we never actually made spoken agreements, you could just tell from their manner, a bit. (Frits)

Usually when a step forward is taken in a sexual contact, this is not spoken about beforehand. There is too much fear of disturbing something. Thus Aad fears that loss of intimacy will result from talking about it explicitly:

> And then we were busy at it. And then, I didn't say, because if you ask that, being the boy, hey I want to do it with you, or something like that, then the girl is going to think, uh-oh or something like that.
>
> Interviewer: Why does she think that?
>
> Just, if a girl has never done it before. And if a boy suddenly says things to her all at once, say they are being really intimate, this might make them more hesitant and distant or something. I think, ... I don't know what she thinks but I just think that as a boy you shouldn't ask this. (Aad)
>
> Talking about what you like and prefer also doesn't fit into the image of lovemaking proceeding naturally and automatically.
>
> Interviewer: In your mind when she is stroking you, do you indicate, "do this"?
>
> No, I don't think so. I'm not a commander or something. [laugh] (Jan)

The taboo on talking does not make taking steps and handling insecurities any easier, especially when the choice of sexual actions is not decided. The basic rules, "do only what you yourself want; have consideration for the boundaries of your partner," in fact demand communication.

Insecurities

Insecurity is involved not only at the point of having sexual intercourse for the first time, but in all aspects of the first sexual encounter – this is what most of the boys interviewed say. Boys with sexual experiences and relationships look back and tell of their insecurities. Boys with little or no experience look forward with apprehension and longing to their first sexual experiences. There is an initial fear of being rejected.

> No, I don't have a lot of experience with it yet, so I don't know when I am being turned down. That would be ... I think I would feel like shit ... but then, I don't know why. (Karel)

> I also think that as a boy you are afraid of failing. If she doesn't want to. Then the whole atmosphere is just gone. If you're busy the whole evening with each other in the dark, just the two of you, cosy. Then if you would ask or suggest or something like that [to go to bed with each other]. Because you can't all at once go and fetch a condom. Then the whole atmosphere can be ruined just like that. (Aad)

At the same time, insecurities are expressed about taking the initiative.

> After that we all went together to the movies, and then I was sitting next to her. I had put my arm on the arm rest, and her arm was under mine, kind of fighting for who could have the arm rest. Then I thought, well, we'll put our arms together, then I nearly reached for her hand, but I thought, well, I better not, she might not be attracted to me, and then I will have ruined the friendship or something. But she'd been thinking exactly the same, "Shall I take his hand or not?" She also only just didn't do it ... (Frits)

And later when they were sitting out on the sidewalk:

> I was starting to have doubts about what to do next, because I had already given her a kiss on the cheek, then I thought, shall I give her a kiss on the mouth now, or a kiss on the cheek again? She was sitting with her back against mine ... Then I turned my head, and then she turned her head as well, well then we started French kissing, so that's how it happened. (Frits)

Every new step, from a kiss on the cheek to a French kiss, causes doubts.
While Frits and his girlfriend both indicate to each other that they are willing to take the next step, Frank comes to the conclusion that his girlfriend doesn't want to go any further. Later he doubts whether his interpretation of her behavior was correct.

Yes, I also saw it a bit as a missed opportunity. I just found her a really nice girl. I was really in love with her, going to bed, finger fucking and genital stimulation I would have been ready to do, but nothing eventuated. I put my hand in her blouse, and maybe she didn't think that was all right. Well, she didn't say, that isn't OK, but I thought she made a movement suggesting rather not, but later I started doubting whether that is what she meant. So yes ... then I don't go on to finger fucking and so on. (Frank)

The boys interviewed differentiate themselves – in the face-to-face setting of the interview[9] from the stereotypical heterosexual male image, not only because they see sex as being more than just coitus, but also because they see sex as going together with a relationship. Most of the boys interviewed indicated they did not want to go to bed with a girl immediately. They first wanted to get to know the girl, and only when there was a sign of a more "permanent" attraction, did they want sexual contact with her, even though this is not how it may always happen – for example, if the girl takes the initiative.

I have to be really sure that it is someone who I will be in love with for a longer period. I mean I don't go to bed with someone already on the first night. Unless it's a friend, a girlfriend who I have known for a long time, who I then develop a relationship with, but not if I meet someone in town and go out with them to a cafe or something like that. I do always have condoms with me, but I don't go to bed straight away ... you can't always be sure ... beforehand. (Willem)

I think that there should be some feeling behind it before I would dive into bed with someone. It's not like saying hi, I'm this and I'm that, and then we do it. You have to get to know each other, and be able to understand each other. You should really care about each other. You see, if you feel like it, then it's nice to do it anyway but ... I'm not really sure, but it's not true that sex is something purely physical. (Ruud)

Sexuality is really quite a big (something) ... with feeling. It is also that you love someone and that you show them by way of sexuality. (Bart)

These boys, therefore, want to express their emotions, their love through sex. For this purpose they especially want to be good lovers; in their eyes technical mastery is very important in order for them to express their feelings toward the girl.

Interviewer: What do you find is important for other boys to know?

How a girl can be aroused, say, as much as possible. That is also the nicest for you, because it is satisfying when she has also found it really nice. (Aad)

Interviewer: Do you find orgasms important?

For myself, not so much, I do like it, but I would rather that she ... She takes first place, and then I get round to myself. But usually I come earlier, because I can't hold out. So I usually come a bit earlier. (Frits)

Interviewer: Do you find it, therefore, a bit performance-oriented because you actually like it the most if she comes? Do you have to achieve this?

Hmm, no, but also yes. But also the idea that she should also be enjoying it. But for boys, coming is the best [part]. For girls, cuddling and more foreplay is a bit more important. So you think about this more as a boy, because girls don't come as quickly as most boys, well, yes, myself then. Then you think that that is also the nicest for her. It is also nice but sometimes she finds cuddling nicer, it's different each time. It also depends on her mood. (Frits)

Usually the boys I spoke with thought more about what the girl would want, than what they themselves wanted. They especially want "to do sex well," and for them this means operating in such a way that the girl experiences pleasure. They hardly stop to think about their own desires, and have no idea of their own boundaries. Marco summarizes this as follows, in answer to the question whether he has ever been dissatisfied with a way of making love:

I don't think that boys are quickly dissatisfied. ... Not me, not as quick as girls ... Boys are happy with everything really, I think. Yes, everything [laugh], if they don't go too far within a normal sexual experience. (Marco)

Boys find it important to be a good lover; they want to have the impression of themselves as being "a good lover": well prepared, with knowledge of the technique, they want to make it as nice as possible for the girl. The image of "the technician," of being proficient, is incompatible with the image of the romantic, who has sex out of love. Their caring and thoughts are oriented to the (assumed) desires of the girl. It seems that boys have interpreted the behavioral code "do only what you yourself want" to mean "do especially what you think the girl wants" within the boundaries set by the girl.

The exception to the rule

In the preceding I have shown how much trouble boys go to, in order to be a good lover, and how they detach themselves from the stereotypical images about male heterosexuality. There is, however, another side to the "ideal lover":

> There came a time when I realized that I had a kind of time-table: I thought, in a month's time we'll do that, and in two months' time that, and in three months that, and after half a year then we'll do that. But then one time we had gone to the movies. When we came back and were lying on the couch, she suddenly put my hand on her breast. This made a proper mess of my whole time planning, because I hadn't planned this until another three weeks' time. At least for myself: then I'm about ready for that, then we are ready. I had been really thinking about her. But when she did that, I reconsidered that I was actually also ... I mean, I'm someone who easily leaves it to others ... – it's easier anyway to leave the initiative to someone else than to take it first yourself. So I felt a bit like – yeah, the leader – that I knew just that little bit more. You know, that you are coaching someone a bit in the sexual experiences and sexual relationship, that you are more able to do that. That's what I thought. And then that was disrupted a bit. Then I thought: uh-oh, then I better ... well OK, I still knew more, and I was more informed, and I had better instruction books, and I knew everything about what was and wasn't nice to do. She didn't know that, and I also knew about how to satisfy myself. I already masturbated and jerked off. So I knew what climaxing was like, which she didn't. In those kind of things, I still had a bit of a head start. (Bart)

For both partners, this is their first sexual contact, and yet the boy still considers himself more experienced than the girl. And even though the boy realizes that he was projecting his own insecurities onto the girl when he looks back on the experience later on, he still stresses that he has more experience: more information from books and experiences with masturbation and with orgasms. So there must be a strong attraction attached to the task he sets himself, to "coach" the girl.

The image of the "successful lover," who ensures good sex is being had, goes beyond that of "the coach" or "supervisor." If talking about sexuality, about the boundaries of yourself and others is not possible, then the only other alternative is to make assumptions about this for the other. The projection of insecurity and your own desires onto another person can remain unnoticed for a long time. In this way the boys' own desires, also often unconscious ones, can be brought in again through the "back door." All this is justified with the motto "as long as the girl is satisfied in the sexual contact." On the one hand, this is rather a stereotype male understanding of caring: boys are supposed to be more experienced, act independently, and know no boundaries (in heterosexual contact). On the other hand, it seems a way for them to master their insecurities – to see themselves as being more experienced than the girl. This is also a strategy for avoiding communication.

It is noticeable that most of the boys interviewed gave a negative impression about the sexuality of other boys:

> If you have all these macho friends, then you have a wholly different view of sex ... You get that from your friends because you don't talk about it with your parents. (Jan)

> At primary school there were these boys in the highest class who were really tough and all that. They would have a girlfriend, but that was only for about two weeks. (Pim)

> What matters is what kind of boys you hang out with. You have these really good boys, you know. But I also have friends, criminal types, ... they only go to a party for the girls. They only want to have some sex and "bye," that's it. (Pedro)

> You have these guys who go on holiday, they feel like it, and think let's get a couple of women and ... every day another one. (Karel)

It seems that boys can articulate their negative impressions about male sexuality quite well, namely when they talk about the sexuality of other boys. These are the "machos," the "criminals," the "tough types" who "use" girls. The boys appear to perceive themselves as "the exception" to the male species:

> Actually, I would like it, if I could talk more about it. I mean, I can talk with women about it so as far as that goes ... I can do that. But I don't think my own experience with this is very normal. Because I feel that I really have to approach this with loving care and so on. (Bart)

Thus these boys start out with negative impressions of male sexuality, about which they themselves then go on to protest. It does not seem possible for them to name positive models, to identify themselves as part of a group of boys, and then go on to differentiate themselves as individuals with their own personal experiences. This suggests that boys cannot name many positive images about male sexuality, with which they are willing to identify themselves in the context of the biographical interview. The boys rebel against the negative stereotyping of male sexuality, at least in conversation with the interviewer, and take the position of being "the exception to the rule" ("I'm different"). The effect of their claim to being an exception is that stereotyping (of other boys) remains intact. But this in turn obstructs communication with other boys about their experience with sexuality, and also explains why the boys interviewed see themselves as "well-informed" and yet doubt whether this is also true for other boys. Communication between boys is constrained by conformity to peer-group pressure, in the context of which they all boast about their accomplishments, radiating a stereotypical image of "male" sexuality.

> Yes, I think it's always like that between boys, that you get a bit of a ranking order. That's how it is in normal society as well, really. The one with the biggest mouth gets to the top. (Frits)

Some of the boys interviewed took the view that when they were in a male peer group, they would join in with the tough talk. When asked why they acted differently in the interview, and were prepared to talk about their personal experiences, they said it was because our contact was a once-only event. Because of this "exceptional situation," the boys felt they had the opportunity to behave freely; by rejecting the formation of negative images, they gained exclusive entry into the terrain of girls as well as boys. A metaphor illustrating the construction of such a space is given in the following account:

> I collect weapons, knives and such, but also cuddly bears. Because half the room is full of military things and the weapons and such, and the other half is full of cuddly toys. This is a bit of a contradiction, so you never know what you should expect from me. (Frits)

Coming out to be straight

In this research, I started out with the expectation that in the absence of clear rules, boys will search for behavioral models and images to help orient themselves when they have their first sexual encounters. Insecurity is the background to this, an insecurity that only grows through lack of communication. Positive images about male heterosexuality that a boy can identify himself with are, however, not mentioned by the boys interviewed. Only negative images remain. Boys joke amongst themselves about sex, and exaggerate their own experiences. Everyone knows it didn't really happen, but the code of the male peer group takes priority. On the other hand, they do want to care well for their girl, to express their own feelings of love, and to be a "good lover or coach."

How do boys do that? With what words can boys describe their own sexuality, given that their impression of the sexuality of other boys is usually negative? In other words, what can the boys do, if no social constructions are available for them to articulate their own experienced or fantasized and positively valued sexuality? This question must also be considered in the context of masculinity. After all, masculinity remains a yardstick for social esteem. A boy will not relinquish the adjective "manly" so easily. Moreover, there exists no construction transcending gender, which would offer the boy an escape from the masculine/feminine dichotomy.

Power in different contexts seems to play a role. Connell (1995) has defined gender as (changeable) social structure in which hegemonic masculinity represents the dominant position of men in relation to women. This hegemony structures not only the relationship of men and women, but also the relationship among men. Behaviors such as the subordination of homosexuality to heterosexuality, and the marginalization of specific types of men (for example ethnic minorities) are included just as much as conformity to hegemonic masculinity.

If we examine the reported behavior of the interviewed boys again in this light, we can tentatively conclude the following. The boy wants to be caring toward the girl. As long as she finds pleasure in sexual activity, he is satisfied. With regard to the girl, he feels that he has to know what she enjoys, and to guide her to satisfying sex. Girls are more demanding in the area of sex than boys, so the boys assume. They construct the sexuality of girls as being more complicated than that of boys, and a good lover knows how to satisfy this sexuality. In this way, the boy acquires a dominant position in relation to the girl. He pays a high price, however, by exposing himself to constant pressure to be a "good lover," while disregarding his own physical pleasure and his own boundaries.

In male peer groups, by contrast, talking about sex has the function "publicly to validate their masculinity to their male friends" (Mac an Ghaill, 1994, p. 92). Talking about sex in (heterosexual) male peer groups serves more the role of establishing hierarchies among boys. The concern for satisfying sex for the girl actually has no place in these discussions. Caring attitudes and masculinity are apparently a touchy subject in the context of the male peer group; precisely when the conversation in the male peer group is about the achievement of masculinity, this theme is avoided. To watch pornographic movies together and make jokes about it, boasting in the awareness that a game of one-upmanship is being played, and denying as a group that insecurity could play a role in the first heterosexual contacts, are rituals that affirm masculinity.

"Coming out to be straight" ought to mean the expression of respect and care for the sexual wishes of girls, and the acknowledgement of their own desires in male peer groups. Then a boy would not need to differentiate between his position in his peer groups, and his position outside them. As it stands, he maintains a negative image of other boys. The boy has to separate himself from the accepted negative image about boys. A solution is offered to him through the images of being "the exception," the "good lover" and "the coach." In this way, he answers to the rules of sexual contact, without departing from the stereotypical image of masculinity: to be proficient in the field of sex, and to be free from insecurities, even though he is constantly talking about his insecurities to the researcher. By doing this, he retains his autonomy in his actions, while paying the necessary price – standing alone as an "exception." In this way, the boy creates room for himself to behave comfortably without losing his identity, with boys as well as girls. He can join the "game" of bragging and control his position within the male peer group, as well as be a good lover and coach. He knows the negative images about male sexuality, and helps to keep these intact by identifying them with other boys, or by following the rules of the game in the group. But "privately," as an "exceptional case," he cuts himself off from the stereotype. So he himself does not carry the burden of these images, and he does not need to conform to the demands of the "macho" image. There is also an element of self-advantage and competition in this: he thinks that he makes an impression on girls, because he is "different from other men," namely "a good lover and coach."

Once the burden of negative images about male sexuality is shaken off in this manner, the question remains whether the images of "a good lover and coach" actually diminish insecurities. By putting his image into perspective with other boys, the boy can gain a certain amount of security. But in the situation where, without any talking, he must know what the girl desires, and how she wants to achieve this, a rather precarious construction becomes evident, in which his own (unconscious) desires can return in the form of projections.

More positive images about male sexuality, about the sexuality of other boys – images with which the individual boys can identify themselves, images integrating caring – would lead, first, to a more conscious image of his own sexual wishes and desires, and, second, to a more honest communication among boys and with their partners. Only then would they not have to constantly run the gauntlet by separating themselves from negative images as exceptions.

Notes

1. English translation by Monica Verburg and Jurriaan Bendien.
2. The studies "Seks in Nederland" (Sex in the Netherlands), better known as the SIN-studies, were carried out in 1968, 1974 and in 1981; see Noordhoff *et al.*, 1969; Kooy *et al.*, 1983. Recent studies are "Jeugd en Seks" (Youth and Sex) by Vogels and Van der Vliet, 1990; and Brugman *et al.*, 1995.
3. My research was conducted at the Department of Women's Studies, Social Sciences at the Utrecht University, Netherlands. I would like to thank Dr. Kathy Davis and Dr. Marianne Grünell for their support of this study.
4. Thirteen interviews were carried out by myself, and two by a student.
5. The youngest was 15.5 years and the oldest was nearly 18. Research shows that of youngsters around 17.7 years of age, about half have had sexual intercourse (van der Brugman *et al.*, 1995).
6. Four boys have a "VWO" (university-oriented) education, five are at "HAVO" schools (higher-level secondary education), five are at "MAVO" schools (middle-level secondary education) and one boy does "VBO" (vocational secondary education).
7. The interviews took place in December 1993 and January and February 1994. In the meantime I implemented the results of my research in methods of sexual education for boys, published in a handbook of boy-specific sexual education, titled *Aan de man brengen* (*Man in Focus*) (Cremer, 1995).
8. The most common questions for which boys call Childline are about the do's and don't's of all forms of sexual interaction (Cremer *et al.*, 1994).
9. As noted below, the interviewed boys say that they behave differently in male peer groups.

References

Brugman, E., Goedhart, H., Vogels, T. and van Zessen, G. (1995) *Jeugd en seks '95*. Utrecht: SWP.
Buysse A. and van Oost, P. (1994) "Rolopvattingen en rolverwachtingen bij 17 tot 21-jarigen ten aanzien van condoomgebruik, initiatiefnemen en mondigheid bij seksueel contact," *Tijschrift voor Seksuologie*, 18, pp. 128-41.
Chodorow, N. J. (1978) *The Reproduction of Mothering Psychoanalysis and the Sociology of Gender*. The Regents of the University of California.
Chodorow, N. J. (1994) *Femininities Masculinities Sexualities, Freud and Beyond*. The Blazer Lectures for 1990. Kentucky: University Press of Kentucky.
Connell, R. W. (1995) *Masculinities*. Cambridge: Polity Press.
Cremer, S. W., in collaboration with Landelijke Werkgroep Signalering (1994) *Over welke seks spreken jongens met de Kindertelefoon?* Onderzoeksverslag, Dordrecht: Landelijk Overleg Kindertelefoon.
Cremer, S. W. (1995) *Aan de man brengen*. Handboek seksuele voorlichting aan jongens. Utrecht: SWP.

Dinnerstein, D. (1983) *Minnotaurus en meermin*. Man-Vrouw regelingen en menselijk onbehagen. Amsterdam: Sara.

Gergen, K. J. (1985) "Social constructionist enquiry: context and implication," in Gergen, K. J. and Davis, K. E. (eds), *The social construction of a person*. New York: Springer.

Glaser, B. G. and Strauss, A. L. (1967) *The Discovery of Grounded Theory. Strategies for Qualitative Research*. Chicago: Aldine.

Kooy, G. A., Weeda, C. J., Schelvis, N. and Moors, H. G. (1983) *Sex in Nederland. Het meest recente onderzoek naar mening en houding van de Nederlandse bevolking*. Utrecht: Het Spectrum.

Mac an Ghail, M. (1994) *The Making of Men. Masculinities, Sexualities and Schooling*. Buckingham, Philadelphia: Open University Press.

Marneth, A. M. (1991) *Ongewenste seks en ambivalente gevolens*. Utrecht: Stichting Wetenschappelijk Onderzoek omtrent Seksualiteit en Geweld.

Noordhoff, J. D. *et al.* (1969) *Sex in Nederland*. Utrecht/Antwerpen: Het Spectrum.

Rademakers J. and Ravesloot, J. (1993) "Jongeren en seksualiteit," in Dieleman, A. J., van der Linden, F. J. and Perrein, A. C. (eds), *Jeugd in meervoud*. Heerlen: De tijdstroom.

Ravesloot, J. and te Poel, Y. (1996) "Het zijn sterke benen die de weelde kunnen dragen ... Praten over seks tussen ouders en kinderen," *Tijdschrift voor Seksuologie*, 20, pp. 37-44.

Shotter, J. (1984) *Social accountability and selfhood*. Oxford: Basil Blackwell.

Strauss, A. and Corbin, J. (1990) *Basics of Qualitative Research, Grounded Theory Procedures and Techniques*. London: Sage.

Vennix, P., Curfs, P. and Ketting, E. (1993) *Condoomschroom*. Delft: Eburon.

Vogels, T. and van der Vliet, R. (1990) *Jeugd en seks, gedrag en gezondheidsrisico's bij scholieren*. Den Haag: SDU.

Chapter 16

"There has always been ..." Gay History in Politics and in Reality

WILHELM VON ROSEN

In 1994 Vatican church politicians and Muslim delegates at the UN
International Conference on Population and Development (ICPD) in Cairo
countered a proposal to include "sexual and reproductive rights and health"
in the Action Program, by bringing about a debate on homosexuality as an
unwelcome and frightening consequence of the proposal. In an interview
with a gay magazine, one of the Danish delegates at the conference, Ebba
Strange, MP, gave an account of the conference and said: "In politics it is
best is to take *reality* as the starting point. ... There has always been
homosexuality. We know that from everywhere. Why not then, allow
people the dignity of a life in accordance with their orientation?"[1]

"Everywhere" and "There has always been" are the beginning of all
good master narratives. "There has always been homosexuality" is a
hypothesis about sex between men that in the modern era – that is since the
1860s – has moved the basis of gay history into the realm of the
transhistorical. History is about that which happens only once, about what
changes, but not about what has always existed. "There has always been
homosexuality" is accordingly the basis for the further hypothesis that gay
history is not the history of homosexuality as such, but (only) a history of
repression and emancipation of something – that is, about repression and
emancipation of an eternal and by nature given homosexuality.

Homosexuality as a location in the body

The more precise determination of this "something" – its ontology and
etiology – is consequently not a historical problem, but a problem that
belongs to the natural sciences. From the viewpoint of the history of
science, homosexuality belonged in medicine, originally in neurology and
psychiatry, later in endocrinology. Lately, the hypotheses of this

"something" have been transferred to biology and genetics. These disciplines mirror the locations within the body where the homosexual "something" has been placed, hypothetically. Concurrently, but with comparatively modest effect in the Nordic countries, a number of theories of the cause of homosexuality have been proposed by the disciplines of psychology. These theories have seen homosexuality as a psychic condition which is partly general, partly particular to certain individuals as the result of the (defective) development of the child as a sexual being.

Since this "something" – the homosexuality of the body – in the course of the 125 years in which the natural sciences have worked on it, has not been located, more precisely determined and demonstrated, it ought to be considered that it is the wrong question. Or differently stated: Is there an adequate logical and linguistic nexus between the question asked (the etiology of homosexuality), and the answers suggested by the individual research projects (their model, their choice of data)?

The point of departure in the nineteenth century was bewilderment. Why, despite hundreds of years of penal legislation and severe punishment, moral condemnation, and social ostracism, had it not been possible to prevent genital sexual relations between men? This question was probably prompted by an increase in the number of cases of pederasty (sodomy with a man or a boy), as a consequence of a change in male sexual behavior, including an increase of male prostitution, in connection with the urbanization of Central Europe. In any case, the answer was soon produced.[2] Pederasty had not been eradicated long ago because it was a behavior which *could not* be prevented, since it was given by nature. During the second part of the century this explanatory model – which originated in Germany – was disseminated and in the main accepted. As an explanation it was in accordance with the tendency of the time, generally to understand crime and immoral behavior as hereditary taint and degeneration of the central nervous system.

What happened shortly after the mid-nineteenth century was, as seen from the point of view of formal logic, that psychiatrists and forensic doctors observed a certain mysterious and inexplicable behavior and then made a generalization on the basis of their observations. The generalization produced a neologism, "contrary sexuality," which around the turn of the century was replaced by "homosexualism" and "homosexuality."[3] The phycisians futhermore proposed the hypothesis that since this behavior was compulsory, combined with effeminacy, and connected to the emotional make-up of the individuals in question, it was in most cases a congenital condition.

The neologism, homosexuality, indicated that the generalization and the whole question of sexuality between men was removed from morality and jurisprudence to medicine. The physicians who published the first articles on homosexuality explicitly stated that this ought to be the consequence of their newly gained insight. Homosexuals did not belong in police stations and courts of law, but in the surgery of the medical practitioner. This in itself implied a statement (not a hypothesis) about the ontology of homosexuality. It belonged to and was part of the body. The hypothesis of the etiology of homosexuality – that in most cases it was congenital – was explicitly formulated.

The data that constituted the basis of the early medical inquiries into male same-sex behavior and produced the generalisation "homosexuality" must now, more than a hundred years later, be considered insufficient. They were extremely few in number and had been obtained and included without consideration of mode of selection or representativness. The observations comprised data which – today at least – would be seen as irrelevant and incongruent: cross-dressing, bad drinking habits, pronounced emotions, memories of childhood and adolescence, psychiatric observation of mental development, and somatic oddities of a presumably hereditary and pathological nature (debility, harelip, phimosis, asymmetrical facial halves), so-called "moral insanity" and *folie circulaire*.[4] To this was added a genealogy that indicated heredity: for example, "the parents were nervous" or "an aunt was insane."[5] Still, in principle there can be no objection to the generalization that was made. Gradually the data were improved, the technique of observation became more sophisticated, and the generalization "homosexuality" remained as a useful logical and linguistic tool for the formulation of hypotheses about the etiology of the observed and generalized data. The hypotheses that have been proposed since then (tested, published, and retested according to various experimental models) were and are accompanied by explicit and usually quite clearly stated reservations. And the hypotheses have not been confirmed. Among the recent attempts to give an answer to the question of the cause of homosexuality was a sensational genetic investigation published in 1993 in the distinguished American journal *Science*.[6]

Why has the question of the cause of homosexuality – the hypothesis that homosexuality is "something" that is embodied in some, but not in all individuals – for so long been so insistently and tenaciously pursued in spite of the absence of results? The reason must be that there is a considerable and general demand for having the question posed, again and again. Hypotheses, serious scientific effort, and cautious interpretation of various tentative results is one thing. But the popular resonance and discursive power of the same hypotheses is quite another. The observed data especially, the homosexuals themselves, have been extremely eager to have the hypotheses of "congenitality" and an innate "something" as the cause of their acts and emotions confirmed by the highest authorities. In this they had, and often still have, an obvious criminological, political, and social interest. It is not surprising that the medical research on homosexuality became characterized by a symbiotic relationship between the researchers and the objects of their research, the homosexuals. In some cases, and usually unknown to the general public, they were one and the same.[7]

Sexual politics, political correctness, deduction, circularity etc.

Homosexuals and their allies in medical science and in the Criminological Movement[8] met with resistance from more traditionally minded segments of Danish society including certain parts of the judicial system and the courts. The judicial outcome of a sensational homosexual scandal in Copenhagen 1906-7 – "The Great Morality Scandal" – was a series of verdicts in which the Criminal Court of Copenhagen disregarded "congenital homosexuality" as a mitigating circumstance, and thereby also disregarded the leading psychiatric authority in the country, professor Alexander Friedenreich, who had officially and semi-publicly made the diagnosis. As a counter-move, Friedenreich and his liberally minded colleagues of jurists on the board of directors of the Danish Criminological Association called a meeting of the association later the same year. On the agenda was one item: "Homosexuality and Criminal Law." Friedenreich and the professor of penal law at the University of Copenhagen, Carl Torp, gave lectures on the subject – and covered very much the same ground. They both argued for decriminalization of sodomy, "the sooner the better." Friedenreich, in his lecture, examined the state of medical science and thereby prepared the ground for the deduction that came to characterize modern European homosexuality. He first said: "In reality there has been presented no decisive argument from either the supporters, or the opponents of homosexuality as a congenital condition." About 15 minutes later, however, he concluded with political correctness: "The large majority of homosexuals have become so because of a congenital predisposition." It seems safe to assume that Friedenreich's statement was a rather blatant example of what during the following decades became the generally accepted "hypothesis" of the cause of homosexuality, at least in the educated, liberal, and scientifically minded segments of the Northern

European population. Congenital homosexuality also became the basis for several decades of unsuccessful research into the hormonal cause of homosexuality. A leading role in this rather sad chapter in the history of medical science was played by the Danish endocrinologist, professor of forensic medicine Knud Sand (1887-1968), whose work became the scientific legitimation for an excessively large number of castrations of sexual offenders (about 660 between 1929 and 1972), and a much smaller, but distressing number of voluntary castrations of homosexuals, as such (at least 19).

In popular discourse the deduction from the generalization "homosexuality" to homosexual individuals gradually became an established fixture in the course of the first half of the twentieth century. The homosexuals' sexual activities, their state of mind, artistic disposition, swishy way of walking, and their sissyfied behavior in general were considered to be explained and caused by the homosexuality that they carried with them and were part of. Thereby the deviant acts and queer emotions of the mysterious homosexuals became explained by "something" that was – scientifically – only *hypothetically* explained as a congenital degeneration of the central nervous system, or hormonal secretion, or certain genes on the x-chromosome. And so – in popular discourse – the hypothesis was multiplied. This also multiplied the possibility of making mistakes, not only regarding the hypotheses, but also regarding all homosexual individuals.

It is not seriously doubted in popular discourse that the cause of homosexuality is located in the body of homosexuals. This is linguistically illustrated by the double meaning of the word "homosexuality": (1) Homosexuality is a generalization of everything connected to sex between individuals of the same sex, from genital sexual acts and a propensity to seduce young men, to sissyness and effemination, cross-dressing and hypermasculinity, artistic talent, cosmopolitan outlook, and general alienation, hypersensitivity, and informal and formal subcultural organization. (2) Homosexuality is the innate bodily or psychic "something" that *causes and explains* (1), that is the hypothesis about the cause of the data from which the generalization in (1) has been deduced. This double meaning of the word "homosexuality" with its incorporated circular explanation (homosexuality is caused by homosexuality) should probably be seen as a – if the not *the* – central feature of the modern European conception of sex between persons of the same sex.

Not everybody accepted the hypothesis about an innate bodily cause as the explanation of why homosexuals were homosexuals. Adherents of traditional morality and social values rejected it as "medical softness" and submitted data and observations that seemed to contradict the hypothesis of congenital (compulsive) homosexuality. A well-known judge, Julius Wilcke, wrote in 1908 that the assertion of doctors and homosexuals did not fit with the observation that in recent years homosexuality had been increasing and spreading in Copenhagen. A medical practitioner, Emanuel Fraenkel, pointed out that homosexuality was a behavior connected with a widely extended and international social network – "a cultural wave" – that was now spreading from Berlin to Copenhagen. They were both very quickly branded as not belonging to the *bona fide* scientific community and their observations were dismissed as biased and prejudiced.

In the long run, homosexuals and their progressive allies were vindicated. Homosexual acts between consenting adults were decriminalized in Denmark in 1933. It may very well be doubted that this happened as a direct result of the efforts of medical science to show that homosexuality was a congenital condition, and that homosexuality was more widespread than generally assumed. A crime does not "automatically" become a non-crime simply because it is caused by the perpetrator's congenital condition, or because the number of "criminals" is high and/or growing. On the other hand, the majority of legislators were influenced by statements of the scientific community and used them as arguments and as a legitimation for decriminalization. Nearly all of the members of the Royal Commission on a New Penal Law were also members of the Danish Criminological Association, and most of them probably attended the meeting in 1907. The decision to decriminalize homosexuals acts (sodomy) was in reality taken already in 1912 with the commission's recommendation in its first report.

There were, however, one or two other points. The Royal Commission recommended not only that male prostitution should be punishable, but also that those who paid for immoral sexual acts with a male should be punished. Although payment for sexual acts could not very well be construed as the (direct) result of a congenital condition, the psychiatrist Sophus Thalbitzer nevertheless succeeded in persuading the government to drop this provision when the bill was introduced in Parliament in 1924. He outlined his reasons for entering the debate by stating that the proposed provision had a certain connection to his own discipline, psychiatry, and that his opinion was shared by all Danish psychiatrists and everybody familiar with the present state of psychosexuality and its perception of homosexuality. "Genuine homosexuality" was always congenital, a sexual variant, and a part of nature which had always occurred among civilized as well as uncivilized nations. He warned against legislation based on opinions that had been left far behind in science and concluded by referring to female prostitution which was not punishable: "There ought to be no provision in Denmark's criminal law that punishes homosexuals only because they are homosexuals."[9] The leader of the government party in Parliament referred to Thalbitzer's article in his speech arguing the bill.[10] With equal success, Thalbitzer a year later published an article in which he propounded the "objections that could be made from the point of view of science" on the bill's treatment of homosexuals in general. He argued against 21 years as the age of consent.[11] In the end it was reduced to 18 years.

It is not easy to estimate the actual extent of Thalbitzer's influence on behalf of science. Was he succesful because he, as a scientist, used the words "science" and "scientific," again and again?[12] It was certainly not generally known that Thalbitzer had recently been elected to an official position in the leadership of the *Wissensschaftlich Humanitäres Komitée* (Scientific Humanitarian Committee), the leading homosexual emancipation organization in Germany.[13] (At the time there was no such organization in Denmark.) In all probability he was also himself a homosexual. To the extent that scientific arguments were the legitimation for decriminalization of homosexual acts, this was in spite of the lack of scientific results.

There is no priviliged discipline. Whether a question belongs in theology, morality, the theory of criminal law, medicine, psychology, or in sociology and history, depends on a qualitative evaluation of the results produced. Do they make sense, and are they meaningful and significant for those who read or hear about them? Do they add to our understanding of ourselves and of the world? While it is not possible in natural science – because of circularity – to say that homosexuals are homosexuals because of their homosexuality, one can very well accept this deduction from a generalization to individuals, not only in sexual politics, but also as the basis for a social and cultural explanation of the causes of homosexuality. Michel Foucault supposedly once said that "anything general does not exist." It does, however, and Foucault was joking.[14]

Symbolic interaction and the definition of homosexuality

Seen in the light of the sociological theories of labelling and symbolic interaction, it poses no problem to say that homosexuals are homosexuals because they are carriers of an "internal" homosexuality. It is not important that the symbol "homosexuality" is also a generalization and that "homosexual" accordingly has been deducted from a black box. The deduction finds its explanation in the social practice and by an analysis of the social interaction in which this symbol is imposed on, contracted, and assumed by certain individuals. In this process – and it is a historical process – homosexuals became homosexuals *because* they had or took part in homosexuality, much in the same way that witches became witches because they had participated in witchcraft and had concluded a pact with the Devil. This gives one an idea of why it might be dangerous to "know too much," or just to pronounce the word "homosexual," and why any utterance had to be accompanied by anger and exorcizing dissociation.[15] In social interaction certain symbols may have a tendency to become infectious, to "jump" like bacteria from one individual to another. The vehicle of contagion is discourse and its master narratives.

The symbol itself, "homosexual, homosexuality," can furthermore be defined in so many ways and with the inclusion of so many auxiliary definitions that *nobody* can feel completely secure. That, probably, was the idea, if not the "intention." That is, the social function of homosexuality was to constitute a threat directed at men and the masculine gender, and especially against young males. It thereby also became a predicted possibility that could become reality. In this regard, the most spacious, if not all-embracing definition of homosexuality was the one produced by the Danish psychiatrist Thorkil Vanggaard, who in 1962 advanced a hypothesis about the so-called "homosexual radical" as a component of all men and the cause of "homosexual feelings and acts of normal men, i.e. men who are otherwise normal heterosexuals."[16] In the modern era homosexuality has been a central element in the disciplining of the European man.

On the one hand homosexuality is mercurially delimited by bisexuality, situational homosexuality, latent and unconscious homosexuality,[17] economic homosexuality (male prostitution),[18] and the above-mentioned "radical/normal homosexuality" and so on. On the other hand there is in modern European-American civilization a strong socio-cultural expectation that individuals are *either* homosexual *or* heterosexual. To be a bisexual or a latent homosexual (or asexual for that matter) is seen as a not quite real state, a temporary, provisional, and unsatisfactory pupal stage that is expected to be succeeded, the sooner the better, by the role of a homosexual or a heterosexual. Those who make the transition from being heterosexuals to being homosexuals are expected to edit their life story by remembering that "in reality" they have "always" been homosexuals. Heterosexuality does not require this kind of legitimation and the transition from being a homosexual to a heterosexual is either not explained, or understood (mostly by others) as being not "real." Socially the role of a homosexual has a tendency to override the heterosexuality of the same individual.

In this minefield of *both* uncertain, not to say fluid, definition of the categories, *and* of mutually exclusive categories – the amorphism of actual sexual behavior and the dimorphism of cultural sexual orientation – the researcher must find his data. To this comes the double meaning of the word "homosexuality" with its incorporated circularity. This makes it a difficult task indeed to establish a satisfactory *logical and linguistic nexus* between single or multiple factors within the body and complicated human socio-sexual behavior and consciousness.[19]

The problem can be seen in the previously mentioned article in *Science* about a possible genetic influence in "at least one subtype of male sexual orientation." The data included in the investigation are presented with evident self-contradiction as being at the same time the object of a description that is "overly simplistic" *and* "a reliable categorization": "describing individuals as either homosexual or non-homosexual, while undoubtedly overly simplistic, appears to be a reliable categorization of the population under study."[20]

It seems clear that "describing" and "categorization" are generalizations of the *social and mental* processes that have led the investigated individuals as "self-acknowledged homosexual men" to be recruited in North American HIV-clinics and through advertising in North American homophile publications.[21] Why it should be of any interest that there might possibly be a genetic explanation for this is not explained.[22] However, the social practice surrounding the publication of the article, the mega-quantity of quotes and comments in the media, indicates an explanation. It is an implied hypothesis that "self-acknowledged homosexual men" recruited in HIV-clinics and through homophile publications in North America are genetically representative of (all) homosexuals, whoever they are. This is not stated in the article, on the contrary, nor in the vast majority of comments in the media, but there can be little doubt that the implied hypothesis is the motivating mainspring of both the research and the publicity. In the power game of discourse there is precious little difference between "We have discovered the cause of homosexuality" and "We have not (yet) discovered the cause of homosexuality."

Although the object of the genetic investigations is the possible genetic influence in *sexual orientation*, it is clearly seen in the linguistic formulation of the publications that *homosexuality* is the interesting part of sexual orientation, for example in the title: "Evidence for a Biological Influence in Male Homosexuality" (LeVay and Hamer, 1994). Since the presence or absence of the same genetic sequence must also be evidence for a biological influence in male *heterosexuality*, one must ask why the hypothesis is never formulated thus. The reason is undoubtedly that the question of the causes of male heterosexuality is not on the agenda and is of no significance or interest in the culture and society in which the research is undertaken and published.

The article by Hamer *et al.* has references to several important articles by historians and sociologists in which the transhistorical and essentialist concept of homosexuality is questioned. However, there is no discussion of this rather central issue and no explicit reflection on language and socio-cultural variations in connection with the concept of "sexual orientation." What does "sexual orientation" mean in cultures that are *not* modern and North American – cultures where one cannot find "self-acknowledged homosexual men" who will answer ads in homophile publications with appeals for participants in a research project? Ancient Greece and the Sambia tribe in New Guinea are two examples, not to mention Mediterranean cultures where "honor" and "shame" imply that only the penetrated person loses his maleness, while the penetrator by this kind of domination confirms and enhances his position as a man. What does it mean to biology that "homosexuality" and "heterosexuality" are categories which historians and sociologists find it impossible to apply outside of modern Europe and North America, and that "homosexual" and "heterosexual" seem to be social roles that do not exist elsewhere in time and space?

Historicity of heterosexuality

What applies to homosexuality also applies to heterosexuality. Since homosexuality did not exist before the end of the nineteenth century, heterosexuality cannot have existed either. But without heterosexuality where would we be right now, all of us? – as the historian David Halperin has asked. He continues:

> How is it possible that until the year 1900 there was no precise, value-free, scientific term available to speakers of the English language for designating what we would now regard, in retrospect, as the mode of sexual behavior favored by the vast majority of people in our culture?[23]

The answer, Halperin writes, lies in "the inescapable historicity of even the most innocent, unassuming, and seemingly objective of cultural representations." Heterosexuality as well as homosexuality carry a heavy load of ideological bagage from modern Northern European and American culture that impedes an understanding of the characteristics and peculiarities of sexual life in other cultures and other periods. The basic problem is that we – as Halperin puts it – "currently lack a theory of taste." And in the absence of a theory it is hardly possible to subject the causes of certain tastes and a certain behavior to intense scientific scrutiny.[24]

But even if one accepts that "homosexual" is not a condition, but a social role, peculiar to the way in which erotic and sexual behavior between persons of the same sex is understood and institutionalized in modern Europe and North America, there remains the (unnamed) genital sexual behavior. One can say, rightly, that there has always been – if not homosexuals – men who had sex with other men and/or erotic feelings for them.[25] This "always" might consequently indicate a biological cause.[26] It probably does. The question is whether it is interesting. While we can accept, but find it of little relevance, that the biological cause of transportation is the biological fact that humans are born, not with a wheel, but with legs, it is probably harder to accept that men have sex with other men because (other) men for genetic/biological reasons are born. Since there are two sexes it follows that there are two sexes with which to have sexual intercourse; men-having-sex-with-men is biologically identical to men-having-sex-with-women. The problem with whether this is "interesting" is that the biological cause of homosexuality – contrary to the biological cause of transportation – is expected to have a dramatic quality that corresponds to the drama surrounding (the fear of) homosexuality.[27] As a cause of homosexuality it is too simple and too obvious. It does not contribute to the drama, it does not solve a riddle of nature, and it does not help set the cultural and social stage on which the existence of the particular and the life of the deviant is played out. It does not meet the expectations of the culture which insistently asks the question. The expectations about what a man is, does, and feels, and what he is not, does not, and does not feel, must be considered to be socially and historically determined. Such expectations will be different in different periods, cultures, social classes, and individuals. The variations in what constitutes gender, in sexual norms, and in sexual behavior, are consequently as many as the variations in religious states, religious dogma, and religious behavior.

Boyish pranks and sexual individuation

It seems that in the Northwestern European culture it has long been acknowledged that boys masturbate and sometimes masturbate together and with each other. Although such behavior has been regarded with fairly severe disapproval, one might say that at the same time it was the only type of sex between individuals of the same sex that was "allowed." By and large it has been ignored as an odious nuisance and boyish pranks. In a criminal case in 1865 involving two grown men who had masturbated each other on the fortification area in Copenhagen, the counsel for the defense said that it was a fact that "this nuisance is all too often committed by school boys, even over the age of criminal responsibility, but nobody has ever so much as considered holding them legally accountable for it."[28] The behavior forbidden by religion and criminal law was sodomy, that it an act by which the male member is inserted in the wrong opening of the body of a woman, in another man, a boy, or an animal, originally also the Devil or a heathen (the same as an animal). In the same way that it was not considered particularly important whether a sodomitical act was committed with a man or with an animal, it was not considered to be of any particular importance whether a man or a boy masturbated himself or another person, for example his wife or a boy.[29] Before the nineteenth century it was not "sexual orientation" that made sexual behavior legal or illegal. Specific acts were either legal or illegal, irrespective of the sex, age, or species of the object. When, towards the end of the eighteenth century, there arose a growing concern about boys' masturbation (inspired by the Swiss physician Tissot and others), this had no connection with whether it happened alone or with other boys. It was solely a medical matter, and consequently a pedagogical matter, since masturbation would have horrible consequences because of loss of bodily fluids.[30]

In the course of the nineteenth century the man/woman parameter in general aquired growing importance as a characteristic element of modernization (urbanization, industrialization, the nuclear family as ideal and ideology). Sexual orientation gradually became the decisive factor for determining what was acceptable and not acceptable, not only regarding specific sexual acts, but also for the understanding of *what* the individuals in question were. The sex of the sexual object thereby became decisive for determining the "real" sex of the sexual subject. This development should probably be seen as a reorganization and specialization of the masculine gender whereby modern man was divided in two: A "real" masculine sex and a supplementary "third sex." The third sex – which was not a proper sex and therefore required special scientific legitimation – existed in Denmark from about 1900 till the mid-1960s. By then a process seems to have begun in which gay men gradually became readopted into the male sex as a subgroup. This corresponds to contemporary changes in the lifestyle of heterosexuals, which more and more came to resemble the lifestyle of homosexual men.[31]

Master narratives

The discursive qualitity in connection with the cause of homosexuality is a measure of the degree to which gays have become integrated into the male sex and thereby are conceived to a lesser degree as deviants and a minority. When (if) the question of the cause of homosexuality is no longer asked, when scientific hypotheses about the etiology of homosexuality are no longer formulated, gays will be fully integrated into one male sex. This will mean that homosexuality as well as heterosexuality will have lost its relevance and be without social significance. Both generalizations will be of historical interest only. In spite of sexual-politically correct invocations in scientific publications on the cause of homosexuality – as they can be read in the article by Hamer *et al.* – all phrases expressing a hypothesis on the biological cause of homosexuality will be master narratives, a discourse which socially and culturally maintains marginalization and indicates that a man may not simply be – a man.

In this connection it may be worth mentioning that the editor of the Danish National Encyclopedia in 1997 objected to the manuscript for the article on homosexuality in which the theories of the cause of homosexuality were not mentioned: "certain information is lacking." The manuscript was circulated among members of the editorial board and they "reacted in the same way." In the opinion of the editors, a section ought to be added to the article "about the biological and psychological theories of the cause [of homosexuality] which have been proposed at various times."[32] It is commendable that a Danish politician – Ebbe Strange in this case – is prepared to support the spread of homosexuality, globally. It should, however, be undertaken with reality as the starting point. Which is not that there has always been homosexuality, but that homosexuality arose in Northern Europe in the second half of the nineteenth century and from there spread to the rest of European-American culture.[33] It is not found everywhere, but is the particular way in which sexual and erotic relations between individuals of the same sex is understood and institutionalized in modern Europe and North America.

Since European-American culture is the globally dominating culture it may be inevitable that homosexuality is spread to other cultures. In some places homosexuality may become a way of being Westernized, a supplement to European dress and consumerism that does not require investment in a formal European education or travels to USA and Europe, but provides *entrée* to an international (European-American) network which the young, the adventurous, and the enterprising may make rewarding and remunerative. It is, however, questionable whether this is really worth the political effort. Homosexuality carries with it a substantial cargo of historical and ideological garbage, notably from European criminal law and medicine. It would be a disgrace to saddle other cultures with it.

Notes

1. "Er seksualitet en menneskeret?" (Is Sexuality a Human Right?), *Pan*, 9 (Copenhagen, 1994), pp. 8-9. Interviewer's emphasis.
2. A number of widely different explanatory models were presented in the middle of the nineteenth century (Heinrich Hössli, 1836; Hans Christian Andersen, 1846; C. F. Michéa, 1849; Arthur Schopenhauer, 1859; Walt Whitman, 1860). The explanatory models presented by J. L. Casper (1852) and K. H. Ulrichs (1864) became the basis for C. F. O. Westphal's article on contrary sexual feeling in 1869. Cf. references in Wilhelm von Rosen, *Månens Kulør. Studier i dansk bøssehistorie 1628-1912* (The Color of the Moon. Studies in Danish Gay History 1628-1912) (Copenhagen, 1993), p. 41 note 78.
3. The term "homosexual" was first coined in 1869.
4. C. F. O. Westphal, "Die conträre Sexualempfindung. Symptom eines neuropatischen (psychopatischen) Zustands," *Archiv für Psychiatrie und Nervenkrankheiten*, 2 (Berlin, 1869), p. 108. Richard von Krafft-Ebing, "Ueber gewisse Anomalien des Geschlechtstriebs und die klinisch-forensische Verwertung desselben als eines wahrscheinlich funktionellen Degenerationszeichens des zentralen Nervensystems," *Archiv für Psychiatrie und Nervenkrankheiten*, 7 (Berlin, 1877), pp. 305ff.
5. Knud Pontoppidan, "Pervers Seksualitet. En klinisk Forelæsning" (Perverse Sexuality. A Clinical Lecture), *Bibliothek for Læger* (Copenhagen, 1891), p. 513.
6. Dean H. Hamer *et al.*, "A Linkage Between DNA Markers on the X Chromosome and Male Sexual Orientation," *Science*, 261 (1993), pp. 321-7. There were also many newspaper articles, for example: "Homoseksualitet kan muligvis arves" (Homosexuality is possibly hereditary), *Politiken*, 17 July 1993. Hamer *et al.* cautiously concluded: "suggesting the possibility of sex-linked transmission in a portion of the population, ... at least one subtype of male sexual orientation is genetically influenced" (p. 321). Cf. Simon LeVay and Dean Hamer, "Evidence for a Biological Influence in Male Homosexuality," *Scientific American*, May 1994, pp. 20-25.
7. The best known example is Magnus Hirschfeld (1868-1935). See below on the Danish psychiatrist Sophus Thalbitzer.
8. The Criminological Movement, from the turn of the century organized in the International Criminological Association, turned the attention of criminology from description and definition of crime and the assumption of a free will to commit an act, good or bad, to the criminal person in order to find the causes

of crime in individual and social circumstances.

9. Sophus Thalbitzer, "Forarbejder til den nye danske Straffelov. En overflødig paragraf" (The Draft of a new Danish Criminal Law. A superfluous article), *Nordisk Tidsskrift for Strafferet*, 1924, pp. 320-22.

10. *Rigsdagstidende 1924-25. Folketinget* (Parliamentary Debates), col. 3858.

11. Sophus Thalbitzer: "Straffelovforslaget og de Homosexuelle" (The Bill for a New Criminal Law and the Homosexuals), *Ugeskrift for Retsvæsen*, 1925, p. 109.

12. Thalbitzer refered to and summarized (and postulated) the hypothesis on the ontology and etiology of homosexuality argued by Hirschfeld in *Die Homosexualität des Mannes und des Weibes* (1914), which contrary to Thalbitzer's claim was by no means generally accepted by the scientific community; cf. Ralf Seidel, *Sexologie als positive Wissenschaft und sozialer Anspruch* (dissertation) (Munich, 1969), pp. 119-21.

13. *Jahrbuch für sexuelle Zwischenstufen*, 1923, p. 195.

14. Didier Eribon, *Michel Foucault* (1989), trans. Betsy Wing (Cambridge, Mass., 1991), p. 139.

15. As a mechanism of social life this has been discussed in essays by Jeremy Bentham and by Villy Sørensen; Louis Crompton, "Jeremy Bentham's Essay on Paederasty," *Journal of Homosexuality*, 3-4 (1978), p. 385. Villy Sørensen, "De normale og de afvigende eller angsten for det normale" (The Normal and the Deviants, or Fear of Normality), in *Hverken-eller. Kritiske betragninger* (Copenhagen, 1962), p. 85.

16. Thorkil Vanggaard, "Normal homoseksualitet og homoseksuel inversion" (Normal homosexuality and homosexual inversion), *Ugeskrift for Læger*, 124 (1962) (Vanggaard's emphasis). T. Vanggaard, *Phallós. A Symbol and its History in the Male World* (New York, 1972).

17. John Boswell accepts "subliminal desire" as operational for the history of homosexuality: "many people are unaware of their own sexual feelings"; John Boswell, *Christianity, Social Tolerance, and Homosexuality. Gay People in Western Europe from the Beginning of the Christian Era to the Fourteenth Century* (Chicago, 1980), pp. 44, 54.

18. The term "economic homosexuality" is not generally employed as a category of homosexuality. Male prostitutes are supposed to be: (1) heterosexuals, or (2) homosexuals (bisexuals), or (3) in transition between (1) and (2). In social life, however, they do constitute a group defined by genital sexual acts caused by economic considerations and they are socially evaluated by this fact.

19. For an overview of methodological problems regarding genetics and sexual orientation, see J. M. Bailey and R. C. Pillard, "Genetics of Human Sexual Orientation," *Annual Review of Sex Research*, 6 (1995), pp. 126-50.

20. Dean H. Hamer *et al.* (1993), p. 322.

21. Ibidem p. 321. - For the more accurate definition of who are and who are not homosexuals, scientists usually apply the Kinsey Scale (and so does Hamer et al). The Kinsey Scale, however, is both too narrowly connected to one

specific social and historical situation, but also in a number of ways without connection to the concepts of homosexual / heterosexual in their wider social and cultural meaning. To use the Kinsey Scale in order to define the data for an investigation of the causes of homosexuality within the body, seems to be as useless as dividing a population on a scale of pedestrian / autocar driver with parametres for self-identification, attraction, and behavior, in order to find the cause of automobilism within the body. - Cf. John H. Gagnon, "Gender Preferences in Erotic Relations: The Kinsey Scale and Sexual Scripts," in *Homosexuality/Heterosexuality. Concepts of Sexual Orientation. The Kinsey Institute Series II,* ed. McWhirter, Sanders Reinisch (New York and Oxford, 1990). Gilbert Herdt, "Developmental Discontinuities and Sexual Orientation across Cultures," ibidem.

22. For a critique of medical and biological research of the cause of homosexuality, see among others William Byrne, "The Biological Evidence Challenged," *Scientific American,* 1994, pp. 26-31; Christian Graugaard, "Når videnska koger over – om normalitet, biologi og sex" (When Science Boils Over - Normality, Biology, and Sex), *Bibliotek for Læger,* 1995, pp. 123-36.

23. David M. Halperin, "Sex Before Sexuality: Pederasty, Politics, and Power in Classical Athens," in Martin B. Duberman, Martha Vicinus and George Chauncey, jr. (eds), *Hidden from History: Reclaiming the Gay and Lesbian Past* (New York, 1989), p. 40.

24. *Ibid.,* pp. 40, 42.

25. This point of view has been emphasized by John Boswell, "Towards the Long View. Revolutions, Universals, and Sexual Categories," *Salmagundi,* 58-59 (1982-83), pp. 94-7.

26. The word "always" covers a very considerable historical variation. On a scale with Ancient Greece, Sambia, and present-day San Francisco at one end, there are at the other end the Scandinavian countries in the seventeenth and eighteenth centuries where sex between men had no or very little social significance and did not occur except as very rare exceptions. See Wilhelm von Rosen (1993), pp.112-15; Jonas Liliquist, "Staten och 'sodomiten' – tystnaden kring homosexualla handlingar i 1600- och 1700-tallets Sverige" (The State and the "Sodomite" – The Silence on Homosexual Acts in Seventeenth and Eighteenth Century Sweden), *Lambda Nordica,* 1 (Stockholm, 1995).

27. It is sometimes assumed that men (males) have sex with women (females) in order to (because of an "instinct") preserve the (human) species. Procreation is undoubtedly a common purpose of genital sexual behavior between persons of different sex. It is, however, equally obvious that very often this is not the purpose. One might add that while intent may be attributed to individual humans, under certain circumstances generalized to a society as a whole, one should probably not attribute "intent" to nature, even if a certain natural mechanism has or may have certain predictable consequences.

28. Wilhelm von Rosen (1993), pp. 390-92, 438-41.

29. This can be seen from a Danish criminal case in 1744 which began with a

charge of sodomy; Wilhelm von Rosen (1993), pp. 86, 103. The case was exceptional in several ways and is the only instance of documented sex between men to be found in Denmark in the eighteenth century.

30. Flemming Bøg, "Hænderne over dynen. Den borgerlige onani-diskurs i slutning en af 1700-tallet" (Hands above the Blanket. The Bourgeois Discourse on Masturbation towards the End of the 18th Century), *Den jyske historiker*, 48 (Århus, 1989); S. Mellemgaard, "Johan Clemens Tode og de hemmelige synders unaturlige natur" (J. L. Tode and the Unnatural Nature of Secret Sins), *Bibliotek for læger*, 1995.

31. Henning Bech, *When Men Meet. Homosexuality and Modernity* (Chicago, 1997), pp. 194-217; H. Bech, "Report from a Rotten State: 'Marriage' and 'Homosexuality' in Denmark," in Ken Plummer (ed.), *Modern Homosexualities: Fragments of Lesbian and Gay Experiences* (London, 1992).

32. Letter 18 February 1997 from The Danish National Encyclopedia to KarinLützen, Henning Bech, and Wilhelm von Rosen.

33. Cf. John D'Emilio and Estelle B. Friedman, *Intimate Matters. A History of Sexuality in America* (New York, 1988), pp. 121-30; George Chauncey, *Gay New York. The Making of the Gay Male World, 1890-1940* (London, 1995), pp. 12-14.

Chapter 17

Coming of Age in England: Black Gay Young Men's Schooling Experiences

MAIRTIN MAC AN GHAILL

Introduction

I can still remember that day when you gave me James Baldwin to read. It changed my whole life. Here was an ordinary black working-class guy who was gay – just like me. And I thought all that stuff that the teachers and kids at school told me about being gay was rubbish. I wasn't mad, it wasn't a phase I was going through and I didn't have to be ashamed of my life. I could really be honest with myself. It's still the best thing that ever happened to me. We need laws to protect gay people but we also need people to read books like Baldwin's, then they will see, gays are not the problem. Like he says, the straights are pushing onto us all their problems, just like the whites do with working-class blacks. But at the same time the white straights would like to be like us. These people are dangerous to us – and to themselves, because they are afraid. And that is the truth.

(Gilroy – African-Caribbean student)

Recent studies in England have highlighted the interrelation between schooling and sexuality as being strategic in the shaping of young people's experiences (Wolpe, 1988; Skeggs, 1991). However, the processes involved in forming and informing young people's subjectivities remain marginalized in relation to policy formulation, school organization and management and pedagogic practice. Of particular concern here is the continuing silence around the issue of how schools help to shape a range of emerging student sexual identities. This is all the more serious at a time of increased state and media projected homophobic moral panics in England. It is against this background that a group of black working-class gay young men provide accounts of their schooling experiences.

This article emerges out of a wider project. During the last decade I have been involved in exploring the construction of young people's identity within schooling contexts (Mac an Ghaill, 1988, 1994). The black young gay men, of Asian[1] and African-Caribbean origin, involved in this qualitative study were aged between 16 and 19 years. They were all attending local post-16 educational institutions. I taught a number of them. Space does not allow for a detailed discussion of the study's methodology, particularly with reference to questions concerning the politics and ethics of researching oppressed groups (see Mac an Ghaill, 1989). Much of the material reported here was collected from observation, informal discussions and recorded semi-structured interviews with the students and their teachers at their schools and colleges. The material is taken from life and school histories that involved discussion of family/kinship networks, peer groupings, work experience, political views/activities and school/college experiences. This methodological approach helped to locate schooling within wider socio-political processes.

My empirical work with young gay students needs to be contextualized with reference to recent theoretical developments. In England during the 1980s particularly, as a result of feminist, gay and lesbian writing and AIDS activism (and more recently the influence of "new queer theory"), the changing nature of men's lives and their experiences were much debated within a range of literatures, drawing upon sex-role, psychoanalysis and gender and power theories (Weeks, 1986; Dollimore, 1991; Sedgwick, 1991; Plummer, 1992; Sinfield, 1994). By the early 1990s we have been provided with theoretical frameworks that enable us to analyze systematically and document coherently the material, social and discursive production of masculinities (Segal, 1990; Brod and Kaufman, 1994). A main argument of this article is that, in order to grasp what is going on in schools with reference to sexual identity formation, it is necessary to bring together young gay people's accounts of schooling and recent theoretical developments in sexual politics. From both these sources sexual/gender categories can be seen as being shaped by and shaping the processes of colonization, racism, class hegemony, male domination, heterosexism and other forms of oppression. In short, sexual/gender relations can be seen as a crucial point of intersection of different forms of power, stratification, desire and subjective identity formation (Fanon, 1967; Hemphill, 1991). The main focus in this theory-led empirical work is a rethinking of sexual/gender categories in relation to the complex interconnections of multiple forms of oppression. Of key significance here is the deconstruction of dominant forms of heterosexuality.

> RAJINDER: One of the plusses of being a black gay person is that you see that you have to try and understand how different oppressions come together. White gays might only be interested in homophobia and blacks only interested in racism, but what is important is looking at the complex ways

homophobia and racism work in schools. And then again how these might effect gays or lesbians or working-class kids in different ways.

Rethinking schooling as a sexualizing agency

As the young men in this study point out, the major problem in the schooling of Asian and African-Caribbean gay working-class students is not their sexuality but the multiple oppressions that pervasively circumscribe their social world. Furthermore, these oppressions are mediated and reproduced both through the existing formal and hidden curriculum, pedagogical and evaluative systems that set out to regulate subordinated young people, and through gender/sexual specific mechanisms, such as the processes of gender/sexual representations and stereotypes, which in turn are "race," class and age specific. Liberal accounts of the curriculum that reduces the heterosexist structuring of schooling to aberrant teacher prejudice are insufficient to explain the complex social interaction of white teachers with black male gay students.

> VIJAY: I don't think teachers really know how deep feelings are about sexuality in schools and it's more complex when they are dealing with black gays. They think it's just about bad stereotypes, but in fact the whole place is organized to exclude gays and lesbians.

Schools can be seen to be sites of historically varying contradictions, ambiguities and tensions. This is highly visible in relation to sexual and gender social ideologies, discourses and practices. Schools function to prepare students for the sexual division of labor in domestic and workplace sites. However, schools do not merely reflect the dominant sexual ideology of the wider society, but actively produce gender and heterosexual divisions (Davies, 1993). At the same time, schooling may be a potential crucial public site that enables individual young people to develop non-traditional sexual/gender identities. Earlier theories in denying the contradictory functions of modern schooling have emphasized a static, ahistorical and over-socialized polarization of gender differences, while also erasing issues of sexuality. In so doing, they have failed to incorporate a more dynamic perspective that sees modern schooling systems as significant cultural sites that actively produce and reproduce a range of differentiated, hierarchically ordered masculinities and femininities that are made available for students and teachers to inhabit. In other words, schooling processes can be seen to form gendered identities, marking out "correct" or "appropriate" styles of being (Butler, 1993). It is suggested here that it is within these historically specific school sexual/gender regimes that we may locate the development of black working-class male gay sexualities (Mac an Ghaill, 1994).

Reconceptualizing complex sexual/gender identity formations

We are only beginning to understand the complex articulation between schooling, young people's cultural formations and sexual/gender identity construction. Feminist theory has enabled us to move beyond the gender/sexual essentialism and determinism of sex-role theory, acknowledging that young people are not such "*tablae rasae*, to be injected or even constructed with the ideology of the day" (Rowbotham, 1989, p. 18). Key texts, such as Connell *et al.* (1982) and Davies (1993) have persuasively presented the case against biologically based and sex-role theories, suggesting that they are inadequate to explain the complex social and psychological processes involved in the development of gendered subjectivities that are underpinned by institutional and wider material powers. Such work acts as a critique of the dominant theoretical and "common-sense" explanations of sexual/gender differences that underpins current pedagogical practice in English schools. These approaches often take for granted definitions of femininity and masculinity that are implicitly assumed to be unitary, universal and unchanging categories. For Davies (1993) one of the major weaknesses of theoretical work on schooling and subjectivity has been inadequate conceptions of sexual/gender identity formation. More recently, theorists drawing on poststructuralism, psychoanalysis and semiology have provided new ways of thinking about subjective identities (Henriques *et al.*, 1984). For example, Hall (1990), in his discussion of the new politics of black culture, has argued that identities are not historically fixed entities but rather that they are subjected to the continuous interplay of history, culture and power.

Earlier feminist research has been very successful in identifying the way in which gender relations operate in favor of male teachers and students and the resulting inequalities experienced by girls and women (Delamont, 1980). Later feminist work has illustrated how dominant forms of sexuality circumscribe female students' and teachers' lives (Skeggs, 1991). However, for the students in this study the "visibility" of gender relations could be contrasted with the "invisibility" of sexuality. At a time when it is common practice for policy documents to subsume issues of sexuality within a more general discourse on gender, there is a need to emphasize that sexual and gender relations are not totally separate, as is usually assumed. In contrast to much policy silence, the young men in this study recognize that sex and sexuality are pervasive within the official and hidden curriculum while at the same time being made "invisible" (Mac an Ghaill, 1991). Staffroom, classroom and playground everyday behavior all serve to carry important messages about sexual identities and practices. Schools treat student sexuality as a latent byproduct of an emerging adult status. When sexuality does "break into" the public arena, it is conceptualized as being natural and normal. At the same time, it remains located within the private sphere, reflecting a popular conception of sexuality as being "special" or "exceptional."

In contrast to schools' attempts to erase sex and sexuality from the formal curriculum, I found that sexuality in schools can be seen as all-pervasive, as it manifests itself in teacher-student relations, within disciplinary practices and within the curriculum. Sex and sexuality reappear in an extensive repertoire of student-student interactions including name-calling, flirting, classroom disruption, harassment of girls, homophobic abuse, playground conversations, desk-top graffiti, and students' dress codes as well as teacher stereotypes and student-teacher interactions. These wide-ranging schooling activities are central in making available dominant and subordinate sexual subject positions. Equally important, the identification of sexuality as part of a wider schooling process reconceptualizes sexuality as a key element of a public agenda that structures school experiences. Presenting sexuality as enmeshed in a set of power relations, serves to highlight that rather than individualizing sexuality, the deployment of sexuality works within social relations of domination and subordination.

> ASSIM: At our school they had a good anti-sexist policy that I think helped the girls. But there was nothing on sexuality. It seems strange when you think of it that they don't see gender and sexuality going together.

> STEPHEN: The teachers try to deny or suppress it but sex is everywhere in school and that includes the way that teachers use it all the time to control kids.

Queer theorists and AIDS activists have argued that sexuality is a key element in the construction of contemporary identities, both internally as a significant dimension of the self, and externally as a social category imbued with cultural expectations by others and as a primary marker of difference (Dollimore, 1991; Sedgwick, 1991; Mac an Ghaill, 1994). More specifically, such work has suggested that heterosexuality is both the assumed reference point of sexual/gender identity formation, while at the same time remaining unspoken. Furthermore, heterosexual relationships and more emphatically homosexual relationships are assumed to refer primarily to intimate sexual relations with the gender of the objects of our desire. What is missing from such "common-sense" perceptions is the fact that heterosexuality and homosexuality are key social, cultural and political arenas in which we are positioned and position ourselves (Butler, 1990, 1993; Dollimore, 1991).

> GILROY: The teachers think that being gay is all about having sex. I think they can't see it's a whole way of living your life, just the same as them. But they just can't see that their being heterosexuals affects the way they see the world, the way they act and everything they do.

Deconstructing heterosexuality

Brah (1992, p. 134) has written very persuasively of the need to problematize the racialization of white subjectivity. It is relevant to apply her argument to the category of sexuality. In English schools there is a tendency to see questions of sexuality as something primarily to do with gays and lesbians. However, it is politically and pedagogically important to stress that both gay and straight people experience their class, gender and ethnicity through sexuality. The sexualization of straight subjectivity is frequently not acknowledged by straights because "heterosexuality" signifies "normality" and dominance. Furthermore, there has been little understanding of sexuality as a relational concept in which different non-essentialist sexual identities are defined in relation to each other, with homosexuality always present in heterosexuality. A major task for educators is to deconstruct the complex social and discursive practices that serve to position teachers and students as "black and white, male and female straights" or "black and white gays and lesbians."

In contrast to the conventional approach within sex-role theory that erases issues of sexuality by subsuming it within a broader discourse of gender, Butler (1993, p. 238) suggests that gender is often spoken through a "heterosexual matrix" in which heterosexuality is presupposed in the expression of "real forms of masculinity and femininity." This provides a useful framework within which to explore the interconnectedness between gender and sexuality as they are lived out in schools. In structuring the attributes of being a "real boy"/"real girl," the various forms of masculinity/femininity that are hegemonic in schools are crucially involved in policing the boundaries of heterosexuality alongside the boundaries of "proper" masculinity/femininity. For example, to be a "real boy" is publicly to be in opposition to and distance oneself from the feminine and the "feminized" versions of masculinity. At an institutional level, student identities are formed in relation to the formal curriculum and the categories it makes available, including the academic/vocational, the arts/science and the academic/sporting polarities. These categories are highly gendered, with the "soft feminine" academic and arts subjects juxtaposed to the "hard masculine" vocational, scientific and sporting options. Similarly, involvement in sport can be read as a cultural index of what it means to be a "real boy," while not to be involved in sport and its associated "lad" subculture is to be a "bit of a poof."

It must be added that it is important not to see heterosexuality as a unitary and cohesive subjectivity. In work on schooling, masculinities and sexualities, Mac an Ghaill (1994) explored the question of what constitutes male students' heterosexual identity. More specifically, he examined the constitutive cultural elements of dominant modes of heterosexual subjectivity that informed male students' performing their sexual apprenticeships within a school arena. These elements consisted of contradictory forms of compulsory heterosexuality, misogyny and homophobia, and were marked by contextual contingency and ambivalence that served to challenge the hetero/homo divide. Male heterosexual identity is a highly fragile socially constructed phenomenon. Hence, the question that emerges is: how does this fragile construction become represented as an apparently stable, unitary category with fixed meanings? Schools alongside other institutions attempt to administer, regulate and reify unstable sexual/gender categories (Foucault, 1979; Skeggs, 1991). Most particularly this administration, regulation and reification of sexual/gender boundaries is institutionalized through the interrelated material, social and discursive practices of staffroom, classroom and playground micro-cultures.

Recent cultural theory reveals a tension between materialist, deconstructionist and psychoanalytic critiques of sexual/gender identity formation. In materialist accounts gender and sexuality are viewed as a matrix of power relations. In contrast, deconstructionist theorists have emphasized that the living of sexual/gender categories and divisions is more contradictory, fragmented, shifting and ambivalent than the dominant public definitions of these categories suggest. As Davies and Hunt (1994, p. 389) assert: "Deconstruction is a strategy for displacing the hierarchy, for revealing the dependence of the privileged or ascendant term on its other for its own meaning: deconstruction moves to disrupt binary logic and its hierarchical, oppositional constitutive force." Psychoanalysis has developed highly productive accounts of the complex psychic investments that individuals have in dominant sexual and gendered discourses (Butler,

1990). At the same time, psychodynamic explanations illustrate the limits of over-rationalist accounts of sexual politics that fail to acknowledge that what we *feel* is as important as what we *know* in relation to the maintenance of dominant gendered and heterosexual discourses and social practices.

James Baldwin (in Troupe, 1989, pp. 178-9), describing more graphically the latter's dependence on gays, points to the political significance of the male body, implying the Freudian insight that extreme personal and cultural antipathy is premised contradictorily on desire and need. He writes:

> the society makes its will toward you very, very clear. ... these are far more complex than they want to realize. That's why I call them infantile. They have needs which for them are literally inexplicable. They don't dare look into the mirror. And that is why they need faggots. They've created faggots in order to act out a sexual fantasy on the body of another man and not take any responsibility for it. Do you see what I mean? I think it's very important for the male homosexual to recognize that he is a sexual target for other men, and that is why he is despised, and why he is called a faggot. He is called a faggot because other males need him.

Much work remains to be done on how schools produce and reproduce male and female heterosexual identities. Currently, cultural theorists have placed on the educational agenda the urgent need for policy responses to acknowledge that key elements of the complexity of the construction of the sexual/gendered identities are the realities of differential power relations and sexual diversity.

As the students point out below, their schooling cannot be reductively conceptualized in terms of a simple binary social system, composed of a juxtaposed white middle-class straight superiority and a black working-class gay inferiority. The relations between them also involve a psychic structure, including such elements as desire, attraction, repression, transference and projection in relation to a racialized "sexual other" (Pajaczkowska and Young, 1992). This echoes one of the main themes of Isaac Julien's film *Young Soul Rebels*. In its exploration of the construction of black masculinity, he focuses upon such issues as white men's ambivalences, transgressions and envy toward black men. There is much work to be done in this area in order to understand the ambivalent structure of feeling and desire embedded within social institutions (Fanon, 1970). In the following accounts the young men discuss the range of split responses from white males to themselves, that were manifested in terms of the interplay between racial and sexual fear and desire and the accompanying contradictory elements of repulsion, fascination and misrecognition (Klein, 1960).

> RAJINDER: Thinking about it, it's very complex. Straight men don't really have a problem with gays, they have a problem with themselves. Straight men seem to fear and love women but fear and hate gay men. Then whites, especially white men, have that fear and hatred for Asians and African-Caribbeans. So, black gay men are a real threat to white straight men. Like James Baldwin says, they act out their fears on us, on our bodies. ... But then there's other complications. Like at our school, you could see some of the white teachers, the men, they really admired the Caribbeans and not just in sport and music, where it was really homoerotic, though of course they could never admit it to themselves. I think for a lot of teachers there, who felt trapped in their jobs, the macho black kids represented freedom from the system. There were anti-school macho whites and Asians but the teachers with their stereotypes fantasized about the Caribbean kids, who they saw as anti-authority, more physical and athletic, everything they couldn't be but greatly admired.

In schooling arenas it is possible to identify different masculine heterosexualities as constitutive of different relationships with African-Caribbean and Asian males and females. In this research, "race" created a number of complexities for white English males in their articulation of particular masculine heterosexualities. Those males who were part of a heterosexual culture that was premised on sexual athleticism, experienced a range of psychic and micro-cultural contradictions because of their racist and homophobic dis-identifications with Asian and African-Caribbean men and women. These dis-identifications limited, restricted and thus contested their claims to a sexual desire that was "uncontrollable." In contrast, those males in sexual cultures who emphasized remaining virgins until they met the "right" person reflected few contradictions in forming relationships with African-Caribbean or Asian females. If African-Caribbean and Asian gay male sexualities are worked out against heterosexuality, it is necessary to see that what we understand as being "heterosexuality" is made up of individual, micro-cultural and institutional complexities. The continuities of relations of domination and subordination embodied in heterosexual practices across different arenas has received vital and necessary critical attention. If schools are constituted by a range of heterosexualities, discontinuities arising between different heterosexualities in different and multiple social relationships need to be taken into account. As Andrew suggests below, mapping out the diverse and incohesive forms of heterosexualities offers an alternative way of identifying the complexities present in the cultural landscape of gay experiences that moves beyond a construction of them as "mere victims."

> ANDREW: It's not a question of all straights being against gays. Like it depends where you meet the straights and whether it's a public or private place. Nor is it a question of all gays being mixed up about their sexuality and straights being sorted out. We need to know more about straights and the different ways they act out their sexual lifstyles. There's a lot of pressure on them to act in certain ways, probably especially when they're not sure about their sexuality.

Gay students as active agents: the complexities of resistance

The students in this study have grown up in a society in which there are no positive images of gay or lesbian people. There is no acknowledgement of gay and lesbian history, sensibility, lifestyle and community. There is no recognition of gay or lesbian achievement. For example, the research showed that when texts written by gays or lesbians were read in school, no reference was made to the authors' sexual orientation. In fact in formal situations homosexuality was rarely discussed and on the few occasions when it was introduced, it was presented in a negative way, most recently in relation to AIDS. For the students this silence, reflecting that in the wider society, pervaded the whole of the formal curriculum, serving to reproduce and legitimate dominant heterosexual hierarchies. From this perspective, heterosexuality was presented as natural, normal and universal, simply because there are no alternative ways of being (Egerton, 1986). The students emphasized the personal isolation, confusion, marginalization and alienation that this engendered. Most significantly, without a positive reference group, they tended to internalize ambivalent negative messages about themselves as gay men.

> DENTON: It's terrible when you're younger, you think you're the only gay person in the world. And everyone is saying all these bad things about gays and lesbians. So, of course, you begin to think some of these things. And then you're really mixed up. Because you think, well this is the way I am and I don't fit into the stereotypes. I'm not suprised so many young gays feel suicidal.

However, there is a danger in examining black gay working-class students' schooling experiences of unintentionally adopting a passive concept of subject positioning, with the student portrayed as unproblematically accepting an over-determined racial and gender/sexual role allocation (Walkerdine, 1990). In fact, as the students here make clear, they are active curriculum and masculine makers. Furthermore, their accounts of schooling help to highlight the complexity of student resistance to cross-cutting multiple forms of oppression, that queer theorists and "post-colonial" writers have suggested (Mercer and Julien, 1988; Bhabha, 1990).

As Cockburn (1987, p. 44) has pointed out: "The social construction of gender is riddled with resistance and the resistance is complex. While some boys refuse the macho mode of masculinity and pay the price of being scorned as a 'wimp' or a 'poofter,' others resist the class domination by means of masculine codes." For African-Caribbean and Asian male students this resistance is also developed in relation to racially administered schooling systems. Here, the students reflected on the specific dynamics and interplay between state schooling and the construction of African-Caribbean and Asian ethnic masculinities. They were aware of how class-based differentiated curricula helped to shape differentiated masculinities, with sectors of black and white working-class students developing compensatory hyper-masculine forms in response to their experience of academic failure. They were also aware of how black students defensively responded to racialized and gendered discourses that constructed juxtaposed images of "weak" Asian and "tough" African-Caribbean males (Mac an Ghaill, 1994).

The students' accounts find resonance in black feminist writing, that has provided ways of understanding power relations that move beyond additive approaches, emphasizing the limitations of conceptualizing experience in terms of competing oppressions. These accounts of the experience of oppressions emphasize the simultaneous relevance of sexuality, gender, "race" and class. As Young and Dickerson (1994, p. 5) argue: "Hierarchies of domination are constructed and experienced simultaneously, their dynamics permeating one another." The exercise of power from a range of structures is refracted through individual experiences as a cohesive form of domination. In order to understand Asian and African-Caribbean gay young men's experiences, we need to take into account the ways that their economic position, their ethnicity and their age constitute *relational configurations* on the social and individual experience and understanding of being gay.

Feminist scholarship in critiquing male ethnographic work on schooling and masculinity has argued that anti-school male student behavior cannot be reductively read as simply a product of resistance, but also acts as a "legitimation and articulation of power and subordination" (Skeggs, 1991). This research has established the widespread forms of sexual harassment experienced by female students and teachers. The students in the study examined the links between the institutional and male peer-group surveillance, regulation and control of female and male gender and sexual reputations. They were surprised at the way in which straight male teachers and students conflated assumed gay behavior with femininity in order to disparage the former. The assimilation of masculine non-macho behavior to feminine behavior was most evident in relation to the ubiquity of the term "poof," which in "denoting lack of guts, suggests femininity-weakness, softness and inferiority" (Lees, 1987, p. 180). Furthermore, they linked this form of "gay-bashing" to the use of the term "Paki" as a form of "Paki-bashing" (physical and verbal attacks on Asians). Both these labels, "poof" and "Paki," have several meanings, sometimes used with a specific sexual or racial connotation, and sometimes used as general terms of abuse. The notoriety and frequency of these labels acted as major mechanisms of policing gender and sexual boundaries with specific implications for straight and gay black youth.

> RAJINDER: Nearly all the tough kids, the really hard lads were in the bottom two bands, especially the bottom one. They got their status by fighting the system that they saw abusing them. Some of the toughest ones were the white kids from the estate, always in trouble with the police and teachers. They were obsessed with proving they were real men, like those kids you talked about with their fighting, football and fucking – that was really them. ... They hated "poofs" and "Pakis" and used to argue with the teachers when they tried to stop fights, say things like, "Sir, he's only a 'Paki' or a 'poof'." They felt that the teachers agreed with them and in some ways they were right. A lot of the men teachers were really into violence but it was official, so that was OK to them. Anything seen as soft in their terms was despised. Like there was all this sexist talk by teachers. They thought that the best way to control a boy was to say to him, "stop acting like a girl." And they always said it loud so all their friends could hear. You see then outside the class the lads could carry on the sexual bullying that the teachers had set up.

There is much evidence from lesbian and gay literature of the physical, psychological and verbal abuse that lesbian and gay people systematically experience in homophobic and heterosexist societies (Burbage and Walters, 1981). The young men in this study report similar personal and institutional experiences of such abuse. However, it is important for educationalists in trying to understand the social positioning of these young people, not to adopt a reductionist pedagogical approach that sees gays and lesbians as mere problems or victims. Without reducing Asian and African-Caribbean gay masculinity to a unitary category, the students provide much evidence in this study to suggest that being gay is in many circumstances a positive and creative experience.

RAJ: It's like when you gave that talk at the university about having several identities. I don't think that most of the people could understand because really everything about them is taken for granted. Their Englishness, their whiteness, their culture, their gender and sexuality – it's just the norm for them. And that's what's really good about being a black gay, you have no choice, you have to question these things. I think what I've learned most in us being together for the last two years, is that the questions can be on our terms, not theirs.

DENTON: I agree. That's why people like James Baldwin and Langston Hughes are so important for us. Yes, the world is going to hate us, but people like them got through and in a lots of ways it was worse, much worse for them. And you feel very proud that they are part of our history ... They've made me more aware of other outsiders who are oppressed in this society. I used to feel really bad about being gay and I still get really down at times. But through being black and gay even if I don't stay gay, I know myself more than white men, than straights do.

Conclusion

The Asian and African-Caribbean working-class gay students here, in exploring the politics of complex difference involving the articulation of homophobia, heterosexism, racism and class oppression, are a sector of the younger generation among whom syncretic black identities are being formed, focusing on social commonalties, as well as on the cultural specificities of personal histories, memories, desires and expectations (Mama, 1992).

ANDREW: Reading through this study it shows, yes we are pushed to the margins of society as black gays. But that doesn't mean we have to accept that position. We can educate ourselves to understand the different oppressions. And you can see here that our position can be positive in helping us to work out ways forward not just for gays and blacks but for others as well, because we are questioning whiteness and heterosexuality that is usually very hidden.

For progressive social activists located within schools, the students suggest political and pedagogical spaces to identify and challenge dominant social practices. In so doing, we may build on their reconstruction of new forms of sexualities.

Acknowledgements

A special thanks to the students who collaborated in the production of this study and especially Rajinder.

Note

1. Asian is used to refer to those students who identified themselves as Indian, Pakistani or Bangladeshi.

References

Bhabha, H. (ed.) (1990) *Nation and Narration*. London: Routledge.
Brah, A. (1992) "Difference, diversity and differentiation," in Donald, J. and Rattansi, A. (eds), *"Race," Culture and Difference*. Milton Keynes: Open University Press/Sage.
Brod, H. and Kaufman, M. (1994) *Theorising Masculinities*. London: Sage.
Burbage, M. and Walters, J. (eds) (1981) *Breaking the Silence: Gay Teenagers Speak for Themselves*. London: Joint Council for Gay Teenagers.
Butler, J. (1990) *Gender Trouble, Feminism and the Subversion of Identity*. London: Routledge.
Butler, J. (1993) *Bodies that Matter, On the Discursive Limits of "Sex"*. London: Routledge.
Cockburn, C. (1987) *Two-Track Training: Sex Inequality and the YTS*. London: Macmillan.
Connell, R. W., Ashenden, D. J., Kessler, S. and Dowsett, G. W. (1982) *Making the Difference: School, Families and Social Division*. Sydney: George Allen and Unwin.
Davies, B. (1993) *Shards of Glass: Children, Reading and Writing Beyond Gendered Identities*. Sydney: Unwin and Allen.
Davies, B. and Hunt, R. (1994) "Classroom competencies and marginal positioning," *British Journal of Sociology of Education*, 15, pp. 389-408.
Delamont, S. (1982) *Sex Roles and the School*. London: Methuen.
Dollimore, J. (1991) *Sexual Dissidence: Augustine to Wilde, Freud to Foucault*. Oxford: Clarendon Press.
Egerton (1986) *Danger: Heterosexism at Work*. London: Greater London Council.
Fanon, F. (1970) *Black Skin, White Masks*. London: Paladin.
Foucault, M. (1979) *The History of Sexuality, Vol. 1*. Harmondsworth: Penguin.
Hall, S. (1990) "Cultural identity and diaspora," in Rutherford, J. (ed.), *Identity: Community, Culture and Difference*. London: Lawrence and Wishart.
Hemphill, E. (ed.) (1991) *Brother to Brother: New Writings by Black Gay Men*. Boston: Alyson Publications.

Henriques, J. (1984) "Social psychology and the politics of racism," in Henriques, J. Hollway, W. Urwin, C., Venn, C. and Walkerdine, V. (eds), *Changing the Subject: Psychology, Social Regulation and Subjectivity*. London: Methuen.

Klein, M. (1960) *Our Adult World and its Roots in Infancy*. London: Tavistock.

Lees, S. (1987) "The structure of sexual relations in school," in Arnot, M. and Weiner, G. (eds), *Gender and Politics of Schooling*. Milton Keynes, Open University Press.

Mac an Ghaill, M. (1988) *Young, Gifted and Black: Student-Teacher Relations in the Schooling of Black Youth*. Milton Keynes: Open University Press.

Mac an Ghaill, M. (1989) "Beyond the White Norm: the use of qualitative research in the study of black students' schooling in England," *Qualitative Studies in Education*, 2 (3), pp. 175-89.

Mac an Ghaill, M. (1991) "Schooling, sexuality and male power: towards an emancipatory curriculum," *Gender and Education*, 3 (3), pp. 291-309.

Mac an Ghaill, M. (1994) *The Making of Men: Masculinities, Sexualities and Schooling*. Buckingham: Open University Press.

Mama, A. (1992) "Black women and the British state: race, class and gender analysis for the 1990s," in Braham, P., Rattansi, A. and Skellington, R. (eds), *Racism and Antisexism: Inequalities, Opportunities and Policies*. London: Sage/Open University Press.

Mercer, K. and Julien, I. (1988) "Race, sexual politics and black masculinity: a dossier," in Chapman, R. and Ruthford, J. (eds), *Male Order: Unwrapping Masculinities*. London: Lawrence and Wishart.

Pajckowska, C. and Young, L. (1992) "Racism, representation and psychoanalysis," in Donald, J. and Rattansi, A. (eds), *"Race," Culture and Difference*. Milton Keynes: Open University Press/Sage.

Plummer, K. (ed.) (1992) *Modern Homosexualities*. London: Routledge.

Rowbotham, S. (1989) *The Past is before Us: Feminism in action since the 1960s*. Harmondsworth: Penguin.

Sedgwick, E. K. (1991) *Epistemology of the Closet*. London: Harvester Wheatsheaf.

Segal, L. (1990) *Slow Motion: Changing Masculinities, Changing Men*. London: Virago.

Sinfield, A. (1994) *Cultural Politics: Queer Reader*. London: Routledge.

Skeggs, B. (1991) "Challenging masculinity and using sexuality," *British Journal of Sociology of Education*, 12 (1), pp. 127-40.

Troupe, Q. (1989) *James Baldwin: The Legacy*. New York: Simon and Schuster/Touchstone.

Walkerdine, V. (1990) *Schoolgirl Fictions*. London: Verso.

Warren, H. (1984) *Talking About School*. London: Gay Teachers Project.

Weeks, J. (1986) *Sexuality*. London: Tavistock.

Wolpe, A. M. (1988) *Within School Walls: The role of discipline, sexuality and the curriculum*. London: Routledge.

Young, G. and Dickerson, B. J. (1994) "Introduction," in Young, G. and Dickerson, B. J. (eds), *Color, Class and Country*. London: Zed Books.

Index

absent fathers 48
addictive behaviour 95−7
advice manuals 50, 60−61, 69−70
AIDS 173, 272, 274, 314
Alcott, William 50
Ali, Muhammad 107
Ang, Ien 148−9
apprenticeship 129
Architectural Digest 158−9
Aristotle 115
Arthur, Timothy 50
asceticism 26−7
asthma 224−34 *passim*
Augustine, St. 21
autobiography 239−41
 women's 240
Awa, Kenzo 130

Bacon, Francis 153, 159
Baldwin, James 312
Barthes, Roland 109, 116−18, 121
baseball 69−71
Baudelaire, Charles 112
Baudrillard, J. 118
Beard, George 63, 65
beards 28−9, 59
Beckett, Samuel 118
Beisser, Arnold 134
Bellah, Robert N. 218
Bennett, Tony 143
Berg Eriksen, Trond 111
bioenergetic analysis 17
biological determinism 269
birthing labor 197−8, 203
bodies, men's xi−xiii
 control over 71
 feminization of 93
 in films 145
 injuries to 111−13
 and masculinity 140−41
 opposed to technology 145−6

physicality of 56, 59
political significance of 312
resemblance to the divine form 28
sexual nature of 52
sins assigned to specific parts
 of 25−6
social construction of 170
sociology of 173−6
symbolism of 101
 and violence 181−5
body painting 119
bodybuilding 93−104, 109−20
 passim, 176
Boëthius, Carl Gustaf 24
Boëthius, Jacob 24−33, 36−7
Bollas, Christopher 210, 213−14
Boscagli, Maurizia 155
Bourdieu, Pierre 111, 150
boxercise 111, 113, 118, 120
boxing 66−9, 107−21
Brende, Joel 179
Bryce, Peter 62−3
bullying 252
Burnap, George 50
Butler, Judith 92, 310

Caillières, Jacque de 35−7
capitalism 55, 70−71
caring labor 195−200
castration 292
Charles Atlas 68
Chesterfield, Lord 36
Chicago "Black Sox" 71
Childline 274−5
Churchill, Winston 201
Cicero 120
Cigar Aficionado 158−9
Clay, Henry 48
Cockburn, C. 315
Cohn, Carol 201, 203
Comfort, Alex 260, 267

Connell, R. W.   243, 274, 284, 308
consumption, culture of   54–5
Conte, Jon   179
Coontz, Stephanie   55
Corliss, Richard   159
Corn, Elliot I.   53, 67
corn flakes   60–61
Coward, Rosalind   141
cowboys   127
Craik, Jennifer   156
Creed, Apollo   144, 147
critical rhetorical induction   115
Cruelty to Animals Act   181
Culverwell, R. J.   52

Daly, Marsha   146–7
Danish Criminological Association
      291
Davies, B.   308, 311–12
Davis, L. J.   238
Davison, A.   239–54 *passim*
deCordova, Richard   142
Deleuze, Gilles   174
De Niro, Robert   158, 160
Details (magazine)   158
Dickerson, B. J.   315
disability   238, 241–4, 249–50
   social model of   242
   for women   244
Douglas, G.   60
Douglas, Mary   141, 161
Drago, Ivan   145
Dyer, Richard   155

Eakins, Thomas   64
Eco, U.   245
Edis, Robert   59
Eliade, Mircea   119
Elias, Norbert   22
Elliot, Gil   172–3
Ellis, John   142
emotionology   24, 32–6
emotions
   history of   38
   men's   xii, 36–7, 58, 155
Epicurean philosophy   35

Esquire   152–3, 157
European Union   217
Evans, George   64
exempla and *exemplars*   115–17, 120
exhibitionism   114

falling, fear of   18–19, 38
fantasies, masculine   127–9
fathers, authority of   199
Featherstone, Mike   118
femininity   22
feminism   xiii, 2–3, 177, 238,
      240, 272–3, 308, 315
   radical   260–61, 265–70
feminization
   of culture   56–9
   of the male body   93
Fiske, G. Walter   66
Fiske, Shirley   133–4
Fletcher, Horace   60
football   137
Foster, Hal   121
Foucault, Michel   21–2, 33, 173,
      233, 294
Fowler, O. S.   58
Fraenkel, Emanuel   293
Frank, Arthur   173
Freud, Sigmund   62, 269
Friedberg, Anne   142
Friedenreich, Alexander   291
Friedman, S. S.   240
Fromm, Erich   116
Fussell, Sam   97–9

Gantz, Bruno   39
Gardner, Augustus Kingsley   52
gay students   314–17
Gelles, Richard   179
gender, men's awareness of   240
gender identity   92
gender roles   100–101
gender studies   1–3
Genet, Jean   113
Gennep, A. van   133
"Genteel Patriarch" model of
      manhood   48, 51

Gentleman's Quarterly 157
Gershick, T. J. 243
Gilman, Charlotte Perkins 63–4
Gledhill, Christine 141–2
Godard, Jean-Luc 199
Graham, Sylvester 50–52, 60, 65
Grass, Gunter 246
Greer, Germaine 260
Grey, Zane 69–70
Griffith, Emile 113
Grinnell, George Bird 65
grounded theory 275
Guattari, Felix 174
Gulf War 180
gym culture 93, 99–104

Haikie, William 60
Hall, G. Stanley 47
Hall, S. 308
Hall, Winfield 60–61
Halperin, David 297–8
Hamer, Dean H. 296–7, 300
Härle, Gerhard 217
health and health care 59–61,
        172–80, 187
hegemonic masculinity 103–4, 177,
        243–4, 254, 274, 284
"Heroic Artisan" model of manhood
        48–9, 54, 67, 69
Herrigel, Eugen 129–31
Holmlund, Chris 156
homosexuality xii–xiii, 47–8, 58,
        216
    congenital 291–3
    decriminalization of 293
    definition of 292, 295–6
    historicity of 297–8
    as a location in the body 288–91
    master narratives of 300–301
    in schools 305–18
    as a social role 297–8
Hopkins, Patrick D. 216
Hudson, Rock 154
Hunt, R. 311–12

hunting 65
Husserl, Edmund 231
Hustler 260
Hutchinson, Woods 65
hydropathy 59

identity work 232
Ikonen, Pentti 209
"ilth" 178
industrialism 23
initiation ceremonies 133–7
"inner-directed" men 54, 59

Jackson, D. 240, 246
James, Henry 56
Jarvis, Edward 622
Jeffords, Susan 146, 155
Johannesson, K. 115
Johansson, Thomas 114
Johnson, Jack 69
Johnson, Virginia 260–65
judo 126–8, 136
Julien, Isaac 312

Kangasniemi, Hanna 144
karaoke 118
karate 126–7, 136–7
Kaye, Elizabeth 153
Keitel, Harvey 158
Kellogg, J. H. 60–62
Kent, William 65
kitsch 111, 113, 118
Klemola, T. 231
Koedt, Anne 265
Kuhn, Thomas 115–16

Lacan, J. 93, 99, 121
Ladies' Home Journal 154
Lahti, Martti 144
Lash, Scott 174
Laurence, William L. 201–2
Lawrence, Maggie 241
Lees, S. 316

legal knowledge and discourse
  174–5
Leggett, T. 131
Leibovitz, Annie 157
LeVay, Simon 296
lifestyle enclaves 219
"lived body" 231, 233
Louis, Joe 107
Lovelace, Linda 260
Lowen, Alexander 16–22, 38
luxury, love of 27

MacFadden, Bernard 56–7, 60, 68
Mac an Ghaill, M. 311
macho image 147–8, 161, 282, 285,
  315
McKeen Cattell, J. 57
McKeever, William 69
McLuhan, Marshall 203
Mahler, Margret 201
make-up, women's 112
Marciano, Rocky 107
"Marketplace Manhood" 48–50, 52,
  58
Marneth, A. M. 273
Marshall, Edward 69
martial arts 126–39
masculinity
  of American men 47–50, 54–5,
    69–71:
  and animal aggression 267–9
  aristocratic ideal of 34–5
  and autobiography 240–41
  and the body 140–41
  crisis of xiii, 23, 49, 66, 154–5
  and disability 238, 241–4
  and dress 156
  and emotions 155
  and fitness 103
  and health 175–6
  internal and *external* 109–10,
    120–21
  as man's nature 109
  and manual labor 116
  middle-class style of 49–50, 70,
    150, 154, 159

in opposition to femininity 58
  and social esteem 284
  and sport 66–7, 70–71, 125–6,
    134, 228–9
  traditional and *new* 100
  and violence 177–8
  and work xiii
  see also hegemonic masculinity
masculinization of the female body
  93
Maslin, Janet 160
Mason, M. G. 240
mass culture 148–9
Masters, William 260–65
masturbation 30, 50–52, 60–62,
  263, 298–9
Matrimonial Causes Act 181
Mayne, Judith 142
meat eating 51, 65
medical knowledge and discourse
  174–5
men's studies 1, 22, 219, 239
Mentor, Will 152
middle-class culture *see*
    masculinity:
    middle-class style of
Middleton, P. 240, 245
Miller, A. S. 243
Miller, N. K. 253
Millet, Kate 260
Mills, Bart 147
mind-body split 38, 131, 170, 176
Mitchell, S. Weir 63
Modleski, Tania 155
Moriarty, Cathy 158
Morris, J. 242, 244
mortality, awareness of 135–6
mortality rates 175
Mosse, George 101
mothers
  relationships with 209–14
  work of 194–5
Muir, John 64
Mulder, Arjen 144
multidisciplinarity in men's studies
  1

"muscular Christianity" 101
"muscular cinema" 140
"muscular masculinity" 243
mushin concept 128
myths 109

narcissism 99–100, 103, 213, 233
National Geographic (magazine) 55
Neale, Steve 154
Neiman, LeRoy 159
neurasthenia 63
New York Herald 66

Oakley, Ann 260
Oates, J. C. 108
O'Brien, Tim 204–6
Oettermann, Stephen 119
ontological dependence 219
ontological security 97
Oppenheimer, Robert 203
orgasm 21
orgasmology 260–70
Orlan 93
"other-directed" men 54, 59

pain, experience of 135–6, 226–7
"Paki" label 316
Paretsky, Sara 199
Parson, Erwin 179
Parton, Dolly 149
patriarchy 33
pederasty 289
Peek, George 50
peer-group pressure 283–5
Peter, Jean-Pierre 16
phenomenology 231, 233
philosophy 35, 198, 231
Pines, Malcolm 209
Platen, Magnus von 28–9
Plato 198, 200
Playboy 260
"poof" label 316

pornography 117–18, 180, 182,
    259–60, 268–70, 275–7,
    284–5
Post, C. W. 60
postmodernism 118–19
pregnancy 195
projective identifications 217
prostitution, male 289, 293
psychoanalysis 312
Pumphrey, Martin 156
Pyke, Rafford 58

quality of life 218

Rambo films 145–52 *passim*, 158,
    161
rape 267–8
rationality 20
Rechardt, Eero 209
Reich, Wilhelm 17
religion 132
Remington, Frederic 64–5
"reproduction", use of term 194
Reuben, David 260
Revel, Jaques 16
Riesman, David 54
rituals 132–5
Robinson, William 62
Rocky films 144–61 *passim*
Rolling Stone 159–60
Roos, J. P. 211
Roosevelt, Franklin 107
Roosevelt, Theodore 64–5, 69
Rowbotham, S. 308
Royal Commission on a New Penal
    Law 293
Ruddick, Sara 194–200
rugby 133
Russell, Kurt 152

Säfve, Torbjörn 107, 111, 119
samurai 127–8, 132, 138
Sand, Knud 292
Sandow, Eugen 68

Sargent, D. A. 66
Sawyer, Roland D. 70
Schindler, Solomon 57
schooling 305–18
  and the formation of sexual/gender
      identity 308–10
  as a sexualizing agency 307–8
Schwarzenegger, Arnold 140
Science (journal) 290, 296
Scorsese, Martin 158
secularization 132
Seidler, Victor J. 154
self-control, masculine 19–21
self-made men 48–52, 56
semen 117–19
Sen, Amartya 173
Sennet, Richard 21
sex manuals 266–7
sex therapy 260–65
sexual dysfunction 263–5
sexual harassment 171, 316
sexual liberation 259–69 *passim*
sexual politics 263, 306
sexual violence 182
sexuality 21
  male 51–2, 62, 141, 268–9,
      282–5
  female 261–2, 269, 284
  in schools 309–12
shame 208–9, 214–15
Silverman, Kaja 140, 150, 156
Sinclair, Upton 55
"sissies" 58–9
Skeggs, B. 316
skinheads 217
social constructionism 2, 170,
      273–4, 315
sodomy 299
soul, the, purity of 25–6
Spalding, A. J. 69
spermatic economy 50, 62
sport 65–71, 125–6, 133–5,
      176, 226–34, 243, 311
  professionalization of 108
  ritual elements in 134–5
Stallone, Sylvester 140–61

stardom and star image 141–5,
      150–57, 161
Starobinski, Jean 118–19
Stauth, Cameron 151
Stearns, Carol Z. 23
Stearns, Peter N. 22–3, 33–4, 38
stereotypes and stereotyping 101–3,
      148, 283, 285, 307
Stern, Daniel 209
Stille, Alfred 58
Stimson, Henry 201
stoic philosophy 35
Strange, E. 288, 300
Sullivan, John L. 69
superhero comics 245
Swedberg, Jesper 29
Swedish Men 24

tacit knowledge 115–17
taekwondo 126–7, 137
Talking Vietnam Blues 204
Tasker, Yvonne 99, 140, 143, 149,
      151, 154
"teenage mutant hero turtles" 127
Teller, Edward 201
Thalbitzer, Sophus 293–4
Thoreau, Henry David 49
Tissot, S.A. 50, 299
Tocqueville, Alexis de 49
Todd, John 50–51
Tomkins, Sylvan 209
Torres, Sasha 155
Trail, Russell 59
Treuniert, Nikolas 214
Turner, B. 174, 242
Tyson, Mike 107, 114

Vanggaard, Thorkil 295
Vanity Fair 157
Veblen, Thorstein 66, 70
Vietnam War 179, 204
violence
  definition of 171–2, 182–3, 187
  forms of 178–80
  and health 172–4, 177–80, 187
  male, towards children 182–3

male, towards other men 250–52
male, towards women 180–85
and masculinity 177–8
men's explanations for 184–7
sociology of 172–5
structural 171–2, 179
Vogue 153–4, 157
voyeurism 267–9

Wacquant, L. J. D. 110–12
Walker, Frances 66
Warhol, Andy 113, 119, 152–3, 159
Weber, Max xi
Wender, Wim 38–9
Westheimer, Ruth 21
Westmoreland, William 204
Wilcke, Julius 293

Wings of Desire (film) 38–9
Wister, Owen 64–5
women's studies 2, 22
Worst, Robert 55
Wright, Adrian 147
Wright, Frank Lloyd 57

Young, Frank 133–4
Young, G. 315
Young Soul Rebels (film) 312
youth rebellion 132

Zappa, Frank 253
Zaragoza, Daniel 113
Zen 131
Ziehe, Thomas 232
Zola, I. K. 242